Multicultural Education

*A Teacher's Guide to Linking Context,
Process, and Content*

Multicultural Education

A Teacher's Guide to Linking Context,
Process, and Content

Second Edition

Hilda Hernández
California State University, Chico

Merrill
Prentice Hall

Upper Saddle River, New Jersey
Columbus, Ohio

Library of Congress Cataloging-in-Publication Data

Hernández, Hilda.
    Multicultural education: a teacher's guide to linking context, process, and content / Hilda Hernández.—2nd ed.
    p. cm.
    Includes bibliographical references and index.
    ISBN 0-13-633538-1 (pbk.)
    1. Multicultural education—United States. I. Title.

LC1099.3 .H47 2001
370.117'0973—dc21   00-030560

Vice President and Publisher: Jeffery W. Johnston
Editor: Debra A. Stollenwerk
Editorial Assistant: Penny S. Burleson
Production Editor: Mary Harlan
Design Coordinator: Diane C. Lorenzo
Cover Design: Rod Harris
Cover Art: Stephen Schildbach
Text Design and Illustrations: Carlisle Publishers Services
Production Coordination: Mary Jo Graham, Carlisle Publishers Services
Production Manager: Pamela D. Bennett
Director of Marketing: Kevin Flanagan
Marketing Manager: Amy June
Marketing Services Manager: Krista Groshong

This book was set in Palatino by Carlisle Communications, Ltd. It was printed and bound by R. R. Donnelley & Sons Company. The cover was printed by Phoenix Color Corp.

Previous edition, entitled *Multicultural Education: A Teacher's Guide to Content and Process,* copyright © 1989 by Macmillan Publishing Company.

Photo Credits: All photos by John McNamara.
Illustration Credits: Frank Hernandez, pp. 1, 55, 137, 157, 191

10 9 8 7 6 5 4 3 2 1
ISBN 0-13-633538-1

Para mi familia
con todo mi amor y cariño

PREFACE

Teaching from a multicultural perspective is in some ways analogous to putting together an elaborate jigsaw puzzle. Even when we can see what the final outcome should be, fitting the pieces together is not an easy task. Some relationships are obvious; others are more difficult to recognize. Slowly, pieces fall into place and a picture begins to emerge. As the remaining gaps are filled, the image becomes clearer, the details easier to discern. The purpose of this book is to help teachers see the big picture, that is, to enhance their understanding of multicultural education and provide the means to make it a truly integral part of life in their schools and classrooms.

A Vision for All Students and Teachers

With excellence and equity as cornerstones, this book presents a vision of what education in a democratic nation can be, should be, and must be for *all* students. It is a vision for the present as well as the future, for multicultural education is about students, teachers, and educational change.

Teaching from a multicultural perspective is knowledge-based and learner-oriented; it contributes to the development of responsibly empowered professionals. These are educators who

◇ better understand the complex social, cultural, and individual factors that affect students' development and performance;
◇ make connections between what they know and how they teach in their own classrooms, whatever the level, setting, or school population; and
◇ effectively apply the precepts of multicultural education to create educational environments that promote excellence and equity.

This is a book for teachers in K–12 instructional settings—elementary and secondary, beginning and experienced. It is for those preparing to enter the profession as well as for educators continuing their professional development. It is for teachers who want to foster excellence and equity wherever they teach, be that in urban, suburban, or rural settings.

A Different Perspective

This book is unique in that it approaches multicultural education from a tripartite perspective linking context, process, and content—dimensions common to all classrooms. Within this framework, we explore the changing context of teaching and the dynamic contexts of home, community, and school. We also examine the "hidden curriculum" enacted through classroom processes and look at the content of textbooks and curriculum from a multicultural perspective. As we do so, teachers will discover a wealth of approaches, strategies, and techniques for effective teaching.

Organization

As the title suggests, this book is a guide to linking context, process, and content in multicultural education. The emphasis is on effective practice based on sound theory and research. The text is divided into four parts. Part I consists of two introductory chapters that provide the foundation for subsequent sections. The first chapter describes what multicultural education is and why it must encompass context, process, and content. It also highlights the challenges inherent in providing a quality education for all students. In the second chapter, attention is focused on the emergence of a new context of teaching, different from both the past and present. This educational transformation is putting teachers at the forefront and demanding a level of professional expertise that makes it imperative that they teach from a multicultural perspective.

The sections on context, process, and content—Parts II, III, and IV—constitute the core of this book. They offer a synthesis of contemporary scholarship complemented by a rich collection of practical information and ideas that teachers can readily apply in K–12 classrooms. Part II comprises two chapters that address the contexts most closely intertwined with the educational process. Chapter 3 explores ways in which teachers can more effectively incorporate home, neighborhood, and community as partners in education. Chapter 4 draws attention to the network of social and cultural factors that weave their way through school and classroom contexts, with important implications for teachers and students alike.

Part III is about the "hidden curriculum" enacted in the socially and culturally organized learning environments we call classrooms. In Chapter 5, we see that how individual students experience classroom life is influenced in significant ways by interaction, social dynamics, management, and organization. In the final section, Part IV, the focus is on content. Chapter 6 looks at textbooks as fundamental components in a multicultural curriculum and offers suggestions on the critical use of instructional materials and media. This sets the stage for Chapter 7, which provides a curriculum development model and related guidelines to facilitate the integration of multicultural perspectives and content throughout the curriculum. This is complemented by ideas on the use of technology to challenge "cultural illiteracy." By way of closure, Chapter 8 addresses the challenge of creating a teaching and learning environment in which all students can achieve academically to their fullest potential.

New to the Second Edition

This second edition builds upon and further refines the conceptualization developed in the original. Students remain the focal point, with continued emphasis on the factors associated with academic performance that fall within the teacher's sphere of influence in schools and classrooms. Every effort has been made to retain what teachers and instructors liked best about the first edition and to revise the text in ways that strengthen the existing foundation by making the links between context, process, and content more transparent.

New to this edition is the expanded treatment of contexts—a new chapter on the changing context of teaching (Chapter 2) and another on school and classroom contexts (Chapter 4). The first underscores recent changes in the context of teaching and their relationship to multicultural education and reflective professional practice. The second examines effective schools, culturally relevant teaching, and special student populations. Among the issues addressed in greater detail are retention, tracking, and high-stakes testing. In combination with the new Application, Extension, and Reflection sections at the end of each chapter, these provide enhanced opportunities for teachers to make the insights and ideas generated through reading the text a more integral part of their professional development.

Chapter 8 on teaching from a multicultural perspective, is also largely new, with an extensive set of teaching strategies for K–12 classrooms—some generic, others related to literacy, language, and mathematics—and sections focusing on learning strategies, learning styles, and multiple intelligences. Additional content in the chapter on textbooks and instructional materials (Chapter 6) provides practical suggestions for using history textbooks, teaching insider perspective, and teaching about religion. The development of a multicultural curriculum now includes sections on technology and the integration of multicultural content. The discussion of school linkages to home, neighborhood, and community contexts has been expanded, as has the treatment of classroom processes. Last but not least, the working definition of multicultural education is new and closely aligned to an updated set of basic assumptions and the underlying theme of a quality education for all.

Acknowledgments

I gratefully acknowledge the contributions others have made in the preparation of this book. First, I am deeply indebted to John McNamara for the artistry of his photographs, which beautifully complement the text. I also want to thank the students, parents, and teachers from New Haven School District, Union City, California, who allowed their photographs to be included as part of this book. If a picture is worth a thousand words, theirs certainly speak volumes. Special thanks go to Frank Hernández for illustrations that capture the theme of multicultural education so elegantly.

I remain most appreciative of all of the individuals who contributed to the first edition of this text, and add to the list those who reviewed this edition at various stages of development. Especially warm thanks to reviewers Lupe Cadenas, California State University; Minerva Caples, Central Washington University; Christian Faltis, Arizona State University; and David J. Szymanski, Peru State College.

I also want to express my gratitude to colleagues in the Department of Education at California State University–Chico for their interest, advice, and support. I am most grateful to Carol Corrody, Jerry Converse, Andy Hanson, Cathryn Huser, Marilyn Niepoth, Maggie Payne, Vic Sbarbaro, Peter Schuler, Paula Selvester, Alayne Sullivan, and Ed Williams for their invaluable comments and feedback. For keeping me on track in the section on teaching about religion, I thank Charles C. Haynes, First Amendment Center, and Bruce Grelle, Department of Religious Studies, California State University–Chico. Thanks, too, to Duarte Silva, Stanford University and Marguerite Clarke, Boston College, for their perceptive observations. I acknowledge the contributions of preservice, inservice, and graduate students at California State University–Chico, and thank all of my students—past and present—for everything they have taught me.

Very special thanks go to Debbie Stollenwerk, my editor at Merrill, for her expert guidance throughout this project. She is everything an author could ask for in an editor: insightful, positive, supportive, helpful, and above all patient. I am also indebted to Linda McElhiney, my development editor early in the revision process, for helping me to see this edition through her eyes. Many thanks to Penny Burleson, Mary Harlan, Carol Sykes, and Jeff Johnston at Merrill, and to Mary Jo Graham, at Carlisle Publisher Services, for their assistance at various points along the way.

For their generosity, I most gratefully acknowledge the contributions of individuals, publishers, and school, state, and government agencies who granted permission for the use of materials reproduced in this book.

Finally, on a personal note, I want to thank my parents, Frank and Hilda Hernández, and my brother, Frank Hernández, for their love, support, encouragement, and patience. In many ways this is their project too, for they have always been at the heart of my own education that is multicultural.

DISCOVER THE COMPANION WEBSITE ACCOMPANYING THIS BOOK

THE PRENTICE HALL COMPANION WEBSITE: A VIRTUAL LEARNING ENVIRONMENT

Technology is a constantly growing and changing aspect of our field that is creating a need for content and resources. To address this emerging need, Prentice Hall has developed an online learning environment for students and professors alike—Companion Websites—to support our textbooks.

In creating a Companion Website, our goal is to build on and enhance what the textbook already offers. For this reason, the content for each user-friendly website is organized by topic and provides the professor and student with a variety of meaningful resources. Common features of a Companion Website include:

For the Professor—

Every Companion Website integrates **Syllabus Manager**™, an online syllabus creation and management utility.

- ◇ **Syllabus Manager**™ provides you, the instructor, with an easy, step-by-step process to create and revise syllabi, with direct links into Companion Website and other online content without having to learn HTML.
- ◇ Students may logon to your syllabus during any study session. All they need to know is the web address for the Companion Website and the password you've assigned to your syllabus.
- ◇ After you have created a syllabus using **Syllabus Manager**™, students may enter the syllabus for their course section from any point in the Companion Website.
- ◇ Clicking on a date, the student is shown the list of activities for the assignment. The activities for each assignment are linked directly to actual content, saving time for students.
- ◇ Adding assignments consists of clicking on the desired due date, then filling in the details of the assignment—name of the assignment, instructions, and whether or not it is a one-time or repeating assignment.
- ◇ In addition, links to other activities can be created easily. If the activity is online, a URL can be entered in the space provided, and it will be linked automatically in the final syllabus.
- ◇ Your completed syllabus is hosted on our servers, allowing convenient updates from any computer on the Internet. Changes you make to your syllabus are immediately available to your students at their next logon.

For the Student–

◇ **Topic Overviews**—outline key concepts in topic areas
◇ **Electronic Bluebook**—send homework or essays directly to your instructor's email with this paperless form
◇ **Message Board**—serves as a virtual bulletin board to post—or respond to—questions or comments to/from a national audience
◇ **Chat**—real-time chat with anyone who is using the text anywhere in the country—ideal for discussion and study groups, class projects, etc.
◇ **Web Destinations**—links to www sites that relate to each topic area
◇ **Professional Organizations**—links to organizations that relate to topic areas
◇ **Additional Resources**—access to topic-specific content that enhances material found in the text

To take advantage of these and other resources, please visit the *Multicultural Education* Companion Website at

www.prenhall.com/hernandez

BRIEF CONTENTS

CONTENTS

PART
I

INTRODUCTION

1   Introduction

> Reality happens to be, like a landscape possessed
> of an infinite number of perspectives, all equally
> veracious and authentic. The sole false
> perspective is that which claims to be the only
> one there is.
>
> *José Ortega y Gasset*

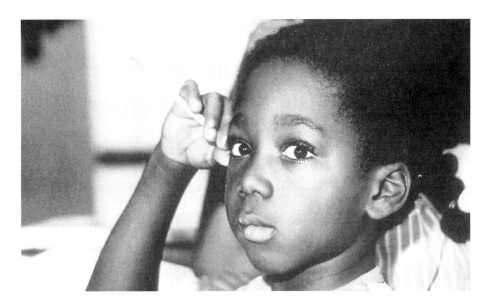

In a democratic nation that celebrates diversity, *excellence* and *equity* must be the cornerstones of education for all students. This is critical to our children's future, and no less important for our society as a whole.

> What the best and wisest parent wants for his own child, that must the community want for all of its children. Any other ideal for our schools is narrow and unlovely; acted upon, it destroys our democracy. (Dewey, cited in 1996, p. 5)

In an increasingly heterogeneous and technologically complex world, the ultimate challenge is to connect meaningfully with every student (Gay, 1996, p. 46).

However, student and teacher demographics provide powerful evidence of the increasing social and cultural distance between students and teachers, a gap accentuated by the growing numbers of students who are African American, American Indian, Asian, and Hispanic, students who are low-income, and students who are English language learners, and a decline in the number of teachers from comparable backgrounds (p. 45). For example, U.S. Department of Education data on teacher and student populations in the public schools in 1993 reveal the following:

	Students	Teachers
White/Non-Hispanic	66%	87%
Black/Non-Hispanic	17%	7%
Hispanic	13%	4%
Asian/Pacific Islander	4%	1%
American Indian/Alaskan Native	1%	1%

(Adapted from Troutman, Jones, & Ramirez, 1999, p. 64)

Many teachers do not share their students' frames of reference because they live in what Gay describes as "different existential worlds," worlds separated by factors such as ethnic and generational differences, residential patterns, social class, experiential background, educational levels, and technological sophistication:

> Although 60% [of teachers] live within the boundaries of the school district where they are employed, only 37% live in the attendance area of the school where they teach. This percentage drops to 17.3 for schools in large systems, where the greater number of ethnically diverse and poor children are enrolled. The overwhelming majority of teachers continue to be Anglo (86.8%). More than 72% are female. By comparison, the student population in public schools is increasingly children of color. (p. 46)

Teachers are the key to educational excellence and equity. If teachers are ever to fulfill the promise, they must understand the dynamics of teaching and learning from within a multicultural framework. Teaching, to be most effective, must be multicultural.

The intent of this text is to introduce teachers and prospective teachers to the complex, dynamic, and multifaceted world of multicultural education. This chapter begins by defining multicultural education. It explains why the focus on linking context, process, and content is central to the implementation of education that is multicultural, and then highlights key assumptions and goals.

WHAT IS MULTICULTURAL EDUCATION?

Since its emergence as a field of study in the 1960s and 1970s, *multicultural education* has been defined in many ways from various perspectives. Some definitions are embedded within specific disciplines, such as education, anthropology, sociology, and psychology. Others represent the views of accrediting agencies and professional organizations concerning what teachers need to teach and what students need to learn. A third type of definition consists of statements developed and adopted by practitioners within schools and at district, county, and state levels. As a result, teachers routinely are confronted with a kaleidoscope of differing views that describe multicultural education as everything from "educational practice" (Pacheco, 1977) to "interdisciplinary process" (*California State Department of Education*, 1979), and "international reform movement" (Banks, 1997).

The differences among definitions are more than a question of semantics. In the final analysis, what teachers do in the name of multicultural education depends upon their point of view. Recognizing the importance of clarity, some have proposed that the designation multicultural education be replaced by such terms as "education that is multicultural" (Grant, 1977; Grant, 1978) "education that is multicultural and social reconstructionist" (Sleeter & Grant, 1999) or "the multicultural facet of education" (Frazier, 1977). These, they argue, better communicate the substance and meaning of the concept. At present, however, *multicultural education*, despite its limitations, remains the most common and accepted term.

In the first edition of this text, I drew from two "classic" definitions to accentuate dimensions of the concept that are particularly important for teachers. The first defines the essence of multicultural education as a perspective that (a) recognizes the political, social, and economic realities that individuals experience in culturally diverse and complex human encounters; and (b) reflects the importance of culture, race, sexuality and gender, ethnicity, religion, socioeconomic status, and exceptionalities in the educational process (National Council for Accreditation of Teacher Education, 1986).

This definition recognizes the multiple realities that exist within the contexts of school and society and the demands this places upon teachers. First, it implies that students must learn to communicate and interact with people of different cultural backgrounds. In this sense, multicultural education is a process through which individuals develop ways of perceiving, evaluating, and behaving within cultural systems different from their own (Gibson, 1984). Second, it requires consideration of those forces that exert a powerful influence on schooling, directly and indirectly. These forces include societal and school factors affecting the priorities and directions of education nationwide and at the state and local levels. Also included are the social and cultural factors that influence how teachers teach and what they teach; how students learn and what they learn.

The second definition complemented the NCATE perspective by focusing attention on multicultural education in relation to curriculum and instruction. According to Suzuki (1984), "Multicultural education is a multidisciplinary educational program that provides multiple learning environments matching the academic, social, and linguistic needs of students" (p. 305). Two essential attributes emerge from this definition. First, from a teacher's point of view, the focus is on learners as individuals characterized by a unique combination of abilities, talents, and instructional needs. Addressing their needs requires the creation of instructional environments genuinely sensitive to many kinds of diversity. Second, from a programmatic standpoint, multicultural education is integrated across disciplines with a strong emphasis on academic achievement as well as social and personal development.

In the ensuing decade, I developed a working definition of my own. In this conceptualization, multicultural education is, first and foremost, learner-centered. It is also professionally empowering. The definition of multicultural education that guides this work is stated as follows:

Multicultural education is a vision of what education can be, should be, and must be for *all* students.

◇ Multicultural education is about *students.* It is about ethnicity, gender, class, language, religion, and exceptionality as influences that shape individuals as cultural beings. It is full development of each learner's unique constellation of intelligences, capabilities, and talents. It is preparing students for citizenship in multiple, interrelated cultural and linguistic communities.

◇ Multicultural education is about *teachers.* It is about ethnicity, gender, class, language, religion, and exceptionality as influences that shape educators as cultural brokers. It affirms the importance of teachers as individuals who can and should make a significant, positive difference in the lives of students within their sphere of influence. It is about teachers as members of a professional community committed to the ideals of educational equity and excellence for all students.

◇ Multicultural education is about significant *educational change.* It is about the complex cultural, political, social, and economic realities that so pervasively and systematically influence everything that happens within schools and classrooms. It is about all facets of the educational enterprise manifested through context, process, and content. Multicultural education reaffirms and extends exemplary practice, and seeks redress for those denied optimum educational opportunities. It is about creating educational institutions that provide dynamic teaching and learning environments reflecting the ideals of equity and excellence.

This operative definition also reflects the two key elements identified by Trueba (1992) as essential if multicultural education is to uphold the democratic principles of equitable treatment for all. The first is an appreciation of U.S. society as fundamentally pluralistic, democratic, and respectful of racial, ethnic, re-

Multicultural education is a vision of what education can be, should be, and must be for all students.

ligious, social, linguistic and cultural differences. The second is a profound commitment to education as the avenue for preparing all citizens to live together in harmony, and to instill in all children an appreciation for the value of the nation's racial, ethnic, and linguistic plurality.

BASIC ASSUMPTIONS

The concept of multicultural education presented in this book is based on a set of related assumptions. By making these explicit, the philosophy that underlies the vision just described is more transparent.

Students

Premise 1   *Multicultural education is for all students.* The development of skills for living in a dynamic society is a continuous, legitimate, and necessary part of the formal and informal educational process. Thus, multicultural education can help prepare students for life in the "real world" beyond the school setting, a world inhabited by individuals and groups with cultures distinct from their own (Gollnick & Chinn, 1986, 1994). It is preparation for life in a society in which there is "no one model American"; a society in which no group lives in a vacuum but rather exists as part of an interrelated whole (American Association of Colleges for Teacher Education, 1973).

A popular misconception regarding most conceptualizations of multicultural education is that it is intended primarily or exclusively for minority students. (For an alternative point of view see Gordon, 1995.) Educational policy in some states has helped to promote such a perception by requiring multicultural education only in districts having at least one school with a 25% minority student population (Baker, 1979). Such policies fail to recognize that developing appropriate skills and attitudes for living in a multicultural society is as critical for the nonminority student as it is for the minority student. Because all students ultimately will need to function in our culturally diverse society, all should be exposed to educational experiences that foster the necessary competencies for doing so.

Premise 2 *Classroom interaction between teachers and students constitutes the major part of the educational process for most students* (Stubbs, 1976). Increasingly, the quantity and quality of interaction between teachers and students are regarded as critical aspects of classroom life. The importance of these dimensions to the instructional process was emphasized in a U.S. Commission on Civil Rights Report (1973), which stated that through student-teacher interaction, "the school system makes its major impact upon the child. The way the teacher interacts with the student is a major determinant of the quality of education [s]he receives" (p. 3). To achieve excellence, teachers must believe in their ability to reach all of their students, to create learning environments in which all students feel that the acquisition of knowledge is an "equal opportunity process" (Webb, 1983, p. 94).

Teachers

Premise 3 *Multicultural education is synonymous with effective teaching for all learners.* Payne (1983) describes multicultural education as "good teaching and good education"; in essence, it is the "natural way to teach" (pp. 98–99). However, multicultural education does not assume that "Good education is good education, period!" (Olsen, 1997, p. 247)—that is, that good teaching is a generic, "one size fits all" enterprise in which what is good for one learner is equally appropriate for other learners. Good teaching and good education do not ignore inclusion and the outcomes of schooling for different groups of learners.

Theory and practice in multicultural education are based on sound educational research. Looking at teaching and learning from a multicultural perspective, teachers acquire a deeper and broader understanding of students as learners and develop an expanded repertoire of strategies and techniques. Multicultural education emphasizes high expectations, adaptation to accommodate individual learner differences, and presentation of all subjects to all students.

A multicultural perspective is a legitimate and necessary part of teaching in all classrooms. Indeed, consideration of sociocultural dimensions in the teaching and learning process is central—not peripheral—to issues of school effectiveness and educational reform. Simply stated, "all teaching should be multicultural" (Gollnick & Chinn, 1994, p. 55).

Premise 4 *It is increasingly important for political, social, educational, and economic reasons to recognize that the United States is a culturally diverse society, and that teaching is a cross-cultural encounter.* Every teacher and every student is a unique cultural being. Each brings to the classroom a distinct combination of beliefs, values, and experiences. These, in turn, influence behavior, perceptions, attitudes, and performance. This is the essence of the connection between culture and the teaching-learning process (Hilliard, 1978).

The classroom is also a setting in which culture is transmitted and individuals are socialized into a well-established, but often invisible, system of behaviors, values, and beliefs. Powerful and dynamic relationships exist between social and cultural factors (e.g., socioeconomic status, ethnicity, gender, language) and schooling. These relationships are so closely intertwined that "in a sense, everything in education relates to culture—to its acquisition, its transmission, and its invention" (Erickson, 1997, p. 33). Whether they realize it or not, teachers are immersed in culture every time they teach or design curriculum: "[issues of culture] may be addressed by educators explicitly and within conscious awareness, or they may be addressed implicitly and outside conscious awareness. But at every moment in the conduct of educational practice, cultural issues and choices are at stake" (p. 34).

If we are ever to realize the goals of excellence and equity, teachers must be able to provide an instructional environment appropriate for learners from diverse backgrounds:

> The school is the only institution through which all children of all cultures can share in the heritage and life of this nation. The teacher who can work only with children from one socioeconomic or cultural group is inadequately prepared to teach in the common school. (Smith, Cohen, & Pearl, 1983, p. 46)

Premise 5 *Next to parents, teachers are the single most important factor in the lives of children* (Smith, Cohen & Pearl cited in Baker, 1983, p. 46). A noted philosopher of education suggests that the three primary functions of schooling are socialization, cultural transmission, and development of self-identity (Green, 1977). Few would argue that teachers play anything less than a central role in all three of these processes.

Individual teachers can and do make a difference in student learning (Good, 1994, p. 312), and to a great extent, they determine the degree to which education is truly multicultural (Frazier, 1977). In fact, recent research reveals that of all the determinants of student achievement, expert teachers' levels of preparation and skill are most important: "skilled teachers are the most critical of all schooling inputs" (Ferguson, 1995, p. 469; 1996, p. 6). Teachers with less than adequate professional preparation are more reliant on rote learning, less adept at managing the complex forms of instruction that foster critical thinking, less skillful in recognizing students' needs and learning styles, and yet more likely to blame the students when their teaching fails (Darling-Hammond, 1996, p. 6).

Darling-Hammond asserts that most classrooms of poor and minority children have teachers who provide instructional experiences that are significantly less effective and engaging than those in other classrooms. This is not meant in any way to disparage or minimize the efforts of successful teachers such as those described by Ladson-Billings (1994). Rather, the point is to recognize that teachers are a most powerful force in children's lives, but also to concede that not all teachers are equally effective in this capacity. In the final analysis, teachers must believe that they can teach all of their students and then go on to teach them.

Educational Change

Premise 6 *The educational system should provide all students with effective teaching, effective programs, and effective schools.* It is important to acknowledge that the educational system in the United States serves many students well. In *The Manufactured Crisis*, Berliner and Biddle (1997) demonstrate that our current system is in many ways effective and compares quite favorably with education in other nations. They join a growing number of educators responding to unfair and unwarranted charges that the public schools are in decline and failing. Debunking contemporary myths about American schools, achievement, and aptitude, Berliner and Biddle challenge assertions that student achievement is in a downward spiral, that our schools fail in comparative studies of student achievement internationally, that most people in the United States are unhappy with their schools, and that those who go into teaching are less able and academically weak. There is little doubt that many students benefit from the educational opportunities created through good teaching, good programs, and good schools.

The basic problem that we face as a nation, however, is that good teaching, good programs, and good schools are not a given for all students. In fact, when Berliner and Biddle discuss the *real* problems confronting public education, they put issues such as unequal support for schools and the challenges of serving a changing student population at the forefront. They note, for example, that "*huge* differences persist in the levels of support given to public schools in this country—differences that are far greater than those found in other advanced countries" (p. 264). Berliner and Biddle go on to say that:

> If America's public-school system were truly to offer *equal* opportunity, it would have to provide *extra* resources for schools serving the poor. Instead, America turns its back on the educational needs of its poorest children and offers them the *worst* public schools in the nation. Moreover, many Americans don't seem to know that this is happening. (p. 267)

The educational system should provide all students with effective teaching, effective programs, and effective schools.

The existence of structural inequalities in access to resources and knowledge has been well documented, but little appreciated: "The fact that U.S. schools are structured such that students routinely receive dramatically unequal learning opportunities based on their race and social status is simply not widely recognized" (Darling-Hammond, 1995, p. 476).

Historical precedent for current realities is strong. "Institutionally sanctioned discrimination in access to educational resources is older than the American nation itself" and was already well entrenched during the colonial period (p. 465). Anyone familiar with the history of education throughout the 19th century and into the 20th century knows that "African Americans faced de facto and de jure exclusion from public schools throughout the nation, as did Native Americans, and, frequently, Mexican Americans" (pp. 465–466). The same holds true for some Asian Americans (Katznelson & Weir, 1985).

Inequalities are most apparent in such areas as teachers, facilities, class size, course offerings, curriculum, instructional materials, equipment, testing and tracking policies and practices (Darling-Hammond, 1995). In her analysis of inequalities and access to knowledge, Darling-Hammond makes some sobering observations with respect to the unequal distribution of well-qualified teachers across urban, suburban, and rural areas. In urban areas, for example, minority and low-income students are most likely to be taught by teachers who are "inadequately prepared, inexperienced, and ill-qualified" (p. 470). Decades of studies have found that disproportionate numbers of poor minority students are taught by the least qualified teachers throughout their school careers (p. 471). The result of this "systematic underexposure to good teaching" has been to put all children in schools with high minority populations at risk (p. 471). Sadly, studies suggest that even the brightest students in these schools appear to have more limited opportunities than their less capable counterparts at better institutions. As Darling-Hammond states, "reducing inequality in learning has to rely on policies that provide equal access to competent, well-supported teachers" (p. 478).

Seeking solutions for these inequalities is further complicated by the widespread assumption that educational inequality is less a function of the school and more a function of the students, and their inability to benefit from what schooling has to offer (Darling-Hammond, 1995). Astuto and Clark (1992) offer this scathing assessment:

> Despite all the rhetoric of the past fifteen years, most people, and most policymakers, believe that the key determinant of school success is family or social or ethnic background. The often asserted public school position that 'all children can learn' is belied by the fact that the American public schools are an efficient sorting machine that reproduces adults in roughly the same social class where they began as five-year-olds entering school.
>
> The issue is not whether schools do, in fact, make a sufficient difference in the lives of children so that most of them can share in the success of this society as adults; they obviously do not do so. The issue is why they do not do so, since they obviously could. (p. 102)

Darling-Hammond suggests that policymakers, educators, and the public at large do not really believe that all students are entitled to receive a "rich, challenging, and thoughtful curriculum":

> If the academic outcomes for minority and low-income children are to change, aggressive action must be taken to change the caliber and quantity of learning opportunities they encounter. These efforts must include equalization of financial resources; changes in curriculum and testing policies and practices; and improvements in the supply of highly qualified teachers to all students. (1995, p. 476)

The substantial differences in educational achievement among groups of students with different backgrounds continue to constitute a complex problem for which no simple, single-factor solutions exist. According to one study, "no matter how the universe of students is divided, the most important factor that is related to earning a bachelor's degree is the intensity and quality of the high school curriculum a student has taken" (Adelman, 1999, p. 99). Along similar lines, Darling-Hammond (1995) observes that "unequal access to high level courses and challenging curriculum explains much of the difference in achievement between minority students and White students" (p. 473). Continuation of this "achievement gap"—as Brown and Haycock (1984) have asserted—does not make educational, economic, or political sense. "All [students], regardless of race, class or economic status, are entitled to a fair chance and the tools for developing powers of mind and spirit to the utmost" (National Commission on Excellence in Education, 1986, p. 2).

Premise 7 *Multicultural education is synonymous with and essential to educational innovation and reform.* Although the aims of the numerous recent initiatives promoting school reform are laudable, many offer less than adequate responses to the challenges facing education today. Consideration of sociocultural factors appears to be the exception, rather than the rule in these reports. Many such calls for reform systematically overlook the sociocultural dimension:

> They neglect the sociocultural influences that, along with traditional matters of curricular offerings and time available for instruction, affect educational outcomes for students. . . . Their potential impact . . . is mediated by the local circumstances in which they are applied; these circumstances are shaped in fundamental ways by the sociocultural influences that permeate the educational process. (McGroarty, 1986, pp. 299–300)

More than a decade later, educators continue to raise similar concerns. It is ironic, says Gay, that multicultural education and cultural pluralism are "conspicuously absent" from most proposals for school reform produced between 1983 (*A Nation at Risk*) and 1991 (*America 2000*) (1995, p. 33). Olsen (1997) describes the political and social discourse of the nineties as silent on issues of exclusion and access:

> A commitment to serving 'all' students is reiterated over and over. The 'all' is intended as a sufficient term to imply inclusion. But beyond the insertion of 'all' in statements about serving students, there has been little leadership or explicit reform dialogue addressing exclusion, equity, and the needs of students related to language and culture. This stems from a pervasive and determined color-blindness, posited as a moral position signaling an end to prejudice and racism. In this scheme, all students are seen as the same. Therefore, there is no need to examine the specifics of language and cultures or how race and ethnicity affect children's experiences in school and society. (p. 246)

Within this context, Olsen finds that educational programs, policies, and pedagogy promoting inclusion and equity are discredited, portrayed as racist, divisive, or seeking special treatment for special interest groups: the voices of advocates are characterized as diverting attention from the real and substantive issues confronting education.

If meaningful educational reforms are to be implemented effectively, social and cultural factors cannot be neglected. Idealists understand that "educational reform must be inspired by the democratic principles on which pluralistic America rests" (Trueba, 1992, p. 107). Pragmatists know that the problems to be addressed are not simple, and solutions that are not responsive to social and cultural differences will have little significant effect. If educational reform efforts respect and reflect diversity, however, the vision of what the future can bring is a powerful one, for "it is in the day-to-day interactions of teachers and students, dealing with a transformed curriculum and attempting to create a transformed, democratic classroom, that the new common culture will be created and continually recreated" (Perry & Fraser, 1997, p. 57). Clearly, "teachers are the key to the success of educational reform" (Astuto & Clark, 1992, p. 98).

LINKING CONTEXT, PROCESS, AND CONTENT

Implementation of multicultural education in the 21st century requires educational reform. Significant educational changes must be rooted within a perspective that enables teachers—individually and collectively—to make professional decisions that foster equity and excellence. To fully realize the possibilities of innovations in education, these changes must encompass not only content but also process (especially human interaction) and organizational structure (Hunter, 1983). This task entails looking beyond curricular content and instructional materials to the context of classroom life and the processes enacted by teachers and students as individuals and members of larger groups.

To teach within the framework of multicultural education requires an understanding of the synergetic relationship of context, process, and content. Content and process represent two sides of the coin that is the world of the school and classroom. By considering both dimensions, teachers can relate seemingly disparate elements into a comprehensive, cohesive, and meaningful whole. From this holistic perspective, the influence of larger social and cultural contexts on classroom processes and content is most easily understood. For those preservice teachers who find it difficult "to delineate dimensions of classroom life or consider what classrooms would look like from a multicultural perspective," this exploration of context, process, and content serves as an organizer to highlight many of the most critical facets (Boyle-Baise & Sleeter, 1996, p. 379).

Context

Context can best be described as encompassing the larger national and global society in which education takes place, as well as the more immediate milieu of home, neighborhood, and community. Shulman (1986) identifies several contexts in which teaching occurs: individual, group, class, school, family, and community. Every context, he notes, is embedded within a larger context: individuals within groups, groups within classrooms, classrooms within schools, and so on. For this reason, to understand life in classrooms, one needs to know more than just the unique dynamics experienced by a particular group of students and their teacher. Also needed are insights about how the students and teacher are "influenced by the larger contexts in which the class is embedded—the school, the community, the society, the culture" (Shulman, 1986, p. 20).

Context affects education in very basic and significant ways. First, many of the real problems in education stem from societal issues whose impact on local schools is powerful and varied. Consider, for example, the unequal support given schools (Berliner & Biddle, 1997). Data on the 1980s indicates that on average local sources accounted for approximately 45% of all funding for public school districts in the United States, with another 45% provided by the states and the rest from federal sources (p. 265). Within and across states, the differences in funding for public education are so great that students in some public schools receive "one-fifth or less the level of support that is provided to public schools in wealthier districts in the country" (p. 265). Berliner and Biddle point out that while affluent and middle-class citizens enjoy the kinds of good educational opportunities that generate satisfaction with the public school system, the poor get the worst schools, limited opportunities, and the feelings of degradation, self-blame, and resentment that this engenders.

Second, as individuals and members of society, we are all influenced by innumerable social and cultural factors. From an educational perspective, some of the more salient include ethnicity, race, gender, socioeconomic status, religion, language, and exceptionality. If we as educators are to provide excellence and equity in the fullest sense, it is not enough to merely appreciate the influence of such factors. Rather, we must make every effort to ensure that the learning environment we create is positively and appropriately responsive to their impact upon us and our students.

Finally, consideration of context also leads educators to focus on students' homes, neighborhoods, and communities. Home, school, and community settings exert a powerful influence on the education of children (Barbour & Barbour, 1997). Although teachers cannot ensure that the influences our students are exposed to outside the classroom will be positive and conducive to learning, we must become increasingly adept at fostering more inclusive linkages between the curricula of the home, community, and school. Doing so demands use of traditional and innovative strategies for working with parents as well as effective models for forging strong and dynamic parent, school, and community partnerships.

Process

Process encompasses the less formal and visible aspects of classroom life, the classroom context in which curricular content is transmitted and the processes involved in doing so. Awareness of the contexts discussed earlier helps explain why individual students experience classroom life differently. Even events that are shared by all students may be interpreted differently according to the particular social, linguistic, or cultural background of the individual. Teachers need to be able to identify how learner preferences, beliefs, attitudes, and behaviors are influenced by culture and how this relationship affects performance. They must also become more aware of how their own preferences, beliefs, attitudes, and behaviors are strongly influenced by their own cultural background and how these in turn affect the way they teach, behave, and interact with students.

Classroom processes are those facets of teaching and learning that involve interaction, organization, social aspects, and management (Shulman, 1986). In the classroom, transactions occur between teachers and students; as Shulman observes, these are social and organizational, academic and intellectual. Processes are important avenues through which sociocultural factors influence students' academic achievement and social development. The creation of learning environments responsive to diversity requires consideration of these four process dimensions.

First, there needs to be greater awareness of how social and cultural factors affect interactional patterns in the classroom and in students' homes and communities. To what extent do students experience equality of opportunity to participate? To what degree is classroom participation a function of ethnicity, gender, socioeconomic status, or academic achievement? What differences in language use exist between the home and the classroom, and in what ways do these relate to instruction?

Second, it is essential that teachers recognize how social aspects such as language attitudes and grouping influence performance and perceptions. How do attitudes toward different varieties of English affect teachers and students? What does research reveal about the advantages and disadvantages of grouping? What does the research tell us about tracking and retention? Who wins, who loses, and why?

Third, accommodating the diversity of needs and abilities students bring to the classroom also requires complementary use of instructional and behavioral techniques. How do content, student behaviors, and instructional strategies and settings relate to the management process? What kinds of strategies have been used in adapting curriculum to meet student needs?

Fourth, in organizing students for instruction, teachers need to be attentive to the ways in which they structure learning activities. How does organization affect student learning? What kinds of strategies have been used to adapt classroom structure and organization to individual needs?

Content

Content encompasses the more formal manifestations of classroom life. It has been defined by Shulman (1986) as the "substance" of teaching and of learning, the specific curricular content and subject matter studied. From his perspective, it is at the "very heart of teaching-learning processes" (p. 8), for teachers and students interact in and through content. It is subject matter and related skills, teaching strategies, and processes. In terms of instruction, content is usually organized as lessons, units, semesters, or years; within these, it is also conceived of as facts, concepts, principles, cognitive strategies, and so forth.

Several aspects of content are relevant to multicultural education. First, if diversity is the hallmark of our global community, then curricular content and instructional materials must assist students in communicating and interacting with people from different cultures. Teachers today are responsible for teaching students about (a) their own cultural heritage and that of other groups; (b) the ways in which culture influences the sum total of each individual's way of life and that of others; (c) similarities and differences among individuals, within and across groups; and (d) attitudes and modes of behavior that can facilitate or impede cross-cultural understanding. To do this effectively, teachers must have specific knowledge about multiple cultures; more importantly, they must have the desire and skills to interact and communicate in different cultural settings and with individuals from diverse cultural backgrounds (Gibson, 1984).

Second, because cultural pluralism is a fact of life in the United States, curricular content and instructional materials must provide multicultural perspectives that reflect the nature of society and the subcultures that constitute it. These include but are not limited to groups defined by ethnicity, gender, age, language, exceptionality, socioeconomic status, and religion. This means that teachers must critically examine the materials they use with respect to the treatment of various groups and topics, and the overt and covert messages they convey. Likewise, teachers will want to help students develop skills in analyzing what they read, hear, and see in instructional materials, through the media, and via technology. This also means that teachers must promote meaningful and authentic learning experiences that take children and adolescents beyond the confines of the classroom to integrate and apply their knowledge in ways that enrich their appreciation of multicultural perspectives.

Third, to teach heterogeneous groups of students, teachers must develop and implement a repertoire of teaching strategies that work for all students successfully, building upon each individual's unique combination of strengths and abilities. Meeting the needs of individual students entails systematic use of effective instructional strategies based upon sound research and practice. It may also require adaptations for language, exceptionality, learning style preferences, or other characteristics, and may affect content, classroom setting, and instructional strategies. Teachers also need to incorporate multiple intelligences, learning styles and learning strategies as an integral part of instruction and assessment.

Finally, teachers must coalesce their knowledge of content and pedagogy to develop an effective multicultural curriculum. Knowing about the processes involved in the construction of knowledge is important as is developing competency in maximizing access to the higher levels of knowledge that empower learners. Also critical are the recurrent processes that guide curriculum development and the infusion of multicultural perspectives across subject areas.

Within the context of classroom life, content and process are powerful allies. The essence of their relationship to equity and excellence is captured in the following statement:

> In the final analysis, it is the kinds of access students of color have to high-status knowledge and the quality of instructional interactions between students and teachers in individual schools and classrooms that define educational quality and indicate who receives educational equality. These processes are what

Multicultural education must embody context, process, and content.

ultimately determine which students are educated for intellectual rigor, personal self-determination, and social empowerment, and which ones are trained for a life of institutional compliance, economic dependence, and the social underclass (*Equality and Excellence,* paraphrased in Gay, 1997, p. 210).

This applies to students from many groups in our society, be they characterized by gender, exceptionality, class, religion, or other variables.

A QUALITY EDUCATION FOR ALL

According to Katznelson and Weir (1985), "mass education has been the country's most important domestic social policy" (p. 207). As we begin the 21st century, one goal of schooling for all—access to public education—has been almost fully achieved. Gone are the days in which children are denied entry into the public schools because of race or ethnicity. With respect to entitlement to state-sponsored schooling, "the democratization of education has been profound" (p. 207).

However, the concomitant egalitarian goal of schooling that provides "a school experience common to all children," that is, a quality education in its fullest sense, is far from reality for all students, facing arguably greater challenges today than in the near or distant past:

Most big-city schools have black and Hispanic majorities. Most suburban districts are overwhelmingly white. White working-class families have joined an exodus from city schools, and their organizations have stopped pressing for common schooling. The more segmented and segregated the schools become, the more uneven are their finances, their curricula, and the capacities of their teachers and administrators. (p. 208) Further evidence of the extent of this disparity is found in international assessments indicating that schools in the United States are "among the most unequal in the industrialized world in terms of spending, curriculum offerings, and teaching quality." (McKnight, Crosswhite, Dorsey, Kifer, Travers, and Cooney; and Educational Testing Service, 1996, p. 6)

The democratic vision of public education as a "repository of egalitarian aspirations and opportunities" is critical in understanding the basic goals of multicultural education (Katznelson & Weir, 1985, p. 27). For generations, the common school has symbolized our abiding faith in education as the key to a better future.

Teachers committed to this vision of quality schooling for all have chosen a path more difficult than they may realize. For example, scholars are divided as to whether the schools can actually transcend class or whether they merely reproduce the existing social structure (p. 14). This gives rise to alternative perspectives and courses of action, such as those presented by Katznelson and Weir (1985), Knapp and Woolverton (1995), and Sleeter (1995). Moreover, the schools are beset by forces that foster social division and inequality. As noted earlier, these are evident in such areas as teacher quality, facilities, class size, instructional materials, and access to curriculum and technology. We have reached a turning point. Looking to the future, today's teachers must grapple with some very disturbing questions. Katznelson and Weir put it bluntly: "Must we compose an elegy for schooling for all? Or shall we fight for this vision and, in doing so, broaden the possibilities of American politics and society?" (1985, p. 222).

If the answer is that this vision is one that we continue to believe in, then educators will need to determine what our goals are going to be, for these will ultimately guide our actions. To this end, the following goals highlight at least part of what needs to be accomplished:

Students

◇ To help students acquire knowledge about a range of cultural, ethnic, and religious groups and develop the attitudes, skills, and abilities needed to function at some level of competency within many different cultural environments. (Banks, 1979; Gibson, 1984)

◇ To develop in students an acceptance of and appreciation for similarities and differences in culture, ethnicity, race, class, gender, religion, and exceptionality. (Manning & Baruth, 2000)

◇ To foster in students a vision of what can be—of a truly democratic society in which cultural diversity and democratic ideals merge to benefit all of its people.

Teachers

⟡ To apply knowledge of sociocultural factors related to the teaching and learning processes to maximize the academic, personal, and social development of all students.

⟡ To give male and female; minority and nonminority; urban, suburban and rural students—all learners from all backgrounds—an opportunity to experience educational equality, success and mobility. (Adapted from Banks, 1995)

Educational Change

⟡ To reform the school and other educational institutions so that students from diverse racial, ethnic, and social-class groups will experience educational equality. (Banks, 1995, p. 3)

These are ambitious, but, hopefully, not unattainable goals. However, they will demand more of teachers than some are willing to give:

> Too many teacher educators (and teachers) believe that they can implement an effective multicultural education program without effecting fundamental change in the classrooms and schools in which they teach. This belief contributes to the superficial and trivial treatment of issues of race, class, and gender in elementary and secondary school classrooms. (Ladson-Billings, 1995, p. 755)

Simply stated, educators "cannot shrink from the responsibility of real change and reform"; those who profess to implement multicultural education programs that are meaningful and powerful will need to challenge the limitations of conventional practice, to go beyond doing "business as usual" (p. 755).

Multicultural education is a vision of what can be—of a truly democratic society in which social equity is a reality; of a truly democratic system in which cultural diversity and democratic ideals merge to benefit **all** of its children. The stakes are high:

> The children who will be in the next century's schools have already been born and, without their knowing so, their educational career may already be "at risk.". . . They are still unaware of the price they will have to pay in school and society because of their linguistic and sociocultural differences. Their silence today about our tardiness to respond to their social, economic, emotional, and especially their educational needs, and our misgivings regarding their place in public schools and their potential contributions to society will speak eloquently tomorrow. In the twenty-first century, these children's voices will be heard as they ask for explanations and solutions, effective educational policies, and a fair share in the social and economic benefits given to other members of American society. (Trueba, 1989, p. v)

The future in Trueba's prediction is already here. It is becoming increasingly apparent that in order to provide a quality education for all, schools must provide an education that is multicultural.

In the final analysis, multicultural education is for all students and all teachers.

SUMMARY

In a pluralistic society, educators must be able to provide all students with a quality education in which *excellence* and *equity* are cornerstones.

◇ Multicultural education—an essential part of schooling in a culturally diverse society—is a vision of what education can be, should be, and must be for *all* students. It is about students, teachers, and educational change. It encompasses the influences that shape individuals as cultural beings and educators as cultural brokers. It strives for the full development of each learner's unique constellation of intelligences, capabilities, and talents, and prepares the next generation for citizenship in multiple, interrelated cultural and linguistic communities. It affirms the importance of teachers as individuals who make a positive and significant difference in the lives of their students, and as professionals committed to the ideals of educational equity and excellence for all students. It demands that we use our understanding of contexts, processes, and content in education to create schools that provide exemplary teaching, dynamic learning environments, and optimum opportunities for all learners.

◇ This view of multicultural education is predicated on several basic assumptions. Multicultural education is for all students. It presumes the cultural diversity of our society, recognizes the pervasive influence of social and cultural factors on teaching and learning, and the centrality of teachers within their sphere of influence in classrooms and schools. Synonymous with and essential to effective teaching and educational reform, multicultural education holds that the educational system is responsible for providing all students with effective teaching, effective programs, and effective schools.

◆ In this conceptualization of multicultural education, the influence of sociocultural factors on education can best be understood by looking at context, process, and content. Through context, teachers can better appreciate the complex interrelationship of social, cultural, economic, and political influences, and their impact on schooling. Content represents the substance of curriculum and instruction; and process comes into play through the often "hidden" interactional, social, managerial, and organizational dynamics of classroom life. Without addressing these three dimensions, any approach that teachers select is incomplete and inadequate. To deal with content alone ignores the "hidden curriculum" enacted in classrooms on a daily basis; to overlook the "intended curriculum" denies the subject matter that is the focal point of classroom life. To ignore the context in which we teach and students learn will frustrate our efforts to ensure that all learners achieve to their capabilities.

◆ Multicultural education has a number of primary goals. Among these are the academic and personal development of students to their fullest potential; the social and cultural development of students as competent, respectful, and responsible participants in a multicultural world; the professional empowerment of teachers; and school reform guided by a dual vision of excellence and equity.

◆ In the final analysis, multicultural education is for all students, teachers, and schools.

APPLICATION, EXTENSION, AND REFLECTION

1. *Defining Multicultural Education.* Gay (1995) observes that there is considerable variation in definitions of multicultural education relative to content, focus, and orientation. She draws on Banks' tripartite definition of multicultural education to identify some of the common attributes in major conceptualizations. The categories are as follows:

   • As a *concept, idea, or philosophy,* multicultural education embodies a set of beliefs and values that recognize the influence of ethnicity and culture upon the lifestyles, experiences, identities, and opportunities of individuals, groups, and nations. Recurrent themes include cultural pluralism, educational equality and excellence. (pp. 27–28)

   • As a *process,* multicultural education is a comprehensive, pervasive, substantive, systematic, and continuous approach to the whole educational enterprise. One recurrent theme is the emphasis on multicultural education as greater in scope than a simple program or product.

- As a *reform movement,* multicultural education emphasizes substantive structural, procedural, and valuative changes in education to reflect social, cultural, ethnic, racial, and linguistic diversity. Recurrent themes include individual empowerment, and social transformation. (pp. 28–29)

Some or all of these elements are typically in evidence in the conceptions of many authors. The following five definitions are illustrative:

> Multicultural education is at least three things: an idea or concept, an educational reform movement, and a process. Multicultural education incorporates the idea that all students—regardless of their gender and social class and their ethnic, racial, or cultural characteristics—should have an equal opportunity to learn in school. . . . [It] is also a reform movement that is trying to change the schools and other educational institutions so that students from all social class, gender, racial, and cultural groups will have an equal opportunity to learn. . . Multicultural education is also a process whose goals will never be fully realized. Educational equality, like liberty and justice, are ideals toward which human beings work but never fully attain. (Banks, 1997, pp. 3–4)

> Multicultural education is an approach to teaching and learning that is based upon democratic values and beliefs, and seeks to foster cultural pluralism within culturally diverse societies and an interdependent world. A comprehensive definition includes the following four dimensions of multicultural education: the movement toward equity, the multicultural curriculum approach, the process of becoming multicultural, and the commitment to combat prejudice and discrimination. (Bennett, 1995, p. 13)

> Multicultural education is a process of comprehensive school reform and basic education for all students. It challenges and rejects racism and other forms of discrimination in schools and society and accepts and affirms the pluralism (ethnic, racial, linguistic, religious, economic, and gender, among others) that students, their communities, and teachers represent. Multicultural education permeates the curriculum and instructional strategies used in schools, as well as the interactions among teachers, students and parents, and the very way that schools conceptualize the nature of teaching and learning. Because it uses critical pedagogy as its underlying philosophy and focuses on knowledge, reflection, and action (praxis) as the basis for social change, multicultural education furthers the democratic principles of social justice. (Nieto, 1996, p. 307)

> A layered concept that includes not only the experiences of particular individuals and groups but also their shared interests and relationships, which, in turn, are embedded in the interconnectedness of all peoples of the world. In its full complexity, then, multiculturalism implies the cultivation of a global view of human affairs. Paradoxically, perhaps, this expanded view of multiculturalism places primary emphasis on the individual and on the importance of individual decisions regarding all issues concerning the welfare of humankind. (García & Pugh, 1992, p. 218).

> In searching for an appropriate understanding of multicultural education in the United States, we must emphasize a type of education that will permit all American children, minority and mainstream, immigrants, refugees, African American, American Indian, Hispanics, and other underrepresented groups (politically disempowered) such as low-income and [handicapped] children, to participate fully in their own development, in their preparation to act as first class American citizens in our social, economic, political and cultural institutions, fully aware that they are genuine member[s] of American society with all rights and obligations that mainstream persons have. This type of education will entail, therefore, not just tolerance for diversity, but commitment to respect it, pride in our collective rich ethnic heritage, and the ability to use [it] in the development of children's talents. (Trueba, 1992, pp. 97–98)

Think about how you would define multicultural education. What does the term encompass and why? What does it mean to you as a teacher? Jot down some of your ideas and compare them with others. How are your views similar? In what ways are they different? Do the differences represent different points of view? How do the elements that you have incorporated in your definition compare to those emphasized in the current literature? In the definition used in this text?

Save your definition. After you finish reading the text, take another look at what you wrote. To what extent has your conceptualization changed? To what extent has it remained the same? If you were to revise your definition, what would it look like? Why?

2. *Historical Development.* Several approaches mark the evolution of multicultural education since its inception. According to the typology developed by Sleeter and Grant (1999), these can be labeled as follows: Teaching the Exceptional and the Culturally Different; Human Relations; Single-Group Studies; Multicultural Education; and Education That Is Multicultural and Social Reconstructionist. Except for the first, these approaches are intended for all students. The following summary of these approaches is based on the discussion by Sleeter and Grant (1999).

Initiated in the 1960s, the approach called **Teaching the Exceptional and Culturally Different** is characterized by efforts to promote the academic achievement of students from minority ethnic groups and lower socioeconomic levels, those with limited English proficiency, and those with other special educational needs. Central to this approach is the adaptation of instruction in regular classrooms to individual differences. Practices focus on the use of culturally relevant curricula, basic skills development, and sensitivity to individual learning styles.

Desegregation efforts provided impetus for **Human Relations,** an approach that emphasizes intergroup relationships and self-concept. This approach is intended to reduce intergroup conflict, promote greater tolerance of individual differences, and foster positive interaction among students.

The curriculum and instruction associated with this approach focus on addressing stereotyping and name-calling, teaching about individual differences and similarities, and recognizing group contributions.

Another approach developed during this period—**Single-Group Studies**—is marked by in-depth study of particular groups (e.g., ethnic and women's studies). This approach attempts to raise social consciousness and promote social action on behalf of specific groups. The perspective of group members is integral to this approach, and instruction centers on the group's history, culture, and concerns. Minority groups are presented as distinct entities and usually are treated separately.

In the 1970s, **Multicultural Education** emerged as a more comprehensive approach. With cultural diversity and equal opportunity as its cornerstones, this approach examines and takes into account the relationships among culture, ethnicity, language, gender, handicap, and social class in developing educational programs. Of all the approaches, this is the most prevalent. In the classroom, content is structured around the contributions and perspectives of different groups. Instruction emphasizes critical thinking skills and uses culturally relevant materials and curricular adaptations. As in other approaches, use of other languages, learning styles, and cooperative learning is prominent.

A more recent approach—**Education That Is Multicultural and Social Reconstructionist**—represents an extension of multicultural education in the direction of more definitive social action. Compared with the other approaches, this one incorporates a much greater curricular emphasis on active student involvement in addressing social issues (e.g., racism, sexism, classism) and on development of problem-solving and political action skills. In addition to curricular adaptations and cooperative learning, instruction emphasizes development of decision-making skills.

As you proceed through the text, try to identify two or three ideas or strategies that might illustrate each of these approaches. Explain why you classified the ideas and strategies as you did and consider how the same idea or strategy might appear under more than one approach. (For more specific information and teaching plans for each of the five approaches, refer to Grant and Sleeter (1998), *Turning on Learning: Five Approaches for Multicultural Teaching Plans for Race, Class, Gender, and Disability.*)

3. *Personal Perspectives.* In discussing the teaching of culturally diverse populations, Etlin (1988) remarked that "to teach them all is to know them all" (pp. 10–11). A good first step in learning how "to teach them all" is to reflect on one's own perspectives. The self-test on cultural sensitivities in Figure 1.1, adapted from Lockart (cited in Etlin, 1988), highlights selected teacher attitudes and behaviors relevant to multicultural education. Respond to each of the questions, then reflect upon your responses.

1. Am I knowledgeable about and sensitive to students' cultural backgrounds, values, and traditions?

2. Have I discarded stereotypes that interfere with my support of students' academic and personal growth as individuals?

3. Do I provide a classroom atmosphere in which students' cultures are recognized, shared, and respected?

4. Do I use culturally appropriate curricular materials to supplement those that treat different groups in a limited or biased manner?

5. Do I give students an opportunity to teach me what I don't know or understand about their cultures? In other words, do learning and teaching operate in both directions in my classroom?

6. Do I involve parents and other community members in classroom activities?

Observations: _____

_____

_____

_____

_____

_____

_____

_____

_____

FIGURE 1.1   Cultural sensitivity.
Adapted from Lockart in M. Etlin, To teach them all is to know them all. *NEA Today,* 6(10), 10–11, 1988.

4. *Professional Competencies.* The creation of schools and classrooms that are optimal learning environments for all students, and the development of educational systems reflecting the ideals of equity and excellence require very specific competencies. The set of questions in Figure 1.2 addresses some of the more salient knowledge, skills, and values involved. Respond to each of the questions, and reflect on the expertise that you already bring to the multicultural classroom. (Note: Answers will vary depending upon where respondents fall along the continuum of professional preparation and experience, from novice to expert teacher.)

5. *React to the Premises.* React to the seven premises presented in this chapter. To what extent do you agree or disagree with the basic assumptions articulated? Why? Compare your notes with a colleague. Then come back to the premises when you have finished reading the text. Has your point of view changed in any way? If so, explain how and why.

1. Have I developed a rationale for multicultural education that provides me with the basis for its implementation in the classroom?

2. Do I understand the interrelationship of context, process, and content in relation to multicultural education?

3. Do I appreciate the influence of sociocultural factors on learning and teaching? To what extent am I able to apply the insights I have to maximize students' academic and social development?

4. To what extent am I cognizant of the interactional, social, management, and organizational dimensions of culturally pluralistic classrooms and their influence on academic outcomes?

5. Do I understand bilingualism and its implications for the education of English language learners?

6. To what extent do I incorporate instructional methods and practices that are culturally appropriate for diverse student populations?

7. Do I have the requisite skills to adapt teaching to meet the needs of individual learners from different backgrounds and with diverse ability levels?

8. To what extent am I able to evaluate, develop, and modify curricular materials in relation to the treatment of social and cultural content?

9. Do I have skills necessary to develop a curriculum that integrates: (a) multicultural perspectives (e.g., ethnicity, gender, socioeconomic status, age, religion, exceptionality); (b) content addressing issues of intercultural and interracial understanding (e.g., cultural awareness, intergroup relations, discrimination and racism); and (c) resources outside the classroom (i.e., home, community, technology).

10. Do I know how to create a learning environment that promotes the academic, linguistic, social, and affective development of all learners?

FIGURE 1.2 Professional competencies.
Source: These questions are adapted in part on Baptiste and Baptiste, 1980 and Suzuki, 1984.

REFERENCES

American Association of Colleges for Teacher Education. (1973). No one model American. *The Journal of Teacher Education, XXIV*(4), 264–265.

Astuto, T., & Clark, D. (1992). Challenging the limits of school restructuring and reform. In A. Lieberman (Ed.), *The changing contexts of education*, Ninety-first Yearbook of the National Society for the Study of Education, Part I. pp. 90–109, Chicago, IL: The University of Chicago Press.

Baker, G. C. (1979). Policy issues in multicultural education in the United States. *Journal of Negro Education, XLVIII*(3), 253–266.

Baker, G. C. (1983). *Planning and organizing for multicultural instruction.* Reading, MA: Addison-Wesley Publishing Co.

Banks, J. A. (1979). Shaping the future of multicultural education. *Journal of Negro Education, XLVIII*(3), 237–252.

Banks, J. A. (1995). Multicultural education: Historical development, dimensions, and practice. In J. A. Banks (Ed.) & C. A. McGee Banks (Assoc. ed.), *Handbook of research on multicultural education* (pp. 3–24). New York: Macmillan.

Banks, J. A. (1997). Multicultural education: Characteristics and goals. In J. A. Banks & C. A. McGee Banks (Eds.), *Multicultural education: Issues and perspectives* (pp. 3–31). Boston: Allyn and Bacon.

Baptiste, M. L., & Baptiste, H. P., Jr. (1980). Competencies toward multiculturalism. In H. P. Baptiste, Jr. & M. L. Baptiste (Eds.), *Multicultural teacher education: Preparing educators to provide educational equity* (pp. 44–72). Washington, DC: American Association of Colleges for Teacher Education.

Barbour, C., & Barbour, N. H. (1997). *Families, schools, and communities: Building partnerships for educating children.* Upper Saddle River, NJ: Merrill/Prentice Hall.

Bennett, C. I. (1995). *Comprehensive multicultural education* (3rd ed.). Needham Heights, MA: Allyn and Bacon.

Berliner, D. C., & Biddle, B. J. (1997). *The manufactured crisis: Myths, fraud, and the attack on America's public schools.* White Plains, NY: Longman.

Boyle-Baise, M., & Sleeter, C. E. (1996). Field experiences: Planting seeds and pulling weeds. In C. A. Grant & M. L. Gómez (Eds.), *Making schooling multicultural: Campus and classroom* (pp. 371–388). Englewood Cliffs, NJ: Merrill/Prentice Hall.

Brown, P. R., & Haycock, K. (1984). *Excellence for whom?* Oakland, CA: The Achievement Council.

California State Department of Education (1979). *Planning for multicultural education as a part of school improvement.* Sacramento: California State Department of Education.

Darling-Hammond, L. (1995). Inequality and access to knowledge. In J. A. Banks (Ed.) & C. A. McGee Banks (Assoc. ed.), *Handbook of research on multicultural education* (pp. 465–483). New York: Macmillan.

Darling-Hammond, L. (1996). The right to learn and the advancement of teaching; Research, policy, and practice for democratic education. *Educational Researcher, 25*(6), 5–17.

Erickson, F. (1997). Culture in society and in educational practices. In J. A. Banks & C. A. McGee Banks (Eds.), *Multicultural education: Issues and perspectives* (3rd ed.) (pp. 32–60). Boston: Allyn and Bacon.

Etlin, M. (1988). To teach them all is to know them all. *NEA Today, 6*(10), 10–11.

Frazier, L. (1977). The multicultural facet of education. *Journal of Research and Development in Education, 11*(1), 10–16.

García, J., & Pugh, S. (1992). Multicultural education in teacher preparation programs. *Phi Delta Kappan, 74*(3), 214–219.

Gay, G. (1995). Curriculum theory and multicultural education. In J. A. Banks (Ed.) & C. A. McGee Banks (Assoc. ed.), *Handbook of research on multicultural education* (pp. 25–43). New York: Macmillan.

Gay, G. (1996). Building cultural bridges: A bold proposal for teacher education. In F. Schultz (Ed.), *Annual editions: Multicultural education, 1996/97* (pp. 45–51). Sluice Dock, Guilford, CT: Dushkin Publishing Group/Brown & Benchmark Publishers.

Gay, G. (1997). Educational equality for students of color. In J. A. Banks and C. A. McGee Banks (Eds.), *Multicultural education: Issues and perspectives* (3rd ed.) (pp. 195–228). Boston: Allyn and Bacon.

Gibson, M. A. (1984). Approaches to multicultural education in the United States: Some concepts and assumptions. *Anthropology and Education Quarterly, 15,* 94–119.

Gollnick, D. M., & Chinn, P. C. (1986). *Multicultural education in a pluralistic society* (2nd ed.). Columbus, OH: Merrill.

Gollnick, D. M., & Chinn, P. C. (1994). *Multicultural education in a pluralistic society* (4th ed.). New York: Merrill/Macmillan.

Gordon, B. M. (1995). Knowledge construction, competing critical theories, and education. In J. A. Banks (Ed) & C. A. McGee Banks (Assoc. Ed.), *Handbook of research on multicultural education* (pp. 184–199). New York: Macmillan.

Grant, C. A. (1977). The mediator of culture: A teacher role revisited. *Journal of Research and Development in Education, 11*(1), 102–117.

Grant C. A. (1978). Education that is multicultural—Isn't that what we mean? *Journal of Teacher Education, XXIX*(5), 45–48.

Grant, C. A., & Sleeter, C. E. (1998). *Turning on learning: Five approaches for multicultural teaching plans for race, class, gender, and disability* (2nd ed.). Upper Saddle River, NJ: Merrill/Prentice Hall.

Katznelson, I., & Weir, M. (1985). *Schooling for all.* New York: Basic Books.

Knapp, M. S., & Woolverton, S. (1995). Social class and schooling. In J. A. Banks (Ed.) & C. A. McGee Banks (Assoc. Ed.), *Handbook of research on multicultural education* (pp. 548–569). New York: Macmillan.

Ladson-Billings, G. (1994). *The dreamkeepers: Successful teachers of African-American children.* San Francisco, CA: Jossey-Bass.

Ladson-Billings, G. (1995). Multicultural teacher education: Research, practice, and policy. In J. A. Banks (Ed.), C. A. McGee Banks (Assoc. Ed.), *Handbook of research on multicultural education* (pp. 747–759). New York: Macmillan.

Lee, M. K. (1983). Multiculturalism: Educational perspectives for the 1980's. *Education, 103*(4), 405–409.

Lewis, A. C. (1999). Washington Commentary, Time for schools to perform. *Phi Delta Kappan, 81*(2), 99–100.

Manning, M. L., & Baruth, L. G. (2000). *Multicultural education of children and adolescents* (3rd ed.). Boston: Allyn and Bacon.

McGroarty, M. (1986). Educator's response to sociocultural diversity: Implications for practice. *Beyond language: Social and cultural factors in schooling language minority students* (pp. 299–334). Los Angeles: Evaluation, Dissemination and Assessment Center, California State University–Los Angeles.

McKnight National Commission on Excellence in Education

National Council for Accreditation of Teacher Education. (1986). *Standards, procedures, policies for the accreditation of professional teacher education units.* Washington, DC: Author.

Nieto, S. (1996). *Affirming diversity: The sociopolitical context of multicultural education.* 2nd ed. White Plains, NY: Longman.

Olsen, L. (1997). *Made in America.* New York: The New Press.

Pacheco, A. (1977). Cultural pluralism: A philosophical analysis. *Journal of Teacher Education, XXVIII*(3), 16–20.

Payne, C. (1983). Multicultural education: A natural way to teach. *Contemporary Education, 54*(2), 98–103.

Shulman, L. (1986). Paradigms and research programs in the study of teaching: A contemporary perspective. In M. C. Wittrock (Ed.), *Handbook of research on teaching* (3rd ed.) (pp. 3–36). New York: Macmillan.

Sleeter, C. E. (1995). An analysis of the critiques of multicultural education. In J. A. Banks (Ed.) & C. A. McGee Banks (Assoc. ed.), *Handbook of research on multicultural education* (pp. 81–94). New York: Macmillan.

Sleeter, C. E., & Grant, C. A. (1999). *Making choices for multicultural education: Five approaches to race, clan, and gender* (3rd ed.). Upper Saddle River, NJ: Merrill Prentice-Hall.

Stubbs, M. (1976). *Language, schools and classrooms.* London: Methuen.

Suzuki, R. H. (1984). Curriculum transformation for multicultural education. *Education and Urban Society, 16*(3), 294–322.

Troutman, P., Jones, W. P., & Ramírez, M. G. (1999). Cultural diversity and the NCATE Standards: A case study. In F. Schultz (Ed.), *Annual editions: Multicultural education* 1999/2000 (pp. 64–67). Guilford, CT: Dushkin/McGraw-Hill.

Trueba, H. T. (1989). *Raising silent voices: Educating linguistic minorities for the 21st century.* New York: Harper & Row.

Trueba, H. T. (1992). Many groups, one people: The meaning and significance of multicultural education in modern America. *Bilingual Research Journal, 16*(3&4), 91–116.

U.S. Commission on Civil Rights. (1973). *Teachers and students. Report V: Mexican-American education study.* Washington, DC: U.S. Government Printing Office.

Webb, K. S. (1983). On multicultural education—how to begin: A practical response to the NCATE guidelines. *Contemporary Education, 54*(2), 93–97.

2 The Context of Teaching

> We must remember that we have every opportunity to transform ourselves and our practice, just as we have every opportunity to stagnate, remaining much the same teachers we were when we began.
>
> *Carol Ann Tomlinson*

In the 21st century, teaching as we know it will be different from the past and present. Social, economic, and demographic changes rooted in the 1980s and 1990s present teachers and schools with increasingly complex challenges and considerable pressures. According to Lieberman (1992), this transformation of our society is also exerting potentially profound effects on teaching and learning. "Teaching is affected not only by what the teacher does, but by the context within which teaching takes place: the kinds of students, the content of the curriculum, and political and social forces within as well as surrounding the school" (p. 6). With the changes that ensue from the transformation now in progress, one thing is certain: our postindustrial society will see a new context for teaching.

What will this **new context of teaching** look like? A look at what is happening in the present provides a glimpse of what is in store for the future, as teachers prepare for "what schools must *become,* not only schools as they *are*" (Darling-Hammond, 1996, p. 6). Analyses of the changing context of education (Lieberman, 1992; Darling-Hammond & Snyder, 1992; Little, 1992) suggest the following:

⬦ Acknowledging that diversity rather than uniformity is the rule, research on teaching is shifting attention from the search for generic rules of effective teaching applicable in all classrooms to better understanding the context of teaching in its myriad manifestations.

⬦ Traditional acceptance of school success for some and failure for others is changing. Simply stated, "there is a growing consensus that the United States cannot maintain its democratic foundations or its standard of living unless all students are much better educated" (Darling-Hammond & Snyder, 1992, p. 13). The schools' new mission—to "ensure high levels of student learning for all"—means that schools must succeed in reaching diverse learner populations (p. 11). Merely delivering instruction, whatever the outcomes, is no longer enough.

⬦ The pendulum is swinging from teacher-directed instruction toward student-centered teaching. In the classroom, approaches to teaching that are student-centered give increasing relevance to the creation of environments that actively engage students in learning, build upon student strengths and abilities, involve students in higher level thinking and problem solving, and make learning more individualized within a group orientation. Outside the classroom, these approaches expand consideration of the teaching context by encompassing other conditions that influence student learning, such as the climate of the school, the participation of parents in the education of their children, and teacher involvement in school governance.

⬦ The role of the teacher is changing in fundamental ways. The tasks are increasingly complex, as teachers assume greater responsibility for their teaching and their students' learning, for making decisions at the school level, defining directions in program development, and confronting pressures from outside the school.

It should come as no surprise then that part of the changing context is a growing move to professionalize teaching further by making demands on teachers to know more, to be heavily engaged in curriculum making and instructional decisions in the school, and to be more involved in reshaping the school to focus on students. (Lieberman, 1992, p. 8)

⬦ Within this new context, teachers are at the forefront. Within this changing context of teaching, a multicultural perspective is an increasingly integral part of the educational transformation that engulfs us all.

The professional role of the teacher is changing in fundamental ways.

ACCOUNTABILITY AND EMPOWERMENT

To appreciate the level of professional accountability demanded of teachers in the new context of teaching, we must first consider the bureaucratic model of accountability currently in place. Darling-Hammond and Snyder (1992) characterize bureaucratic accountability as displaying these critical attributes:

The Bureaucratic Model

◇ The purpose of accountability is "to ensure equal education through the development of uniform, standardized procedures." (p. 16)
◇ Underlying assumptions include the belief that students in all educational settings will respond similarly and predictably to mandates imposed by those at the top of the hierarchy; that the rules and procedures developed in response to these mandates can be fully and faithfully implemented by teachers; and that the outcomes can be effectively monitored through a complex of regulatory and inspection systems.
◇ Within this model, teachers are accountable for implementing curricular and testing policies, whether or not these are appropriate for all learners. As a result, adherence to standardized procedures takes precedence over meeting the individual needs of learners, and heavy reliance on standardized

testing to monitor progress and promote conformity renders test scores as the primary outcome of schooling rather than higher-order skills and performance.

◇ The potential for failure is great, as neither teachers nor students develop the skills nor enjoy the opportunities conducive to productive teaching and learning.

The impact of the bureaucratic model on teachers has been described as follows:

> At the risk of oversimplifying a complex situation, it seems that what might be termed a "natural" problematic change in the context of teaching, that of a differing clientele, gave rise to a "constructed" change in which authorities outside the classroom specified how teachers were to handle the problem. The "constructed" change not only failed to solve the problems of the "natural" change; it created a new context and role for teachers which led to greater problems, including dissatisfaction with job and workplace and a decline in rewards. In some instances, the demoralization brought about by the "constructed" change was so overwhelming that some teachers who were perceived to be talented and effective left the classroom while others who remained became dysfunctional. (Cohn, 1992, p. 132)

More recently, a growing number of policymakers are reaching the conclusion that regulations are not going to transform schools: "only teachers in collaboration with parents and administrators, can do that" (Darling-Hammond, 1996, p. 5).

Teacher Accountability

Darling-Hammond and Snyder (1992) envision a different future, one with accountability at all levels geared toward equity and excellence. In their model of accountability for learner-centered teaching in Figure 2.1, **teacher accountability** is paramount. Because the complex decisions related to classroom life can best be made by teachers, the primary responsibility and commitment is theirs. Characterized by teaching practices that are knowledge-based and learner-oriented, professional accountability is enhanced through teacher inquiry and collaborative problem solving. Teachers routinely evaluate and reflect upon what happens within the school community. They ask themselves why it is happening, and whether current practices are achieving the desired results. The profile of such a teacher might look like this:

> A professionally responsible teacher may decide that some or all of her students would be better taught using books other than a mandated text that is poorly constructed, at the wrong reading level, or biased in its depiction of certain racial, ethnic, or cultural groups. She may be aware that the learning styles of some of her students would be better addressed by one set of teaching methods or materials than another prescribed for general use. She would insist, in line with professional knowledge about assessment, that no decision about any student be made solely on the basis of a single test score or other standardized measure. (p. 22)

In the final analysis, professional accountability in the new context of teaching will require more of teachers than ever before. With greater authority and re-

---

Accountability model for learner-centered schools.

Level	*Responsibilities*
State	Provides schools equal and adequate resources
	Ensures enforcement of equity standards and standards of professional certification
School district	Adopts local policies and accounts for their implementation
	Provides for equitable distribution of school resources
	Develops processes for responding to the needs and concerns of parents, students, and school faculty/staff
School	Accounts for equitable internal distribution of resources
	Adopts policies based upon professional knowledge
	Establishes means for ongoing staff learning
	Develops processes for identifying problems and solutions as part of continuous improvement
	Responds to ideas from parents, students, and staff
Teacher	Identifies and meets the needs of individual learners based on professional knowledge and the application of standards of practice appropriate to instructional goals
	Engages in continuous evaluation of his/her own practices and those of colleagues
	Seeks new knowledge and constantly revises strategies to meet student needs more effectively

---

FIGURE 2.1

Source: Adapted from L. Darling-Hammond and J. Snyder, 1992, Reframing Accountability: Creating Learner-Centered Schools. In A. Lieberman (Ed.), *The Changing Contexts of Teaching*, Ninety-first Yearbook of the National Society for the Study of Education, Part I (pp. 25–26). Chicago, IL: The University of Chicago Press.

sponsibility based at the school level to address increasingly complex student needs, it will be incumbent upon teachers to link context, process, and content in their search for answers. As Darling-Hammond and Snyder observe,

> at its best teaching knowledge is context- and content-specific. Thus, uniform policy decisions about teaching methods and school processes cannot meet the needs of varying school and student circumstances. Improving student and school achievement demands discretionary decisions safeguarded by professional accountability. (p. 24)

Responsibly Empowered Professionals

The scenario for responsibly empowered professionals assuming the expanded roles and responsibilities created by the transformations just described is exciting as well as challenging. With teacher empowerment come opportunities for greater "autonomy, responsibility, choice, and authority" (Lawrence Lightfoot,

Responsibly empowered professionals know their discipline as well as they know their students.
("Teacher, are you sure this is how the seafarers drank water long ago?")

1986, pp. 9–28). With teacher empowerment comes greater demands on teachers to know their discipline as well as they know their students.

According to Lichtenstein, McLaughlin, and Knudsen (1992), when teachers are empowered through professionally relevant knowledge they develop "a sense of authority and a belief that they can make a difference" (p. 49). This sense of efficacy complements their competence in professional domains. Thus, believing that they can actually make a difference, and having the relevant professional and subject matter knowledge and skills to deliver on the promise inspires performance.

> As far as professionally empowered teachers are concerned, the walls of the classroom are an illusion. The meaningful focus of teacher development may include the classroom, but also necessarily transcends it. We ought no longer to confuse where teachers work with how they work; knowledge gained outside the classroom informs (and is informed by) knowledge teachers gain within the classroom. Both sources of knowledge are essential to teacher empowerment. (p. 56)

Responsibly empowered professionals will be lifelong learners, fully cognizant of the fact that how they learn and what they do with what they know directly and indirectly affects their students. Research on teacher learning suggests that it entails enhancing pedagogical skills, changing beliefs and attitudes, and acquiring knowledge as well as transforming classroom practice as the result of new learning (Grossman, 1992, p. 180). For teacher learning to make a difference, however, teachers must "situate their new knowledge and understanding within the context of their actual classroom" (p. 181). Empowered teachers see the connections between what they learn and what they do, as learning is brought to bear upon classroom practice. Those who are not empowered learners do not see the relevant relationships that would enable them to transform their practice in light of what they have learned. Learning to teach from a multicultural perspective can be a critical part of this process.

DEVELOPING A MULTICULTURAL PERSPECTIVE

In the day-to-day life of the classroom, teachers perceive issues and challenges differently and respond accordingly. In a given situation, some teachers may be troubled by what they see, while others are complacent or indifferent. Teachers' perspectives reflect both prior school and general life experiences (Boyle-Baise & Sleeter, 1996, p. 373). They are likened to a filter through which we interpret information and experiences, and define how we approach teaching. Teacher perspectives reflect the interconnectedness of thought, behavior, context, and situation. In more precise terms teacher perspective has been defined as "a theory of action that has developed as a result of the individual's experiences and is applied in particular situations" (Ross, cited in Boyle-Baise & Sleeter, 1996, p. 373).

Research suggests that teachers who work effectively with diverse populations operate from a different perspective than those who are less effective (Boyle-Baise & Sleeter, 1996, pp. 373–374). Ladson-Billings (1994) refers to this as "culturally relevant teaching." Various studies suggest that preservice teachers are particularly prone to regard their perspective as normative. It is more difficult for them to accept the fact that theirs is only one point of view, an outlook on reality that may not provide an accurate picture of children's learning, homes, and communities, especially when these are different from their own. Moreover, preservice teachers tend to define "good" teaching primarily in terms of maintaining order and covering textbook content. When learners do not perform well, their failure is attributed to home environment, attitude, or ability. Social inequality is explained most often in terms of either "cultural deprivation" and lack of effort, or personal attitudes and prejudice; the impact of institutional structures is largely ignored.

By contrast, effective teachers are more likely to construct their teaching perspectives by drawing on the cultural group of the learners. This is evidenced by systematic use of adults within a cultural community as primary sources of information, teaching in a manner congruent with learners' experiences and styles, and perceptions of students' homes and cultural backgrounds as assets. Effective teachers understand how to draw relevant information from the social and cultural context and then use what they learn to enhance effectiveness. They develop a teacher perspective that is, in effect, multicultural.

Maintaining a healthy equilibrium between a heart that cares and eyes that are critical is essential to teaching from a multicultural perspective.

How teachers think powerfully affects how their students will learn. Eby's (1998) comparison of more and less effective teachers makes this point most succinctly. "From my observations of dozens of schools and hundreds of teachers, the less successful and less effective teachers seem to be those who think very little, believe that very simple answers exist for every question, and think that they know it all and have all the answers" (p. 6). By contrast, "successful, effective teachers tend to reflect actively and productively about the important things in their careers, their educational goals, the classroom environment, and their own professional abilities" (p. 6).

Teaching from a multicultural perspective demands a pedagogy that balances "a caring heart and critical eyes" (Wink, 1997, p. 147). Reflective teaching helps teachers to maintain a healthy equilibrium between these seemingly disparate yet complementary elements.

> Teaching can be done as badly as anything else. It can be wooden, mechanical, mindless, and wholly unimaginative. But when it is sensitive, intelligent, and creative—those qualities that confer upon it the status of an art—it should, in my view, not be regarded, as it so often is by some, as an expression of unfathomable talent or luck but as an example of humans exercising the highest levels of their intelligence. (Eisner, cited in Henderson, 1996, p. 160)

REFLECTIVE TEACHING

Reflective teaching can be used to foster development of a teacher perspective that enhances effectiveness with cultural and social groups different from one's own (Boyle-Baise & Sleeter, 1996; Gillette, 1996). When teachers reflect upon their teaching, they are involved in questioning, processing, and internalizing concepts, intensely engaged in "a process of knowing how we know": "it is the only chance we have to discover our blindness and to recognize that the certainties and knowledge of others are, respectively, as overwhelming and tenuous as our own" (Maturana & Varela, 1987, p. 27).

It is easy to see why Dewey's ideas about reflection in teaching have become an integral part of many approaches to multicultural education (Grant & Gómez, 1996; Powell, Zehm, & García, 1996). For Dewey (1933), reflective action sets reflective teachers apart from those for whom teaching is imitation and unquestioned acceptance of traditional practice, whatever the outcomes. Reflective thought is characterized by "active, persistent, and careful consideration of any belief or supposed form of knowledge in the light of the grounds that support it and the further conclusions to which it [leads]" (Dewey, 1933, p. 9).

Eby's (1998, pp. 7–8) analysis of Dewey's statement draws our attention to the specific traits that characterize the teacher as **reflective thinker:**

active	=	energetically engages in a vigorous search for knowledge and solutions to classroom problems
persistent	=	is rarely content with easy answers and simple solutions; habitually and purposefully in pursuit of more knowledge and superior ways to teach
careful	=	is deeply concerned with improving professional performance and learner outcomes, academic and psychosocial
belief or supposed form of knowledge	=	maintains an appropriate level of skepticism in regards to pedagogical theories and practices; open to new ideas that prove their value and appropriateness in meeting learner needs
in light of the grounds that support it	=	gathers data, weighs evidence, applies criteria and draws conclusions when making judgments

For Dewey, attitude is a critical element in reflective teaching, a pivotal factor in the way in which individuals recognize and respond to problems. In his characterization of reflective teachers, Dewey placed particular emphasis on open-mindedness, whole-heartedness, and responsibility, all key attitudes in *translating thought into action* (Eby, 1998, p. 8). In the following definitions, notice

how Dewey (1933) embeds reflection upon teaching within the educational, social, and political context in which it occurs:

◇ *Open-mindedness:* This attitude involves "an active desire to listen to more
sides than one; to give heed to facts from whatever source they come; to give
full attention to alternative possibilities; to recognize the possibility of error
even in the beliefs that are dearest to us" (p. 30).

◇ *Whole-heartedness:* "When anyone is thoroughly interested in some object
and cause, he[she] throws himself [herself] into it; he[she] does so, as we say,
'heartily,' or with a whole heart. The importance of this attitude or disposi-
tion is generally recognized in practical and moral affairs. But it is equally
important in intellectual development." (p. 31)

◇ *Responsibility:* "To be intellectually responsible is to consider the consequences
of a projected step; it means to be willing to adopt these consequences when
they follow reasonably from any position already taken." (p. 32)

Reflective teaching marked by context sensitivity is an integral part of decision making. Teachers' interactions with students are "embedded in many subtly unique and overlapping contexts"—the perspectives of supervisors,
parental expectations, community norms and values, and societal trends, to
name a few (Henderson, 1996, p. 12). The importance of context is illustrated in
this recollection from Wink (1997):

Context. Context. Context. I will never forget when I first understood this. A
seventh-grade boy, Jim, had been misbehaving in my class. I called his mother
to come and visit with Jim and me. When she finished with the two of us, I
never *ever* saw him in the same way. I had been introduced to his world. I understood a little better how students read their world and respond to it. (p. 119)

As decisionmakers, teachers need to consider the circumstances specific to
the setting in which their decisions are made. The reader's application of information from this text is illustrative. To effectively adapt general ideas to practice
in particular situations, teachers must be sensitive to the contexts in which they
are working. Those who choose to ignore the complex nuances of the classroom,
school, home, and community contexts may be inadvertently undermining their
own efforts.

The development of reflective thinking is an intellectual process that must be
nurtured over time. Beginning teachers appear to engage in reflection at various
levels. In an analysis of reflective papers written by beginning teachers, Ross
(1989, p. 26) identified three distinct levels of reflection. At the lowest level, student teachers concentrated on describing practice, emphasizing simple solutions
to complex problems. At the next level, they demonstrated the ability to critique
and analyze practice. Only at the highest level, was practice evaluated from multiple perspectives (e.g., teacher, student, parent). Only thinking at this level displayed sensitivity to the multiple factors that determine outcomes, awareness of
the complexity of decisionmaking, and appreciation for the pervasive impact of

In the 21st century, teaching as we know it will be different from the past and present.

Teachers must prepare for what shcools will become, not only for what they are today.

To effectively adapt general ideas to practice, teachers must be sensitive to the interplay of contexts within their own classroom.

their actions. Although all of the beginning teachers demonstrated the capacity to reflect at these three levels, reflections at the two lower levels were most characteristic of their thinking.

For a select group of teachers, sophisticated reflective practice will eventually lead to transformative teacher leadership. As defined by Henderson (1996), this is "a type of leadership in which teachers function as agents of fundamental change," working "to help initiate and sustain progressive decision-making and to facilitate the necessary organizational changes that must accompany this sophisticated reflective practice" (pp. 20–21). Realistically, not all teachers will have the inclination or opportunity to be "catalysts for personal and organizational change" at this level (p. 217). For Henderson, this ideal is best fostered within a professional learning community in which teachers collaborate with others as they develop expertise in a broad range of areas such as staff development, curriculum, collaboration, organizational structure, and policy leadership. The process toward transformative teacher leadership can begin at the preservice end of the experiential continuum and continue throughout one's career, culminating in the creation of collaborative cultures supportive of reflective practice, and individual and collective teacher inquiry. Borrowing from Sirotnik, these are teachers that can make schools the centers of change, rather than a target for change. (For those who choose the path of transformative teacher leadership, Henderson provides strategies appropriate for different stages of professional development, for teachers in schools that are centers of inquiry, and for those working in institutions that are not supportive of teachers as responsibly empowered professionals.)

In the final analysis, reflective teaching is teaching at its best. As Liston and Zeichner (1996) observe, teachers grapple with many issues that both engage their minds and affect their hearts:

> Teaching is work that entails both thinking and feeling; those who can reflectively think and feel will find their work more rewarding and their efforts more successful. Good teachers find ways to listen to and integrate their passions, beliefs, and judgments.

THREE BASIC STRATEGIES

Three basic strategies that can be used to foster reflective teaching are daily reflection, reflective writing, and inquiry activities (California Foreign Language Project, 1991, pp. 2–4).

Daily reflection should be an integral part of a teacher's routine in reviewing each day's teaching experiences. The questions highlighted here are illustrative of those used to facilitate reflection.

Smyth (1989) asserts that if teachers are to "uncover the forces that inhibit and constrain them, they need to engage in four forms of action with respect to teaching" (p. 2). These actions are represented by the following four stages and their corresponding questions:

◇ DESCRIBE   What do I do?
◇ INFORM   What does this mean?
◇ CONFRONT   How did I come to be like this?
◇ RECONSTRUCT   How might I do things differently? (pp. 2, 5–6)

Additional questions may be used to facilitate reflection on teaching within the broader educational, social, and political contexts involved:

◇ If I do not do things differently, what will the effect be for the students, now and in the future?
◇ Will this effect be different for different students?
◇ How can I connect my efforts to those of others and to larger societal issues related to equity, justice, and human rights? (Gillette, 1996, pp. 406–407)

In order to help teachers come to know themselves as professional educators, Henderson (1996) uses the following questions to promote pragmatic and critical reflection:

◇ How would I like this classroom to feel today?
◇ What parts of the lesson may lead to confusion or frustration for the students?
◇ What do I know about various students that can help them work peacefully today? (p. 142)

Teachers can use **reflective writing** to facilitate critical analyses of and reflections on teaching. Journal writing is frequently used to stimulate this type of reflection by providing a written account over an extended period of time. Henderson (1996) suggests that teachers start by recording personal insights, questions, and concerns related to the students and classroom in their journals. For greater clarity and direction, he encourages teachers to be specific as they focus on aspects of the classroom community. He also recommends that colleagues share their reflections by reading each other's journals.

There are many opportunities to incorporate reflection in much of the professional writing teachers already do. For example, personal and professional histories (Smyth, 1989) and practical personal philosophies of education (Powell, Zehm, & García, 1996) are recommended as reflective writing activities for preservice and inservice teachers. For those involved in teacher preparation, professional development, or graduate programs, many observations, assignments, and projects provide rich opportunities for reflection. The same holds true for many of the curriculum, technology, subject matter, and program projects that teachers routinely engage in through their schools, districts, and state departments of education. The questions in Figures 2.2 and 2.3 can be used to stimulate reflection on a wide variety of topics.

---

1. How would you describe the

    a) learning experience,

    b) strategy, or

    c) theory and practice?

2. What did you learn from the experience?

3. What experience does this remind you of?

4. What factors influenced this experience?

5. Why do you think that this particular outcome occurred?

6. What other possible outcomes could there have been?

7. What alternative approaches can you "imagine"?

8. What would you like to learn more about? (CFLP, 1991, 3)

FIGURE 2.2 Questions for reflection—general.
Source: California Foreign Language Project. (1991). "Reflective Education: An Introduction and Guidelines for Use in Teachers' Professional Growth and Development." Eighth Annual Summer Seminar for Foreign Language Teachers.

Boyle-Baise and Sleeter (1996) observe that teachers need to understand how institutions (such as schools) perpetuate inequality and at the same time be able to visualize alternative structures that do not. They provide the following questions to help preservice teachers examine their own perspectives:

1. What group(s) serves as the main culture of reference for teaching?

2. What is known about the aspirations, cultural patterns, and strengths of particular groups (as defined by ethnicity, class, gender, etc.)?

3. In what ways should teaching relate to students' life experiences?

4. To what extent are the notions of educational equality and equity integrated into beliefs and actions?

The following are illustrative of the types of questions used in reflecting on different dimensions of classroom life:

Classroom Environment (Aesthetic/Visual)

1. What kinds of people seem welcome here?

2. Does the room reflect the children and teachers' work and interests?

3. Are there stereotypes, or are groups of people omitted?

Curriculum

1. What information, skills, and attitudes are emphasized?

2. To what extent is the information correct, nonstereotypic, and unbiased?

3. To what extent is it weighted toward the accomplishments of one group?

4. What messages are sent about race, social class, and gender through the information, skills, and attitudes that are "important to know" as compared to those regarded as "nice to know?"

Discipline Procedures

1. What is considered appropriate behavior?

2. For which cultural group(s) are these expectations similar to behavioral norms in students' homes?

3. Who is suspended most often, for what offenses?

4. Are suspensions proportionate to the population of particular groups in the school?

FIGURE 2.3   Questions for reflection—teaching within a framework that is multicultural and social reconstructionist.

Source: Questions from Boyle-Baise, M., & Sleeter, C. E. (1996). Field experiences: Planting seeds and pulling weeds. In C. A. Grant and M. L. Gomez (Eds.), *Making schooling multicultural: Campus and classroom*, pp. 379–380. Upper Saddle River, NJ: Merrill/Prentice Hall.

The students in my introductory course on multicultural education are asked to develop a professional growth project that will "make a difference" for them personally and professionally, and hopefully for others as well. Students in the course represent the full spectrum of professionals teaching kindergarten through community college, undergraduate to graduate students, preservice and student teachers to expert teachers. By design, the projects are limited in scope and duration. The intent is to provide opportunities for the application and extension of knowledge and skills related to multicultural education.

The following are examples of the types of projects students have developed:

◇   Two language arts teachers, interdisciplinary team teaching partners, worked with the school's ESL teacher to bring students in their classes together. Concerned with what they had observed on campus (e.g., occasional racial tension, the isolation

of English language learners, the lack of communication between ethnic and racial groups, stereotyping within the school and community), the two teachers decided to:

   a. assess their eighth grade students to determine what they knew and wanted to find out about people from a different culture;
   b. prepare their students for interviews with two or three English language learners as consultants (e.g., provided background information, brought in a guest speaker, developed the questions and protocol for the interviews);
   c. develop a teacher observation/evaluation rubric to focus their observations of the actual interviews;
   d. assess what the students had learned by asking all participants in the interviews for written reflections; and
   e. evaluate the learning outcomes.

2. A community college instructor, unfamiliar with the rural community in which he was teaching adult education classes, concentrated on learning about the culture of his students and the town in which they lived and worked. He first interviewed three local educators from the small town's major ethnic groups. This enabled him to better understand the social, economic, and cultural dynamics within the community. He then surveyed his students, adult English language learners, to identify their specific language needs within the context of their community (e.g., settings, situations). Finally, he visited the home of one of his students, learning first hand about the man's need for English skills specific to ranch work and the farm machinery he was responsible for operating and maintaining.

FIGURE 2.4   Professional Growth: Sample Projects.

Inquiry activities enable teachers to study their own teaching and their students' learning. Inquiry is an essential part of continuous professional growth: "For when teachers observe, examine, question, and reflect on their ideas and develop new practices that lead toward their ideals, students are alive. When teachers stop growing, so do their students (Barth, cited in Henderson, 1996, p. 4). Because inquiry activities are context-sensitive, meaningful insights can emerge from teachers' critical study of their own schools and classrooms.

The inquiry activities highlighted in Figure 2.4 were designed and carried out successfully by pre- and inservice teachers, and graduate students in my multicultural education classes. These teachers and instructors are in a variety of positions inside and outside of educational systems in the area, and are representative of educators at different points along the experiential continuum.

To assist teachers in their exploration of ideas from the text, activities for application, extension, and reflective practice have been incorporated as a part of every chapter in a special section entitled *Application, Extension, and Reflection.* Readers at different levels of professional development are encouraged to select and adapt the activities that best meet their interests, needs, and circumstances. The best ideas always come from teachers themselves, for "when teachers engage in continuous professional study, they no longer need to be told how to teach. They become responsibly empowered professionals" (Sergiovanni, paraphrased in Henderson, 1996, p. 4).

IN THE REAL WORLD

As teachers identify the salient issues in their school context, they are advised to consider the institutional environment in which they work and the nature of their activities. Teachers may need to "safeguard" themselves by developing strategies appropriate to their particular situation, especially in institutions that are not supportive of teachers as responsibly empowered professionals. This holds particularly true when delving into politically sensitive areas (e.g., race, ethnicity, and class) or in moving outside the confines of your own classroom (see Henderson, 1996; Herr, 1999; Oakes, Wells, Yonezawa, & Ray, 1997). Teachers need to be well versed in the literature specific to the issues, and to understand the school culture and processes of educational change. Examining detracking efforts in 10 racially mixed schools, Oakes et al. describe the struggles of reform-minded educators, and the normative and political obstacles they faced in taking their schools beyond the traditional limits of equal educational opportunity. They observe that "Most of the change literature, useful as it is to schools generally, is silent on matters of race and social class, and the politics of altering the distribution of access and achievement" (p. 66).

Even experienced teacher researchers may encounter unforeseen difficulties. As an example, Herr (1999) describes the complications that arose when she embarked on teacher research at the middle school in which she was a teacher and counselor. A research project that started out with the intention of improving educational practice and contributing to the school's commitment to diversity eventually focused on issues of institutional racism. Details of her experiences illustrate the professional dilemmas she faced both as a teacher/counselor and as a researcher. The "real world" challenges that teacher researchers encounter in critically analyzing the institutions in which they teach should not be underestimated. How teachers perceive their position within the school context will be a critical factor in determining how they proceed as researchers:

> Practitioners must make their peace with how much of a challenge to the status quo they wish to be. Some are more skillful and in stronger positions to take stands on issues than others. However, if practitioner research is not done with a critical spirit, it runs the risk of legitimating what may be—from the perspective of equity considerations—unacceptable social arrangements. (Anderson et al., cited in Herr, 1999)

In Herr's case, the real and the ideal faces of the institution were in conflict. Acceptance of the status quo would require that she forsake deeply held personal and professional beliefs and "betray" the students she sought to empower; opposition to "unacceptable social arrangements" put her at odds with the institution.

SUMMARY

- ◇ In the 21st century, teaching as we know it will be different from the past and present. The transformation of society occasioned by social, economic, and democratic changes in recent decades is creating a new context for teaching. In this changing context, diversity is the rule, rather than the exception; achieving high levels of learning for all students is the norm. As student-centered teaching replaces teacher-directed instruction, the professional role of teachers will change in fundamental ways.
- ◇ The level of professional accountability demanded of teachers in this new context of teaching is high and will demand more of teachers than ever before. As greater authority, autonomy, and responsibility is based at the school level in order to address increasingly complex student needs, teachers will rely heavily on practices that are knowledge-based, context- and content-specific, and learner-oriented.
- ◇ Responsibly empowered professionals are lifelong learners characterized by their command of relevant professional and subject matter knowledge, and the concomitant sense of efficacy this competence engenders. Teaching from a multicultural perspective with "a caring heart and critical eyes" is a critical part of their professional profile.
- ◇ Reflective teaching is essential to developing a multicultural perspective. The teacher as reflective thinker is proactive, persistent, careful, and deliberate in making decisions related to practice. Decision making is also

context-sensitive, that is, appropriate to the educational, social, and political contexts in which teaching occurs. Three basic strategies that are widely used to foster reflective teaching are daily reflection, reflective writing, and inquiry activities.

◇ In the real world, it is important for teachers identifying salient issues within their school context as the focus of inquiry activities to consider the institutional environment in which they work and the nature of their activities. This holds particularly true for teachers in institutions that are not supportive of teachers as responsibly empowered professionals and for those delving into politically sensitive areas.

APPLICATION, EXTENSION, AND REFLECTION

1. *Reflecting on Personal/Professional Knowledge and Experiences.* An important step in developing a multicultural teaching perspective involves reflecting on one's own cultural identity and values, professional knowledge and life experiences, and their relationship to the classroom. Although articulated in many different ways, the importance of knowing oneself—both as a person and as a professional—is basic to effective teaching. The following statements are among the more eloquent expressions of this belief:

   • A central task in reflection entails an examination of our own theories and beliefs. These theories and beliefs . . . are formed and arise from our past experiences, our received knowledge, and our basic values. Part of reflective teaching entails an introspective and critical analysis of those experiences, understandings, and values. (Liston & Zeichner, 1996, p. xviii)
   • The most fundamental building block in a pedagogy of ownership is acknowledgment of the life experiences and voices of our students. (O'Laughlin, 1992, p. 338)

   The critical examination of personal and professional experiences can make teachers more cognizant of life experiences that foster development of a multicultural perspective, while helping to dispel superficial, "dysfunctional," or stereotypical ideas that can impede its development. "Reflective teachers put personal and professional values in the foreground of their decisionmaking, rather than in the background hidden behind their behaviors." (Henderson, 1996, p. 113)

   a. *Reflect.* Before you begin writing, examine your personal and professional values and experiences. Use the questions in Figure 2.5 to stimulate and focus your reflections, but do not try to address each and every one. They are intended as prompts to help you generate ideas.

SET I

1. What is the role of school in your life (e.g., significant positive or negative experiences; school in relation to academic, social, cultural, class, or religious experiences; participation in peer groups and extracurricular activities; cultural diversity of peer group(s); personal accomplishments)?

2. How did the social class (i.e., socioeconomic status) of the community where you grew up influence the schools you attended?

3. How does social class (i.e., socioeconomic status) influence the schools where you now teach or will do your field experience work?

4. What other social and/or cultural factors influence the schools where you now teach or will teach?

5. What was the relationship between the social class of the schools you attended and the school's/schools' academic missions?

6. In what way(s) did your schools demonstrate, or fail to demonstrate, educational equity for students?

7. In what way(s) did your schools reflect diversity (e.g., cultural, racial, religious, linguistic, gender, academic, social class)?

8. In what ways did significant positive and negative teacher role models in elementary and secondary schools influence you as an individual and as a professional?

9. In what ways did your family's values influence your perspective on education (e.g., educational background, attitudes toward education, value of schooling and education, support for schooling and education)?

10. With respect to prior experiences and present interaction with culturally diverse groups, what is the quantity and quality of your interaction with various groups?

11. What do you think about teaching in culturally diverse classrooms?

SET II

1. "How long has your family" (or ancestors) "been on this continent?"

2. "Where did your family" (or ancestors) "come from before joining the drama 'of the Americas'? Or, were they always here?"

3. "How many generations of your family, on both sides, have lived in the U.S.A.?" In the state in which you are now living?

4. "What languages were or are spoken in your (childhood) home? What languages are spoken in your current domicile?"

5. "At this point" in your professional preparation or graduate program, "do you have any opinions about multicultural education?"

FIGURE 2.5   Personal/professional knowledge and experiences.

Set I: Adapted from R. R. Powell, S. Zehm, & J. García. 1996. Field experiences: Strategies for exploring the diversity in schools (pp. 45, 50–51). Englewood Cliffs, NJ: Merrill/Prentice Hall and

Set II: Adapted from L. Davidman. 1996. Multicultural education: A movement in search of meaning and positive connections. In Fred Schultz (Ed.), *Annual editions: Multicultural education, 1997/98* (p. 107). Guilford, CT: Dushkin/McGraw Hill.

    b. *Relate.* Drawing from your reflections, discuss the relationship between your personal-professional knowledge and experiences, and your teaching diverse populations. Specifically,

       1. What is the relationship between your life experiences, your beliefs about teaching, and your classroom instruction?

       2. Assess how prior and current experiences inside and outside of school settings influence your beliefs about teaching and your academic/social interactions with students.

       3. Consider how these influences affect (or will affect) your classroom environment.

2. **Defining Your Professional Development Goals.** Identify two or more objectives that can serve as the focal point for your professional development in the area of multicultural education. These should represent your "top priorities" in developing the competencies you need to be more effective with diverse learners. You may choose to focus on context (e.g., learning about the community in which you teach or enhancing linkages with the homes of all your students), process (e.g., analyzing your interaction with students), and/or content (e.g., developing curriculum materials and identifying resources that you can use to teach about religion; exploring Internet resources that can be incorporated to teach about ethnicity). Look at the examples in Figure 2.4 for more ideas. (Note: Individual objectives will vary subject to professional preparation and prior experiences.)

Develop a plan describing how you propose to address each area and evaluate your success in meeting the professional objectives you have set for yourself. Use the following chart to help you.

Personal/Professional	What I Propose to Do	How I Will Proceed	How I Will Define Success
Objectives			
1.			
2.			
3.			
4.			

REFERENCES

Boyle-Baise, M., & Sleeter, C. E. (1996). Field experiences: Planting seeds and pulling weeds. In C. A. Grant & M. L. Gómez (Eds.), *Making schooling multicultural: Campus and classroom* (pp. 371–388). Englewood Cliffs, NJ: Merrill/Prentice Hall.

California Foreign Language Project. (1991). *Reflective education: An introduction and guidelines for use in teachers' professional growth and development.* Eighth Annual Summer Seminar for Foreign Language Teachers, Santa Barbara, CA.

Cohn, M. (1992). How teachers perceive teaching: Changes over two decades, 1964–1984. In A. Lieberman (Ed.), *The changing contexts of teaching,* Ninety-first Yearbook of the National Society for the Study of Education, Part I (pp. 110–137). Chicago, IL: The University of Chicago Press.

Darling-Hammond, L. (1996). The quiet revolution: Rethinking teacher development. *Educational Leadership, 53*(6), 4–10.

Darling-Hammond, L., & Snyder, J. (1992). Reframing accountability: Creating learner-centered schools. In A. Lieberman (Ed.), *The changing contexts of teaching,* Ninety-first Yearbook of the National Society for the Study of Education, Part I (pp. 11–36). Chicago, IL: The University of Chicago Press.

Davidman, L. (1997). Multicultural education: A movement in search of meaning and positive connections. In Fred Schultz (Ed), *Annual editions: Multicultural education, 1997/98* (pp. 104–108). Guilford, CT: Dushkin/McGraw-Hill.

Dewey, J. (1933). *How We Think: A Restatement of the Relation of Reflecting Teaching to the Educative Process.*Boston, MA: D. C. Heath and Company.

Eby, J. W. (1998). *Reflective planning, teaching, and evaluation, K–12* (2nd ed.). Upper Saddle River, NJ: Merrill/Prentice-Hall.

Gillette, M. D. (1996). It's got to be in the plan: Reflective teaching and multicultural education in the student teaching semester. In C. A. Grant & M. L. Gómez (Eds.), *Making schooling multicultural: Campus and classroom* (pp. 389–409). Englewood Cliffs, NJ: Merrill/Prentice Hall.

Grant, C. A., & Gómez, M. L. (Eds.). (1996). *Making schooling multicultural: Campus and classroom.* Englewood Cliffs, NJ: Merrill/Prentice Hall.

Goodness in Schools: Themes of Empowerment. *Peabody Journal of Education, Vol. 63, No. 3,* Spring 1986, pp. 9–28).

Grossman, P. (1992). Teaching to learn. In A. Lieberman (Ed.), *The changing contexts of teaching,* Ninety-first Yearbook of the National Society for the Study of Education, Part I (pp. 179–196). Chicago, IL: The University of Chicago Press.

Henderson, J. G. (1996). *Reflective teaching: The study of your constructivist practices* (2nd ed.). Englewood Cliffs, NJ: Merrill/Prentice-Hall.

Herr, K. (1999). Unearthing the unspeakable: When teacher research and political agendas collide. *Language Arts, 77*(1), 10–15.

Ladson-Billings, Gloria. (1994). *Dreamkeepers: Successful teachers of African American children.* San Francisco, CA: Jossey-Bass Inc.

Lichtenstein, G., McLaughlin, M. W., & Knudsen, J. (1992). Teacher empowerment and professional knowledge. In A. Lieberman (Ed.), *The changing contexts of teaching,* Ninety-first Yearbook of the National Society for the Study of Education, Part I (pp. 37–58). Chicago, IL: The University of Chicago Press.

Lieberman, A. (1992). Introduction: The changing context of education. In A. Lieberman (Ed.), *The changing contexts of teaching,* Ninety-first Yearbook of the National Society for the Study of Education, Part I (pp. 1–10). Chicago, IL: The University of Chicago Press.

Liston, Daniel P. and Kenneth M. Zeichner. (1996). *Culture and Teaching.* Mahwah, NJ: Lawrence Erlbaum Associates, pp. xii.

Little, J. W. (1992). Opening the black box of professional community. In A. Lieberman (Ed.), *The changing contexts of teaching,* Ninety-first Yearbook of the National Society for the Study of Education, Part I (pp. 157–178). Chicago, IL: The University of Chicago Press.

Maturana, H. R., and Varela, F. J. (1987). *The Tree of Knowledge.* Boston: New Science Library, p. 24.

Oakes, J., Wells, A. S., Yonezawa, S., & Ray, K. (1997). Equity lessons from detracking schools. In A. Hargreaves (Ed.), *Rethinking educational change with heart and mind,* 1997 ASCD Yearbook (pp. 1–26). Alexandria, VA: Association for Supervision and Curriculum Development.

Powell, R. R., Zehm, S., & García, J. (1996). *Field experiences: Strategies for exploring diversity in schools.* Englewood Cliffs, NJ: Merrill/Prentice-Hall.

Ross, Dorine Doerre. (1989). "First Steps in Developing a Reflective Approach." *Journal of Teacher Education,* March–April, Vol. XXXX, No. 2, pp. 22–30.

Smyth, John. (1989). Developing and Sustaining Critical Reflection in Teacher Education. *Journal of Teacher Education,* Vol. XXXX, No. 2, March-April, pp. 1–9.

Wink, J. (1997). *Critical pedagogy: Notes from the real world.* White Plains, NY: Longman.

PART

II

CONTEXT

Linking Home, Neighborhood, and Community Contexts

My voice is heard. I've made a difference for my children.

June Cavarretta (Parent volunteer)

Teaching is a process of getting to know the students . . . of learning about them and learning from them. That is what most of this chapter is about. What occurs in the classroom clearly is an important part of education, but the curriculum imparted in the schools is only part of the picture. All students experience a very pervasive and influential "education" outside the classroom.

The purpose of this chapter is to help teachers learn about students' cultural identities and backgrounds, and the broader, sociocultural context in which their students live and learn outside the classroom, most specifically at home and within their neighborhoods and communities. It is also intended to help teachers make connections between the classroom, home, community, and larger society.

STUDENTS' CULTURAL BACKGROUNDS: WHAT TEACHERS NEED TO KNOW

French politician Edouard Herriot once observed that "culture is what remains when one has forgotten everything else." In many respects he was right, for much of what is culture influences our lives in ways beyond our awareness at a conscious level. In his classic works on the subject, Hall (1959, 1969) used terms such as "silent language" and "hidden dimension" to describe various aspects of culture. Cultural influences are pervasive, and their impact on the educational process is significant.

Before proceeding, think about how you would define culture? Which elements of culture are most obvious? Which are largely invisible to those within? Compare your ideas with the overview in Figure 3.1 and the exploration of the different faces of culture in Figure 3.2.

Depending in part on their background, preparation, and personality, teachers approach cultural diversity in the classroom with a wide range of emotions and attitudes. That the potential for cultural conflict exists when teachers and

---

To anthropologists, the term *culture* refers to the complex process of human social interaction and symbolic communication. It is "a *dynamic, creative,* and *continuous process* including behaviors, values, and substance *learned* and *shared* by people that guides them in their *struggle for survival* and gives meaning to their lives" (Arvizu, Snyder, & Espinosa, 1980, p. 5). Culture provides security to group members, while enabling people to adapt to change. Cultural influences sometimes are obvious and visible, as in certain actions and speech patterns; in other cases, they are almost "invisible," as in patterns of thinking, feeling, and perceiving.

Although definitions of culture are as diverse as they are numerous, anthropologists agree on certain basic points (Mukhopadhyay, 1985). First, they share the view that culture is created collectively by humans and consists of interrelated components: material artifacts (e.g., technology, shelter, transportation); social and behavioral patterns (e.g., social, economic and political organization); and mental products (e.g., conceptual systems, rules for action, values and goals). Second, they agree that culture is a universal, human phenomenon that is cumulative, integrated, pervasive, and psychologically real. As Mukhopadhyay (1985) observes, "It structures how we actually *experience* reality" (p. 19).

Many common perceptions of culture capture only pieces of the concept, such as arts and artifacts, behaviors, social structure, language, history, technology, and symbols. Culture is more than mere objects or material goods, items that can be bought, sold, and exchanged. It defies compilation in a "laundry list" of traits and facts. Because it is shared and learned, culture goes beyond an individual's genetic heritage. Nor would it suffice to limit the concept of culture to the ideal and romantic heritage of a people (as expressed in music, dance, and celebrations) or to the "cultured" class associated with knowledge of the arts, literature, and manners (Arvizu et al., 1980; Cross Cultural Resource Center, 1979).

FIGURE 3.1   Culture.

Culture has different faces, some highly visible, others hidden from view. In anthropology, important distinctions are made between ideal and real culture, implicit and explicit culture (Arvizu et al., 1980). *Ideal* culture refers to what people say they believe or how they think they should behave. Aspects of ideal culture frequently are expressed in proverbs, stories, myths, sayings, and jokes. These may contrast sharply with the real culture, which is how individuals actually behave in specific situations. This is one reason descriptions of group "cultural traits" often seem idealized or stereotypic. Not surprisingly, knowledge of actual cultural patterns within a local community often provides greater insight about how individuals behave in real situations than do idealized cultural descriptions.

It is equally important to realize that some elements of culture operate at a conscious level of awareness, whereas others do not. *Implicit* (covert) culture includes elements hidden or taken for granted to the extent that they are not easily observable or consciously recognized by individuals. Values, attitudes, fears, assumptions, and religious beliefs are common elements of implicit culture. *Explicit* (overt) culture, on the other hand, is visible and can be described verbally. It includes styles of dress and housing, speech, tools, and concrete behaviors. In the classroom, teachers are aware of differences in how students dress for school and whether they speak with an "accent." They are much less likely to be aware of values and attitudes students hold, and in some instances, they may not be cognizant of their own.

Anthropologists also distinguish insider and outsider views of culture (Arvizu, Snyder, & Espinosa, 1980). The *insider* view is the perspective individuals have of their own culture. Members of a cultural group possess in-depth knowledge, common understandings of what is significant, and perceptions based upon a shared conceptual foundation. A group's history and literary heritage provide insider views of the culture in which they were created. In approaching other cultures, however, individuals take an *outsider* view, a comparative perspective grounded in familiar knowledge, attitudes, and perceptions.

How do various cultural elements appear to an outsider? The following passage by Miner (1979) describes in a tongue-in-cheek way how Nacirema concern with dental hygiene might be interpreted by an outsider:

> The Nacirema have an almost pathological horror of and fascination with the mouth, the condition of which is believed to have a supernatural influence on all social relationships. Were it not for the rituals of the mouth, they believe that their teeth would fall out, their gums bleed, their jaws shrink, their friends desert them, and their lovers reject them. They also believe that a strong relationship exists between oral and moral characteristics. For example, there is a ritual ablution of the mouth for children which is supposed to improve their moral fiber. (p. 175)

In reading this passage, at what point did you recognize that Nacirema is American spelled backwards?

FIGURE 3.2 The different faces of culture.

students do not share the same beliefs, values, and behaviors is a reality in all classrooms; classroom conflict cannot be entirely eliminated—whether students are culturally, ethnically, or socially homogeneous or heterogeneous. Gay (1981) suggests that *points of potential conflict can be identified*. With knowledge of cultural differences and satisfactory observation skills, teachers can recognize at least some of the values, attitudes, and behavioral patterns that may give rise to potential problems. Once identified, these can be addressed in such a way as to enhance rather than impede the instructional process.

What, then, can teachers do to enhance their effectiveness in culturally pluralistic settings? First, they need to develop *an awareness of culture in themselves,* both as individuals and as teachers. This usually is a prerequisite to acceptance of the reality and validity of cultural differences, a first step in dealing with diversity in the classroom (Arvizu, Synder, & Espinosa, 1980; McGroarty, 1986; Saville-Troike, 1978). Second, teachers need to develop *an awareness of culture as it is manifested in their students,* both as individuals and members of different cultural groups. To understand how culture influences what happens in their classrooms, teachers must have "local cultural knowledge about a group's history, economic circumstances, religions and social organizations, socialization practices, conceptualization of social competence and language uses" (McGroarty, 1986, p. 315). Third, teachers need to know which *sociocultural factors influence the teaching and learning process and how they do so.* Teachers who develop their cultural knowledge and insights will be prepared to devise effective strategies for working with all students, whatever their backgrounds and capabilities.

Cultural Identity

As Adler (1977) observes, every culture has its own internal coherence, integrity, and logic. Each is an intertwined system of values, attitudes, beliefs, and norms that give meaning and significance to both individual and collective identity. To varying degrees, all persons are culturally bound and conditioned. Within a particular culture, they derive a sense of identity and belonging, a guide for behavior.

An individual's cultural identity is based upon a number of traits and values related to national or ethnic origin, family, religion, gender, age, occupation, socioeconomic level, language, geographic region, residence (e.g., rural, suburban, or urban), and exceptionality (Gollnick & Chinn, 1986, 1994). It is determined in large part by the interaction of these primary elements and the degree to which individuals identify with different subcultures. Microcultures are cultural groups whose members share some political and social institutions, as well as certain distinctive cultural patterns, that are not generally a part of the culture common to the larger society. Figure 3.3 illustrates how different elements contribute to an individual's microcultures identity and how individuals differ in the emphasis they place on the microcultures to which they belong. For example, even though both persons represented in Figure 3.3 are middle-class, Catholic, Italian American women who live in New York City, one identifies strongly with her ethnic and religious microcultures, whereas the other identifies most strongly with the female microculture.

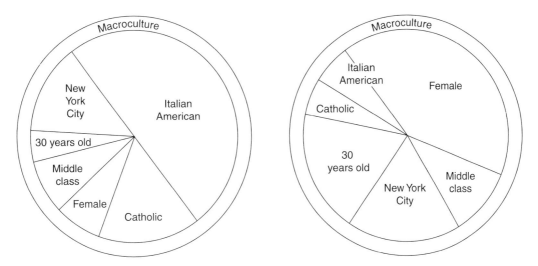

FIGURE 3.3 Cultural identity is based on one's membership in numerous microcultures.
Source: D. M. Gollnick and P. C. Chinn, *Multicultural Education in a Pluralistic Society* (2nd ed.). Copyright 1986 by Merrill. Reprinted with permission.

What does your cultural identity "circle" look like? Given that examining one's cultural identity is a useful first step in dealing with diversity in the classroom, take this opportunity to create your own representation following the guidelines in Figure 3.4.

McLeod (1997) tells us that identity is developed in the family and sustained through the interaction of the individual and society. How we identify ourselves is malleable and dynamic, influenced by factors such as inter-group relations and power differentials among groups. "It is a changing, individual framework within which we place our experience of the social world and attempt to give it meaning" (p. 121). McLeod asserts that members of dominant groups often find it difficult to understand the significance of defining identity. For them, the framework developed within the family and further shaped by wider social spheres (e.g., neighborhood, community, society) is normally quite congruent with their experiences in the outside world and with definitions presented by mass media and in other cultural representations. In fact, "where our experience of the world is consistent with the norms of society at large the frame of identity tends to blend in with the background and disappear" (p. 121). However, members of minority groups are likely to discover that this does not hold true for them. They may be defined and viewed by those outside the group in ways that are not congruent with how the groups define and view themselves. As individuals, they may find it necessary to change the understandings of the world that they bring to the wider social spheres in order to better align with the perspective of the majority.

According to Garza and Lipton (1982), an individual's cultural environment affects the range of stimuli and experiences to which the person is exposed. It

1. Listed below are different microcultures. *Identify* the microcultures to which you belong and fill in the blanks with the appropriate information.

   _____   nationality

   _____   ethnicity

   _____   race

   _____   gender

   _____   class

   _____   religion

   _____   age group

   _____   geographic region

   _____   urban/suburban/rural

   _____   other: _____

   _____   other: _____

   _____   other: _____

Now, put a check next to the microcultures with which you identify most strongly, that is, the microcultures that most influence your cultural identity.

2. Using Figure 3.3 as a model, *draw* a circle on your paper to represent your cultural identity. Use segments of the circle to *represent* the relative contributions of the different microcultures in defining your cultural identity. The microcultures you checked as most important should appear as the largest segments. When you finish, your circle should look like your personalized version of one of the models in Figure 3.3.

3. Compare your representation with those of others in the class. I always ask for volunteers (at least eight) to draw their circles on the board and explain the importance of the various segments depicted. In what ways are they similar? How do they differ? What does this tell you about how different individuals are likely to respond to different issues related to multicultural education?

4. As noted earlier, one prerequisite to acceptance of the reality and validity of cultural differences is the development of an awareness of culture in ourselves, both as individuals and as teachers. This exercise is also a strategy that teachers can use in their own classrooms. In pairs or small groups, brainstorm how you might use it with your students. For example, university students in one art education class use it as the starting point in creating a collage and essay that depicts who they are as individuals. In teaching literature, the diagram might be used to represent the cultural identity of characters in stories read in class.

FIGURE 3.4   Cultural identity exercise.

Sources: Categories adapted from a handout from Los Angeles in the World, prepared by the IHC Center, Los Angeles.

Everyone is multicultural to varying degrees, yet unique in terms of specific cultural characteristics.

also influences the repertoire of responses available in a given situation and the likelihood that the individual will act or behave in a particular way. Chicanos, for example, experience multiple cultural influences. Some influences certainly exert a greater effect than others, but all contribute to the Chicano "cultural equation": Chicano = Mexican influence + Anglo influence + unique Chicano influence + influences from other cultures (Garza & Lipton, p. 422).

Whenever different cultures are in contact, ongoing processes such as acculturation and change are likely to operate. In addition, variations within microcultural groups (e.g., socioeconomic status, gender, age, region, religion), and the interactions between them, further fragment the cultural environment individuals experience (Laosa, 1977). Such variation at the individual level helps to explain why many of the issues that confront educators in culturally diverse societies are so complex and multifaceted: *"Everyone is multicultural to varying degrees with [the] specific cultural characteristics of each individual being unique"* (Garza & Lipton, 1982, p. 422).

Students' Cultures

To better understand the lives of their students, teachers need to learn about the history and culture of different groups represented in their classrooms. When confronted with such a task, however, you may find it difficult to decide just how to begin. What areas of culture are important? What kinds of information are most useful? In addition to general information about various cultural groups in the United States, teachers will want to know more about those in their local community. Saville-Troike (1978) has developed a set of questions that can help teachers identify what they need to know (Figure 3.5). Applicable to a wide range of groups, the questions focus on sociocultural elements relevant to education—differences related to language, ethnicity, religion, and other cultural characteristics.

Because these questions cover areas central to any discussion of culture in the classroom, they have many possible applications. First, teachers can use the questions to reflect on their own culture. In fact, Saville-Troike suggests that teachers answer some of the questions, based on their own experiences, before trying them out with others. Such introspection might be followed by comparing and contrasting answers with family, friends, and colleagues. In this manner, teachers can become more aware of their own beliefs, behaviors, and values and can see how such concepts as real and ideal culture, and implicit and explicit culture apply in their own lives. In the process, the relationship between culture and context will become more clearly defined.

Second, Saville-Troike also recommends use of these questions to guide observations in the classroom, around the school, and in other settings. Informed observation can increase teachers' understanding of classroom events and form the basis for modified teaching strategies that are culturally appropriate and instructionally sound. Some of the questions in Figure 3.5 are especially useful as the focal point of observations: What constitutes a positive response by a teacher to a student? What methods do parents use when teaching children at home? What genres of language are most common in the home? One question, for example, addresses the role of language in social control and the significance of using the first as opposed to the second language. A common observation among teachers in bilingual classrooms is that some students respond better when reprimanded in their home language. In this situation, observation can be used to guide language choice in the disciplining of students.

Third, the questions in Figure 3.5 can also be used to enhance instruction in a wide range of subjects. Activities incorporating some of the questions can be exciting and rewarding, and the possibilities for student projects are endless. Adding a cultural perspective on foods, for example, can give added depth to a unit on nutrition. At the secondary level, students from cultural groups that traditionally use herbal medicines may enjoy doing research to trace the origin of folk remedies used in the home.

Saville-Troike (1978) offers some guidelines and precautions for use of the questions in Figure 3.5. There are no correct or incorrect responses to the questions—only answers that are different. There are no absolutely safe questions about culture. Any question that focuses on culture—even one that appears to be objective

General

1. What are the major stereotypes that you and others have about each cultural group? To what extent are these accepted by members of the group being typed?

2. To what extent and in what areas has the traditional culture of each minority group changed in contact with the dominant American culture? In what areas has it been maintained?

3. To what extent do individuals possess knowledge of or exhibit characteristics of traditional groups?

Family

1. Who is in a "family"? Who among these (or others) live in one house?

2. What is the hierarchy of authority in the family?

3. What are the rights and responsibilities of each family member? Do children have an obligation to work to help the family?

4. What are the functions and obligations of the family in the larger social unit?

5. What is the degree of solidarity or cohesiveness in the family?

The Life Cycle

1. What are criteria for the definition of stages, periods, or transitions in life?

2. What are the attitudes, expectations, and behaviors toward individuals at different stages in the life cycle?

3. What behaviors are appropriate or unacceptable for children of various ages? How might these conflict with behaviors taught or encouraged in the school?

4. How is language related to the life cycle?

5. How is the age of children computed? What commemoration is made of the child's birth (if any) and when?

Roles

1. What roles within the group are available to whom, and how are they acquired? Is education relevant to this acquisition?

2. What is the knowledge of and perception by the child, the parents, and the community toward these roles, their availability, and possible or appropriate means of access to them?

3. Is language use important in the definition or social marking of roles?

4. Are there class differences in the expectations about child role attainment? Are these realistic?

(continued)

FIGURE 3.5 Survey of cultural group characteristics.

FIGURE 3.5   *(continued)*

Interpersonal Relationships

1. How do people greet each other? What forms of address are used between people in various roles?

2. Do girls work and interact with boys? Is it proper?

3. How is deference shown?

4. How are insults expressed?

5. Who may disagree with whom? Under what circumstances?

Communication

1. What languages, and varieties of each language, are used in the community? By whom? When? Where? For what purposes?

2. Which varieties are written? How widespread is knowledge of written forms?

3. What are the characteristics of "speaking well"? How do these relate to age, sex, context, or other social factors? What are the criteria for correctness?

4. What roles, attitudes, or personality traits are associated with particular ways of speaking?

5. What is considered "normal" speech behavior?

6. Is learning language a source of pride? Is developing bilingual competence considered an advantage or a handicap?

7. What is the functionality of the native language in the environment?

8. What gestures or postures have special significance or may be considered objectionable? What meaning is attached to making direct eye contact? To eye avoidance?

9. Who may talk to whom? When? Where? About what?

Decorum and Discipline

1. What counts as discipline in terms of the culture and what doesn't?

2. What behaviors are considered socially acceptable for students of different age and sex?

3. Who (or what) is considered responsible if a child misbehaves?

4. Who has authority over whom? To what extent can one person's will be imposed on another? By what means?

5. How is the behavior of children traditionally controlled, to what extent, and in what domains?

6. What is the role of language in social control? What is the significance of using the first versus the second language?

FIGURE 3.5   *(continued)*

Religion

1. What is considered sacred and what secular?

2. What religious roles and authority are recognized in the community? What is the role of children in religious practices?

3. What taboos are there? What should *not* be discussed in school? What questions should *not* be asked? What student behaviors should *not* be required?

Health and Hygiene

1. Who or what is believed to cause illness or death?

2. Who or what is responsible for curing?

3. How are specific illnesses treated? To what extent do individuals utilize or accept modern medical practices by doctors and other health professionals?

4. What beliefs or practices are there with regard to bodily hygiene?

5. If a student were involved in an accident at school, would any of the common first aid practices be unacceptable?

Food

1. What is eaten? In what order? How often?

2. What foods are favorites? What taboo? What typical?

3. What rules are observed during meals regarding age and sex roles within the family, the order of serving, seating, utensils used, and appropriate verbal formulas (e.g., how, and if, one may request, refuse, or thank)?

4. What social obligations are there with regard to food giving, preparation, reciprocity, and honoring people?

5. What relation does food have with health? What medicinal uses are made of food, or categories of food?

6. What are the taboos or prescriptions associated with the handling, offering, or discarding of food?

Dress and Personal Appearance

1. What clothing is typical? What is worn for special occasions? What seasonal differences are considered appropriate?

2. How does dress differ for age, sex, and social class?

3. What restrictions are imposed for modesty?

4. What is the concept of beauty or attractiveness? What characteristics are most valued?

5. What constitutes a compliment? What form should it take?

6. Does the color of dress have symbolic significance?

FIGURE 3.5 *(continued)*

History and Traditions

1. What individuals and events in history are a source of pride for the group?

2. To what extent is knowledge of the group's history preserved? In what forms and in what ways is it passed on?

3. Do any ceremonies or festive occasions commemorate historical events?

4. How and to what extent does the group's knowledge of history coincide with or depart from scientific theories of creation, evolution, and historical development?

5. To what extent does the group in the United States identify with the history and traditions of their country of origin? What changes have taken place in the country of origin since the group or individuals emigrated?

6. For what reasons and under what circumstances did the group or individuals come to the United States (or did the United States come to them)?

Holidays and Celebrations

1. What holidays and celebrations are observed by the group and individuals? What is their purpose (e.g., political, seasonal, religious)?

2. Which are especially important for children and why?

3. What cultural values are they intended to inculcate?

4. Do parents and students of immigrant children know and understand school holidays and behavior appropriate for them (including appropriate nonattendance)?

Education

1. What is the purpose of education?

2. What methods for teaching and learning are used at home (e.g., modeling and imitation, didactic stories and proverbs, direct verbal instruction)? Do methods vary with the setting or according to what is being taught or learned?

3. What is the role of language in learning and teaching?

4. Is it appropriate for students to ask questions or volunteer information?

5. What constitutes a positive response by a teacher to a student?

6. How many years is it considered normal for children to go to school?

7. Are there different expectations by parents, teachers, and students with respect to different groups? In different subjects? For boys versus girls?

Work and Play

1. What range of behaviors are considered "work" and what "play"?

2. What kinds of work are prestigious and why? Why is work valued?

FIGURE 3.5 *(continued)*

3. Are there stereotypes about what a particular group will do?

4. What is the purpose of play?

Time and Space

1. What beliefs or values are associated with concepts of time? How important is punctuality? How important is speed of performance when taking a test?

2. Is control or prescriptive organization of children's time required (e.g., must homework be done before watching television; is bedtime a scheduled event)?

3. How do individuals organize themselves spatially in groups (e.g., in rows, circles, around tables, on the floor)?

4. What is the spatial organization of the home?

5. What is the knowledge and significance of cardinal directions (North, South, East, West)? At what age are these concepts acquired?

6. What significance is associated with different directions or places (e.g., heaven is up, people are buried facing West)?

Natural Phenomena

1. What beliefs and practices are associated with the sun, moon, comets, and stars?

2. Who or what is responsible for rain, lightning, thunder, earthquakes, droughts, floods, and hurricanes?

3. Are particular behavioral prescriptions or taboos associated with natural phenomena? What sanctions are there against individuals violating restrictions or prescriptions?

4. How and to what extent does the group's beliefs about natural phenomena coincide with or depart from scientific theories?

5. To what extent are traditional group beliefs still held by individuals within the community?

Pets and Other Animals

1. Which animals are valued, and for what reasons? Which animals are considered appropriate as pets? Which are inappropriate and why?

2. Are particular behavioral prescriptions or taboos associated with particular animals?

3. Are any animals of religious significance? Of historical importance?

4. What attitudes are held toward individuals or groups holding different beliefs and behaviors with respect to animals?

5. Which animals may be kept in the classroom? Which may not, and why?

Art and Music

1. What forms of art and music are most highly valued?

FIGURE 3.5   *(continued)*

2. What media and instruments are traditionally used?

3. What forms of art and music are considered appropriate for children to perform or appreciate?

4. Are there any behavioral prescriptions or taboos related to art and music (e.g., depiction of the human form; desecration of living things)?

5. How and to what extent may approval or disapproval be expressed?

Expectations and Aspirations

1. How is success defined?

2. What beliefs are held regarding luck and fate?

3. What significance does adherence to the traditional culture of the group have for the individual's potential achievement?

4. What significance does the acquisition of the majority culture and the English language have?

5. Do parents expect and desire assimilation of children to the dominant culture as a result of education and the acquisition of English?

6. Are the attitudes of community members and individuals the same as or different from those who speak for the community?

Source: M. Saville-Troike, 1978, *A Guide to Culture in the Classroom.* National Clearinghouse for Bilingual Education.

and innocuous on the surface—may touch upon areas that individuals (e.g., students, parents, community members) feel are personal, sensitive, or even threatening under certain circumstances. Use of ethnographic techniques such as interviewing, observation, and participation is highly recommended.

These questions have been widely used by teachers for decades. Of course, the relative importance of specific information in any of the 20 areas covered will vary for individuals within and across different groups as well as by subject and grade level. In physical education, for example, the questions listed under Health and Hygiene have been of particular interest. Swisher and Swisher (1986) argue that promoting equity in physical education requires that teachers consider more than motor development; they also need to understand relevant student attitudes, values, and beliefs, which can be revealed by asking additional questions such as the following:

◇ Why do some students approach competition differently from other members of their peer group?
◇ Why do certain students prefer to watch activities before demonstrating that they can do the task?

◇ How culturally appropriate a mode of interaction is coeducational participation? (p. 37)

In other content areas, teachers can supplement the questions in Figure 3.5 with some of their own, designed to provide information relevant to instruction in specific areas.

As teachers come to better understand their students culturally, they are often impressed by how eloquent children and adolescents can be in expressing what their culture means to them. In telling about their culture, students reveal a great deal about themselves. The following student essay by Angela Asilo serves to illustrate this point (Figure 3.6):

Everyone Should Have An Asian Grandmother

Angela Asilo, 8

Searles Elementary School, Union City

I am happy to tell you about my "Nanay" Catalina. She lives in the eastern corner of Manila. My family is lucky to have a grandmother like Catalina. "Nanay" Catalina brings the Philippines to us in Union City, California.

In March, I always remember my seven-year-old birthday fiesta. I had it in "Nanay's" house near Manila. We went close to a beach. I ate all day. In the morning, I had champurado. That's chocolate with rice. For lunch, I had sinigang with rice, a stew of vegetables like peas mixed together with chicken. That's really healthy for you! We finished the day with a dinner of pansit, noodles with hot dogs. Mmmmm! I'm craving for them even now! Pansit is good for long life.

The fun wouldn't end. People danced using long sticks. Then grandma had a large gift of a purple, yellow and white dress. When she put it on me, it was really beautiful. Before the end of my special day, "Nanay" explained "The Spiders Game" to me. We had time to watch the winning spider spin a web. At home in Union City, I use lady bugs on a pencil, but it's not the same.

When the clock struck twelve, I had to go to sleep. "Nanay" put her hand or "mano" on my forehead to say good night and to bless me. I love "Nanay" Catalina and her land.

At Searles School, I have fun sharing these stories about the Philippines with my friends. Everyone should have a "Nanay" like Catalina.

First Place, K–6th Grade

FIGURE 3.6
Source: Asian Pacific Fund, San Francisco, CA, *Growing Up Asian in America, Prize Winning Essays and Artwork,* 1997, p. 1.

In the next two sections, the discussion shifts to the more immediate sociocultural contexts in which students live: proceeding first from the individual to home and family, then to the neighborhood and community. We will look at what families do to support and encourage education, what teachers and families can do together and within their communities to promote educational excellence and equity. Learning about students' families, neighborhoods, and communities is essential for all teachers. When teachers and students come from different ethnic or socioeconomic levels, such knowledge is "critically" important (Grant, 1981).

HOME AND FAMILY

Recognizing that teachers and families are partners in the educational enterprise "acknowledges that neither families nor schools alone can educate and socialize children for their work in society" (Hidalgo, Bright, Siu, Swap, & Epstein, 1995, p. 515). Low-income, minority parents can and should feel empowered in their relationships with schools, as should all parents. An African American mother captured this idea in her response to a question about the importance of the school's role in the way she raises her fifth-grade child:

> Yes, myself and the school, play a very important part together because we're work-ing on the same thing, and that is to see a child get an education, to show the child that we care, and to let them know also what they're doing wrong. We both play very, very important roles in their lives. (Bright, cited in Hidalgo, et al., 1995, p. 507).

Research on family environments and involvement in their children's edu-cation reveals some key findings that are often at odds with assumptions ac-cepted as "conventional wisdom":

◇ Family practices pertaining to the education of their children are more impor-tant to student success in school and in general than are family structure, class, or factors such as race, parent education, family size, and age of the child.

◇ Families are able to compensate for limitations in resources—material or monetary—through strengths in fostering supportive relationships with their children, and by supervising / guiding their children's education.

◇ The more effectively schools involve families, the less parental behavior or student performance can be explained as a function of status variables.

◇ When schools create partnership programs, the participating families value the help, their numbers increase, and their children's performance, attitudes and behaviors improve. (Hidalgo et al., 1995, p. 499).

Literature reviews of family influence and family-school community con-nections for four ethnic groups—Puerto Rican, African American, Chinese, and Irish—reveal a great deal about similarities and differences within and across groups (Hidalgo et al., 1995).

◇ **Generalizations about cultural group differences are often erroneous and invalid for many families within any particular group.** Differences *within* racial and ethnic groups may be greater than differences *between* groups. Within groups, families differ in terms of factors such as class, recency of im-migration, proficiency in English- and the native-language, educational background, residence, neighborhood ethnicity, parents' age, intermar-riage, and other indicators of assimilation or acculturation. The influence of such factors on family attitudes and behaviors pertaining to children's education may be equal to or greater than variables such as country of origin, race, or ethnicity. This also holds for family factors related to support for children's education, reliance on extended families and community networks, and direct family involvement with children's learning. (p. 514)

◇ **Educational research and practice will learn more from better understanding the successes of children and families, than from focusing on their failures.** Some variables common to families from all groups appear to outweigh the potential effects of other factors. Not surprisingly, these include "the presence of reading matter at home, family praise and guidance for being a good student and getting good grades, and family support for many literacy activities such as reading, writing, word games, and stories." (pp. 514–515)

◇ **Within their families, children are taught about their multiple memberships—about the bicultural or multicultural identity that coalesces ethnicity and mainstream America.** (p. 515)

◇ **In addition to the personal characteristics of students and their families, the school plays an important role in determining whether and how all families become involved in their children's education.**

It is the school's leadership in fostering a home-school partnership that determines whether all families—whatever their educational and cultural backgrounds—are "empowered" as strong and effective partners in their children's education. First and foremost, parents "want to know *how to help their own child at home each year*" (p. 515) and schools need to respond appropriately. It is wrongheaded to heavily promote parent involvement at the school site *at the expense of* practices that focus on the home. The optimum program provides a more balanced approach that engages parents at home and, to the extent possible, at school.

◇ **To be effective, home-school partnership programs must respond to all families with appropriate practices, meeting common as well as more specific needs.** Ideally, schools will have a broad repertoire of practices, some apropos for all families, some designed to enable different groups to reach common goals, and yet others uniquely tailored to address particular family situations. Hidalgo et al. (1995) capture the essence of their findings in these words:

> . . . the differences in the nature and extent of family involvement and influence on children's education and on children's learning are not simply the result of fixed, unchangeable, culturally determined values and practices, but are likely to be explained by variations in family factors, community contexts, and school programs that systematize and organize practices of partnership. (p. 515)

Multicultural education has a critical role to play in the partnerships that link schools and families (Hidalgo et al., 1995, pp. 516–517). On the one hand, it is imperative that school and family partnerships be regarded as essential components of multicultural education. This contributes to the success of both the students and the programs. On the other hand, it is critical that these partnerships draw from multicultural education in their design and implementation. This serves to ensure student access in school and the successful involvement of all families. Partnerships should also include primary caretakers such as grand-parents, guardians, and foster parents.

Six specific types of activities have been identified as the most salient in partnership programs designed with these kinds of links in mind.

Activities that foster school and family partnerships . . .

◇ enable families to create home environments supportive of student learning;
◇ inform parents about school programs and the progress of their children;
◇ enlist parents and volunteers as an audience for school events;
◇ engage parents in learning activities with their own children at home;
◇ empower parents through membership in groups involved in decision-making, governance, and advocacy; and
◇ facilitate collaboration with community groups affiliated with the school. (Hidalgo et al., 1995, pp. 517–518)

Selected activities are provided in the sections that follow in relation to home visits, parent involvement, and parent/teacher communication.

Home Visits

The teacher's task has been described as that of determining for each student what is known, what is possible, and what is important (Wallace, 1981). Home visits are one of the best ways teachers can learn what is familiar and significant to their students. As Wallace points out, "When you know the articles, personal space, name of personalities, family members, smells, and shades of color and light that surround a person, a whole new perspective on that person opens up and you can greatly increase your teaching potential" (p. 92). I still remember many of the home visits I made as a teacher: the people, the sights, the sounds, the smells, and the tastes. Whether to make a "social call" or to report on a student's progress, the home visit can have a positive impact on teaching and enhance rapport with students and parents alike.

For those thinking about making home visits, Grant (1981) offers the following suggestions:

◇ Determine whether home visits are welcome in your school community.
◇ Schedule an appointment ahead of time.
◇ Dress as you would for school.
◇ Keep the visit short, from 20 to 30 minutes.
◇ Avoid questions that may be regarded as "prying."
◇ Say something positive about the student.

For many teachers, scheduling a home visit for each student is an unrealistic goal (e.g., at the secondary level). If this is the case, one or two visits per month to selected students' homes usually is feasible and can provide valuable information. The following account from a Vo-Ag teacher eloquently captures the change in perspective that can result:

In the school setting, parents can provide a role-model when they serve as resource persons for classroom activities.

> Karl's dad was crippled (sic) in a tractor accident, but it never occurred to me that Karl would be living in a trailer on two acres. When he told me he lived in the country and talked about his prize lambs I had pictured a big farm. He dressed the part and obviously was a friend of the other boys whose parents were farmers and ranchers. Now I know that in order to keep those hopes alive, I must build carefully on their (Karl and his dad's) well-tended sheep project crowded carefully onto that small acreage. (cited in Wallace, 1981, p. 92)

While home visits are an integral part of effective practice in many schools, some teachers may encounter situations in which visits to student homes are not recommended. Teachers will need to use personal and professional judgment to assess the appropriateness of home visits in light of local circumstances (e.g., school policies). As the discussion of home and family moves into parent involvement, it will become increasingly evident that home visits are just one of many ways to foster effective partnerships between family and school.

Parent Involvement

Generally speaking, parent involvement refers to activities by parents, both in the home and school, that are intended to support and promote students' school performance and well-being (Simich-Dudgeon, 1987). Within the school setting, parents typically provide classroom assistance, serve as resource persons, accompany classes on field trips, and participate in parent-teacher organizations, advisory committees, and other decision-making bodies. At home, they teach, tutor, and provide an environment conducive to learning.

Although opinion surveys indicate that both the public and teachers generally favor increased contact between parents and school (Hoover-Dempsey, Bassler, & Brissie, 1987), actual levels of parent involvement are generally regarded as low. This is true despite the potential benefits of parent involvement on the achievement, behavior, attendance, attitudes, and study habits of students. Overall, teachers at the elementary level try harder and in more diverse ways to encourage parent involvement than do those at the secondary level (Epstein & Becker, cited in Simich-Dudgeon, 1987).

It is believed that the degree to which parents participate in school-based efforts is related to factors such as school socioeconomic status and teachers' belief in their ability to teach effectively and in students' capacity to learn (Hoover-Dempsey et al., 1987). In general, the higher the socioeconomic status and teachers' belief in themselves and their students, the greater the levels of participation. However, these factors do not appear to affect rates of parent involvement at home. For this reason, researchers suggest that efforts to increase and improve home-school linkages—particularly in areas serving predominantly low-income families—should complement school-based activities with "specific, task-related parent-child involvement at home" (Hoover-Dempsey et al., 1987, p. 432).

Research supports the importance of home-based parent involvement and school efforts to encourage and enhance parents' efforts. Simich-Dudgeon (1987) mentions the following pertinent findings:

◆ Parental encouragement, activities, and interest at home, as well as parental participation in schools and classrooms, have a positive influence on achievement, even after accounting for student ability and socioeconomic status.
◆ Parents involved in academic activities with their children at home gain knowledge that makes them better able to assess the quality of teaching their children receive and to help with academic tasks.
◆ The results of parent involvement in tutoring English language learners are consistent with those for native English-speaking students and their families. To be most effective as home tutors, all parents—regardless of ethnic language—need school support and direct teacher involvement.

More recent research provides some very interesting findings and signals a number of meaningful directions for teachers and schools to pursue. It now appears that parental involvement at home and at school do *not* contribute equally to children's learning (Finn, 1998). Surprisingly, research has not related parental involvement in school with student achievement on a consistent basis (p. 23). However, in terms of influence on children's academic achievement, research has documented the importance of parental engagement at home. Research also reveals the specific types of behavior parents engage in at home that are most strongly linked to school performance.

**What Can Parents Do at Home
to Promote Their Child's Performance?**

Parents can

✔ actively manage, organize, and monitor the child's time;
✔ assist the child with homework;
✔ talk with the child about school matters; and;
✔ read to the child and let the child read to them.

Although families will vary in their approach to these tasks, each one is crucial. Moreover, studies of student resilience suggest that "many of these same behaviors explain why some students succeed academically despite the adversities posed by poverty, minority status, or native language" (Finn, 1998, p. 21).

Taking a closer look at each of these areas serves to highlight the forms of parental engagement that make a difference. In terms of managing and organizing time, Finn finds that the parents of successful students are actively involved in the following ways (p. 21):

How Parents Can Help Students Organize Their Time

Parents can help their children by

✔ assisting with the organization of daily and weekly schedules;
✔ checking normal routines on an ongoing basis;
✔ monitoring how children use their time;
✔ staying informed regarding children's school activities, school performance, and assigned homework;
✔ allocating a time and place for completing homework assignments;
✔ monitoring where children are, with whom, for how long, etc.; and
✔ exercising appropriate control over nonacademic activities such as watching television.

Parents' engagement with homework enables them to demonstrate an interest in what their children are doing and provides an opportunity for direct involvement in their academic development (Finn, 1998, p. 21). More specifically, parents

◇ ensure that homework assignments are done;
◇ discuss assignments and clarify details;
◇ review for accuracy;
◇ assist with completion of assignments as appropriate; and
◇ teach and tutor their children.

Parent-child discussions of life at school entail regular conversations that cover a broad range of areas (Finn, 1998, pp. 21–22). It is not only important that

Parent involvement can have a very positive influence on the development of literacy and math skills.

parents talk with their children; it is also imperative that they share problems as well as accomplishments. Discussions might include

◇ providing support and guidance when difficulties arise;
◇ helping children to persevere in resolving problems related to academic work or interpersonal relationships; and
◇ engaging in joint decision making when appropriate (e.g., in picking projects or, in later grades, selecting courses).

Research on reading at home consistently supports the relationship of both parents reading to their children and children's reading to their parents to the development of literacy skills (Finn, 1998, p. 22). The effectiveness of having children read aloud to their parents, a practice long recognized by teachers, has been confirmed by a number of studies over many years. In a 2-year experiment conducted in England, children in schools in multiethnic and linguistically diverse areas of London read aloud to their parents on a nightly basis. Their progress was compared with that of children working with a reading specialist and with others receiving no intervention treatment at all. Findings revealed just "how powerful the sharing of literacy experiences can be" (Cummins, 1984, p. 238). First, the researchers found that parental involvement was feasible and practical for virtually all parents, including those who were nonliterate and those with limited proficiency in English. The willingness of parents to participate in home collaboration was not hindered by limitations in their own reading or English language skills, nor did these factors impede children's ability to progress. Second, children who regularly read to their parents outperformed those receiving instruction from a reading specialist and those who did not participate. Teachers observed greater interest in learning and improved behavior among the home readers. Third, parents, for the most part, "expressed great satisfaction" with this type of involvement, and teachers reported that home collaboration was beneficial for pupils regardless of performance level. The practice was considered so worthwhile that after the experiment was over, teachers chose to continue home collaboration and were joined by teachers from the other groups (Cummins, 1984).

In certain situations, teachers may need to be flexible, creative, and persistent in their efforts to encourage these literacy practices. This is clearly illustrated in the account of one kindergarten teacher's efforts to promote home literacy presented in Figure 3.7. As demonstrated in this case, creating the conditions necessary to realize the full potential of a program for every student in the classroom sometimes proves to be a real test of a teacher's determination and problem-solving skills.

Literacy in the Home

Debra Burgett

In the fall of 1997, I was hired by a very small school district to teach kindergarten. My class was made up of 24 eager little faces, one-third of which were English language (EL) learners.

At that same time a program was started for our primary-aged children to encourage reading. Each grade level would set certain parameters in which the students could earn a T-shirt for reading, either a certain number of pages, words or books. We kindergarten teachers, knowing our students could not read books yet, altered the program a bit. For our kids, being read to is one of the most important steps in learning to read, so our rules for the T-shirt was they had to have someone read 50 books to them. A form would have to be filled out with the name of the book, the person who did the reading and the student's signature. Then they had to draw a picture of their favorite part.

A note was sent home in both English and Spanish, the only other language spoken in my class. Right away, forms began coming in and I made up a big poster with our classroom mascot, Winnie-the-Pooh. One honey pot for each book read would track the progress until the 50th spot was in Pooh's hand, eagerly waiting at the end of the board. Every couple of days we'd count the honey pots for each student. I really wanted to encourage our little guys to earn a T-shirt just like the big kids. The students would get very excited to see the spaces fill up and were very encouraging to each other. There were obvious blank spots forming. Not one of my EL students had brought back any of the forms. (This is not to say that my English-speaking kids were whizzing through.) Most brought a few the first week or two and then things slowed down.) I tried more encouragement with these students and then I brought in one of the T-shirts to hang on the wall to entice them to get busy. Nothing was working. Then one day we gave away our first T-shirt, in fact we gave away two on the same day. Now the

(continued)

FIGURE 3.7

FIGURE 3.7   *(continued)*

children had the reading fever! Forms were coming everyday . . . but not from my EL kids. I wondered about what to do, but to be honest I just took it to be a lack of desire to participate in the program on the part of both the kids and the parents.

I knew that in learning to read, being read to is the first, most important step. The children have to develop a love of reading and books. They have to hear the vocabulary and see the left to right tracking. . . . A lot of books, not only text but story books, reflect a culture that my EL students haven't become completely familiar with. This would make comprehension more difficult and I feared with my young students, they might not develop that love of reading that I was so eager to instill.

One day as I was putting more honey pots on our poster, one of my EL students came to me and wanted me to put up a honey pot for her. I told her that I would love to and all she had to do was to get mom to read to her and fill out a form. She got a very sad look on her face and walked away. My heart was breaking.

That same day when the ESL teacher came for the pull-out program, I asked her if she would be willing to read to the kids, in Spanish (because a few of my students could not speak English), and let them fill out a form to start earning a T-shirt. She was so excited at the idea they began reading every day. I finally had all eight names, with honey pots, on our poster! However, there were still no reading forms coming from home.

Then one day, one of the EL students, who speaks English well and is in my top reading group, came up to me and said that her mother wanted to know if I had any books in Spanish that they could borrow because her mom doesn't understand a lot of the words in English. Her question hit me like a ton of bricks. I'd broken the first law of teaching . . . . never assume anything. What I had assumed was apathy, was really a lack of materials, and most likely too much pride for the parents to come to me to say they had no books in the home. This little girl comes from a very stable family where the dad works all year and while not wealthy, they seem to live a little better than most of the other Hispanic families in my class. I realized if she didn't have books, the chances were pretty great that the other students did not either. I now had a new mission and a project for my class.

My first step was to quickly get some books to her but our school library doesn't allow kindergartners to check out books. I went to the library myself that afternoon and checked out every age-appropriate book written in Spanish. Then I went to the ESL teacher and asked her if she had any books she could let the children take home. She had a small collection of first reader-type books. We began signing out books, and to make the children learn responsibility and keep the flow of limited supplies moving, they had to bring them back the next day. Our poster began to fill up. It was so rewarding to see how supportive the families really were of the program. Every day these kids were bringing in reading forms, and it was a special day for me and the ESL teacher when I was able to give away the first T-shirt to an EL student. One day one of the students came to school and asked if we had any harder books, because her mom was tired of reading the baby books!

A wonderful aspect about the program for all the students is not only are they reading, but I know for at least a short time, some quality time is being spent between the parents and the children. Sometimes in our busy lives, I'm afraid reading to the kids at bedtime or any time gets put aside as something that can be discarded.

I still needed to get books permanently into these homes. I tracked down a book club through Scholastic that has an order form in Spanish to order books written in Spanish. The

FIGURE 3.7 *(continued)*

books are fairly inexpensive ranging from .75 cents to $6.00. Free books can be earned for the classroom depending on the size of the orders, and I have been able to purchase a few for our classroom library. Several of the families have placed small orders which is really exciting. Small steps lead to miles crossed.

Just as I was feeling so successful with my new program, I discovered a glitch. There were two boys, cousins, who still were only bringing back forms if the ESL teacher read to them, nothing was coming from home. Doing a little investigating I discovered that the parents of these boys had not had much schooling and could not read, in either language. This was to be phase two of my program.

This second phase involves finding "Reading Buddies" for my students who have non-reading parents or family. I went to the fifth grade teacher who sends some of her students to the second and third grade classrooms to listen and help those readers. We set up reading buddies for my students as well, but these fifth graders read to my students instead of vice-versa. Then the students with their reading buddies fill out the form to earn the T-shirt.

I am so pleased with this program and its success. To date I have 11 out of 20 who have earned T-shirts, of those four are EL students and two other EL students who were making good progress, have moved to another community.

My goal for the summer is to purchase as many books in Spanish as I can to build up my Spanish library. I want to be able to have a good supply to let my students begin borrowing the first week of school.

. . . . I have learned a lot about my students and myself with this project. I've learned that lack of participation does not mean a lack of interest and in the future I will immediately look for reasons. I can look back on this year with success because this one program was so successful.

May 1998

Source: D. Burgett, 1998, *Literacy in the Home.* Unpublished paper. California State University—Chico.

Edwards and Young (1992) propose that teachers and administrators build on family and community strengths by creating a network of multiple partnerships. Their recommendations include the following:

◇ Use of home/school strategies based upon the strengths of families and knowledge of their own children;
◇ Use of preventive strategies that foster closer relationships with families, supporting children's development in and out of school;
◇ Exploration of multiple models for reaching out to families and service agencies; and
◇ Use of community resources as an integral part of the standard school routine such that children's immediate needs are met promptly.

Teachers can encourage parent involvement at home in many ways. One approach is the use of materials specifically designed for home use; a good example is *Family Math* by Stenmark, Thompson, and Cossey (1986). This book contains many enjoyable activities that parents and children (K–8) can work on together to develop problem-solving skills and math understanding.

Parent/Teacher Communication

The very nature of the educational process makes the relationship between home and school an important one. As Rich (1998) observes, genuine school reform "is not somewhere 'out there.' It's in every classroom and in every home" (p. 39). Parents are an integral part of efforts to improve student performance, their insights critical to educational change.

What do parents think? What do parents want and expect from their children's teachers? What are their concerns? According to Rich (1998), three basic concerns seem to be foremost in the minds of parents: these are teachers' knowledge of and commitment to (a) *teaching,* (b) their *children,* and (c) *parent communication* (p. 37). To delve deeper into parents' perceptions, Rich suggests that educators survey parents, asking them questions that are useful in identifying what they are doing well and in facilitating communication in areas of mutual concern. She reports that this is already being done in Anchorage, Alaska, and Rochester, New York, as part of larger parent involvement programs. The questions used are framed around the kinds of typical parent concerns highlighted in the three areas of Figure 3.8.

Although the questions have implications as an evaluative tool, this is not the application that is being proposed here. For our purposes, the questions show promise as a reflective tool. Reading over this set of parent questions is enough to prompt most reflective professionals to speculate as to how their students' parents would respond. In what areas am I communicating most effectively? What might I do to improve? Am I communicating with some parents more effectively than others? Are there issues that need to be addressed before they turn into problems? Asking a few well chosen questions, perhaps informally or even with selected individuals, may help to pinpoint existing or potential concerns.

If parents are asked to characterize effective teachers, many of the behaviors addressed in the questions are certain to be mentioned in a positive way. Yet even the most experienced teachers have had occasion to address parental concerns—real or perceived—ranging from the need to provide clarification for homework assignments, standards, or expectations to being accessible and responsive when called upon to discuss children's progress or problems. Making it a point to take the *initiative* in asking parents for their input may help teachers to better identify what different parents need and expect from us. According to one series of studies, a frequent complaint from parents from all socioeconomic levels is that teachers and principals come across as "patronizing" and "talking down to us": "They liked those with a 'personal touch.' They wanted educators just to be real" (Lindle, cited in Brandt, 1998, p. 30). Ad-

---

Teaching (pp. 37–38)

Does the teacher . . .

✔ appear to enjoy teaching and believe in what he/she does in school?
✔ set high expectations and help children attain them?
✔ make expectations and standards for student learning clear?
✔ know the subject matter he/she teaches and how to teach it?
✔ create a safe classroom where children are encouraged to pay attention, participate in class, and learn?
✔ deal with behavior problems fairly and consistently?
✔ assign meaningful homework?
✔ make homework assignments clear?
✔ provide enough time for the completion of assignments?
✔ return homework assignments in a timely manner?

Children (p. 38)

Does the teacher . . .

✔ understand how my child learns and try to meet his/her needs?
✔ treat my child fairly and with respect?
✔ contact me promptly with any concerns about my child's academic and behavioral performance?
✔ provide helpful information during conferences?
✔ tell me how my child is doing in class?

Communicating with Parents (pp. 38–39)

Does the teacher . . .

✔ provide clear information about class expectations?
✔ use a variety of communication tools to report progress and student needs?
✔ work with me to develop a cooperative strategy to help my child?

Is the teacher . . .

✔ accessible and responsive when I call or want to meet?

FIGURE 3.8 Questions for Parents.
Source: Adapted from D. Rich, (1998). "What Parents Want From Teachers," 1998, *Educational Leadership,* 55(8), pp. 37–39.

dressing the areas of greatest concern to parents through effective partnerships may serve to mitigate such perceptions.

Rich indicates that it is too early to report on the results of the "parent report cards" being used in Anchorage and Rochester. At this point, the Anchorage Public Schools report that the response rate from parents was about 50%, with input from the parent surveys used as the basis for ongoing discussions at each school site (most typically about curriculum) and in identifying differing perceptions between parents and children on areas such as school safety.

NEIGHBORHOOD AND COMMUNITY

In this section, the emphasis is on making connections between the school context and that of the neighborhood and community. Learning about the sociocultural environment beyond the school is essential, particularly at a time in which many educators live outside the communities in which they teach. This section focuses on how teachers can develop a better understanding of the neighborhood and community context beyond the school, and how they can foster strong and supportive connections between the classroom, school, and community.

Neighborhood and Community Environments

Neighborhood visits enable teachers to become familiar with the neighborhood and community environment experienced by their students (Wallace, 1981). In some cases, much can be learned about an area by walking or driving through it; if students are bused to the school, a bus ride may provide useful information about their neighborhoods. In schools with extended service areas, teachers may choose to focus on a single neighborhood, one they do not know well.

The need for the information such visits provide is becoming increasingly evident. In one study, most teachers surveyed did not know how and where students were spending their time outside school, nor were they aware of available community resources (Grant, 1981). Careful and directed observation and analysis of students' immediate surroundings—the places they spend their time out of school—can have educational payoffs. "Tying into and building onto" what students already know "yields high educational gain and is a way of subtly showing respect for the background and lifestyle of every student" (Wallace, 1981, p. 96).

There are different ways of planning neighborhood walks according to the time available and specific interests. Teachers who are apprehensive about visiting an unfamiliar neighborhood can arrange to be accompanied by someone who is familiar with the area. For example, two teachers who were hesitant about visiting a particular area in a large city arranged to walk through the neighborhood with a doctor whose office was located there. They later reported that their neighborhood walk "gave us a different feeling about the area, a different attitude" (Hays & Hays, 1981, p. 102). Another strategy is to use student "tour guides." For example, one teacher who toured the favorite haunts of junior high students guided by student volunteers observed, "I immensely enjoyed the walks with the kids, they were quite enlightening" (Elner, 1981, p. 108).

In undertaking these visits, teachers will want to identify the physical surroundings familiar to students and consider their possible classroom applications. To facilitate the observation process, Wallace (1981) encourages teachers to note such things as homes, fences, doors, windows, architectural styles, lot sizes, paths, streets, gardens, animals, buildings, stores, industries, junk, water, mail, fire, police, furniture, lighting, religious institutions, music, art, toys, gathering places, landmarks, foods, and cars. The number and age of people visible in the area and their activities also should be noted. For those with an inclination to map the area, color codes can be used to distinguish the location of various types of structures and areas around the school (Anderson, 1979). These features include public community agencies, religious or political organizations, housing, places where children and teenagers play, places where adults gather (e.g., unemployed, senior citizens), major industries and businesses, etc.

Teachers may even find it useful to ask students to map their own neighborhoods. Information gleaned from such an activity can provide valuable insights about areas and structures that are familiar to the students and those that are not. What do children know about their own neighborhoods and the surrounding areas? What appears to be most important and meaningful? From their perspective, what are the "boundaries" of their neighborhood? Finally, if teachers want even more detailed information, questionnaires can be used to explore community demographics, and concerns (Anderson, 1979).

Note: Before asking students to do this activity, map your own neighborhood or perhaps the neighborhood of the school where you teach or would like to teach. Think about your own knowledge of the neighborhood and its people.

Community Study: Oral History

A community's most important resource is its people. One way that teachers can effectively tap this resource is through oral accounts of individuals' life experiences. It has been defined as "the recollections and reminiscences of living people about their past . . . The materials of oral history are the raw data of historical scholarship—history as primary sources with the warts, wrinkles, and inconsistencies. Rich in personal triumph and tragedy, it is a history of the common person, the undocumented but not inarticulate" (Sitton, Mehaffy, & Davis, 1983, p. 4).

In the context of multicultural education, this technique enables students to develop a deeper understanding of culture and community by participating in "the systematic collection of a uniquely personal history—the history of common people" (Mehaffy, 1984, p. 470). Use of life histories helps students to recognize and understand the changes and constants elders have experienced over a lifetime and the ways people cope with problems and conflicts. From a cultural perspective, life histories serve a dual purpose by illustrating both the commonality and diversity of roles, values, and experiences within groups (Gibson & Arvizu, 1978). Within the family context, they are a record of family heritage and traditions for younger generations, providing "a sense of belonging, of identity, . . . a place in space and time" (Grenier, 1985, p. 6A).

Benefits of Classroom Oral History Projects

☑ Classroom oral history enables teachers to bring curriculum and community together; it makes history come alive as textbooks and classroom converge with the faces and realities of the student's own community (p. 12).

☑ Classroom oral history projects can encompass much more than local history with applications well beyond the study of history (p. 14).

☑ By engaging students in authentic research on their family, ethnic, and community heritage, classroom oral history engenders a personal motivation for the study of history. In the process, students identify more strongly with their heritage and experience greater self-worth (p. 16).

☑ Classroom oral history projects enable students to develop important academic and interpersonal life skills using strategies consistent with current directions in education (p. 17).

☑ The products of classroom oral history projects are authentic and valuable contributions to families, community, school, and historical scholarship.

Source: Sitton, Mehaffy, & Davis, 1983. pp. 12, 14, 16, 17, 20.

Guidelines for Enhancing the Value of Life History Projects*

1. *Begin by interviewing someone you know.* Create an atmosphere that is informal and comfortable.

2. *Prepare for the interview.* Meet with the person before doing an interview. Explain the purpose of the interview and how the information will be used. Find out about the person's life so that you can guide the interview without being directive.

3. *Develop an outline of topics to be covered in the interview.* Common topics include personal items (e.g., place of birth; information regarding parents, schooling, and work); recollections of major historic events that occurred during the person's life (e.g., where were you when . . .); and special qualities, knowledge, or experiences. Topics relevant for family research include the origin of the family surname and its meaning; naming traditions; stories; famous or notorious family members; family recipes; and family members' childhood experiences, religion, politics, schooling, marriage, courtship, etc.

4. *Use questions sparingly.* Although useful for providing structure and clarification, questions tend to produce a stilted interview if used in excess. In general, keep questions short, and avoid those that can be answered by a simple "yes" or "no." "Who, what, where, when, and how" questions elicit more elaborate answers and hence, more information.

5. *Take notes during the interview.* Check information for accuracy.

6. *Limit the length of the interview to no more than 1 hour.* If all areas of interest cannot be covered in one session, schedule a series of interviews. Doing a

---

* Adapted from Gibson and Arvizu (1978), Mehaffy (1984), and Smith and Otero (1982). (See Sitton, Mehaffy, and Davis (1983) for a complete oral history guide for teachers.)

complete life history requires a considerable amount of time. Students may want to focus upon a particular period in or aspect of an individual's life (e.g., the experiences of international students, immigrants, or longtime residents in the community; the educational experiences and orientations of several generations in the same family).

7. *Practice the interviewing technique.* Students can start by interviewing their teacher or each other. Once skills are developed, invite a community elder to the classroom for an interview. Ask students to record information and work together to check its accuracy. Encourage students to interview family members such as grandparents, aunts, and uncles.

Life histories are an effective tool for family and community study. Figure 3.9 provides a typology of project options developed by Sitton et al. (1983). The possibilities are almost endless. Multiple histories can provide the basis for preparation of a local history, documenting the experiences of a cross-section of the community's population. The technique also serves as a vehicle for integrating multicultural concepts with skills development in history, language arts, and other subject areas. Life history projects also enhance students' self-identity, awareness of their neighborhood and history, and research and writing skills (Mehaffy, 1984).

Self

• Oral autobiography (student's own)

Family

• A memory book (students interview one or two of their grandparents)
• Family life histories
• Family genealogy
• Family oral history
• Family archive project
• Comprehensive family history
• Family cookbook and social history
• Exploring family roots

School and Neighborhood

• Oral history of the school
• Oral history of the home neighborhood (individually or in teams, students trace the history of a block, street, or neighborhood)

Community

• Living history—classroom interviews of community consultants
• Researching the origins of local place names

(continued)

FIGURE 3.9   Oral history projects: a typology.

FIGURE 3.9 *(continued)*

- Oral histories of local buildings
- Historic photographs and oral history
- The community at war
- A mainstreet oral history
- An oral history of a local industry
- An immigrant's oral history
- Environmental oral history
- The local effects of national events
- The oral history of a significant event
- Chronicling recent local events with oral history
- Studies in community social history
- Social history: ethnic variations
- The study of a local campaign or election

Oral Life History

- General
- Topical focus
- Chronological focus
- Student focus (peers or younger children, perhaps siblings or cousins)
- Folk/popular artist

Political Studies

- A controversy retrospective
- Local lives in politics
- Local political roles
- The structure of local politics
- Local political meetings
- Political folklore

Folklore Studies

- A self-interview
- Student folklore
- Children's folklore
- Family folklore
- A community-wide collection
- Ethnic variations in folklore

Other

- An oral history of traditional crafts
- Trades and professions project
- Institutional or organizational histories
- Ethnic history projects

Source: Adapted from T. Sitton, G. L. Mehaffy, and O. L. Davis, Jr., 1983, *Oral History.* Austin, TX: University of Austin Press, pp. 45–67.

The products of these projects can be shared with other classes, published in school literary publications, incorporated in library collections, displayed in community museums, and used as the basis for other activities. Potential products from classroom oral history projects include community oral history archives, publications (e.g., Foxfire books), local media productions, community-specific curriculum materials, and research on historical problems (Sitton et al., 1983). The projects are as diverse as the people whose recollections and reminiscences they capture, and the communities whose people, places, and events they document. Cultural journalism produced from student-produced oral history materials is inner city and rural, small town, and suburban. Its regional and cultural richness is evidenced by the original—*The Foxfire Book* (Nacoochee School in Rabun Gap, Georgia) and succeeding generations of projects such as *Tsa'Aszi* (Navajo), *Kalikaq Yugnek* (Eskimo), *Sombras del Pasado* (Mexican American), *Nanih Waiya* (Choctaw), *Mo'Olelo* (Hawaiian), and *Lagniappe* (Cajun/Creole) (p. 10).

Jessica Oliver's award-winning essay about her great-grandmother incorporates the kind of personal information that students can generate through life history projects (Figure 3.10 pp. 90–91). In this case, a middle school student writing on the theme of "Growing Up Asian in America," provides an example of how powerful such accounts can be.

One of the earliest life history programs instituted in the public schools is the Foxfire project in rural Georgia, which began with a focus on Appalachian traditions; similar projects now number more than 200 nationwide (Mehaffy, 1984). Elementary school students in North Carolina and California have published texts based upon oral history projects, and others have initiated Living History programs. As part of an ongoing process of community study, life histories can bring a personal quality to the dynamics of ethnicity and enhance students' awareness of cultural diversity at the local level (Cortés, 1981).

Community Partnerships

The educational literature is replete with examples of how schools and communities are working together as partners to make a difference in the education of their children. (As an example, see the May 1998 issue of *Educational Leadership* on engaging parents and the community in schools.) Such partnerships take a variety of forms, and the changes they produce may be subtle or dramatic. According to Hatch (1998), community involvement can contribute to the academic achievement of students through:

◇ *increased support for learning* as manifest through improvements in the physical environment of the school, additional resources, and development of a stronger constituency of advocates;
◇ *improved student, teacher, and parent attitudes and higher expectations;* and
◇ *enhanced learning experiences* that engage students, parents, and teachers. (pp. 16–19)

Remembering Ma-Má
Jessica Oliver, 11
Francisco Middle School, San Francisco

Ahhh . . . The sweet aroma of incense . . .

It beckons my memory to when I was little, watching my Great-Grandmother burning incense and praying to Quan Yin (the Chinese Goddess of Mercy), Sahm Bo Fut (the Three Gods), and for the loss of her husband, Chung. She would put a little tiny spoon of cooked rice in three tiny bowls, and she would put tea in three other tiny cups. Also, she would put fruits and steamed chicken on the altar to pay her respects to the gods and goddesses of the kitchen. Gracefully, she would lean down and chant these words over and over again, holding her prayer beads: "Na Mo Au Lae Tau Fut." These words tingled in my ears so peacefully, and they sounded like a soothing lullaby.

I was determined to understand what she was doing. So I asked her what those peaceful words meant: the enlightenment and energy within. Also, she said that she was praying for me to have health, happiness, and a good education.

What I love about Ma-Má (the Chinese name for Great-Grandmother in a respectful way) was that not only was she my Great-Grandmother, but she had a good sense of humor. Sometimes Ma-Má would make funny faces that would just make me hysterical. Whenever Ma-Má was mad at someone, she would make a face at them when they weren't looking. She would scrunch her nose closer to her eyes like a wrinkled raisin and tighten her mouth like she just ate a super lemon (sour candy). Then she would stick out her two fingers and point at him/her. When the person turned to look at Ma-Má, she would smile like an innocent angel.

What makes Ma-Má so special to me is that she would always explain about how she came from China, about my ancestors, and my Chinese heritage. Ma-Má told me lots of stories. She also told me about her life in China. This is what she told me:

Ma-Má was born in 1907 in Canton. She had 9 brothers and sisters. Her family was very poor and always had to share whatever they had with each other. When Ma-Má was 21, her father arranged a marriage, and she was very mad. She wanted to stay and help her mother to work and support her family, but she couldn't disobey her father, so she married Yéa-Yéa (Great-Grandfather), and they fell deeply in love. After that, she had three sons, but two died from lack of food.

Shortly after, Yéa-Yéa had to go to San Francisco for a business trip because he was an opera star. But they never realized that they would be separated for 32 years! Every day Ma-Má grieved. They couldn't contact each other. Also, it was during war time, so there was hardly any food for Ma-Má and her son. She was always really thoughtful about her son (my grandfather, Gong-Gong). Sometimes she wouldn't eat anything and give it all to Gong-Gong and to her nieces. One of Ma-Má's brothers died, and he had a little girl whom nobody wanted because they thought she was too much trouble. Ma-Má didn't want to see her little niece, Sau Ying, die so she adopted her. Ma-Má had to knit sweaters and make match boxes to buy food. Her neighbors were eating dead human babies and rats to survive. But Ma-Má didn't have the heart to eat babies and rats, so she cut down trees and boiled the insides of tree trunks for food.

After 22 years, Ma-Má, Gong-Gong, and Sau Ying finally found a way of escaping from China to go to Hong Kong. Yéa-Yéa would always send money to Ma-Má, but her brothers

(continued)

FIGURE 3.10

FIGURE 3.10 *(continued)*

would always steal her money. She would never know because she didn't know how to read or write.

Many years passed. One day, Yéa-Yéa finally contacted Ma-Má's brother (in Hong Kong) and he found out that Ma-Má, Gong-Gong, and Sau Ying were staying there. Yéa-Yéa tried for 10 years to bring her to the United States. Finally, in the summer of 1966 they were once again reunited!

Without her great love and encouragement, many lives, such as those of my aunts and uncles would have been lost. She kept on telling them to stay strong through the War and Communism. I remember she would encourage me to bear through my problems, especially when my parents were divorced and my dad wouldn't come to see me. When my cousins made fun of me because I wasn't full-blooded Chinese, and I didn't look Chinese, Ma-Má would sing to me and tell me that it was okay to be a multi-cultural person. She would cry with me and tell me to keep my head high and be proud of who I am. She also told me not to follow her and be an illiterate. An education could take me anywhere I wanted, and that I couldn't be cheated by others with my money.

Ma-Má's dream was to be reunited with her husband, Yéa-Yéa. Their love stayed alive even though they were separated from each other for 32 years. Yéa-Yea could have easily forgotten about Ma-Má and married someone else in America, but their love kept them strong. They never forgot the hope of one day seeing each other again. She also dreamed of living in a place with no war, Communism, or starvation. She hoped one day to see her son married, and she wanted to live long enough to see her grandchildren born. I will fulfill the rest of Ma-Má's dreams as much as I possibly can. She dreamed for me to be the best person I could be and to respect my mother with dignity.

My dream is to become a singing star and follow in Yéa-Yéa's footsteps. I also hope I can become as patient as Ma-Má and never give up on my dreams, exactly the way she never gave up for 32 years!

People in China expected Ma-Má to marry a rich person who had a good education and was a doctor, instead of an opera singer. They doubted that she would survive the war. They expected she would remarry.

People expect me to be an All-American person, to know nothing about the Chinese culture, and speak only English. I'll never be just an All-American. I want to learn all there is to know about Chinese culture.

It is beneficial for me to be an Asian American growing up in America. Not only do I know the American culture, but I know my Chinese cultural background, and I know how to speak fluent Chinese. I'm proud to learn how to chant these soothing lullabies like Ma-Má did. She really reminds me of Quan Yin; she knew the meaning of mercy, too. Another benefit to being Asian in America is that I can read and write, get a good education, and I have a lot more opportunities than Ma-Má had.

. . . Now the sweet aroma of incense is fading away, and Ma-Má has gone with it. But I'll always remember her and treasure her in my heart . . . Quan Yin smiles on me with Ma-Má's face.

First Place, Ages 6–11

Source: Asian Pacific Fund, San Francisco, CA, *Growing Up Asian in America, Prize Winning Essays and Artwork,* 1996, pp. 1–2.

Engaging members of the community in partnerships with the schools can make a difference in the education of its children.

Community partnerships with schools reflect the diverse concerns and needs areas they serve. The following examples of *public and professional engagement,* to use Thompson's (1998) term, are merely illustrative of some of the possibilities:

◇ **Community-action alliances:** The Alliance Schools, a network of low-income communities in Texas, developing a constituency of advocates—parents, community leaders, and educators—to improve student achievement. (Hatch, 1998)

◇ **Intergenerational partnerships:** The "100 Grandparents" program in which adult volunteers (senior citizens) engage in read-aloud activities with children in grades K–2, Marion County Public Schools, Florida. (Smith, 1998)

◇ **Public and professional engagement:** Collaborative action involving different stakeholders in school reform (the Panasonic Foundation's principles and strategies for real engagement). (Thompson, 1998)

◇ **School-to-work programs:** Ho'ala Na Pua, a multidisciplinary program built around Hawaiian culture and seafaring, Konawaena High School, Kealakekua, Hawaii (Hickcox, 1998); connecting school learning with workplace expectations through the Relevance Counts Institute and Teachers in Business program with school districts in Minnesota. (Bottge & Osterman, 1998)

◇ **Community-based technology programs in rural areas:** Programs using technology to provide "a window to the world" for students, their parents and communities, such as those in a remote Inuit community—Igalaaq (the Inuktitut word for "window"), Leo Ussak Elementary School, Rankin Inlet, Canada (Belsey, 1998)—and a rural coal mining town—Christopher Elementary and High School Districts, Christopher, Illinois. (Corley, 1998)

SUMMARY

◇ Cultural influences are pervasive in education, their impact on educational processes significant. The first step in dealing with diversity in the classroom is to develop an understanding of culture in ourselves, both as individuals and as teachers.

◇ Getting to know students is an ongoing process for all teachers. An important part of this process is to develop an understanding of culture in students, both as individuals and as members of different cultural groups. As teachers learn about students' cultural identities and backgrounds, they better appreciate what culture means to them. As teachers learn about students' homes, neighborhoods, and communities, they better understand the sociocultural contexts outside the classroom in which students live and learn.

◇ Teachers and families are partners in the educational enterprise. Research suggests that "conventional wisdom" is often at odds with reality when it comes to identifying family practices that support the academic success of children. Schools can foster effective partnerships with parents both at home and at school. Since parental involvement at home influences children's academic achievement, schools can promote student performance by providing meaningful support for efforts in the home. Along similar lines, communication between parents (e.g., caretakers, guardians) and teachers is another integral part of the effort to improve student achievement.

◇ Teachers can make important connections with the community they serve. They can begin by learning about the neighborhood environments in which their students live. Recognizing that a community's most important resource is its people, teachers can use oral history as a powerful tool for family and community study. Schools and communities can also work together in partnerships that contribute directly to academic achievement or indirectly by addressing other salient needs and concerns.

APPLICATION, EXTENSION, AND REFLECTION

1. **Cultural Groups.** Using selected questions from the survey of cultural group characteristics in Figure 3.5, interview two students or adults (volunteers) from one or two cultural and linguistic backgrounds different from the mainstream. What did the interviews reveal about the culture(s)? How did culture impact on their schooling? What insights did you gain from the interviews that can be applied in the classroom?

2. **Oral History.** Practice the interviewing technique presented in this chapter with family members, friends, or colleagues. Complement information from this chapter with other sources that you may have, and develop an oral history activity for classroom use. The typology in Figure 3.9 highlights some of the many possibilities that you may want to explore. Reflect on what you and your students learn from doing an oral history.

3. **Parent Interviews.** Using the questions for parents, in Figure 3.8, interview two parents (volunteers) with school-age children. From their perspective, what are the particular strengths of their child's teacher(s)? What kinds of concerns, if any, do they express? What insights do the parents' perspectives offer you as a teacher? In class, compare the responses of parents from different groups and backgrounds. How are their experiences and concerns similar and different?

4. **Community Engagement.** Identify the community partnerships with school(s) in your area. To what extent do the projects identified provide real engagement for the various constituencies? What are the major strengths and limitations of current patterns of engagement? What might be done to improve the existing partnerships? Are these changes likely to take place? Why or why not?

REFERENCES

Adler, P. S. (1977). Beyond culture identity: Reflections upon cultural and multicultural man. In R. W. Brislin (Ed.), *Culture learning* (pp. 24–41). Honolulu: University of Hawaii Press.

Anderson, J. (1979). Community analysis field study. In H. P. Baptiste, Jr. & M. L. Baptiste (Eds.), *Developing the multicultural process in classroom instruction* (pp. 208–212). Washington, DC: University Press of America.

Arvizu, S. F., Snyder, W. A., & Espinosa, P. T. (1980, June). *Demystifying the concept of culture: Theoretical and conceptual tools.* Bilingual Education Paper Series, 3(11). Los Angeles: Evaluation, Dissemination and Assessment Center, California State University—Los Angeles.

Asilo, A. (1997). Everyone should have an Asian grandmother. *Growing Up Asian in America, Prize Winning Essays and Artwork* (p. 1). San Francisco, CA: Asian Pacific American Community Fund.

Belsey, W. (1998). Igalaaq: Window to the world. *Educational Leadership, 55*(8), 68–70.

Bottge, B. A., & Osterman, L. (1998). Bringing the Workplace to the Classroom. *Educational Leadership, 55*(8), 76–77.

Brandt, R. (1998). Listen first. *Educational Leadership, 55*(8), 25–30.

Burgett, D. (1998). *Literacy in the home.* Unpublished paper. Chico: California State University—Chico.

Cavarreta, J. (1998). Parents are a school's best friend. *Educational Leadership, 55*(8), 12–15.

Corley, T. K. (1998). Tapping into technology in rural communities. *Educational Leadership, 55*(8), 71–73.

Cortés, C. E. (1981). The societal curriculum: Implications for multiethnic education. In J. A. Banks (Ed.), *Education in the 80's: Multiethnic education* (pp. 24–32). Washington, DC: National Education Association.

Cross Cultural Resource Center (1979). Culture posters. Sacramento: Department of Anthropology, California State University—Sacramento.

Cummins, J. (1984). *Bilingualism and special education: Issues in assessment and pedagogy.* San Diego: College Hill Press.

Elner, E. (1981). A neighborhood walk. In W. E. Sims & B. Bass de Martínez (Eds.), *Perspectives in multicultural education* (pp. 104–108). Lanham, MD: University Press of America.

Finn, J. D. (1998). Parental engagement that makes a difference. *Educational Leadership, 55*(8), 20–24.

Garza, R. T., & Lipton, J. P. (1982). Theoretical perspectives on Chicano personality development. *Hispanic Journal of Behavioral Sciences, 4* (4), 407–432.

Gay, G. (1981). Interactions in culturally pluralistic classrooms. In J. A. Banks (Ed.), *Education in the 80's: Multiethnic education* (pp. 42–52). Washington, DC: National Education Association.

Gibson, M. A., & Arvizu, S. F. (1978). *Demystifying the concept of culture: Methodological tools and techniques.* Monograph II. Sacramento: Cross Cultural Resource Center, California State University-Sacramento.

Gollnick, D. M., & Chinn, P. C. (1986). *Multicultural education in a pluralistic society* (2nd ed.). Columbus, OH: Merrill.

Gollnick, D. M., & Chinn, P. C. (1994). *Multicultural education in a pluralistic society* (4th ed.). New York: Merrill/Macmillan.

Grant, C. A. (1981). The community and multiethnic education. In J. A. Banks (Ed.), *Education in the 80's: Multiethnic education* (pp. 128–139). Washington, DC: National Education Association.

Grenier, (1985). Oral history gives you a place in space and time. Life/Style section. *Chico Enterprise Record,* September 28. p. 6A.

Hall, E. T. (1959). *The silent language.* Greenwich, CT: Fawcett Publications.

Hall, E. T. (1969). *The hidden dimension.* Garden City, NY: Anchor Books, Doubleday & Company, Inc.

Hatch, T. (1998). How community action contributes to achievement. *Educational Leadership, 55*(8), 16–19.

Hays, O., & Hays, S. (1981). A neighborhood walk. In W. E. Sims & B. Bass de Martínez (Eds.), *Perspectives in multicultural education* (pp. 101–104). Lanham, MD: University Press of America.

Hickcox, A. K. (1998). The canoe is their island. *Educational Leadership, 55*(8), 58–59.

Hidalgo, N. M., Bright, J. A., Siu, S-F., Swap, S. M., & Epstein, J. L. (1995). Research on families, schools, and communities: A multicultural perspective. In J. A. Banks (Ed.) & C. A. McGee Banks (Assoc. ed.), *Handbook of research on multicultural education* (pp. 498–524). New York: Macmillan.

Hoover-Dempsey, K. V., Bassler, O. C., & Brissie, J. S. (1987). Parent involvement: Contributions of teacher efficacy, school socioeconomic status, and other school characteristics. *American Educational Research Journal, 24* (3), 417–435.

Laosa, L. M. (1977). Multicultural education—How psychology can contribute. *Journal of Teacher Education, XXVIII* (3), 26–30.

McGroarty, M. (1986). Educator's response to sociocultural diversity: Implications for practice. *Beyond language: Social and cultural factors in schooling language minority students* (pp. 299–334). Los Angeles: Evaluation, Dissemination and Assessment Center, California State University—Los Angeles.

McLeod, D. (1997). Self-identification, pan-ethnicity, and the boundaries of group identity. In F. Schultz (Ed.), *Annual editions: Multicultural education, 1997/98* (pp. 121–124). Guilford, CT: Dushkin/McGraw-Hill.

Mehaffy, G. L. (1984). Oral history in elementary classrooms. *Social Education, 8*(6), 470–472.

Miner, H. M. (1979). Body ritual among the Nacirema. In E. C. Smith & L. F. Luce (Eds.), *Toward internationalism* (pp. 173–178). Rowley, MA: Newbury House. (Reprinted from *American Anthropologist,* American Anthropological Association; 1956, *58*(3)).

Mukhopadhyay, C. C. (1985). Teaching cultural awareness through simulations: Bafa Bafa. In H. Hernández & C. C. Mukhopadhyay, *Integrating multicultural perspectives into teacher education* (pp. 100–104). Chico: California State University—Chico.

Oliver, J. (1996). Remembering Ma-Má . *Growing Up Asian in America, Prize Winning Essays and Artwork* (pp. 1–2). San Francisco, CA : Asian Pacific Fund.

Rich, D. (1998). What parents want from teachers. *Educational Leadership, 55* (8), 34–39.

Saville-Troike, M. (1978). *A guide to culture in the classroom.* Rosslyn, VA: National Clearinghouse for Bilingual Education.

Simich-Dudgeon, C. (1987). Involving limited-English-proficient parents as tutors in their children's education. *ERIC/CLL News Bulletin, 10*(2), 3–4, 7.

Sitton, T., Mehaffy, G. L., & Davis, Jr., O. L. (1983). *Oral history.* Austin, TX: University of Austin Press.

Smith, G. R., & Otero, G. (1982). *Teaching about cultural awareness.* Denver: University of Denver, Center for Teaching International Relations.

Smith, J. (1998). It takes 100 grandparents. *Educational Leadership, 55*(8), 52–53.

Stenmark, J. K., Thompson, V., & Cossey, R. (1986). *Family math.* Berkeley, CA: University of California Press.

Swisher, K., & Swisher, C. (1986). A multicultural physical education approach. *Journal of Physical Education, Recreation and Dance, 57*(7), 35–39.

Thompson, S. (1998). Moving from publicity to engagement. *Educational Leadership, 55*(8), 54–57.

Wallace, G. (1981). Cultural awareness: Interaction of teachers, parents, and students. In W. E. Sims & B. Bass de Martínez (Eds.), *Perspectives in multicultural education* (pp. 89–112). Lanham, MD: University Press of America.

CHAPTER

4 School and Classroom Contexts

To teach them all is to know them all.

Etlin (1988)

I n Latin, the term *contextere* means "to weave together" (Cole & Griffin, 1987, p. 7). The image of context as a network of invisible threads aptly describes the texture of contextual factors in education. Imagine students in a classroom engaged in a cognitive task; context encompasses those innumerable interrelated factors that operate at multiple levels beyond the task itself. It includes "All the factors that might influence the quality of time spent on the task, ranging from the arrangement of a lesson in the curriculum, to the relation of the classroom to the school as a whole, and to the relation of the school to the community of which it is a part" (pp. 6–7).

Contexts can be represented as dynamically embedded within each other as illustrated in Figure 4.1. The classroom is nestled within a multitude of increasingly broader contexts outside the school that include parents, district, community, and more (adapted from Cole & Griffin, p. 7). In this text, exploration of the classroom context involves *process*—interaction, social dynamics, organization,

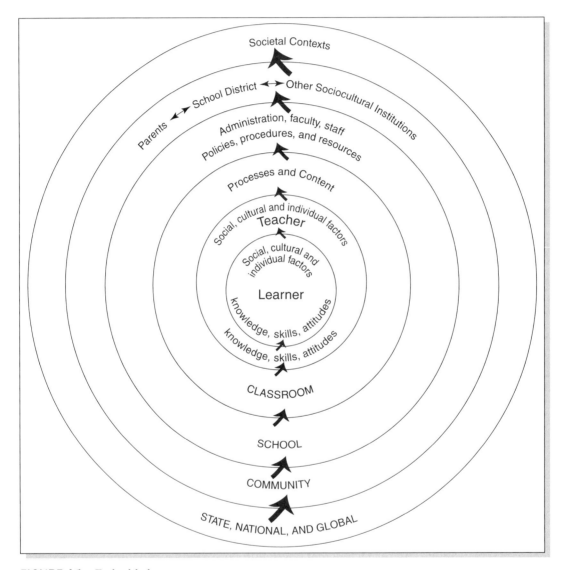

FIGURE 4.1   Embedded contexts.
Source: Adapted from M. Cole and P. Griffin (Eds.), Laboratory of Comparative Human Cognition, *Contextual Factors in Education.* Copyright © 1987 by Wisconsin Center for Education Research, School of Education, University of Wisconsin—Madison.

and management—and *content*—curriculum, instruction, and materials. This text is organized to draw our attention from contexts outside the school proper—societal, community, and home—to those inside the school and classroom.

While there are many important contextual factors, only some of those that influence school performance are directly related to schools and fall within the purview of educational policy and practice. Cole and Griffin (1987) cite parental stress and family circumstances (e.g., illness, marital conflict, financial problems, absentee parent) as examples of factors beyond our control as educators. While recognizing their importance, given the parameters of this text, emphasis is given to factors whose institutional links to the schools are strongest and most accessible to the influence of teachers. It is hoped, however, that connections fostered within these contexts will in turn facilitate the efforts of service providers (e.g., social services, religious institutions) more directly involved in dealing with this other "set" of factors.

As researchers and educators focus attention on contextual factors, they recognize the need for recontextualization at different levels. According to Cole and Griffin (1987), this involves:

> recontextualizing individual tasks; recontextualizing the social organization of the instructional process, emphasizing the special case of linguistic and social variations and social organization; recontextualizations afforded by the advent of computers in education; the school as a distinctive cultural organization; and, finally, links between schools and various nonschool settings. (p. 14)

In the previous chapter, we considered some key reconceptualizations that involve the linkages between schools and students' homes and communities. In this chapter, we first explore the interaction of contextual factors in schools and classrooms, most specifically in relation to academic achievement and school effectiveness.

CONTEXTUAL FACTORS AND ACADEMIC ACHIEVEMENT

In the United States, as in many other countries, cultural groups differ in terms of overall educational achievement. Explaining the influence of social and cultural differences on academic performance is not a trivial matter because the solutions proposed to address the situation are clearly contingent upon assumptions made in accounting for the observed variance. Sue and Padilla (1995) have examined four common explanations for the academic underachievement of some minority groups. These are presented in Table 4.1.

For obvious reasons, the *genetic inferiority* explanation is the most destructive and negative. It is based on the assumption that certain populations are incapable of performing intellectually on a par with other groups. This perspective assumes that innate intelligence can be measured adequately and that differences between groups are due primarily to heredity. It denies the potential

TABLE 4.1   *Perspectives on Differential Academic Achievement Among Cultural Groups*

Perspective	Attribution of Blame	Primary Solutions
Genetic Inferiority (minorities fail to do well because they are genetically inferior)	The groups themselves, not society	No solutions are possible because little can be done to change heredity
Cultural Deficit (minorities fail to do well because their culture is viewed as deficient)	The groups themselves, as well as social prejudice and discrimination	Train minorities to be less deficient and eliminate prejudice and discrimination
Cultural Mismatch (minorities fail to achieve because their cultural traits are incompatible with those in the U.S. mainstream)	No one; cultures just happen to be different	Change groups so that they can participate in the mainstream, but also change schools in order to better accommodate and ameliorate the mismatch
Contextual Interaction (minorities fail to achieve because of unfortunate interaction of many factors)	No one factor, group, or institution; outcomes produced through the interaction of many factors such as circumstances, cultural values, etc.	Change one or more of the factors or the context to alter interactions and thereby change the outcomes

Source: Adapted from S. Sue and A. Padilla, "Ethnic Minority Issues in the United States: Challenges for the Educational System." In *Beyond Language: Social and Cultural Factors in Schooling Language Minority Students*, p. 42. Copyright © 1986 by California State Department of Education [Evaluation, Dissemination and Assessment Center]. Reprinted by permission.

of those identified as "genetically inferior," a list that over the years has included African-Americans, Chinese, Hispanics, Native American, Jews, Italians, Greeks, Yugoslavs, and others (Sue & Padilla, 1995). Equally detrimental is the notion that, except for genetic engineering, nothing can be done to significantly alter a situation attributed to heredity. More recent manifestations of this line of reasoning are evidenced in *The Bell Curve* (Herrnstein & Murray, 1994). (For various analyses and critiques in response to the book's controversial findings and conclusions, see Fraser 1995).

Those who adopt a *cultural deficit* interpretation ascribe deficiencies to the minority culture itself or to the effects of racism and discrimination on the group. From an educational perspective, what is perhaps most critical about this explanation is the perception that minority group members are "lacking the cultural competence necessary for dealing with academic and social challenges"

(Sue & Padilla, 1986, p. 44; 1995, p. 44). The group's perceived deficiencies are emphasized, while existing strengths, competencies, and skills are downplayed. Characterizations stress social, psychological, and economic problems, among them drug addiction, criminal behavior, alcoholism, personality disorders, laziness, and so on. Intervention strategies focus on compensating for deficits—both presumed and real—and challenging discriminatory practices and ethnic stereotypes. Hence, although programs developed from this point of view recognize that people are capable of adapting and achieving, they take on a deficit perspective. Compensatory or remedial in approach, the programs make it incumbent upon members of the target group to change in order to improve their status.

In contrast to the cultural deficit view, the *cultural mismatch* explanation assumes that cultures are inherently different but not necessarily superior or inferior to each other. Skills learned in one's culture may range from highly functional to nonfunctional or maladaptive in relation to another culture. This viewpoint is used to explain both academic and economic success and failure. Chinese and Japanese Americans are seen to benefit from parallels in Confucian and Protestant work ethics. For other groups, educational underachievement is thought to occur because the cultural traits of the ethnic group do not match those of the dominant culture as reflected in schools. Thus, the educational performance of minority groups is related to the degree of congruence between group values and traits and those of the education system: the better the match, the greater the likelihood that the level of academic achievement will be high.

Efforts to improve the performance of minority students are aimed at increasing the congruence between schools and ethnic cultures; changes in both are usually necessary. There is pressure for groups to acculturate, to become "Americanized." Language-minority students learn English, but are allowed use of the primary language in the early stages so as to keep up with their peers.

Sue and Padilla (1986, 1995) find this viewpoint to be intuitively appealing, but too simplistic in its explanatory power and excessive in its espousal of strict acculturation. In reality, there is more of a convergence or divergence of interacting cultural and social factors rather than simply an accommodation of cultural traits. Ethnic groups experience historical and socioeconomic circumstances which present their members with unique opportunities and obstacles. Since cultures are not static, these circumstances are constantly changing, sometimes in ways that are more favorable, sometimes less.

According to the *contextual interaction* explanation, educational achievement is a function of the interaction between two cultural orientations—the cultural values of the larger society and those of the ethnic minority group. The behaviors, beliefs, and perceptions of individuals within specific minority groups are influenced by the more-or-less fortuitous social, economic, and political circumstances they experience. Over time, the changes in beliefs and behaviors that result from cross-cultural interaction may enhance or impede achievement: "The key to understanding achievement is the change that occurs because of the interaction between different cultures" (Sue & Padilla, 1986, p. 49; 1995, p. 49). For example, a group's experiences with discriminatory occupational patterns can enhance or devalue the importance of education, depending on how the group responds. From this perspective, groups are not assumed to be culturally superior or inferior; adaptation to the dominant culture does not call for loss of the ethnic culture.

This focus on interaction provides a more holistic, comprehensive, and dynamic view than do other explanations of differential academic achievement. Within this framework, solutions to educational problems require changes in the larger society as well as in the schools, ethnic groups, and communities. At the societal level, dealing with differential achievement patterns requires the elimination of discrimination and prejudice and greater appreciation for cultural diversity. At the local level, significant improvement in educational outcomes for minority-group students depends on school reform (e.g., changes in teacher attitudes toward minority students; adaptations in curriculum and instruction; use of culturally unbiased testing procedures) and the adaptation of ethnic minority students and groups to the institutions of American society.

In the final analysis, explanations of differences in academic achievement patterns among cultural groups are not easily separated from sociocultural considerations. Recent scholarship rejects a single cause approach in explaining group differences. The need to examine relationships between sociocultural factors (e.g., language, socioeconomic status, racism, prejudice, cultural conflict) and the societal and school contexts in which they appear is becoming increasingly evident (Cortés, 1986; Sue & Padilla, 1986). The reason is simple: Factors that explain differences in one setting have often been found to lack explanatory power in another. Take language as an example. The performance of English language learners is influenced by variables such as socioeconomic status, language attitudes, and school orientation. The mere presence of a native language other than English does not explain the observed variability in school performance within and across different language-minority groups. Table 4.2 highlights many of the critical elements involved in contextual interaction.

Teachers and students operate within a school context that exerts considerable power—directly and indirectly—on classroom processes. Effective schools are characterized by effective teaching, and they support it. Culturally relevant teaching further defines successful teachers of children and adolescents from minority backgrounds. Formal and informal school policies and practices related to the organization of instruction at the school level (such as grade levels based on age, tracking, and retention) also impact what happens at the classroom level in profound ways.

TABLE 4.2 *School and Society*

Societal Context: The Societal Curriculum	
Family	Community
Institutions	Mass media
Heritage	Culture/ethnicity
Language	Educational level
Attitudes	Perceptions
Socioeconomic status	
Other sociocultural factors	

School Context: The School Educational Process		
Educational Factors	**Instructional Elements**	**Student Qualities**
Theoretical rationale	Goals Objectives	Academic skill and knowledge
Underlying assumptions	Curriculum design Staff development	Language proficiency and attitudes
Administrative knowledge	Parental involvement Evaluation plan	Prosocial skills Life goals
Fiscal/material/ district policies	Placement Counseling	Health/nutrition Motivation
Teacher knowledge skills attitudes expectations	Methodology Textbooks/materials	Sociocultural attributes Self-image

Outcomes
Academic achievement
Language proficiency
Prosocial skills
Self-image
Other cognitive/affective skills

Source: C. E. Cortés, "The Education of Language Minority Students: A Contextual Interaction Model." In *Beyond Language: Social and Cultural Factors in Schooling Language Minority Students.* Copyright © 1986 by California State Department of Education [Evaluation, Dissemination and Assessment Center]. Reprinted by permission.

CONTEXTUAL FACTORS, EFFECTIVE SCHOOLS, AND SUCCESSFUL TEACHING

The processes that occur in a school as a whole and in individual classrooms can and do influence educational outcomes significantly. Teachers know this from personal observation, and researchers have demonstrated that it is so (Erickson, 1986; Good & Brophy, 1986; Knapp & Woolverton, 1995; Ladson-Billings, 1994). School variables are important determinants of student achievement, for the characteristics of student populations such as socioeconomic level and minority-group status are not sufficient to predict how students will actually perform. What transpires at the school level must be taken into account because differences among schools, as among teachers, significantly affect students and their achievement. Moreover, since the vast majority of the variation in student achievement—from 70 to 90%—actually occurs within schools, overall school effectiveness clearly is contingent upon effective teaching at the classroom level (Cohen, cited in Good & Brophy, 1986, p. 581).

Significant differences in pupil performance across classrooms at the elementary level have been observed among groups historically marked by persistent and disproportionate school failure. Although the probability that children from low-socioeconomic backgrounds and "at-risk" groups will underachieve in school is "powerfully influenced" by social processes and individual differences, their school performance also is subject to considerable influence by individual teachers (Erickson, 1986).

Two excerpts from Ladson-Billings' (1994) interviews with successful teachers of African American students serve to illustrate this point. In the teachers' own words:

> I have children in here who other teachers told me could not read. Heck, *they* told me they couldn't read. But I look them squarely in the eye in the beginning of the school year and tell them, you *will* read, and you will read *soon*. I tell my entire class we all have to know how to read and it's everybody's responsibility to make sure that everyone learns to read well. I pair up the better readers with the poorer ones and tell them that *the pair* gets a reading grade. They are allowed to do any number of things to help each other read. Although the school doesn't want us to do it I let them take their readers home. I also use some of those old, out-of-date basals as at-home readers for them. All students have a reading log in which they list what they read aloud to their parents the night before. The parents sign the logs. I award prizes for completing the reading logs. You may have noticed how quiet things got when the reading lesson began. I'm pretty easy-going about a lot of things, but I keep my reading time sacred. (pp. 114–115)

> I don't believe in telling students that they are doing well when they aren't. Some teachers come into this district and think that they're doing the children a favor by sticking a star on everything. They don't care that they're rewarding mediocrity. But in doing so, they're really just setting the kids up for failure because somewhere down the road they're going to learn that that A was really a C or a D.

> What I try to do is find those things the children really are good at and acknowledge them in the classroom. That means knowing about their sports and church activities. . . . I have had coaches, ministers, Scout leaders, family members—you name it—in here to tell the class about the excellence of class members. (p. 99)

Unfortunately, "positive teacher influence on the achievement of children at risk seems to be the exception rather than the rule" (Erickson, 1986, p. 125). Compared to other developed countries, the United States does not fare as well as might be expected. For example, Erickson (1986) reported that the relationship between social class and school achievement is greater in the United States than in Italy, Sweden, Finland, Japan, and Flemish-speaking Belgium. Although teachers can have a significant impact on children at risk, the dramatic possibilities of their "powerful" positive influence are not being realized systematically in U.S. schools.

While responsibility for this situation is shared by teachers and administrators within schools, schools are also strongly influenced by contextual factors beyond their direct control. For example, the conditions under which teachers work in the United States are in part determined by the social class of the communities they serve, the students they teach, and the teachers themselves: "Teachers in lower- and working-class contexts are more likely to experience severe resource constraints, receive fewer rewards for good work, see fewer incentives to work hard, have less autonomy, and work within a professional culture that discourages complex forms of teaching" (Knapp & Woolverton, 1995, p. 565).

Nevertheless, the situation just described need not and should not continue. There are spheres of influence that do fall within teachers' control, and it is particularly critical that teachers maximize their effectiveness at the classroom level, even under less than optimum conditions. Successful teachers know how to make the most of their time with children in the classroom. Less successful teachers do not. This is exemplified in one study of schools in low-socioeconomic districts with predominantly White and Black student populations identified as high or low achieving on the basis of academic performance (cited in Good & Brophy, 1986). In this study, various classroom elements were assessed and associated with achievement level. In high-achieving schools, whether predominantly White or Black, the features highlighted in Figure 4.2, p. 106 prevailed. The major findings of this study thus illustrate how classroom processes such as those discussed in Chapter 5 can contribute to educational outcomes, either positively or negatively.

The importance of classroom processes, especially teacher behaviors related to student achievement, is further demonstrated by research examined by Brophy (1982). Teachers know that the characteristics and attributes of effective teaching defy easy description. "Effective" teachers are not "ordinary" teachers: they are more dedicated, better organized, and more efficient in classroom management. That students in their classrooms experience more academic success is the "cumulative result of daily planning, thorough preparation, and simple hard work" (Brophy, 1982, p. 529).

In high-achieving schools:

- students spent most of their class time productively involved in instructional activities.
- teachers believed that, with few exceptions, students were capable of mastering the content and expected them to do so.
- teachers used reinforcement patterns that provided appropriate rewards and encouraged higher levels of achievement.
- heterogeneous or flexible grouping procedures were implemented.

In low-achieving schools:

- the quantity and quality of instruction varied considerably among classrooms (e.g., some teachers had managerial problems; in many classrooms, students engaged in limited productive, task-relevant work and academic interaction).
- students considered to be less capable were "written off."
- performance expectations were low.
- teachers' reinforcement practices were variable and sometimes inappropriate.
- grouping procedures often were used for management rather than instructional purposes and provided for little mobility among groups.

FIGURE 4.2   Compare and contrast: school characteristics.
Source: Study cited in T. L. Good and J. E. Brophy (1986). School effects. In M. C. Wittrock (Ed.), *Handbook of Research on Teaching* (3rd ed., pp. 570–602). New York: Macmillan.

Effective teachers know how to make the most of their time with students to help them excel.

In a study that looks specifically at successful teachers for African American children, Ladson-Billings (1994) highlights the basic tenets of culturally relevant teaching. She characterizes such pedagogy as intellectually, socially, emotionally, and politically empowering—educational practice that uses culture to promote academic and cultural excellence (pp. 17–18). A tripartite vision guides educators in a culturally relevant school: their goals are to (a) provide educational self-determination; (b) honor and respect students' home culture; and (c) help students understand the world as it is and enable them to make it better. In the classroom, culturally relevant teaching is distinguished by the way teachers see themselves and others, by their relationships with students, their appreciation of knowledge, and their instructional practices. The critical attributes of the exemplary teachers in Ladson-Billings' study are summarized in Figure 4.3.

Clearly, the teachers' actions have a strong influence on students.

Conception of Self and Others

Teachers with culturally relevant practices:

✔ have high esteem and high-regard for others
✔ see themselves as part of the community, see teaching as giving back to the community, and encourage their students to do the same
✔ see teaching as an art and themselves as artists
✔ believe that all students can succeed
✔ help students make connections between their community, national, and global identities
✔ see teaching as "digging knowledge out" of students

Social Relations

Culturally relevant teachers:

✔ establish teacher-student relationships that are fluid and "humanely equitable"
✔ extend the teacher-student relationship to interactions beyond the classroom and into the community
✔ are careful to demonstrate a connectedness with each of their students
✔ encourage a community of learners
✔ encourage students to learn collaboratively and expect them to teach each other and take responsibility for each other

Conceptions of Knowledge

Culturally relevant teaching:

✔ views knowledge as something that is continuously re-created, recycled, and shared
✔ views knowledge critically
✔ is passionate about knowledge

(continued)

FIGURE 4.3 Culturally relevant teaching.

FIGURE 4.3 *(continued)*

☑ helps students develop necessary skills
☑ sees excellence as a complex standard that takes student diversity and individual differences into account

Basic Tenets of Instruction

☑ Teachers help students whose educational, economic, social, political, and cultural futures are most tenuous to become intellectual leaders in the classroom
☑ Teachers make students apprentices in a learning community rather than teach in an isolated and unrelated way
☑ Teachers legitimize students' real-life experiences by making them part of the "official" curriculum
☑ Teachers treat students as the competent learners they demonstrate they are
☑ Teachers and students participate in a broad conception of literacy that incorporates both literature and oratory
☑ Teachers provide instructional "scaffolding" to move students from what they know to what they need to know
☑ Teachers and students engage in a collective struggle against the status quo
☑ Teachers are cognizant of themselves as political beings
☑ Teachers display in-depth knowledge of both the students and the subject matter
☑ Teachers make instruction the focus of the classroom
☑ Teachers believe that real education is about extending students' thinking and abilities

Source: Synthesis of research findings from G. Ladson-Billings, 1994, *The dreamkeepers: Successful teachers of African-American children.* San Francisco, CA: Jossey-Bass.

SCHOOL POLICIES AND PRACTICES

Within schools, formal and informal school policies and practices related to the organization of instruction can foster or impede the creation of culturally relevant learning environments. Some policies and practices are the product of local circumstances and decisions, while others are so widespread that the underlying beliefs and assumptions remain largely unquestioned. Among the latter are policies and practices based upon the belief that "students need to be held to standards of performance at specific grade levels and at graduation" (Astuto & Clark, 1992, p. 96). According to Astuto and Clark, three assumptions embedded within this belief provide the basis for educational practices that research suggests are "dysfunctional":

◇ the use of grade levels as the basis for grouping students for instruction;
◇ the use of retention as a means for enforcing arbitrary levels of academic achievement; and

◇ the tracking of students into different levels of curricula as a way of dealing with those unable to meet arbitrary grade-level standards.(p. 96)

Astuto and Clark are struck by the "absurdity" of organizational practices that rely on students' age for placement in grades with "arbitrary, but uniform, curricula and tests"; such practices, they argue, violate all we know about variations in the developmental progress of children and adolescents, including obvious gender-related differences in maturation (p. 96).

> One thing is certain. The practices derived from these beliefs have contributed directly to the conversion of the American public school into a sorting machine dominated by the economic status of the student's family. If we were serious about maximum achievement opportunities within American public schools, we would be forced to find alternatives to organizing students by age-based grade levels, emphasizing performance on standardized tests as a measure of progress and achievement in school, and enforcing arbitrary standards of achievement for students within and at the end of their school experience. We would have to abandon the most popular policy tools now in use at national and state levels in the reform of American education. (pp. 96–97)

In the sections that follow, we take a closer look first at ability grouping, tracking, and retention, and then at their relationship to high-stakes testing.

Ability Grouping and Tracking

> . . . in one district I know, teachers resist being placed in the 'trash' track. This raises lots of very difficult questions that can only be answered by looking critically at the entire context. What is the 'trash' track, you ask? It is the 'track' that has been (consciously or unconsciously) assigned less status and power and prestige. I know many teachers in this district who resist ever being placed on this track. I know teachers on this track who feel 'less.' Who are the students who are placed in this track? You already know the answer: students from lower socioeconomic communities and ethnic minorities. (Wink, 1997, p. 121)

As defined by Wheelock (1994), *tracking* is used to describe "the practice of sorting secondary school students into different programs of study," such as vocational, general, or college preparatory (p. 1). *Ability grouping* refers to similar sorting practices at the elementary and middle school levels, as students are placed "into classes or work groups based on their perceived ability levels (average, below average, above average)"; in the differentiated classes, students are commonly exposed to different curricula and instruction (p. 75). In the minds of many educators, tracking and ability grouping are interchangeable in that they both involve judgments about students' intellectual abilities and their academic potential, and concomitant decisions as to appropriate curricula and instruction (Oakes, cited in Wheelock, 1994). To avoid confusion, it should be noted that as used in this context, ability grouping is not synonymous with *flexible grouping*, the accepted and widespread practice of short-term, skill-specific instructional grouping within classrooms (Findlay & Bryan, 1975; Wheelock, 1994).

Wheelock characterizes tracking and ability grouping as common and pervasive sorting practices, citing the following data to illustrate just how widespread they are:

◈ At the elementary level, one estimate suggests that some form of ability grouping is evident in 60% of the schools. (Between-class ability grouping or pull-out are widely used in Chapter 1, special education, and gifted/talented programs.)

◈ At the middle school level, principals report ability grouping in 82% of their schools, with approval from teachers in school leadership teams at 72%.

◈ At the high school level, by one estimate 80% of all schools offer tracks that provide students different learning opportunities. (pp. 7–8)

In schools and districts in which these practices are commonplace, the stage for tracking is set by ability grouping in the lower grades. Goodlad observed that after the first few months of the first grade, students were rarely regrouped for instruction in math and reading:

> One of the reasons for this stability in group membership is that the work of upper and lower groups becomes more sharply differented with each passing day. Since those comprising each group are taught as a group most of the time, it is difficult for any one child to move ahead and catch up with children in a more advanced group, especially in mathematics. (cited in Wheelock, 1994, p. 12)

As what is initially a modest gap between groups widens, the real and perceived distances become greater over time. By the time they enter high school, students are separated into tracks that offer very distinct academic and occupational learning experiences.

Most research suggests that the disadvantages associated with tracking and ability grouping, particularly for students at the middle and lower levels, far surpass the benefits. This is evident in terms of expectations; student achievement, self-esteem, and motivation; access to knowledge, quality instruction, and challenging learning environment. Several important generalizations have emerged from research on tracking and ability grouping. The following discussion is based largely on findings summarized by Findlay and Bryan (1975), Hallinan (1984), and Wheelock (1994).

The most commonly stated basis for instructional grouping is student ability. For teachers, the basic motivation is a desire to establish homogeneous groups which are easier to teach. At the elementary level, pupils usually are placed into different ability groups within the classroom; at the secondary level, tracking into separate classes is the more typical pattern. The dominance of this pattern is such that heterogeneous ability groups are rare. In actual practice, however, the assignment of students to tracks or ability groups depends, to a considerable extent, on factors other than the ability or academic achievement of students as individuals. Group assignments often are influenced by school and classroom characteristics such as achievement distribution and organizational and management considerations. In her analysis of one district, Oakes reported that "in practice all ability groups—high, average, and low—include students whose test scores range from the lowest to the highest percentiles" (cited in Wheelock, 1994, p. 9).

Students in low groups generally have quantitatively fewer and qualitatively inferior opportunities to learn than those in higher levels. In one study of secondary schools, for example, students in higher tracks spend 80% or more of their time involved in instruction (Oakes, cited in Sleeter & Grant, 1988, p. 21). Instruction in these tracks was clear, varied, and focused on higher thinking skills and content necessary for college. Those in lower tracks, however, spent less of their time on instruction (67%), and did half as much homework as did students in high tracks. Instruction provided in lower tracks was characterized by considerable rote memorization and routine activities and emphasized basic education skills. Commenting on the absence of Shakespeare in the curriculum of students in lower tracks, Oakes notes that "Shakespeare wrote plays for audiences far less literate than most 9th, 10th, and 11th grade low-track American high school students" (cited in Astuto & Clark, 1992, p. 96).

In schools, education is differentially distributed across groups and tracks (Mehan, 1988). During instruction, student behavior varies according to track and ability level. In particular, more task-related interactions occur in higher ability groups than in lower groups, in which off-task behaviors are common.

> Students at lower levels look around and see themselves grouped with others who have been sorted according to the same low expectations. Not surprisingly, when these groups include students placed together "for behavioral reasons," teachers often must spend as much time controlling students as teaching them. (Wheelock, 1994, p. 11)

Students in remedial classes also tend to have teachers with less teaching experience. In one study, researchers found 42% of the remedial, vocational, and general mathematics sections taught by teachers with five years or less experience as compared to 19% of the sections in pre-algebra and Algebra 1 (McDonnell et al., cited in Wheelock, 1994, p. 12).

Significant differences in student social status exist both within and between different tracks and ability levels. Because academic status contributes to the social status of students among peers, the hierarchy defined by grouping influences the social position of students within the classroom and school. It is not surprising that assignment to low-ability groups "carries a stigma that is generally more debilitating than relatively poor achievement in heterogeneous groups" (Findlay & Bryan, 1975, p. 20). In the United States, both socioeconomic status and ethnicity influence placement in tracks; in general, low-income and minority students are found in disproportionate numbers in lower groups and tracks and middle-income students in average and higher groups (Sleeter & Grant, 1988; Winn & Wilson, 1983). "In tracked schools, African American and Latino students typically are missing from top-level classes"(Wheelock, 1994, p. 9). Research also suggests that homogeneous grouping increases social-class differences, whereas heterogeneous grouping appears to reduce them (Findlay & Bryan, 1975).

- The assignment of students into high, middle, and low ability groups appears to be influenced by socioeconomic status: "Children from low income or one parent households, or from families with an unemployed worker, are more likely to be assigned to low ability groups." (p. 27)
- Given comparable low grades and poor test scores, children from families with low incomes are more consistently placed into lower groups than those from middle- or high-income families (parent intervention is a factor here).
- Given comparable low grades and adequate test scores, children from low-income families are placed into lower groups whereas similar children from middle-income families are tracked into middle level groups.
- Research studies "consistently and robustly document" the negative effects of ability grouping within classrooms on students in average and low ability groups: "With respect to instructional processes and student motivation, behavior, and achievement, there is not a single observational study that shows positive consequences for low-track students." (p. 28)
- Inappropriate grouping can exacerbate what are fairly minor differences early in children's school careers into major differences in succeeding years.

FIGURE 4.4   Research highlights: ability grouping.
Source: Synopsis of research on ability grouping in M. Cole and P. Griffin (Eds.), Laboratory of Comparative Human Cognition, 1987, *Contextual factors in education*, pp. 27–28. Prepared for Committee on Behavior and Social Sciences and Education, National Research Council. Madison, WI: Wisconsin Center for Education Research, School of Education, University of Wisconsin—Madison.

Instructional grouping usually hinders learning and academic achievement among students consistently assigned to low groups. This negative effect of grouping is most pronounced for low-ability groups. In these groups, students may be "restrained more by poor-quality instruction or amount of time spent off-task than by any limitations in ability to learn" (Hallinan, 1984, p. 236). Some students—particularly those from lower socioeconomic levels and members of minority groups—also may experience a lowering of self-esteem and changes in attitudes toward school when they are placed in low-ability groups (Winn & Wilson, 1983). Indeed, the only students for whom ability grouping appears to have any beneficial effects in terms of academic achievement are those placed in high-ability groups and tracks.

Along similar lines, Cole and Griffin (1987) highlight important findings from research on ability grouping in Figure 4.4.

Economic, legal, and educational imperatives are demanding that teachers committed to the ideal of higher standards for all students explore alternatives to ability grouping and tracking. Economic realities—today's and tomorrow's—dictate that "all students should be prepared for postsecondary education to be competitive in the marketplace" (Wheelock, 1994, p. 16). Court cases in states such as Alabama, California, and Illinois are addressing concerns directly related to tracking. One court order shaping educational reform in Alabama states that:

Schools shall not track students, relegate particular students to a general track of undemanding courses, or design coursework that forecloses educational and occupational options. Programs shall not result in de facto tracking and shall include safeguards to ensure that factors such as socioeconomic status, race, gender, and disability do not limit or determine students' post-high school pursuits. (Wheelock, 1994, p. 18)

A growing number of prominent groups and organizations are calling for an end to tracking and strict ability grouping. Among these are the National Governors' Association, the Council for Basic Education, the Education Commission of the States, the Carnegie Council on Adolescent Development, the National Commission on Secondary Schooling for Hispanics, the Quality Education for Minorities Project, and the Common Destiny Alliance (Wheelock, 1994, pp. 18–20). Efforts to raise achievement levels and implement educational reforms are contingent on changes in grouping practices.

In their own classrooms, teachers can begin to address grouping practices in several ways. First, teachers must provide constancy in the quality of instruction across levels (Hallinan, 1984). Accounting for the academic performance of individual students requires examination of the mode of instruction and learning climate within levels. Teachers need to ensure that students in low-ability groups have access to quality instruction and "high-status knowledge" (i.e., the academic skills, content, attitudes, and experiences that characterize informed, educated, and productive members of society) (Hallinan, 1984; Nevi, 1987). Teachers should avoid labeling, allow for mobility across groups, and consider status effects in assigning peer groups (Hallinan, 1984). Use of descriptive labels for groups should be avoided because it serves only to ascribe characteristics that may be inaccurate and damaging. Students should be reassigned to different groups if their learning rates, performance, and motivation change.

The negative effects of status expectations on learning by low-ability and low-status students can be reduced by use of strategies such as cooperative learning, complex instruction, and tutoring. Students also need to recognize (a) that each group contains students with differing qualities and abilities and (b) that group assignments are relative, subject to achievement distributions within each class. At the school level, alternative procedures for planned heterogeneous grouping can be explored (Findlay & Bryan, 1975).

Although unusually effective schools have been found to employ a wide variety of arrangements in grouping students for instruction, several studies suggest that an overriding concern in these schools has been the design and implementation of instructional interventions that serve low achievers (Levine & Lezotte, 1995). Among the particularly effective arrangements reported in the research are those highlighted in Figure 4.5.

Wheelock (1994) observes that "untracking is not an end in itself but a means to the end of improving learning for everyone" (p. 23). Educators in untracked schools share a commitment to achieving success for all learners in heterogeneous classrooms and providing equal access to high-level knowledge through multifaceted teaching strategies. Their efforts are guided by the belief

☑ Providing special assistance to low readers in small "parallel" classes
☑ Providing "parallel scheduling" of reading instruction in small groups
☑ Targeting resources to individualized and small group instruction
☑ Assigning two teachers to Chapter I classes of students with low readers
☑ Making widespread use of credentialed teachers to provide small group instruction and tutoring in reading and at the primary level
☑ Providing learning opportunities—developmental and remedial—within and beyond the regular school day
☑ Reducing the size of classes in the primary grades (e.g., 20–22 or less in urban schools)
☑ Placing retained pupils in transitional classes or units taught by specially prepared teachers who can target their needs and help the children rejoin their peers
☑ Substituting special help in algebra (a "gatekeeping" course) for time allocated to study hall and physical education so that low achievers can perform to the required standard
☑ Using tutoring, after-school, and/or summer school learning sessions to address gaps in students' prior knowledge in anticipation of the introduction of content and skills in regularly scheduled classes
☑ Having paraprofessionals provide supplementary support for low achievers
☑ Using common reading periods that allow across- and within-grade grouping of elementary students on the basis of performance (pp. 531–532)

FIGURE 4.5   Effective intervention arrangements for low-achievers.
Source: Synthesis of research findings presented in D.U. Levine and L.W. Lezotte, 1995, "Effective schools research." In James A. Banks (Ed.) and Cherry A. McGee Banks (Asso. Ed.), *Handbook of research on multicultural education*, 531–532. New York: Macmillan.

that all children can learn at high levels and that the schools are responsible for helping them do so. In untracked schools, the teachers' belief that "all students can learn" is paramount (p. 24).

By all accounts, effective untracking is a very complex, and sometimes difficult, process in which educators must contend with a myriad of constraints in various contexts (Kohn, 1998; Wheelock, 1994). As Wheelock suggests, it entails "far more than simply regrouping students or substituting one curriculum or instructional strategy for another" (p. 55). In general, conditions favorable to untracking efforts include the following:

◇ support at all levels of school-based leadership,
◇ generous time for staff development,
◇ a multiyear blueprint for change,
◇ an implementation plan that phases in changes by grade, team, or department, and
◇ supporting policies at the school, district, and state levels.

There is no one model or prescription for change (Wheelock, 1994). Each school faces its own unique set of challenges, and creates programs uniquely designed for its student population. As they chart this new course, educators find that changes in one area of the school precipitate changes in other areas. Changing expectations and outcomes occasion the need for coaching and tutoring support. New learning and teaching strategies require an overhaul of the curriculum. Organizational structures and routines are altered, the responsibilities of counselors change, and assessment approaches are revamped.

In summary, tracking and ability grouping appear to have a largely negative impact on the educational and career opportunities of students, as well as their social and emotional development. Given the negatives associated with the allocation of "different learning experiences to different groups according to perceptions of their capacity to learn," these widespread practices often do more harm than good (Wheelock, 1994, p. 2). Teachers must recognize and make every effort to eliminate or at least minimize the negative academic and social effects involved in the grouping of students. Grouping for instructional purposes must contribute to the goals of helping students reach their full potential, as individuals and members of society, and of providing equality of educational opportunities. There are a variety of instructional interventions that have been demonstrated to work effectively for students in general and for low achievers in particular. In some schools and districts, untracking is becoming an integral part of school improvement and educational reform. According to Wheelock (1994), "in addressing the imperative for equity, untracking schools find excellence. In finding excellence, they realize equity" (p. 73).

The Myths About Retention

Retention is the educational practice of keeping a student in the same grade for an additional year of instruction, that is, repeating that grade. Children typically refer to grade retention as "flunking," although adults regard the term as pejorative (Shepard & Smith, 1989, p. 1). Four questions will be used to frame this discussion of retention, first to explore your own beliefs about retention and how they compare to what other teachers believe, then to examine what educational research reveals and consider alternatives to grade retention.

What are your beliefs about retention? In order to help you determine what you think about retention, you are asked to respond to the exercise in Figure 4.6. This will provide an opportunity for you to reflect on your own beliefs and later to see whether or not your beliefs and assumptions are consistent with what educational research tells us about retention.

How do your beliefs compare with those of other teachers? Having better defined your own beliefs about retention, we will look at how they compare to those of other teachers. On this issue, if you found yourself in support of retention, your position is widely shared: "educational professionals and the public are almost universally in favor" of retention (House, 1989, p. 204).

In one study of students, parents, and educators in a large city in the Southwest, 74% of the principals, 65% of the teachers, and 59% of the parents surveyed answered that children unable to meet grade level requirements should be retained (Byrnes, 1989, p. 111). When asked to check the three most salient

Indicate whether the following statements are **TRUE** (T) or **FALSE** (F):

_____ **1.** In the nineteenth century, grade retention was so widely practiced that it affected over 70 percent of all students. (p. 5)

_____ **2.** There has never been a period in our history in which holding students to strict promotion standards has not also been accompanied by the segregation of pupils by ability and the departure of large numbers of students from school by the eighth grade. (p. 5)

_____ **3.** There are no national data available on the number of students retained in grade each year. (p. 6)

_____ **4.** Retentions reached an all time low in the early 1970s. (p. 6)

_____ **5.** The negative effect of retention is greater with respect to achievement than it is for personal adjustment, self-concept, or attitude toward school. (p. 10)

_____ **6.** From a historical perspective, repeating kindergarten is a very recent phenomenon. (pp. 10–11)

_____ **7.** The number and types of children retained in grade differs greatly from one school to another, well beyond any biological or sociological factors specific to the children themselves. (p. 11)

_____ **8.** Teachers almost universally endorse retention. (p. 147)

_____ **9.** Retention in grade has no benefits for either school achievement or personal adjustment. (p. 215)

_____ **10.** Retention is strongly related to later dropping out of school. (p. 215)

_____ **11.** Retention increases the probability of dropping out of school by 20 to 30 percent. (p. 215)

_____ **12.** Two years in kindergarten—even when one year is labeled a "transition" program—fail to enhance achievement or solve the problem of inadequate school readiness. (p. 215)

_____ **13.** Children promoted in kindergarten suffered no disadvantages compared to similar children with two years of kindergarten. (p. 216)

_____ **14.** The age-grouped grade is neither universal nor historically inevitable. (p. 220)

_____ **15.** The threat of failure is a poor motivator, especially for students from minority and lower socioeconomic backgrounds. (p. 224)

_____ **16.** Schools that retain also segregate students by tracking and special education placements at higher rates than low-retaining schools. (p. 225)

_____ **17.** Educators are unable to predict which children will benefit from retention. (p. 226)

_____ **18.** Correlations of successful retention with chronological age, gender, or size are larger in teachers' minds than they are in the results of careful empirical research. (p. 227)

Answer Key: All items are TRUE.

FIGURE 4.6   What are your beliefs about retention?
Source: Selected chapters from *Flunking Grades: Research and Policies on Retention* (1989). Lorrie A. Shepard and Mary Lee Smith (Eds.), New York: Falmer Press.

characteristics observed in children selected for retention, the teachers and principals responded as follows (listed in order by frequency of response): developmentally immature, low self-esteem, low motivation, lack of English proficiency, low intelligence, discipline problem, learning disabled, shy and non-assertive, and emotionally unstable (p. 112). Clearly, academic achievement is only part of the equation for retention.

What do teachers say when they are asked for their views on retention? In a study by Smith (1989), kindergarten teachers were asked about the children in their classes who seemed to be candidates for retention, the decisions involved, and the consequences of those decisions. The dominant belief among the teachers interviewed was that retention benefits the pupil. Social, academic, and personal benefits were attributed to a number of factors related to the pupil's being older and more experienced. Retention was believed to enable the child to assume leadership, gain self-confidence, achieve academically, integrate socially, and become familiar with the classroom environment and routine. In one teacher's words,

> I tend to get the children who are repeating, and it's just like night and day for most of them. The first year they just don't cooperate, have no idea what's going on, and the second year is just like a new child just walked in. (p. 140)

Retention was perceived as almost a preventative measure, one that would keep the child from struggling through school, and experiencing stress and frustration; help the child to avoid subsequent retention; and enable the child to deal with peer pressure. In another teacher's words,

> If he doesn't [get retained], school's going to be a struggle for him. You think about on down the road what is school going to be like for this child. If he is struggling right now in kindergarten what will it ever be like in first or second grade? (p. 141)

Teachers also draw on personal experience, as the following excerpt illustrates:

> We held our first son back, number one because he was a boy and because we felt from observing him that he didn't have the maturity. We didn't want him to meet with failure, we wanted him to be a year older to cope. And of course then in junior high and high school ages we were delighted because he's had the maturity that so many of the kids haven't had to say no and to be his own man. (p. 141)

Teachers were unable to recall negative repercussions nor stigma attached to retention in kindergarten. They also expressed concerns over the potentially negative consequences of promoting a child who should be retained (e.g., failure, special education referrals, retention in a later grade). The following are typical:

> There's not the stigma of failure in kindergarten, so that is the time to do it. (p. 142)

> When I think about them going into first grade, it would have been failure, failure, failure. (p. 142)

Some teachers recognize that certain conditions may mitigate the benefits of retention, most specifically, the response of the teacher, parents, and child to the retention decision. Although retention was deemed to be effective for children who are immature, special education was preferred for children with educational disabilities, low motivation, or limited intellectual ability. This is how two teachers saw it:

> If the parents let the child know they are happy with the decision . . . if they're not happy and there's a lot of wavering on it, then I think it's almost—then I think it is probably harmful to the child. Because they are going to read that from the parent. And the kids really will read what you are feeling. And if you accept it, they accept it. So it depends on how the parent approaches the child. (p. 143)

> You see some parents just think retaining a child is a terrible stigma, you've labeled them for life. And you have to correct a lot of these attitudes. (p. 144)

Teachers minimized or failed to acknowledge negative consequences attributable to retention, and typically underestimated the children's feelings of failure, disappointment and confusion. Their endorsement of retention was such that if they were to err in making a decision, they preferred that it be on the side of retention rather than promotion.

Of the teachers interviewed, remarkably few expressed concerns about school factors—teacher, curriculum, and structure—that enter into the decision-making process. Some teachers are concerned about what other teachers will think: "Teachers at all levels worry that, if they promote children who have not mastered grade-level skills, the next grade teacher will send the promoted but incompetent children back to them or otherwise vilify the socially promoting teachers" (Smith & Shepard, 1989, p. 218). Of the teachers in the Smith study, the following response was atypical . . .

> I have a lot of trouble failing anyone. It means I haven't done my job. I feel it's my job to take all the kids who come in and teach them what they need even though they are behind in their development. (Smith, 1989, p. 147)

Smith offered some tentative explanations to account for the near unanimity of support for retention among kindergarten teachers (pp. 147–150). First, the information that teachers have access to is incomplete and misleading. Teachers are most likely to see children who are retained shortly after the decision has been made, when the children are still dealing with familiar content and routines. How the children would have fared had they been promoted is in the realm of the hypothetical. Moreover, teachers lack data as to what happens to these children at later stages in their school careers, little knowledge of the increased probability that they will drop out of school. Second, kindergarten teachers are responding to expectations that children entering first grade are ready to read. Retention is used to "protect" children who are neither ready nor competent to deal with this common standard and the externally imposed curriculum that goes with it. Unwilling or unable to question whether the standard literacy-focused kindergarten curriculum is inappropriate for some learners, the teachers opt instead to retain the children least likely to succeed within the prevailing structure. Third, some kindergarten teachers are more capable than others at managing the great diversity of ages, backgrounds, and experiences they face in the classroom. Some teachers respond by trying to achieve greater homogeneity through programs and policies, believing at some level, that these efforts will not be in vain. However, "ability grouping benefits the most able group while restricting the amount and frequently the quality of instruction received by the least able group. Many teachers fail to realize that, even with such tracking policies there will always be a child who is the youngest, the smallest, the least able and the least mature in any group of children" (p. 220). As compared to high retaining teachers, kindergarten teachers retaining few pupils were more likely to provide productive learning experiences for all of their children and less likely to use tracking and segregation to deal with the heterogeneity of their classes.

What does the research on retention reveal? We will now examine what most teachers do not know about retention—what the educational research reveals. The findings appear to be as consistent and one-sided against the practice of retaining children in grade as public and professional opinion are in favor: "few practices in education have such overwhelmingly negative research findings arrayed against them" (House, 1989, p. 204). House further observes that this is a rather unique situation, in that educational practice is normally ahead of research in the field. In this case, however, he finds that research evidence appears to be more sound than professional judgment.

As recapitulated by Smith and Shepard (1989), the research findings indicate that

◇ *"Retention in grade has no benefits for either school achievement or personal adjustment."* (p. 215)

> Smith and Shepard report that when similar students are compared, those who are promoted achieve as well as or better than those who are retained. The same holds true when the children are compared in terms of personal and psychological adjustment, self-concept, school attitude, and attendance. Time appears to be a factor, as the long-term effects of retention are more strongly negative than the short-term effects. (It should be noted that the limited number of studies in which retention appeared to be advantageous were found to be either "poorly controlled or employed populations of unusually bright pupils with questionable need for retention." (p. 215)

◇ *"Retention is strongly related to later dropping out of school."* (p. 215)

> Significantly more dropouts than graduates have been retained in grade. Controlling for achievement, socioeconomic status, and gender, retention increases the likelihood of dropping out by 20 to 30%.

◇ *"Two years in kindergarten, even when one year is labeled 'transition program,' fail to enhance achievement or solve the problem of inadequate school readiness."* (p. 215)

Although the philosophies behind transition programs and traditional kindergarten programs differ, the outcomes for children taking an additional year between kindergarten and first grade are no different than for those pupils retained in kindergarten for a second year. This applies whether the children are characterized as immature or slow learners. In addition, promoted children were not at a disadvantage when compared to similar pupils with two years of kindergarten.

◇ *"From the students' perspective, retention is conflict-laden and hurtful."* (p. 216)

In clinical interviews, children retained in grade perceive their "flunking" as punishment. They express anger, sadness, and fear of the emotional reactions of family and teasing from peers. The parents of children retained in kindergarten cite adjustment problems and negative experiences.

This final conclusion is one that is not fully appreciated by many teachers. According to Roderick (1995), "grade retention is perhaps the strongest message that a teacher and a school can send to a student that she or he is not making the grade and is not as capable as other children, a failure that is permanent and cannot be remediated by extra effort" (p. 2).

It is important that teachers hear what children have to say about retention. In one study, Byrnes (1989) surveyed the attitudes of 71 nonpromoted children in grades 1, 3, and 6. Asked about their feelings, over 80% responded "sad," "bad," and "upset" (p. 116). The children explained what it means to be retained in their own words (p. 116):

Anna(first grade)	Sad, it's not fun not to pass.
Victor (first grade)	I'm afraid to tell someone I flunked. On my birthday I'll be embarrassed. I don't want it to come because then the teacher will ask how old I am.
Janis (third grade)	Real sad. Kids start calling me names.
Ellen (sixth grade)	Sad. Friends were going on and I was staying.
Herberto (sixth grade)	Terribly bad.

When asked whether they were punished for being retained, 47% replied "yes" (p. 117). Pupils told the interviewers (pp. 116–117):

Angela (first grade)	They were mad and real sad. They spanked me and [I got] grounded. I didn't get to go to Disneyland.
Tommy (first grade)	Mad! Dad paddled me and kicked me out of the house.
Miguel (first grade)	They were sad. They said, "Be good at school."
Will (first grade)	They didn't care. They were mad at school because my teacher didn't teach me barely anything.
Veronica (third grade)	Mad! They said I didn't try hard. No TV for a month. I couldn't go anywhere. I got grounded.

| Robert (sixth grade) | They were mad. They said that I better pass cause I need a good education. |

Asked why they were retained, the children's responses varied (p. 118). The most frequent response was that they were "not getting good grades ." Behavior problems (14%), work habits (13%), missing school (11%), "not knowing English" (9%) and "I don't know why" (9%) were also common responses. Among the responses that were difficult to categorize are these two:

| Frankie (first grade) | I ran out of medicine [Ritalin] for the last two weeks and didn't do any work. I think that's why. |
| David (third grade) | The first time I came to school I couldn't see real well. I have glasses now. (p. 119) |

The perceptions of one half of the first graders and two thirds of the third and sixth graders were fully or partially consistent with school records as to the reasons for nonpromotion. The remaining children misidentified the reasons for retention in part because they were not told or were given misinformation.

Retention often affects more that one child within a family. In Byrnes' study, three quarters (76 percent) of the children retained had older or younger siblings who had also repeated a grade. In two cases, all five siblings in one family and six in the other had been retained at least once.

Information on the parents of 60 children who had been retained indicated that two thirds accepted and supported retention. However, for one third of the children, one or both parents were initially opposed to non-promotion. These parents believed that retention was not the best way to address their child's needs, did not feel that their child had a problem, or asserted that the teacher had failed to do a good job. Most of the dissenting parents eventually went along with the decision.

Finally, many teachers are not aware of just how many students are affected by retention. Roderick (1995) reports that retention rates and proportions vary considerably by race and gender. The following figures highlight this point:

In 1992, for example, almost 40% of all 14-year-old males were overage for grade compared to 20% of all females. Over one-half of black 14-year-old males and fully 48.5% of Hispanic males were enrolled below ninth grade. (p. 1)

Figure 4.7 shows the percentage of enrolled students from 6 to 14 years old who are overage. Table 4.3 presents proportions for students at ages 6, 9, and 14 by race/ethnicity and gender. Roderick attributes the increase in retention rates over the last two decades to (1) the adoption of stricter promotion policies, commonly tied to test performance; and (2) increasing academic demands in kindergarten and first grade (p. 2). Given the current climate, this pattern is likely to continue.

What alternatives to student retention are available? It is ironic that retention has put teachers in the position promoting accountability for achievement mastery with a practice that is arguably not in the best interest of many students

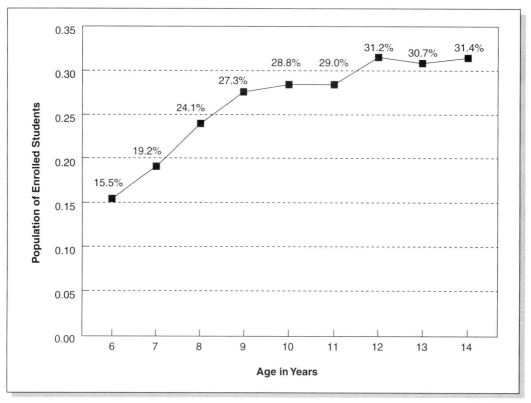

FIGURE 4.7   Student population: percentage overage.
Source: U.S. Department of Commerce, Bureau of the Census. *School Enrollment: Social and Economic Characteristics of Students: October 1992*, Table 3. Current Population Reports, Series P-20, no. 474. Reported in M. Roderick, Grade retention and school dropout's policy debate and research questions. *Research Bulletin* (no. 15), December 1995. Bloomington, IN: Phi Delta Kappa, Center for Evaluation Development and Research.

(Smith & Shepard, 1989, p. 219). Although retention decisions are difficult for many teachers and the available options seem limited for students who are candidates for nonpromotion, there are some possible solutions worth exploring. This is particularly important in light of current trends toward "higher" standards and accountability through standardized testing. Retention is likely to remain a serious issue, and teachers are looking for alternatives. Whatever decision teachers make regarding promotion, many students will need help.

Among the alternatives identified by Smith and Shepard are the following:

1. *Provide teachers with access to data on the effects of retention.*   Concerned teachers in a school district can begin by examining what is happening in their own schools. They can look for the answers to retention questions of importance to them and their students: How are the retained children performing in the short-term? over the long-term? Are they dropping out of school at higher rates? How do the children feel about nonpromotion? How do the parents feel? What are the perceptions of teachers in the schools?

TABLE 4.3   *Student Population: Proportion Overage by Race/Ethnicity and Gender*

Age Modal Grade Year	Age 6 First 1984	Age 9 Fourth 1987	Age 14 Ninth 1992
All Males	13.2	32.4	39.6
All Females	8.9	20.6	20.5
White	11.1	26.0	29.4
Male	13.3	31.8	33.5
Female	8.7	20.0	20.5
Black	12.3	32.6	41.8
Male	14.2	40.2	52.0
Female	10.4	25.5	30.4
Hispanic	10.5	28.6	33.2
Male	7.9	30.3	48.5
Female	13.4	27.2	15.8

Source: U.S. Department of Commerce, Bureau of the Census. *School Enrollment: Social and Economic Characteristics of Students.* Current Population Reports, Series P-20, selected years. Reported in M. Roderick, Grade retention and school dropout's policy debate and research questions. *Research Bulletin* (no. 15), December 1995. Bloomington, IN: Phi Delta Kappa, Center for Evaluation Development and Research.

Subject to what their findings reveal, the teachers can come together to explore issues raised, generate alternatives, and pursue appropriate action.

2. *Review the decision-making processes and procedures used in retention.* Especially in high retaining districts, teachers and administrators may need to reconsider the decision-making process itself to ensure that the practices being used do not raise legal issues. This would include safeguards to prevent use of invalid indicators such as gender and size and to ensure that retention does not have a disproportionate effect on certain groups of children (e.g., as defined by socioeconomic status or ethnic group). Smith and Shepard argue that a basic tenet in special education should apply to retention as well: "any treatment must unambiguously benefit the child to warrant a decision that separates the child from his or her peers" (Heller, Holtzman, & Messick, cited in Smith & Shepard, 1989, p. 227).

3. *Address parental issues in retention.* Principals and teachers both believe that the final say in decisions regarding retention should be theirs, and many parents accept their professional recommendations, albeit reluctantly at times (Byrnes, 1989, p. 113). The socioeconomic status of the parents appears to be a factor, however, in that higher income parents want a stronger voice in making promotion decisions.

Teachers need to identify the parent issues that are most salient in their school. Parents can and should have an active and informed voice in retention decisions (Smith & Shepard, 1989). However, this is not always the case, particularly in schools in which there is a tendency to pressure parents into agreeing with a retention recommendation. In some cases, parents opposed to retention have insisted on promotion, removed children from one school and placed them in another, and even relocated entirely to another area. Parents who are less empowered or less involved may have fewer options in dealing with retention decisions.

There are other potential issues. Smith and Shepard cite the problem of academic redshirting, a practice described as keeping a child legally able to enter kindergarten out of school for an additional year. This is usually done with boys, who because of a birthdate near the enrollment cutoff, are likely to be among the youngest, smallest, and most immature in the class. Teachers often share the parents' concerns and support their decision to delay. What parents and teachers may or may not appreciate is that the academic advantage age may offer initially will disappear by the end of third grade; hence, for the individual child "the only possible lasting advantage might be to the boys' athletic career" since interscholastic sports are determined by grade level (p. 229).

4. *Provide promotion plus remediation.*   Providing children with tutoring, summer school, in-class or pull-out individualized instruction is more cost-efficient and effective than retention. Shepard and Smith cite the example of one district that requires a plan stipulating the remediation to be provided for each child for whom promotion is in question. The bottom line is that neither option—retaining immature and low-achieving students without remediation nor promoting them without addressing their academic needs—is likely to provide a satisfactory solution.

5. *Provide opportunities for later acceleration of nonpromoted students.*   For retained students who achieve academically and are socially and psychologically prepared to rejoin their peers, schools need to develop procedures to facilitate acceleration later in their school careers. This is particularly important for students who are not sufficiently challenged by educational experiences and academic content intended for younger learners. Specially-designed intensive individual or group instruction can be used to provide access to the content these students need in order to move up to the next grade.

6. *Initiate district policy changes through collaborative efforts.*   Administrators and teachers need to work together to make the kinds of changes that are necessary and supported by parents and pupils. This includes decisions related to academic demands in kindergarten (especially literacy-focused curriculum), accountability, school organization, testing and assessment, as possible starting points. Eliminating retention in and of itself is not a panacea. The implications of any proposed action will have to be considered in light of its potential effects on teachers and students.

It should be noted that many of the suggestions offered here are compatible with the existing structure of most schools. Byrnes (1989) has found that most principals and teachers are not supportive of alternatives requiring more significant changes in the school structure (p. 114). Hence, the scope of policy changes proposed and subsequently implemented will certainly vary from one district to another.

High-Stakes Testing

With the current emphasis on assessment in education, issues related to tracking and retention also need to be considered in light of the impact of high-stakes testing, particularly in regards to its effects on minority students and other special populations. Madaus and Clarke (in press) describe the ubiquitous nature of testing from entry into the school system through exit: "The range of high-stakes testing programs is expansive; from 'readiness' testing for entrance to kindergarten, to tests required for promotion and graduation, to teacher, school, and district accountability, to teacher testing for certification".

In their review of approximately three decades of trend data on the test performance of minority students and others not traditionally well served by the educational system, Madaus and Clarke conclude that

1. "High-stakes, high-standards tests do not have a markedly positive effect on teaching and learning in the classroom";
2. "High-stakes tests do not motivate the unmotivated";

Testing is a pervasive part of the school experience from entry through exit.

3. "Contrary to popular belief, 'authentic' forms of high-stakes assessments are not a more equitable way to assess the progress of students who differ in race, culture, native language, or gender"; and

4. "High-stakes testing programs have been shown to increase high school dropout rates—particularly among minority populations."

Given the increasingly greater role of large-scale testing in making high-stakes decisions that "significantly affect the life chances of individual students," the National Academy of Sciences, through its National Research Council, was asked by Congress to conduct a study and recommend methods, practices, and safeguards to ensure that new and existing tests used to assess . . .

◇ student performance are not utilized in a discriminatory manner nor in inappropriate ways in regards to promotion, tracking, and graduation;

◇ comprehension in reading and mathematics provide the most accurate information on students' achievement in reading and mathematics skills. (Heubert & Hauser, 1999, p. 273)

Recommendations in the report pertain to all schools and school systems in which "tests are used for student promotion, tracking, or graduation" (Heubert & Hauser, 1999, p. 274). Teachers and administrators who want to ensure appropriate use of high-stakes tests will find the Council's recommendations (presented in Figure 4.8) useful in developing policies and procedures at the local level.

General Recommendations

1. Accountability for educational outcomes should be a shared responsibility of states, school districts, public officials, educators, parents, and students. High standards cannot be established and maintained merely by imposing them on students.

2. If parents, educators, public officials, and others who share responsibility for educational outcomes are to discharge their responsibility effectively, they should have access to information about the nature and interpretation of tests and test scores.

3. A test may appropriately be used to lead curricular reform, but it should not also be used to make high-stakes decisions about individual students until test users can show that the test measures what they have been taught.

4. Test users should avoid simple either-or options (e.g., retention or promotion) when high-stakes tests and other indicators show that students are doing poorly in school, in favor of strategies combining early intervention and effective remediation of learning problems.

5. High-stakes decisions such as tracking, promotion, and graduation should not automatically be made on the basis of a single test score but should be buttressed by

(continued)

FIGURE 4.8   Ensuring appropriate use of high-stakes tests.

FIGURE 4.8 *(continued)*

other relevant information about the student's knowledge and skills, such as grades, teacher recommendations, and extenuating circumstances.

6. In general, large-scale assessments should not be used to make high-stakes decisions about students who are less than 8 years old or enrolled below grade 3.

7. All students are entitled to sufficient test preparation so their performance will not be adversely affected by unfamiliarity with item format or by ignorance of appropriate test-taking strategies. Test users should balance efforts to prepare students for a particular test format against the possibility that excessively narrow preparation will invalidate test outcomes.

8. High-stakes testing programs should routinely include a well-designed evaluation component. Policymakers should monitor both the intended and unintended consequences of high-stakes assessments on all students and on significant subgroups of students, including minorities, English-language learners, and students with disabilities (e.g., dropout rates).

Tracking

1. As tracking is currently practiced, low-track classes are typically characterized by an exclusive focus on basic skills, low expectations, and the least-qualified teachers. Students assigned to to low-track classes are worse off than they would be in other placements. This form of tracking should be eliminated. Neither test scores nor other information should be used to place students in such classes.

2. Since tracking decisions are basically placement decisions, tests and other information used for this purpose should meet professional test standards regarding placement.

3. Because a key assumption underlying placement decisions is that students will benefit more from certain educational experiences than from others, the standard for using a test or other information to make tracking decisions should be accuracy in predicting the likely educational effects of each of several alternative educational experiences.

4. If a cutscore is to be employed on a test used in making a tracking or placement decision, the quality of the standard-setting process should be documented and evaluated.

Promotion and Retention

1. Scores from large-scale assessments should never be the only sources of information used to make a promotion or retention decision. No single source of information— whether test scores, course grades, or teacher judgments—should stand alone in making promotion decisions. Test scores should always be used in combination with other sources of information about student achievement.

2. Tests and other information used in promotion decisions should adhere, as appropriate, to psychometric standards for placement and to psychometric standards for certifying knowledge and skill.

FIGURE 4.8   *(continued)*

3. Tests and other information used in promotion decisions may be interpreted as evidence of mastery of material already taught or as evidence of material at the next grade level. In the former case, test content should be representative of the curriculum at the current grade level. In the latter case, test scores should predict the likely educational effects of future placements—whether promotion, retention in grade, or some other intervention options.

4. If a cutscore is to be employed on a test used in making a promotion decision, the quality of the standard-setting process should be documented and evaluated—including the qualifications of the judges employed, the method or methods employed, and the degree of consensus reached.

5. Students who fail should have the opportunity to retake any test used in making promotion decisions; this implies that tests used in making promotion decisions should have alternate forms.

6. Test users should avoid the simple either-or option to promote or retain in grade when high-stakes tests and other indicators show that students are doing poorly in school, in favor of strategies combining early identification and effective remediation of learning problems.

Awarding or Withholding High School Diplomas

1. High school graduation decisions are inherently certification decisions; the diploma should certify that the student has achieved acceptable levels of learning. Tests and other information used for this purpose should afford each student a fair opportunity to demonstrate the required levels of knowledge and skill in accordance with psychometric standards for certification tests.

2. Graduation checks should provide evidence of mastery of material taught. Thus, there is a need for evidence that the test content is representative of what students have been taught.

3. The quality of the process of setting a cutscore on a graduation test should be documented and evaluated—including the qualification of the judges employed, the method or methods employed, and the degree of consensus reached.

4. Students who are at risk of failing a graduation test should be advised of their situation well in advance and provided with appropriate instruction that would improve their chances of passing.

5. Research is needed on the effects of high-stakes graduation tests on teaching, learning, and high school completion. Research is also needed on alternatives to test-based denial of the high school diploma, such as endorsed diplomas, end-of-course tests, and combining graduation test scores with other indicators of knowledge and skill in making the graduation decision.

Using the Voluntary National Tests for Tracking, Promotion, or Graduation Decisions

1. The voluntary national tests (VNT) should not be used for decisions about the tracking, promotion, or graduation of individual students.

FIGURE 4.8 *(continued)*

2. If the voluntary national tests are implemented, the federal government should issue regulations or guidance to ensure that VNT scores are not used for decisions about the tracking, promotion, or graduation of individual students.

Participation and Accommodations: Students With Disabilities

1. More research is needed to enable students with disabilities to participate in large-scale assessments in ways that provide valid information. This goal significantly challenges current knowledge and technology about measurement and test design and the infrastructure needed to achieve broad-based participation.

2. The needs of students with disabilities should be considered throughout the developmental process.

3. Decisions about how students with disabilities will participate in large-scale assessments should be guided by criteria that are as systematic and objective as possible. They should also be applied on a case-by-case basis as part of the child's individual educational program and consistent with the instructional accommodations that the child receives.

4. If a student with disabilities is subject to an assessment used for promotion or graduation decisions, the IEP team should ensure that the curriculum and instruction received by the student through the individual education program is aligned with test content and that the student has had adequate opportunity to learn the material covered by the test.

5. Students who cannot participate in a large-scale assessment should have alternative ways of demonstrating proficiency.

6. Because a test score may not be a valid representation of the skills and achievement of students with disabilities, high-stakes decisions about these students should consider other sources of evidence such as grades, teacher recommendations, and other examples of student work.

Participation and Accommodations: English-Language Learners

1. Systematic research that investigates the impact of specific accommodations on the test performance of both English-language learners and other students is needed. Accommodations should be investigated to see whether they reduce construct-irrelevant sources of variance for English-language learners without disadvantaging other students who do not receive accommodations. The relationship of test accommodations to instructional accommodations should also be studied.

2. Development and implementation of alternative measures, such as primary-language assessments, should be accompanied by information regarding the validity, reliability, and comparability of scores on primary-language and English assessments.

3. The learning and language needs of English-language learners should be considered during test development.

FIGURE 4.8   *(continued)*

> 4. Policy decisions about how individual English-language learners will participate in large-scale assessments—such as the language and accommodations to be used—should balance the demands of political accountability with professional standards of good testing practice. These standards require evidence that such accommodations or alternative forms of assessment lead to valid inferences regarding performance.
>
> 5. States, school districts, and schools should report and interpret disaggregated assessment scores of English-language learners when psychometrically sound for the purpose of analyzing their educational outcomes.
>
> 6. Placement decisions based on tests should incorporate information on educational accomplishments, particularly literacy skills, in the primary language. Certification tests (e.g., for high school graduation) should be designed to reflect state or local deliberations and decisions about the role of English-language proficiency in the construct to be assessed. This allows for subject-matter assessment in English only, in the primary language, or using a test that accommodates English-language learners by providing English-language assistance, primary language support, or both.
>
> 7. As for all learners, interpretation of the test scores of English-language learners for promotion or graduation should be accompanied by information about opportunities to master the material tested. For English-language learners, this includes information about educational history, exposure to instruction in the primary language and in English, language resources in the home, and exposure to the mainstream curriculum.

Source: Jay P. Heubert and Robert M. Hauser (Eds.). (1999). *High Stakes: Testing for Tracking, Promotion, and Graduation* (pp. 278–298). Washington, DC: National Academy Press.

SPECIAL POPULATIONS

A school's capacity to successfully meet the many needs of the diverse student population it serves is one important measure of its effectiveness. In this section, the focus is on selected populations, specifically, English language learners, educable mentally retarded and learning disabled learners, and gifted and talented learners. Often identified as populations not adequately served in schools, these learners are routinely affected by school policies, procedures, and assessments directed specifically at them—some determined locally; others in response to state and federal mandates. Although the students that comprise these populations cannot be defined strictly along ethnic, racial, gender, or class lines, social and cultural factors often play an important role in what happens to these students throughout their school careers.

English Language Learners

Think back to your first day of school. It's an exciting one for many children; a trying one for others. Especially for a child who does not know the language

A school's capacity to successfully meet the many needs of the diverse student population it serves is one important measure of its effectiveness.

used in the school, the whole experience can be painful. After fifty years, Cárdenas (1986) still vividly recalls his first days in school:

> In the mid-1930s, without an adequate knowledge of the English language, I was placed in an all-English first-grade instructional program. I still remember how I felt. The experience was not merely uncomfortable, unpleasant, or challenging; it was traumatic, disconcerting, and terrorizing. (p. 360)

For older students, moving to a new community and starting classes in a new school can also be a stressful and frightening experience. The first day of school in a new country is even more difficult, as this original account from a Southeast Asian student looking back on her first day at school in the United States suggests:

> A very scary experience, long ago when I first came to the United States. My uncle took me to _____ High School to enrolled. After we enrolled my uncle took me to the classroom then he go home and let me stayed in the classroom. I was very scare because the teacher was sitting in front the classroom. I looked at him, he was big and tall. When he came near me and I looked at his mouth and nose, and his mouth were opened and his talking to me but I did [not] know what he talking about and I was very scared and when he looked at me and came near me, I did cries but my tear were came out to my face. After that day I came home and I never go back to school until one year later. That was a very scary experience for me at that time. (Yang, 1987)

Historical and Contemporary Perspectives

The role of native languages in the schooling of English language learners has been in the past and continues to be in the present a "hot" issue in education (and politics). The passage of Proposition 227 in California, establishing a legal mandate that instruction be "overwhelmingly" in English, is just one example from recent headlines. Distinguishing between myth and reality in debates on educational policy and practice related to language issues is not always easy. Debates, whether on talk shows, in the editorial page of the local newspaper, or at the kitchen table, often are intense and emotional, to say the least. Regrettably, certain oft-repeated arguments are based on limited or inaccurate perceptions of what the educational experience has been for students whose primary language is other than English. Because these beliefs are widely held, they sometimes confound and confuse real issues in the education of English language learners. These myths clearly warrant the attention of educators, particularly those who teach English language learners.

The first myth—the *submersion myth*—relates to the rather pervasive belief that English language learners share similar experiences and can make a uniformly smooth transition to English instruction in the public schools (McConnell, 1982; Tyack, 1974). It is often expressed something like this: My parents (grandparents, great-grandparents, etc.) came here from the Old Country in 19__. They spoke no English when they came. In the public school they attended, they were taught only in English, and they never had any problems.

The approach to schooling of language-minority students reflected in this myth is generally known as submersion. Submersion, or the "sink-or-swim" model, is the practice of placing English language learners in classes designed for native speakers. This is done with no modification in input or content to accommodate second-language learning. Students are expected to acquire English as they deal with content just like other students. As the appellation suggests, those who succeed swim; the others sink. Underlying the submersion approach is the assumption that the more language-minority students are exposed to English, the faster and better they will develop proficiency in the language. While this notion may appear to have intuitive appeal, it is not supported empirically. In general, research has shown that many language-minority students exposed to this type of situation tend to lose their mother tongue faster than they acquire proficiency in English (Trueba, 1981).

Although many children have done well under these circumstances, many others have not done as well as most Americans would like to believe. Among immigrant groups, the actual documented progress of English language learners suggests a very different picture from what is commonly depicted. Immigration to the United States reached its peak between 1900 and 1910. In 1911, the U.S. Immigration Service reported, based on a study of over 2 million children of immigrant families, that 43% of the children whose parents were from non-English-speaking countries were one or more grade levels behind in school, whereas 26.7% of native White children and 29.9% of those from English-speaking countries were below grade level. The percentages (by nationality) of children below grade level were even higher for those not born in the United States: German, 51%; Russian Jews, 59.9%; and Italian, 76.7% (Cohen, cited in Fillmore & Valadez, 1986; McConnell, 1982).

Dropout rates provide another important indicator of how immigrants fared in schools. Here, too, the percentages of immigrant children not completing their education were considerably higher than those of native-born, English-speaking students. A 1926 study conducted in Hartford, Connecticut, found that 66% of immigrant children from non-English-speaking countries, but only 36% of the native-born, non-Hispanic White students, in the high schools dropped out by their junior year (McConnell, 1982). Rothstein (1998) finds that: "Far from immersing themselves in English, immigrant groups did much worse than the native-born, and some immigrant groups did much worse than others" (p. 674).

People have forgotten how bad the situation was for some children and for some groups. According to Rothstein, "the poorest performers were Italians" (p. 674). A few examples of the disproportionate academic underachievement of Italian immigrant children earlier in this century will suffice:

◇ In 1931, about 40% of all students who entered high school graduated; for Italian students, the graduation rate was 11%. (p. 674)
◇ On a consistent basis, averages for Italian immigrant children on IQ tests administered in the 1920s, were reported at about 85, as compared to 102 for native-born students. (p. 674)
◇ The first special education classes in New York were established to deal with "the challenge of educating Italian immigrant children." (p. 674)
◇ In 1921, half of the "learning disabled" (by today's terms) special education children in New York schools had fathers who were born in Italy. (Sarason & Doris, cited in Rothstein, 1998, p. 674)
◇ In the year 1910, approximately one third of the adult male immigrants from Southern Italy were unskilled laborers. (p. 674)

The plight of Italian immigrant children during this period helps to illustrate the point that, historically, "we've never successfully educated the first or even second generation of children from peasant or unskilled immigrant families"(p. 675). In New York City, Italian American levels of persistence in schooling began to rise in the 1930s (Cohen, cited in Olneck, 1995). Today, we cannot easily distinguish group differences in the educational distribution of "the descendants of eastern, central, and southern European immigrants from those of northern and western European immigrants (Lieberson & Waters, cited in Olneck, 1998, p. 322).

In the face of such clear-cut data demonstrating the historical underachievement of many language-minority students in U.S. schools, why does the popular myth to the contrary persist? One possible explanation lies in certain changes that have taken place in American society. In the past, dropout rates were high, not only for English language learners but also for the student population as a whole. Early in this century, secondary schools were still rather elitist institutions: less than 10% of the high-school-age population was in school; only about 1 in 20 graduated by age 17 (U.S. Commission on Civil Rights, 1975). In California, 18% of immigrant children were not even enrolled in schools in 1913 (Hartmann, cited in U.S. Commission on Civil Rights, 1975). At that time, completing high school was not the economic and social imperative that it is today because the job market provided relatively ample opportunities for those with a limited education. Hence, the educational experiences of past generations, although in reality often difficult and limited, are likely to be perceived in a positive light because most immigrant children, even if they did not fare very well in school, did find a place in the workforce. However, the extent to which the limited schooling attained by immigrants and their children restricted their access to professions and occupations requiring more education has been largely overlooked.

Many Americans also assume that all language-minority students are immigrant children. In reality, language-minority groups in the United States today are quite diverse. For some groups, recent immigration has indeed provided a major source of vitality and growth (e.g., Asian Americans). For others, language maintenance has not depended on immigration but rather on continued usage in geographically isolated language communities (e.g., Native Americans). In still other groups, present-day language patterns represent a combination of recent immigration and continued usage of another language by established nonimmigrant populations (e.g., Hispanics).

The historical experiences of immigrants and the diversity among language-minority groups today, thus, belie the common misconception that all English language learners face the same linguistic (and cultural) barriers and respond to them in the same way. The demonstrable differences in the school performance of different European immigrant groups in the past, as well as among Asian Americans, Hispanics, and other language-minority groups at present, have no single, definitive explanation. Some educators believe that variability in school achievement among language-minority students may be related to patterns of intergroup relations within the society as a whole as well as differences within groups (Ogbu & Matute-Bianchi, 1986; Cruz, cited in Schreiner, 1985). (For more complete information on specific groups, refer to *The Handbook of Research on Multicultural Education.*)

According to the *English-only myth,* the incorporation of native languages and cultures other than English are recent phenomena (Baca & Cervantes, 1984; McConnell, 1982). The basic argument goes something like this: Today's language-minority populations are making demands that differ markedly from years ago. My parents (grandparents, great-grandparents, etc.) had to learn English as a second language, and they did not ask that their language be used in the schools.

Those who voice this belief may be ignorant about or denying how their ancestors actually felt. This view also overlooks the integral part that language plays in fostering individual and group identity. The actual experience is that strong attachments to language are commonplace and natural, in the United States and other countries. Immigrant—particularly in the first and second generations—and ethnic language groups alike have often experienced a strong need and desire to preserve their native language. To the extent that bilingualism is valued in our society, such loyalty to a native language can be viewed as a positive phenomenon. To the extent that bilingualism is viewed as indicating a less than total commitment to American culture and values, it may be resented and disparaged.

Language loyalty, which encompasses the symbolic attachment individuals feel toward their native language and everything that it represents, is a phenomenon that cuts across linguistic and ethnic groups. In fact, some historians claim that the Pilgrims' fear that their children would stop using English contributed to their decision to leave Holland and set sail on the Mayflower (Crawford, 1991, p. 19). Historically, shifts in language usage among most immigrants to the United States have followed a general pattern: acquisition of English in the first generation, bilingualism in the second, and displacement of the native language by English in the third. In more recent years, this pattern has been accelerating; for some, the shift is taking place within two generations.

The English-only myth also ignores the fact that the use of languages other than English for instructional purposes has a long tradition in the United States. Historically, native languages were often incorporated into religious instructional programs and private schools before finding their way into public schools. Contrary to popular belief, the use of languages other than English in schools has not been limited to any single national or ethnic group, nor has it been confined to the present period in history, although the languages involved have changed with shifts in immigration and demographic patterns. In the

The next generation's skills for living in a pluralistic society and a multilingual global community are being developed today. Bilingualism is an important part of that future.

nineteenth century, German, Polish, and Scandinavian languages were at the forefront; today, the emphasis is on Spanish as well as Asian and Native American languages.

Even a cursory glance through the history of American education demonstrates that a bilingual tradition has existed in the public schools for many years. In the nineteenth century, for example, bilingual programs were prevalent in many communities with large German populations (Hernández, 1982). For decades, Germans constituted the largest non-English-speaking immigrant group in the nation, and between 1820 and 1910, 6 million Germans arrived in the United States (Zeydel, 1961). In 1850, they represented 75% of the foreign-born non-English-speaking population; even in 1880, when 3.4 million non-English-speaking inhabitants were foreign born, 60% were German (Kloss, 1977). Initially, German immigrants tried to establish schools modeled upon those in Germany, and numerous private schools were created and supported in cities with large German populations (e.g., Cincinnati). In 1860, Germans in St. Louis preferred their own schools to the city's by a ratio of four to one. At the time, there were 38 private schools, almost all parochial, and use of German in these institutions was the norm (Troen, 1975). It is worth noting that the German private schools waned in importance only after the public schools improved in quality and yielded to pressure from the German community to make the teaching of German part of the curriculum. By 1900, at least 231,700 students were studying German in public elementary schools in the Midwest (Tyack, 1974). Over the years, the role of German in the schools underwent considerable change: at the outset, serving as a language of instruction; later as a subject. Many programs existed for years, even decades. Decline of these programs came with changes in immigration patterns and the advent of World War I.

One fundamental tenet of the early bilingual German programs was the goal of language maintenance: "The Germans wanted their children to know English, but they did not want them to lose the German language and the traditions of German culture" (Herrick, 1971, p. 61). The German community was politically active in promoting use of their native language as a means of instruction in the public schools. Efforts were also made to convince English-speaking citizens of the scholarly, economic, and cultural value of learning a second language, and the advantages of initiating the study of a foreign language at an early age (*School Report: Chicago, 1900*).

The point to be made here is that the desire to have instruction provided in the native language, generally in addition to but not in lieu of English, has been widely shared among immigrant and ethnic groups. In the nineteenth century, "many immigrant children, not just Germans, did not attend school at all if they could not have classes in their native language" (Rothstein, 1998 p. 675). This is not intended to suggest that all groups have been equally successful in achieving their goals. Such is not the case, especially among nonimmigrant groups. In fact, until fairly recently, few language-minority students received special assistance in schools. To ignore the existence of this bilingual tradition in U.S. schools, however, limits current thinking about the schooling of today's language-minority students and falsely suggests that a monolithic English-only policy existed in the past.

Once upon a time there was a cat that lived in a large house. Fond of chasing mice, the cat was especially intent on catching a certain mouse that always seemed to just elude him, escaping into the nearest little hole. As the mouse remained in his hideaway, safely out of reach, the cat could do nothing but wait for another chance and hope that next time things would be different. Shortly after another successful escapade, the mouse heard barking outside his hole. Certain that the cat had departed, he ventured confidently out of his hiding place. To his surprise, the mouse immediately found himself in the tight grasp of his old nemesis. In a trembling voice, he asked where the dog was. Pleased with his long-awaited triumph, the cat responded that there really was no dog. He was, you see, bilingual. The moral of this story, at least from the cat's perspective, is that being bilingual definitely can have its advantages.

FIGURE 4.9   A fable.
Source: Adapted from *BBC Modern English* (1976), 2(10), 34. Cited in Tiedt and Tiedt (1986). Illustration by Frank Hernandez.

From local schools to the national political arena, the pendulum has swung back and forth on issues of language in the education of English language learners for years. It continues to do so.

By way of conclusion, here is a short fable about a cat and a mouse (Figure 4.9).

Special Education Populations

Within the school-age population, rough estimates indicate that almost 11% of all students—nearly 5 million of the approximately 45 million elementary and secondary students enrolled in the 1980s—were in need of some special education services (Gage & Berliner, 1988). These included children and youth with a wide variety of needs that required adaptations in their educational programs. Learning disabled, speech impaired, and mentally retarded youngsters accounted for about 86% of all the school-age students with disabilities; emotionally disturbed children accounted for 8%; the remainder had hearing, visual, orthopedic, or other health impairments or multiple disabilities (Gage & Berliner, 1988).

Within the student population that requires special education, many children were still underserved by existing programs in the mid-1980s. In fact, those receiving services probably represented less than half of all eligible children in the United States (Baca & Cervantes, 1984). Those least likely to receive appropriate services were children 3 to 5 years of age; secondary students and individuals between the ages of 18 and 22; emotionally disturbed, migrant, and foster children; military dependents; and incarcerated youth (Cárdenas & First, 1985). More recently, Gonzalez, Brusca-Vega and Yawkey (1997) report that by the mid 1990s, over 5 million children and youth—approximately 6.4 percent of children and youth under 21—were actually receiving special education services. These numbers represent an increase of about 2 percent in the period

An estimated 11% of school-age children are in need of some special education services.

following passage of the Individuals with Disabilities Act of 1990, PL 101-476 (p. 24). Although more difficult to document, disparities in services provided minority students and English language learners still exist (p. 26).

Gonzalez et al. (1997) define the term *disability* as "a physical and/or cognitive impairment that significantly limits the ability of an individual to participate in one or more of the major activities of life, including working, learning, and caring for one's self" (p. 21). It is important for teachers to remember that the vast majority of students in special education programs have disabilities that "do not necessarily reflect diminished intellectual capacity" (Wang, Reynolds, & Walberg, 1986, p. 30). For example, in the state of New York, about three quarters of the 286,000 students in special education are identified as learning disabled or as having a speech, visual, or orthopedic impairment; these disabilities are not necessarily associated with limitations in the students' capacity to perform academically (Wang et al., 1986). The fact that these students must be identified in order to provide the assistance and resources they need should not—in and of itself—adversely affect teacher and peer perceptions and expectations regarding their mental abilities.

Another general point about students in special education programs is that boys significantly outnumber girls among those classified as having disabilities. Phipps (1982) reports that about 85% of the students in public school programs for the learning disabled, educable mentally retarded, and behavior disordered are boys. In a study of gender differences in referrals for one

California school district. Phipps found that teachers' perceptions of boys' conduct and behavior was a significant factor in their identification for placement in special education. Numerically, boys outnumber girls in programs for the educable mentally retarded by a ratio of 1.2 to 1; in learning disabled programs by 3 or 4 to 1 and even higher (MacMillan, Keogh, & Jones, 1986). To some extent, the decision to refer a student for special education appears to be an index of teacher tolerance, and a tacit admission that the student is not likely to benefit instructionally in a particular classroom setting (Shinn, Tindal, & Spira, 1987).

Less than 20% of the children in special education are identified on the basis of objective, medically defined criteria—that is, "rigorous physical or physiological measures" (Wang et al., 1986, p. 27). Classifications such as *educable mentally retarded* and *learning disabled* are to a large extent socially determined. Among recipients of special education services, about 19% are classified as educable mentally retarded and 36% are classified as learning disabled (MacMillan et al., 1986). Thus, the majority of learners in special education are classified by largely subjective criteria, which to some extent may be associated with socioeconomic variables. As Gelb and Mizokawa (1986) note, "Social context . . . is at least as important as the inner qualities of individuals in creating mild 'handicaps'" (p. 552). It is these learners—that teachers are most likely to encounter through mainstreaming in regular classrooms. For many of these children, the regular classroom environment represents the least restrictive educational environment mandated by PL 94-142, the Education for All Handicapped Children Act of 1975, which ensures all children and youth with disabilities a free and appropriate public education. Today, approximately 94 percent of students with disabilities are served in general education settings, that is, in regular classrooms with and without outside support, or in separate classes (Tonzalez et al., 1997, p. 25).

Mental Retardation

As defined by the U.S. government, mentally retarded refers to individuals "having significant sub-average general intellectual functioning existing concurrently with deficits in adaptive behavior and manifested during the developmental period" (cited in Baca & Cervantes, 1984, p. 43). Teachers must recognize that to a large extent, mental retardation is a "social status" defined primarily on the basis of two characteristics: social incompetence and cognitive impairment (Manni, Winikur, & Keller, 1984).

The mildly retarded are those at the lower end of the normal distribution: They are "*normal* in the sense that differences between them and higher-IQ children are differences of *degree*, not *kind*" (MacMillan et al., 1986, p. 687). By contrast, learners characterized as severely retarded have intellectual limitations directly attributable to chromosomal anomalies or brain damage (MacMillan et al., 1986). The social incompetence and cognitive impairment of such individuals are evident at home, in the school, and within the community. Overall, however, they represent a relatively small proportion of children and youth in special education.

That the proportion of culturally different students classified as mentally retarded on the basis of IQ tests is higher than their representation in the general population has been recognized for some time. Dunn (cited in Baca & Cervantes, 1984) concluded that in the 1960s, about 60–80% of the pupils in classrooms for the "retarded" were from "low-status" backgrounds. These pupils included a disproportionately high number of African Americans, Native Americans, Mexican Americans, and Puerto Ricans; children from broken homes; and youngsters from nonstandard-English-speaking and non-middle-class environments. This same pattern was still prevalent in the early 1980s, according to Ysseldyke, Algozzine, and Richey (cited in Amos & Landers, 1984): "The number of minority and low socioeconomic children thought to evidence academic difficulties and behavior problems was at least twice as high as the number of high-socioeconomic status children and girls; estimates for boys were medial" (p. 145).

This nationwide pattern, however, sometimes is not observed within specific populations. Among some minority groups with a home language other than English, for example, children who are fluent in English may be overreferred to special education programs, whereas those with limited English proficiency (for whom assessment is more problematic) may be underreferred (Ochoa, Pacheco, & Omark, 1983). In general, there appears to be agreement that although the disproportionately high numbers of minority children and English language learners classified as educable mentally retarded have been reduced to some extent in recent years, problems persist (Baca & Cervantes, 1984; MacMillan et al., 1986). Even today, they "are likely to be either overidentified, underidentified, or misidentified as having disabilities" (Gonzalez et al., 1997, p. 7).

Learning Disabled

Individuals classified as learning disabled generally are characterized by one or more of the following: "notions of brain damage, hyperactivity, mild forms of retardation, social-emotional adjustment, language difficulties, subtle forms of deafness, perceptual problems, motor clumsiness, and above all, reading disorders" (Farnham-Diggory, cited in Cummins, 1984, p. 82). Estimates of the incidence of learning disabilities among the general population range from 2 to 20%; government estimates place the incidence as high as 26% (Cummins, 1984; MacMillan et al., 1986). It is not surprising that the category of students with specific learning disabilities is now the "largest and fastest growing" (Gonzalez et al., 1997, p. 25).

Learning disabled students usually are identified on the basis of (a) a discrepancy between what appears to be their potential and their actual classroom performance or (b) a dysfunction related to the learning process that is not attributable to environmental, cultural, economic, and other conditions (MacIntyre, Keeton, & Agard, cited in Cummins, 1984). In general, the academic problems of the learning disabled primarily involve language and literacy, and most of these students are placed in regular classes.

Students identified as learning disabled account for the largest proportion of Whites placed in special education, nearly 40%; about 26% of Blacks in special education classes are considered learning disabled (Collins & Camblin, 1983). The largely subjective criteria used to classify students as learning disabled have resulted in overidentification in general and variability in identification among different populations. Thus, it is difficult to determine whether minority children as a group are overidentified as learning disabled. Some researchers have reported that they have not been (MacMillan et al., 1986), whereas others cite evidence that some groups (e.g., Hispanics) have been overrepresented (Ortiz & Yates, cited in Cummins, 1984).

At present, students who are learning disabled cannot be consistently differentiated from those who are not (Cummins, 1984; Gelb & Mizokawa, 1986). Some question the multifold increase in the numbers of learning disabled students and hypothesize that this labeling may be an inappropriate response to academic underachievement resulting from instructional inadequacies (Gage & Berliner, 1988). Others question the purposes and needs served by identifying certain students as learning disabled while not identifying others who are "very much their twins" (Ysseldyke et al., cited in Sleeter, 1986).

Classroom Learning Environment

Because most learning disabled students are mainstreamed in regular classrooms, the learning environment provided by teachers is crucial to their academic achievement. Despite the difficulties in formally identifying students with learning disabilities, regular classroom teachers should be prepared to recognize and address the special needs of these students.

To achieve this objective, Gage and Berliner (1988) recommend careful examination of student behaviors and the instructional context in which they occur. Specifically, Gage and Berliner suggest that teachers begin by observing and describing student behaviors in different contexts. After examining the child's behavior and comparing it with that of other children, teachers need to determine whether it falls within the range of typical behavior for the age group. If the child appears to have a learning disability or behavior problem that may require treatment, a decision is made regarding consultation and referral. If a student is eventually classified as learning disabled and treatment is indicated, then an individualized learning plan is developed and implemented.

Teachers also should assess the effectiveness of their own instructional methods and explore alternative instructional strategies before looking for ways "to explain children's academic difficulties in terms of cognitive processing deficits" (Cummins, 1984, p. 5). Gonzalez et al. (1997) characterize this as a movement away from looking for learning problems within children labeled as "difficult-to-teach" and in the direction of educators as advocates, taking on greater responsibility for changing the external factors within their control (p. 238). Pedagogy is increasingly regarded as the key element in promoting academic achievement for students in special education. Appropriate pedagogical approaches, used effectively, can help students assume greater control over their own learning and develop what Cummins refers to as a sense of efficacy (i.e., a belief in their own ability to succeed) as learners. Inappropriate or ineffective instructional strategies may unintentionally undermine academic achievement.

Pedagogy is increasingly regarded as the key element in promoting academic achievement for students in special education.

If all students are to achieve academically and develop a sense of efficacy, teachers must provide facilitative teaching and learning environments; they must also believe that they can teach all students within that environment. Creating this "ideal" classroom, Cummins argues, requires a realignment of instructional strategies based on the principles of language and knowledge acquisition. Ideally, the classroom environment should empower students, promote academic achievement, and heighten teachers' own sense of effectiveness in promoting the learning of all students. From Cummins' perspective, the promise inherent in emphasizing instructional factors is the belief that these elements, at least in principle, are more easily changed than presumed cognitive deficits in the child.

What would this classroom environment look like? In the context of bilingual special education, an instructional model emphasizing language, literacy, and cognition would have the following characteristics as described by Cummins (1984):

◇ Substantive and meaningful teacher-student interaction in both oral and written forms
◇ Promotion of peer interaction through cooperative learning
◇ Emphasis upon meaningful language use rather than correctness of form
◇ Incorporation of language development as an integral part of all content areas
◇ Increased emphasis on development of higher level cognitive skills
◇ Use of approaches that promote intrinsic rather than extrinsic motivation

Schools serve many populations—learners representing a broad range of capabilities and talents. As Amos and Landers (1984) suggest, a "marriage" between special and multicultural education would provide teachers with knowledge, skills, and attitudes to increase educational opportunities for all learners. "Such a marriage should also enhance the efforts to serve more learners with differences in the mainstreams of our educational system" (p. 146). Likewise, a union of gifted and multicultural education would contribute to the schools' effectiveness in the teaching of unusually creative and gifted learners. It is to this group that attention now turns.

Gifted and Talented Learners

Gifted and talented students are set apart from others by unique abilities, talents, interests, and psychological maturity; tremendous versatility and complexity; and a special sensitivity to the school environment (Correll, 1978). Under the law, giftedness is defined in terms of capability for high levels of performance, intellectual ability, academic aptitude, creative and productive thinking, leadership, and unusual talent in the visual and performing arts (Cheney & Beebe, 1986); some definitions also have included psychomotor and kinesthetic abilities.

Students who are gifted and talented require specific programs and services to fully develop their abilities. Presently, there are at least 30 distinct program alternatives for teaching gifted and talented students. These include, but are not limited to, Saturday and summer programs, special classes and schools, acceleration, ability grouping, enrichment, resource teachers, televised instruction, tutoring, self-directed and independent study, community-based programs, counseling, mentoring, and parent programs (Getzels & Dillon, cited in Torrance, 1986).

As strange as it may seem, gifted children are frequently not recognized in schools. In one study at the junior high school level, more than half of the gifted students identified by researchers were not nominated by teachers (Pegnato & Birch, 1959). To assist teachers in identifying gifted and talented students, Gage and Berliner (1988) recommend that they look for the following attributes and behaviors:

◇ Demonstrations of talent through creative efforts or performance
◇ Extensive knowledge and curiosity in diverse areas of interest
◇ The capacity to focus on problems or activities for prolonged periods of time
◇ The ability to relate problems to their solutions and to produce ideas that are original and inventive
◇ The ability to think independently and in abstract terms
◇ Command of a large vocabulary and accelerated learning of basic skills and reading

Giftedness is manifest in many forms including intellectual ability, academic aptitude, creative and productive thinking, leadership, and the visual and performing arts.

Not only are many individual gifted students overlooked, but certain groups of students have traditionally remained unrecognized and underrepresented in gifted programs. Among these are underachieving, low-socioeconomic, and minority students; creative and/or divergent thinkers whose abilities are not effectively assessed through existing procedures; and learning disabled and students with other disabilities (Richert, 1985). Smutny and Blocksom (1990) also identify gifted girls as a population "at risk". Despite efforts to establish a rationale and appropriate approaches for identifying and educating creative and gifted learners from diverse populations, current educational responses have been described as ambivalent (Torrance, 1986). In general, state and local authorities have been reluctant to broaden the criteria for identifying gifted and talented students in ways that would assure inclusion of greater numbers of gifted students from these underrepresented populations (Torrance, 1986). The IQ test remains the single most important measure used to identify students for gifted programs; some argue that educators still rely on "a 1900's definition of intelligence and an IQ test largely unchanged since 1930" (Hatch & Gardner, 1986, p. 147; Sternberg, 1986).

That the participation of minority students in gifted programs is disproportionately small in relation to their numbers in the student population as a whole has been well established (Mercer, 1976). In the mid-1980s, enrollments in gifted programs nationally suggested that groups such as African Americans, Hispanics, and Native Americans were underrepresented by 30–70% (Richert, 1985). The results of one study in New Jersey, for example, indicated that social conditions related to racial and ethnic group and socioeconomic status tended to circumscribe access of minority and low-socioeconomic students to gifted/talented programs (McKenzie, 1986). In another study, Evans de Bernard (1985) found that only one Hispanic child was placed in a gifted class over an 8-year period in a New York City school district in which Hispanic students constitute a large segment of the student population.

As Torrance (cited in Masten, 1985) points out, "There is a great deal of [unrecognized] giftedness among the culturally different and the waste or underuse of these resources is tragic" (p. 83). The tragedy affects not only individuals, whose unusual talents and abilities are not nurtured to fruition, but also society, which is deprived of the fullest possible range of creative, innovative thinking. An important first step in correcting this situation is to compare what is known about identifying and teaching creative and gifted learners with what is typically done in U.S. schools.

Treffinger and Renzulli (1986) made just such a comparison between educational research and theory and common educational practice. Their analysis reveals the following, rather startling, discrepancies:

We know that . . .	*We continue to . . .*
1. Ability cannot be represented by single score or a single measure.	Use scores as the primary basis for determining access to special programs.
2. Many human talents are independent.	Consider giftedness primarily in academic terms.
3. Aptitudes and talents are dynamic potentials, which can be developed in appropriate settings.	Think of giftedness as a fixed and permanent endowment, which individuals either have or do not have.
4. Most students benefit from instruction involving thinking processes at different levels.	View "thinking skills" as the exclusive purview of a select group of students.
5. Broadening the definition of giftedness would promote the identification and development of many more students with special talents and abilities.	Limit special instruction and services to a select few labeled as gifted based on quite restrictive, culturally biased criteria.

SUMMARY

◇ As noted at the outset, the image of context as a network of invisible threads aptly describes the texture of contextual factors in education. The classroom is nestled within a multitude of increasingly broader school and societal contexts embedded one within each other.

◇ For educational reforms to be effective, it is imperative that teachers better understand the influence of social and cultural differences on academic performance. Educators are moving away from perspectives that ascribe the academic achievement patterns of some groups to inferiority and cultural deficit toward more holistic, comprehensive, and dynamic interpretations of the interaction of complex and interrelated sociocultural factors. It is increasingly evident that single cause approaches to explaining group differences and their attendant solutions are simplistic and inadequate. Effective educational change demands much greater attention to context and to the interplay of multiple school and societal factors.

◇ Differences among schools as among teachers significantly affect students and their achievement. In the classroom, successful teachers know how to make the most of the time they have with their students. Effective teachers are more dedicated, better organized, and more efficient classroom managers. Their students experience greater success, as evidenced in the vision of culturally relevant teachers who strive for educational self-determination, honor and respect students' home culture, and help students to understand the world as it is and enable them to make it better.

◇ School policies and practices can foster or impede the creation of culturally relevant learning environments. Given the current climate regarding the use of high-stakes tests, it is time for educators to reexamine deeply embedded assumptions related to ability grouping and tracking, promotion and retention. It is also time to review policies and procedures at the local level to ensure appropriate and nondiscriminatory use of high-stakes tests.

◇ A school's capacity to successfully meet the many needs of the diverse student populations it serves is one important measure of its overall effectiveness. Among the populations that traditionally have not been well served in schools are English language learners, students in special education programs, and gifted and talented learners.

◇ The role of native languages in the schooling of English language learners—immigrant and native born—has been in the past and continues to be in the present a hotly debated issue. Historically, although bilingual programs were instituted in some areas, the dominant approach to the education of English language learners was submersion. Despite myths to the contrary, this did not provide an optimal learning environment for many students. In fact, people have forgotten how bad the situation was for some children and some groups. The desire to have instruction provided in the native language, generally in addition to but not in lieu of English, has been widely shared among immigrant and ethnic groups. To ignore the existence of this tradition limits educators' options in the schooling of English language learners.

◇ The student population served by special education programs is itself widely diverse. It includes students who are learning disabled, mentally retarded, and emotionally disturbed, and those with visual, hearing, speech, and physical impairments. It is important to recognize that the majority of children and youth in special education programs do not have disabilities that imply diminished cognitive abilities. To a degree, both the mentally retarded and learning disabled categories are subjective and socially determined classifications in which socioeconomic variables are at least as important as individual characteristics. As with other learners, a learning environment emphasizing language, literacy, and cognition is the key to enhancing academic achievement.

◇ Students in gifted education bring unique abilities, talents, and needs to the classroom. As a group, gifted learners are frequently unrecognized, especially among minority populations. Actual educational practice in providing for the gifted and talented continues to be several years behind current research and thinking in the field.

APPLICATION, EXTENSION, AND REFLECTION

1. *Reflections on Differential Outcomes.* Sue and Padilla (1995) provide us with a scholarly analysis of differences in educational performance. While contextual interaction offers a way of accounting for the dynamic social and cultural factors involved, the understanding that practitioners develop through academic and professional experience may or may not be consistent with this explanation. In education, there are often gaps in what we know, what we believe, and what we do.

   The focus of this reflective activity is to examine different frames of reference in explaining educational outcomes. Interview two or more teachers to find out how they account for differences in academic achievement within and between groups. For underachieving groups, what strategies do they suggest? What forms of intervention do they think are most effective? Reflect on what this tells you about their frame of reference in explaining educational outcomes. Which of the academic explanations best describes the teachers' perspectives? Explain.

2. *Labels.* In the 1960s, the prevailing definition and characterization of the so-called "culturally disadvantaged" student was standard content in texts for student teachers. As a student teacher, I still remember "being taught" that I was among the "culturally disadvantaged," that is, according to the description Hoover (1968) used to identify students who share my cultural heritage (see Figure 4.10). On a personal level, I found this extremely offensive, and totally inconsistent with how I regarded my cultural heritage. From a professional perspective, the implications of Hoover's words became even clearer when I went on to teach in an urban elementary school. One of my second graders had been tested for admission into a program for gifted students. When his test scores came back, they were strong, but below the level required for acceptance into the program. In discussing the results with me, the specialist advised that the pupil might still be admitted to the program if I were willing to maintain that the child was "culturally disadvantaged." I refused. Reflecting upon what happened, it later occurred to me that the specialist doing the

"Cultural disadvantage" is a relative term. Such youngsters can be found in almost all schools; they tend to be concentrated in certain rural areas and in large, industrial cities.

A portrait of the culturally disadvantaged has been offered by Reissman. Such an individual (1) is relatively slow in cognitive tasks, but is not stupid; (2) appears to learn more readily through a physical, concrete approach (often is slow but may be persistent when the content is meaningful and valued); (3) often appears to be anti-intellectual, pragmatic rather than theoretical; (4) is traditional, superstitious, and somewhat religious in a traditional sense; (5) is from a male-centered culture, except for a major section of the Negro subculture; (6) is inflexible and not open to reason about many of his beliefs (in the categories of morality, diet, family polarity, and educational practice); (7) appreciates knowledge for its practical, vocational ends, but rarely values it for its own sake; (8) desires a better standard of living with personal comforts for himself and his family, but does not wish to adopt a middle class way of life; (9) is deficient in auditory attention and interpretation skills; (10) reads ineffectively and is deficient in the communications skills generally; and (11) has wide areas of ignorance, and often is suggestible, although he may be suspicious of innovations.

By the beginning of secondary school, according to Bloom, Davis, and Hess, the typical disadvantaged adolescent is reading at a level of approximately three and one-half years below grade level. He is considerably retarded in all school subjects, has difficulty in problem solving and abstract thinking processes, and is generally apathetic toward learning tasks. Moreover, he seldom participates in extra-class activities other than athletics. His vocational goals are ill defined. In all probability he has developed hostility and rebellion against school authorities. Essentially having given up hope for the future, he turns to the peer society for an exciting and rewarding life free from adult supervision and control. Such individuals may band together and "strike back" at a most frustrating school experience.

Cultural deprivation should not be equated with race. Although a large number of Negro children are likely to be disadvantaged, it has been estimated that as many as one-third of the Negro children in the large U.S. cities are at least equal of white norms for educational development. Havighurst suggests that in racial and ethnic terms, the groups are about evenly divided between whites and nonwhites. They consist mainly of the following:

1. Negroes from the rural South who have migrated recently to the northern industrial cities.

2. Whites from the rural South and the southern mountains who have migrated recently to the northern industrial cities.

3. Puerto Ricans who have migrated to a few northern industrial cities.

4. Mexicans with a rural background who have migrated into the West and Middle West.

5. European immigrants with a rural background, from Eastern and Southern Europe.

(continued)

FIGURE 4.10   Who are the culturally disadvantaged?

FIGURE 4.10 *(continued)*

> Although Havighurst places the number of the disadvantaged at about 20 percent of the school population, he estimates that at least 30 percent of the children in such cities as New York, Chicago, Philadelphia, Washington, Detroit, Cleveland, and Baltimore fall into this category.
>
> **AUTHOR'S NOTE:** Language usage is that of the original text and does not reflect current norms with respect to gender, race, and ethnicity.

Source: Kenneth H. Hoover (1968). *Learning and Teaching in the Secondary School* (2nd ed.) (pp. 475–476). Boston: Allyn and Bacon.

testing had found it easier to label the child than to question the assessment measures and appropriateness of practices being used by the district to evaluate students for the program.

Today's teachers must continue to deal with the consequences of labels assigned to students in different groups After reading Hoover's description of the "culturally disadvantaged" in Figure 4.10 and discussing its underlying assumptions, generate a list of terms currently in vogue ("at-risk," "limited-English proficient," "culturally and linguistically diverse") and reflect on the meanings associated with some of these labels. Which have positive connotations? Which carry negative denotations? What are the implications of subscribing to the assumptions inherent in use of these and other terms? What are the programmatic and policy implications for you and your students?

3. *Effective Teaching.* Based upon observations of typical teachers and students involved in routine classroom activities in inner-city schools, Brophy (1982) identified a set of teacher behaviors that consistently promotes student learning. These teacher behaviors are common elements in effective basic skills instruction; for many experienced teachers, Brophy's findings validate practices they have found to be successful in their own classrooms. They also attest to the fact that teachers make a difference.

   The questions in Figure 4.11 focus attention on the attitudes and skills underlying the behaviors identified by Brophy. They can serve as an informal guide for teachers to evaluate their own classroom practices, taking into account variations in setting (urban, rural, suburban), class size, composition, group dynamics, and so forth. Reflect on what they reveal about your teaching.

4. *Retention.* What do administrators, teachers, parents, and students at your school think about retention? Speak with other teachers, and if possible, with students and parents as well. Compare their responses to those cited in the text. To what extent are the responses from your informants consistent with the research presented in this chapter?

Yes	No	
		Teacher expectations, role definitions, and sense of efficacy
☐	☐	Do you accept responsibility for teaching all students?
☐	☐	Do you believe in students' ability to learn?
☐	☐	Do you believe in your own ability to teach all students?
☐	☐	Do you persevere in finding methods and materials that work?
☐	☐	Do you view student difficulties with a positive attitude, as challenges rather than failures?
		Student opportunity to learn
☐	☐	Do you allocate most available class time to instruction?
☐	☐	Do classroom organization and management maximize learning time?
		Classroom management and organization
☐	☐	Do you establish an efficient classroom learning environment?
☐	☐	Do you involve the students in academic activities?
☐	☐	Do you use effective group management techniques?
☐	☐	Do you instruct students on classroom procedure and routines?
☐	☐	Do you convey expectations clearly and follow through consistently?
☐	☐	Do you hold students accountable?
		Curriculum pacing
☐	☐	Do you engage students in meaningful tasks?
☐	☐	Do you match student achievement levels with assigned tasks?
☐	☐	Do you aim for success rates of 90–100% on independent seatwork?
☐	☐	Do you aim for success rates of at least 70–80% on large-group instruction?
		Active teaching
☐	☐	Do you provide active instruction in large- and small-group settings (e.g., demonstrate skills, explain concepts, conduct activities and reviews)?
		Teaching to mastery
☐	☐	Do you provide opportunities for practice and application following active instruction?
☐	☐	Do you monitor student progress and provide feedback and remediation?
☐	☐	Do you teach the basic skills thoroughly?
		Supportive learning environment
☐	☐	Do you maintain a strong academic focus and high standards?
☐	☐	Do you demand that students do their best?
☐	☐	Do you provide a pleasant, friendly, and supportive atmosphere?

FIGURE 4.11 Self-assessment of classroom practices.

Source: Drawn from J. E. Brophy, 1982, Successful teaching strategies for the inner-city child. *Phi Delta Kappan*, 63(8), 527–530.

Strongly agree	Agree	Neither agree nor disagree	Disagree	Strongly disagree		
						Conceptions of Self and Others (p. 34)
SA	A	NA	D	SD	1.	Teachers are technicians, and teaching is a technical task.
SA	A	NA	D	SD	2.	Teachers should promote achievement as a means for helping students escape their community.
SA	A	NA	D	SD	3.	Failure is inevitable for some students.
SA	A	NA	D	SD	4.	Teachers should strive to homogenize students into one "American" identity.
SA	A	NA	D	SD	5.	Teaching, like "banking," is "putting knowledge into" students' heads.
						Social Relations (p. 55)
SA	A	NA	D	SD	6.	Teachers should encourage students to learn individually and in isolation.
SA	A	NA	D	SD	7.	Teachers should encourage competitive achievement.
SA	A	NA	D	SD	8.	Teachers should make connections with some students.
SA	A	NA	D	SD	9.	Teacher-student relationships should be fixed, hierarchical, and limited to formal classroom roles.
						Conceptions of Knowledge (p. 81)
SA	A	NA	D	SD	10.	Knowledge is static, and conveyed from teacher to student.
SA	A	NA	D	SD	11.	Knowledge is infallible.
SA	A	NA	D	SD	12.	Teachers should be detached, neutral about content.
SA	A	NA	D	SD	13.	Students need to demonstrate prerequisite skills before they are taught challenging content.
SA	A	NA	D	SD	14.	Excellence exists independently from students' diversity or individual differences.

If you found yourself to be in disagreement with these statements, this may suggest that you may be less assimilationist and more culturally relevant in your teaching. All of these statements were used by Ladson-Billings (1994) to characterize less successful teachers of African American children. They are in opposition to the teacher behaviors and belief system described earlier in the chapter. To what extent does her characterization of culturally relevant teaching apply to you?

FIGURE 4.12 Culturally relevant teaching: beliefs.
Drawn from G. Ladson-Billings, 1994, The *Dreamkeepers: Successful teachers of African American Children.* San Francisco, CA: Jossey-Bass.

5. *Culturally Relevant Teaching.* How do you see yourself as a teacher? To what extent would you describe your teaching as culturally relevant? Read the statements in Figure 4.12 and determine to what extent you agree or disagree with each one.

REFERENCES

Amos, O. E., & Landers, M. F. (1984). Special education and multicultural education: A compatible marriage. *Theory Into Practice, XXIII* (2), 144–150.

Astuto, T., & Clark, D. (1992). Challenging the limits of school restructuring and reform. In A. Lieberman (Ed.), *The changing contexts of teaching,* Ninety-first Yearbook of the National Society for the Study of Education, Part I (pp. 90–109). Chicago, IL: The University of Chicago Press.

Baca, L. M., & Cervantes, H. T. (1984). *The bilingual special education interface.* St. Louis: Times Mirror/Mosby.

Brophy, J. E. (1982). Successful teaching strategies for the inner-city child. *Phi Delta Kappan, 63*(8), 527–530.

Byrnes, D. A. (1989). Attitudes of students, parents and educators toward repeating a grade. In Lorrie A. Shepard & Mary Lee Smith (Eds.), *Flunking grades: Research and policies on retention* (pp. 108–131). New York: Falmer Press.

Cárdenas, J. A. (1986). The role of native-language instruction in bilingual education. *Phi Delta Kappan, 67*(5), 359–363.

Cárdenas, J. A., & First, J. McC. (1985). Children at risk. *Educational Leadership, 43* (1), 5–8.

Cheney, M., & Beebe, R. J. (1986). Gifted education: Continuing controversies. *ERS Spectrum, 4*(3), 12–17.

Cole, M., & Griffin, P. (Eds.), Laboratory of Comparative Human Cognition. (1987). *Contextual factors in education.* Prepared for Committee on Research in Mathematics, Science, and Technology Education, Commission on Behavior and Social Sciences and Education, National Research Council. Madison, WI: Wisconsin Center for Education Research, School of Education, University of Wisconsin—Madison.

Collins, R., & Camblin, L. D., Jr. (1983). The politics and science of learning disability classification: Implications for Black children. *Contemporary Education, 54* (2), 113–118.

Correll, M. (1978). *Teaching the gifted and talented.* Bloomington, IN: Phi Delta Kappa Educational Foundation.

Cortés, C. E. (1986). The education of language minority students: A contextual interaction model. In California State Department of Education, *Beyond language: Social and cultural factors in schooling language minority students* (pp. 3–33). Evaluation, Dissemination and Assessment Center, California State University—Los Angeles.

Crawford, J. (1991). *Bilingual education: History, politics, theory, and practice* (2nd ed.). Los Angeles: Bilingual Educational Services, Inc.

Cummins, J. (1984). *Bilingualism and special education: Issues in assessment and pedagogy.* San Diego, CA: College Hill Press.

Erickson, F. (1986). Qualitative methods in research on teaching. In M. C. Wittrock (Ed.), *Handbook of research on teaching* (3rd ed., pp. 119–161). New York: Macmillan.

Etlin, M. (1988). To teach them all is to know them all. *NEA Today, 6*(10), 10–11.

Evans de Bernard, A. (1985). Why José can't get in the gifted class: The bilingual child and standardized reading tests. *Roeper Review, VIII* (2), 80–85.

Fillmore, L. W., & Valadez, C. (1986). Teaching bilingual learners. In M. C. Wittrock (Ed.), *Handbook of research on teaching* (3rd ed., pp. 648–685). New York: Macmillan.

Findlay, W., & Bryan, M. (1975). *The pros and cons of ability grouping.* Bloomington, IN: Phi Delta Kappa Educational Foundation.

Fraser, S. (1995). *The bell curve wars: Race, intelligence, and the future of America.* New York: BasicBooks.

Gage, N. L., & Berliner, D. (1988). *Educational psychology.* (4th ed.). Boston: Houghton Mifflin.

Gelb, S. A., & Mizokawa, D. T. (1986). Special education and social structure: The commonality of "exceptionality." *American Educational Research Journal, 23* (4), 543–557.

Gonzalez, V. R. Brusca-Vega, & Yawkey, T. (1997). *Assessment and instruction of culturally and linguistically diverse children with or at-risk of learning problems: From research to practice.* Needham Heights, MA: Allyn & Bacon.

Good, T. L., & Brophy, J. E. (1986). School effects. In M. C. Wittrock (Ed.), *Handbook of research on teaching* (3rd ed., pp. 570–602). New York: Macmillan.

Hallinan, M. (1984). Summary and implications. In P. L. Peterson, L. C. Wilkinson, & M. Hallinan (Eds.), *The social context of instruction* (pp. 229–240). Orlando, FL: Academic Press.

Hatch, T. C., & Gardner, H. (1986). From testing intelligence to assessing competencies: A pluralistic view of intellect. *Roeper Review, VIII* (3), 149–150.

Hernández, H. (1982). Parallels in the history of American bilingual education. *Chabot College Journal, 4*(2), 33–39.

Herrick, M. (1971). *The Chicago schools.* Beverly Hills, CA: Sage Publications.

Herrnstein, R. J., & Murray, C. (1994). *The bell curve: Intelligence and class structure in American life.* New York: The Free Press.

Heubert, J. P., & Hauser, R. M. (Eds.). (1999). *High stakes: Testing for tracking, promotion, and graduation.* Washington, DC: National Academy Press.

Hoover, K. H. (1968). *Learning and teaching in the secondary school.* (2nd ed.). Boston: Allyn and Bacon.

House, E. R. (1989). Policy implications of retention research. In Lorrie A. Shepard & Mary Lee Smith (Eds.), *Flunking grades: Research and policies on retention* (pp. 202–213). New York: Falmer Press.

Kloss, H. (1977). *The American bilingual tradition.* Rowley, MA: Newbury House.

Knapp, M. S., & Woolverton, S. (1995). Social class and schooling. In James A. Banks & Cherry A. McGee Banks (Assoc. Eds.), *Handbook of research on multicultural education* (pp. 548–569). New York: Macmillan.

Kohn, A. (April 1998). *Only for My Kid: How Privileged Parents Undermine School Reform. Phi Delta Kappan,* Vol. 79, No. 8, pp. 569–577.

Ladson-Billings, G. (1994). *The dreamkeepers: Successful teachers of African American children.* San Francisco, CA: Jossey-Bass.

Levine, D. U., & Lezotte, L. W. (1995). Effective schools research. In James A. Banks & Cherry A. McGee Banks (Eds.), *Handbook of research on multicultural education* (pp. 525–547). New York: Macmillan.

MacMillan, D. L., Keogh, B. K., & Jones, R. L. (1986). Special education research on mildly handicapped learners. In M. C. Wittrock (Ed.), *Handbook of research on teaching* (3rd ed., pp. 686–724). New York: Macmillan.

Madaus, G., & Clarke, M. (in press). The adverse impact of high stakes testing on minority students: Evidence from 100 years of test data. In G. Orfield & M. Kornhaber (Eds.), *Raising Standards or Raising Barriers? Inequality and High Stakes Testing in Public Education*. New York: The Century Foundation.

Manni, J. L., Winikur, D. W., & Keller, M. R. (1984). *Intelligence, mental retardation and the culturally different child*. Springfield, IL: Charles C. Thomas.

Masten, W. G. (1985). Identification of gifted minority students: Past research, future directions. *Roeper Review, VIII* (2), 83–85.

McConnell, B. B. (1982). In grandpa's day. *NABE News, V*(5), 10.

McKenzie, J. A. (1986). The influence of identification practices, race and SES on the identification of gifted students. *Gifted Child Quarterly, 30* (2), 93–95.

Mehan, H. (1988, April). Teacher education issues session. Linguistic Minority Project Conference, Sacramento, CA.

Mercer, J. R. (1976, May). *Identifying the gifted Chicano child*. Paper presented at the First Symposium on Chicano Psychology, University of California, Irvine.

Nevi, C. (1987). In defense of tracking. *Educational Leadership, 44*(6), 24–26.

Ochoa, A. M., Pacheco, R., & Omark, D. R. (1983). Addressing the learning disability needs of limited-English-proficient students: Beyond language and race issues. *Learning Disability Quarterly, 6* (4), 416–423.

Ogbu, J. U., & Matute-Bianchi, M. E. (1986). Understanding sociocultural factors: Knowledge, identity, and school adjustment. *Beyond language: Social and cultural factors in schooling language minority students* (pp. 73–142). Evaluation, Dissemination and Assessment Center, California State University—Los Angeles.

Olneck, M. R. (1995). Immigrants and education. In James A. Banks & Cherry A. McGee Banks (Eds.), *Handbook of research on multicultural education* (pp. 310–327). New York: Macmillan.

Pegnato, C. W., & Birch, J. W. (1959). Locating gifted children in junior high schools: A comparison of methods. *Exceptional Children, 25* (7), 300–304.

Phipps, P. M. (1982). The LD learner is often a boy—Why? *Academic Therapy, 17* (4), 425–430.

Richert, E. S. (1985). Identification of gifted students: An update. *Roeper Review, VIII* (2), 68–72.

Roderick, M. (1995, December). Grade retention and school dropout: Policy debate and research questions. *Research Bulletin*, No. 15. Bloomington, IN: Phi Delta Kappa Center for Evaluation, Development, and Research.

Rothstein, R. (1998). Bilingual education: The controversy. *Phi Delta Kappan, 79*(9), 672–678.

School Report: Chicago, 1900. (1900). Chicago: H. Anderson, Printers. pp. 235–241.

Schreiner, T. (1987, December 18). Hispanic students: Educator sees 5 types. *San Francisco Chronicle.*

Shepard, L. A., & Smith, M. L. (Eds.). (1989). Introduction and overview. *Flunking grades: Research and policies on retention* (pp. 1–15). New York: Falmer Press.

Shinn, M. R., Tindal, G. A., & Spira, D. A. (1987). Special education referrals as an index of teacher tolerance: Are teachers imperfect tests? *Exceptional Children, 54* (1), 32–40.

Sleeter, C. E. (1986). Learning disabilities: The social construction of a special education category. *Exceptional Children, 53* (1), 46–54.

Sleeter, C. E., & Grant, C. (1988). *Making choices for multicultural education.* Columbus, OH: Merrill

Smith, M. L. (1989). Teachers' beliefs about retention. In Lorrie A. Shepard and Mary Lee Smith (Eds.), *Flunking grades: Research and policies on retention* (pp. 132–150). New York: Falmer Press.

Smith, M. L. , & Shepard, L. A. (1989). Flunking grades: A recapitulation. In Lorrie A. Shepard & Mary Lee Smith (Eds.), *Flunking grades: Research and policies on retention* (pp. 214–236). New York: Falmer Press.

Smutny, J. F. and Blocksom, R. H. (1990). *Education of the gifted: Programs and perspectives.* Bloomington, IN: Phi Delta Kappa Educational Foundation.

Sternberg, R. J. (1986). Identifying the gifted through IQ: Why a little bit of knowledge is a dangerous thing. *Roeper Review, VIII* (3), 143–147.

Sue, S., & Padilla, A. (1986, 1995). Ethnic minority issues in the United States: Challenges of the educational system. *Beyond language: Social and cultural factors in schooling language minority students* (pp. 35–72). Evaluation, Dissemination and Assessment Center, California State University— Los Angeles.

Tiedt, P. L., & Tiedt, I. M. (1986). *Multicultural teaching.* (2nd ed.). Boston: Allyn and Bacon.

Torrance, E. P. (1986). Teaching creative and gifted learners. In M. C. Wittrock (Ed.), *Handbook of research on teaching* (3rd ed., pp. 630–647). New York: Macmillan.

Treffinger, D. J., & Renzulli, J. S. (1986). Giftedness as potential for creative productivity: Transcending IQ scores. *Roeper Review, VIII* (3), 151–154.

Troen, S. K. (1975). *The public and the schools: Shaping the St. Louis school system, 1838–1925.* Columbus, MO: University of Missouri Press.

Trueba, H. (1981). Bilingual education: An ethnographic perspective. *California Journal of Teacher Education, VIII*(3), 15–41.

Tyack, D. B. (1974). *The one best system.* Cambridge, MA: Harvard University Press.

U. S. Commission on Civil Rights. (1975). *A better chance to learn: Bilingual-bicultural education.* Clearinghouse Publication 51. Washington, DC: U.S. Government Printing Office.

Wang, M. C., Reynolds, M. C., & Walberg, H. J. (1986). Rethinking special education. *Educational Leadership, 44* (1), 26–31.

Wheelock, A. (1994). *Alternatives to tracking and ability grouping.* Arlington, VA: American Association of School Administrators.

Wink, J. (1997). *Critical pedagogy: Notes from the real world.* White Plains, NY: Longman.

Winn, W., & Wilson, A. P. (1983). The affect and effect of ability grouping. *Contemporary Education, 54*(2), 119–125.

Yang, M. (1987). A very scary experience. Unpublished manuscript.

Zeydel, E. H. (1961). The teaching of German in the United States from colonial times to the present. In *Reports of surveys and studies in the teaching of modern foreign languages.* New York: Modern Language Association of America.

PART
III
PROCESS

5   Classroom Processes

> Classrooms . . . are places in which the formal and informal
> [social] systems continually intertwine.
>
> *Frederick Erickson (1986, p. 128)*

eaching and learning occurs in a variety of contexts—individual, group, class, school, home, community, and so on. Within the classroom context, two interrelated curricula are negotiated by teacher and students. The first is visible, transmitted through the formal structure of academic content, planned learning experiences, and instructional materials. The second, to some extent, is invisible, hidden in the interactional, social, management, and organizational aspects of classroom life. Together, these curricula establish "what schools are for, what purposes they are designed to accomplish" (Shulman, 1986, p. 8).

The intent in this chapter is to examine the "hidden" curriculum, that is, the behaviors of teachers and students and the transactions between them. As teachers and students enact the formal curriculum, they must also deal with the informal curriculum, which gives direction and structure to classroom life. Teachers must recognize the effect of the elements of this curriculum, and be able to manage them, if they are to create an environment that enhances all students' academic performance and self-concept. This cannot be accomplished by focusing on the formal curriculum of content and materials alone.

CLASSROOMS: A CLOSER LOOK

Classrooms are socially and culturally organized learning environments (Erickson, 1986). Teaching in pluralistic classrooms demands heightened awareness of the classroom processes that constitute the hidden or invisible curriculum. The more visible the dynamics of these processes become, the more significant their role in multicultural education. Descriptions of the hidden curriculum focus on the tacit values, attitudes, and unofficial rules of behavior students must learn to participate and succeed in school (Eggleston, 1977; Stubbs, 1976). These central components embody the real knowledge transmitted by the hidden curriculum and reflect the patterns of communication and participation deemed appropriate by both teachers and peers. From a sociological perspective, the initiation of students into this curriculum has been associated with developing skills related to the following (Eggleston, 1977; Jackson, cited in Gay, 1996):

1. Functioning in "crowds," but working in solitude
2. Developing work habits and using time productively
3. Being patient and passive, obedient, conforming and compliant
4. Accepting assessment by others (teachers and peers)
5. Competing to gain praise, rewards, and esteem from teachers and peers
6. Living in a hierarchical society with clearly defined power relationships and being differentiated in the process
7. Collaborating with other students to control the speed and progress of what is presented by the teacher in the official curriculum
8. Sharing the norms for and meanings of participation in classroom activities

To better understand the interplay of these competencies and others within the instructional environment, teachers need to examine in detail the interactional, social, management, and organizational dimensions of the classroom. They also need to recognize how ethnicity, socioeconomic status, gender, and other aspects of culture influence and interact with classroom processes.

INTERACTIONAL DIMENSION

Teacher Expectations

The relationship between teachers' perceptions of student academic ability, their expectations about how students will perform, and their interaction with individual students is very complex. *Teachers' expectations* have been defined as inferences drawn from current knowledge of students to predict anticipated behavior or academic achievement (Good & Brophy, 1997, p. 79). Teachers hold expectations—positive and negative—relative to individuals, groups, and entire classes (p. 14). Teacher expectation effects may take the form of self-fulfilling prophecies, in which the teacher's expectation creates the conditions that cause the expectation to be fulfilled, or sustaining expectation effects in which the expectations that students will continue to exhibit established learning and behavior patterns are so strong that these are assumed to exist even when this is no longer the case (p. 80). It is critical that teachers acknowledge the existence of expectations; it is no less important that they be cognizant of the actions that these expectations may produce.

Some studies support the view that teacher expectations affect outcomes such as student achievement, class participation, and social competence (Good, 1981; Wilkinson, 1981). The College Board's National Task Force on Minority High Achievement attributes the lack of achievement among capable minority students to racial prejudice manifest through low expectations "leading some teachers and counselors to ask less of 'underrepresented' minority students, including discouraging them from taking demanding college-preparatory courses in high school" (Lewis, 1999, p. 100). However, other research has shown that not all teachers are "equally susceptible to the biasing effects of interpersonal expectations" (Rosenthal & Babad, 1985, p. 39).

According to Good (1981), an important contribution of research on teacher expectations has been the "identification of specific ways in which some teachers treat high and low students differently" (p. 416). The research in Figure 5.1 indicates that certain identifiable behaviors may signal the differential treatment of students (Good & Brophy, 1997, pp. 90–91).

Good and Brophy caution that there is considerable variability across individual teachers, and that these behaviors are not characteristic of all classrooms. Teachers may be totally unaware of their behavior or they may interpret their actions as supportive rather than prejudicial. In some circumstances, these behaviors are highly appropriate responses and not indications of negative expectations. They suggest that there may be reason for concern if the differential treatment of students is large and occurs across a broad front: "Such a pattern suggests that the teacher is merely going through the motions of instructing low-expectation students, without genuinely trying to encourage academic progress" (p. 91).

Low achievers are likely to experience more variations in teacher communication patterns than high achievers (Good, 1981). For example, some teachers criticize or disparage low achievers' incorrect responses, whereas others reward answers that are marginal or even wrong. Such wide variation in teacher behaviors tends to make low achievers uncertain and tentative. By junior high school, some less successful students become passive learners, reluctant to ask for clarification and assistance from teachers.

Sociocultural factors seem to be closely associated with teacher expectations and the differential treatment of students. As Gollnick and Chinn

1. Allowing less wait-time for low-achieving students to respond to teacher questions.

2. Opting to give low-achieving students the answers or calling on other students to respond rather than providing clues, or repeating/rephrasing the question.

3. Providing inappropriate reinforcement of unacceptable behavior or incorrect responses from low-achieving students.

4. Being more critical of low-achieving students' failure.

5. Praising low-achieving students less for their accomplishments.

6. Not providing feedback to public answers from low-achieving students.

7. Interacting with low-achieving students less often and giving them less attention.

8. Providing fewer opportunities for low-achieving students to respond to questions or limiting the questions asked to those that are less difficult and require no analysis.

9. Failing to seat low-achieving students close to the teacher.

10. Making fewer demands of low-achieving students.

11. Providing more private than public interaction with low-achieving students; providing more direct organization and supervision of their tasks.

12. Providing differential treatment in the administration/grading of tests/assignments; displaying bias in the handling of borderline responses by accepting questionable answers from high achievers, but not from low-achieving students.

13. Engaging in less "friendly" interactions with low-achieving students (e.g., less smiling, fewer nonverbal signs of support).

14. Answering the questions asked by low-achieving students more briefly and less thoroughly.

15. Communicating attentiveness and responsiveness nonverbally (e.g., leaning body forward, nodding head) less often and making less frequent eye contact.

16. Limiting use of strategies that are effective but time consuming with low-achieving students when time available is limited.

17. Accepting and using fewer ideas from low-achieving students.

18. Providing low-achieving students a poor curriculum (limited/ repetitive content, emphasis on factual recall, recitation, and drill and practice).

FIGURE 5.1   Behaviors characteristic of differential treatment of high- and low-achieving students. Source: Adapted from the list of behaviors in T. L. Good and J. E. Brophy, *Looking in classrooms*, (7th ed.). New York: Longman. 1997 (pp. 90–91).

(1994) point out, students from lower socioeconomic backgrounds tend to be overrepresented among the ranks of low achievers. They cite research showing that teacher expectations—as evidenced through patterns of ability grouping and classroom interaction—also may be influenced by nonacademic student characteristics such as dress, language, cleanliness, and family stability. Generally, such influences tend to work to the disadvantage of students from lower socioeconomic backgrounds and those speaking minority languages or nonstandard dialects of English.

It comes as no surprise that disproportionate numbers of students from certain ethnic minority groups are underachievers. Sadker, Sadker, and Klein (1991) report that many studies support the contention that most teachers do not "expect" children from racial and ethnic minorities to do as well as 'White' children:

> Lower teacher expectations for minority student performance have been attributed to a variety of factors, including less effective use of standard English . . . , perceived less physical attractiveness . . . , perceived lower achievement of the minority groups as a whole being ascribed to each member . . . , and miscommunication of both verbal and nonverbal messages due to cultural differences. (pp. 301–302)

Drawing on examples of actual incidents will illustrate this point on a more personal level. Delpit (cited in Good & Brophy, 1997, p. 87) shares the following account of one child's experience:

> One evening I receive a telephone call from Terrence's mother, who is near tears. A single parent, she has struggled to put her academically talented fourteen-year-old African American son in a predominantly white private school. As an involved parent, she has spoken to each of his teachers several times during the first few months of school, all of whom assured her that Terrence was doing "just fine." When the first quarter's report cards were issued, she observed with dismay a report filled with Cs and Ds. She immediately went to talk to his teachers. When asked how they could have said he was doing fine when his grades were so low, each of them gave her some version of the same answer: Why are you so upset? For him, Cs are great. You shouldn't try to push him so much. (p. xiii)

Contrast this with Ladson-Billings' (1994) account of what happened to her son early in his school career:

> When my son was in first grade he was the only African American child in his class. His teacher, an African American woman, seemed particularly tough on him. As a young parent I was dismayed at what I saw as unfair treatment. In a parent-teacher conference she said to me, "I've seen too many black children, particularly boys, get messed over in this school. I'm being hard on him because he's got to be tough enough to endure." I didn't like what she said but I knew she was right. I could not shield my son from the realities of racism. He *did* indeed need a school experience that made him better prepared than his white peers. (p. 139)

Both real-life scenarios underscore the need for teachers to examine their own expectations—positive and negative—and whether these affect their interaction with students in the classroom.

In summary, then, teacher expectations and perceptions of students are important facets of classroom interaction. These expectations and perceptions

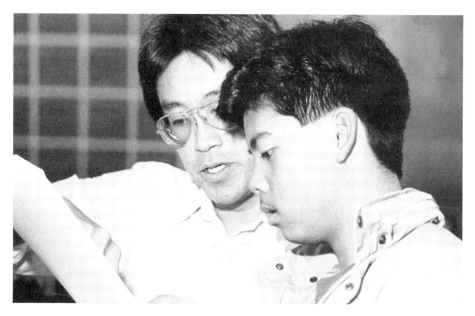

The relationship between teacher expectations and student learning outcomes is complex.

often are influenced by the sociocultural characteristics of students and may be reflected in differential treatment of students by teachers in ways that continue, even promote, inequalities of information and skills that exist when children start school (Cazden, 1986). In addition, cultural differences often affect how students respond to and interact with teachers and other students within schools. The effects of cultural differences on classroom interactions and patterns of differential treatment are discussed further in the next two sections.

Effects of Cultural Differences

Given the pervasiveness of culture in determining patterns of social behavior in general, the existence of variations among cultural groups in the formal and informal rules governing interaction between individuals should come as no surprise. Such variation may cause problems for students when classroom interactional patterns are not consistent or compatible with those that children experience in their homes and community. In some cases, stylistic variations in what, how, and when something is said may be minor and remain largely unnoticed by teachers and students alike. In other cases, however, cultural variations in interactional patterns can interfere with learning, particularly in the primary grades. Hymes (1981) observed that the differences typically recognized by school and community are the most visible symbols of culture, the most stereotypic of conventions. The less visible aspects of culture associated with everyday etiquette and interaction and with expressions of rights, obligations, values, and aspirations through norms of communication are commonly overlooked. "One can honor cultural pride on the walls of a room yet inhibit learning within them" by overlooking and not accommodating to such cultural differences in communication and interpersonal interactions (Hymes, 1981, p. 59).

In Native American communities, for example, the classroom learning environment may be structured according to rules not shared by the community to which the students belong. Such discontinuities between school and community can affect teachers and students alike and may be reflected in classroom (a) *tempo* (e.g., how quickly teacher and students interact); (b) *management* (e.g., how teachers control and monitor behavior, what kinds of behaviors are used to intervene, how teachers define what constitutes paying attention, how the attention is focused, how much time is given for students to respond); (c) *organization* of students (e.g., whole class, small groups, group project, one-on-one with the teacher); and (d) *participation* (e.g., frequency of volunteering and responding, willingness to interrupt other speakers) (Mohatt & Erickson, 1981; Philips, 1983).

Especially critical in the Native American communities observed by researchers were instructional demands that students respond competitively and individualistically. Within the Odawan community, these appeared to violate cultural norms emphasizing cooperative and group effort. Hence, sensitivity to the culture of Odawan students demands recognition of less obvious aspects of "interactional etiquette," such as avoiding direct commands and refraining from placing students in the "spotlight" (Mohatt & Erickson, 1981). On the Warm Springs Indian Reservation, Philips (1983) found that one-on-one contact between students and teachers or aides and the use of group projects and cooperative learning activities were most compatible with the interactional patterns of the students' culture.

In their interactions with students, *teachers should aim to maintain the integrity of the home culture while respecting the demands of the school* (Mehan, 1988). Bridges are built to incorporate cultural elements in ways that provide support for students as they learn to deal with the instructional patterns of the classroom. In the Kamehameha Early Education Program (KEEP), for example, classroom practices capitalize on the cognitive and linguistic abilities children bring to the classroom (Au & Jordan, 1981). This program begins with the storytelling approaches that the children experience in their own homes; then a gradual transition is made to the traditional school format of children reading texts and responding to questions posed by the teacher. Similar strategies for establishing links between home and school can work in many settings when teachers are familiar with prevailing cultural patterns.

Heath (1983) described how teachers in the Piedmont Carolinas developed knowledge of communication styles in different communities and used it in adapting the methods and materials related to language and literacy in the classroom. These teachers "constructed curricula from the world of the home to enable students to move to the curricular content of the school" (p. 340). Three strategies used by these teachers were (a) to use knowledge familiar to students to provide a foundation for classroom information; (b) to involve students in identifying and examining familiar ways of knowing and to help them translate these into the labels, concepts, and generalizations used in the school; and (c) to provide opportunities for students to explore how language is used to organize and express information.

As this discussion suggests, the classroom is a complex communicative environment. Classroom interaction has several important elements: communication between teachers and students and among peers; the construction of contexts and meanings; levels of student participation; and evaluation of student ability (Morine-Dershimer, 1985). The cultural background that students bring to the classroom can influence their interpretation of and response to each of these elements.

At the very heart of the educational process in most classrooms is communication between teacher and students. This communication influences students' ability to assimilate curricular content:

> The actual (as opposed to the intended) curriculum consists in the meanings enacted or realized by a particular teacher and class. In order to learn, students must use what they already know so as to give meaning to what the teacher presents to them. Speech makes available to reflection the processes by which they relate new knowledge to old. But this possibility depends on the social system, the communication system, which the teacher sets up. (National Institute of Education, 1974, p. 1)

Patterns of Differential Treatment

Few would argue that within the same classroom the possible experiences of individual students can differ significantly. In one study, the researchers concluded that students "in the same classroom, with the same teacher, studying the same material were experiencing very different educational environments" (Sadker & Sadker, 1986, p. 513). They found, across a range of grade levels, subject areas, classroom settings, and student populations, that about one fourth of the students were silent and did not interact with the teacher at all. The majority of students interacted with the teacher only once during a class period; fewer than 10% of the students had three or more exchanges with the teacher. Such variations in teacher-student interactional patterns have been associated with gender, ethnicity, and achievement level. In many cases, these differences lie beyond the conscious awareness of teachers.

In a summary of research on gender differences in elementary classrooms, Lindow, Marrett, and Wilkinson (1985) reported general, though not universal, agreement that (a) teachers tend to interact more with boys than girls and (b) a significant proportion of the attention focused on boys is negative. The generally observed pattern is that boys are "more active and salient in classrooms" and receive "more of almost any kind of interaction with the teacher that may be measured," including criticism and praise and behavioral, procedural, and academic exchanges (Brophy, 1985, p. 120). This pattern is attributed more to gender role-related differences in student behaviors than to teacher intent, as the pattern is usually observed whether the teacher is male or female. It should also be noted that although boys as a group receive more teacher attention, high-achieving boys tend to receive more positive attention (e.g., approval, questions, detailed instructions, and active teaching attention) than low-achieving boys, who often receive negative feedback such as criticism and reprimands (Brophy & Good, cited in Sadker & Sadker, 1982).

A more recent synthesis of research on gender equity in teacher-student interaction supports these findings and provides additional insights (Sadker, Sadker, & Klein, 1991, pp. 295–307). Some of the more important conclusions emerging from work in this area are presented in Figure 5.2.

---

1. Gender-different teacher behaviors—quantity and quality—have been documented from the beginning of children's school careers at the preschool level through college and university classes.

2. Studies at all educational levels report a higher frequency of teacher interaction with male students: "males are both given, and through their behaviors attract, a higher number of teacher interactions" (p. 298). This disparity appears to increase with age, as studies generally report greater discrepancies in the distribution frequency at secondary and postsecondary levels than at the elementary level.

3. There is inequity within genders as well as between males and females. Studies reveal that teachers interact more with high-achieving boys and boys with behavior problems than with other boys and girls; interact more with high-achieving boys than with high-achieving girls. In reality, many boys and many girls enjoy only limited interaction with the teacher. Another familiar pattern is the disproportionate attention that a select few students receive in many classrooms (pp. 298–299).

4. Ethnicity, racial background, and socioeconomic status are other factors that enter into the interaction equation. Majority group students—male and female—fare better than those from minority groups. The tendency is for majority males to interact more often and more productively with the teacher, while interaction with minorities and females is less frequent and specific (pp. 299, 301). Along similar lines, students from lower income backgrounds are less likely to receive positive or productive interaction from the teacher.

5. How teachers respond to student comments is as important to creating learning opportunities and successful outcomes as the number of questions asked or frequency of interaction. Student achievement and attitudes are affected by teacher praise and corrective comments. Effective praise is specific, sincere, informative, and related to student performance. It conveys the importance of the students' accomplishments and acknowledges effort or ability. Corrective comments are most effective when they (a) focus explicitly on performance, (b) create an environment in which mistakes are accepted and viewed as part of the learning process, (c) offer specific directions for improvement, and (d) encourage students to persist in their efforts to succeed (p. 300).

FIGURE 5.2   Research highlights: gender equity in student-teacher interaction.
Source: Drawn from pages 296–300 in the review of literature by M. P. Sadker, D. M. Sadker, and S. Klein. The issue of gender in elementary and secondary education. In G. Grant (Ed.), *Review of research in education*, Vol. 17 (pp. 269–334). Washington, DC: American Educational Research Association, 1991.

Teachers may be surprised to learn that academically, "girls are the only group in our society that begins school ahead and ends up behind" (Sadker, Sadker, & Long, 1997, p. 139).

The differential treatment of students by teachers is also related to ethnicity in some classrooms. One of the most frequently cited studies supporting this conclusion involved 429 classrooms in urban, suburban, and rural schools in California, New Mexico, and Texas. Major findings indicated that schools in the Southwest "are failing to involve Mexican American children as active participants in the classroom" (U.S. Commission on Civil Rights, 1973, p. 43). Other studies of interactions in interracial classrooms also have found differences in teachers' treatment of students and variations in student friendship patterns, although the results are less consistent than in the case of gender differences (Schwanke, 1980). In one study of elementary pupils in a multiethnic community, Morine-Dershimer (1985) found that pupils with higher academic status participated more frequently than others in class discussions and their comments were attended to more carefully by peers. In the classes observed, ethnic minority pupils had lower academic status; when they participated, their contributions to discussions received significantly less attention than those of other students.

It is clear that students experience different learning environments in the classroom, although the effects of these differences on educational outcomes and student self-concept have not been fully delineated. Some of the variation is accounted for by student and teacher characteristics. Other variations may result from culturally influenced patterns associated with ethnicity, language, socioeconomic status, and gender. Some differential treatment in classrooms is inevitable; in many situations, it is beneficial. Educators must be willing and able to determine whether differential treatment represents "helpful individualization, or detrimental bias" (Cazden, 1986, p. 447). *The best way for individual teachers to do this is to be aware of and to monitor interactional patterns in their own classrooms.*

Monitoring of Interactions

It is not enough to merely know that teacher expectations and interaction patterns influence classroom effectiveness. In reality, teachers are not cognizant of their use of behaviors and even when they have some degree of awareness, they often fail to appreciate the consequences of their actions (Good & Brophy, 1997). This lack of awareness of the behaviors themselves and the effect they have on students mitigates against effective teaching. This happens for a number of reasons, among these the fast pace and complexity of classroom life, and limitations in the professional preparation of teachers in analyzing classroom behavior.

Observations of interactional and discourse patterns in a classroom can clarify how individual students and groups of students respond to different teacher behaviors and how the teacher, in turn, responds to them. Based upon such observations, teachers can begin to identify behaviors they wish to target for modification and explore alternative strategies for doing so. When there appear to be culturally related differences in the interactional patterns expected in the classroom and those that students experience within their homes and/or community, additional observations in other settings may be appropriate.

Teachers who decide to monitor and examine their own patterns of interaction first need to *determine the kind of interaction information* they want to collect. They may want to concentrate their attention on one or more aspects of interaction mentioned earlier (e.g., treatment of boys and girls) or focus on other dimensions (e.g., questioning strategies; teacher feedback to student contributions). Good and Brophy (1997) emphasize the importance of simplifying the observational task. They recommend that beginning observers do so by initially limiting their study to a few students such as

◇ Two high, middle, and low achievers—one male and one female at each level—for a total of six students
◇ A specific group of learners (e.g., low achievers). (p. 49)

Second, they must *select an observation technique* to help them to describe their interaction with students. Whatever the approach, it should provide useful and accurate information, and within the parameters given, be as simple to use and interpret as possible. For example, Good and Brophy (1997) suggest that teachers observing the six high, middle, and low achievers focus on information related to questions such as the following:

> How often do they raise their hands?
> Do all students approach the teacher to receive help, or do some seldom approach?
> How long does each reading group last?
> Are the students involved in their work? How long do they work independently at their desks?
> How often are students in different groups praised?
> What do students do when they finish their work, while other students are still completing theirs? (pp. 49–50)

They also recommend restricting the number of specific behaviors to be observed at a given session, concentrating on perhaps five to ten behaviors at the outset.

Third, teachers must *decide how to collect the information* they need. There are a number of options available. Teachers working independently can record activities on audiotape or, with assistance, on videotape. Peer observations also can be used to enhance information obtained through self-monitoring. Colleagues can exchange observation visits as an alternative to the use of recordings. Some teachers have devised ways of involving student assistants or individual members of the class in recording information for some of their observations, as appropriate.

Numerous approaches to monitoring classroom interactions have been developed. Among those designed for teacher use are approaches for examining interactions directed at boys and girls (Sadker & Sadker, 1982), language choice in bilingual settings (Legarreta-Marcaida, 1981), and verbal and nonverbal aspects of ethnicity (Longstreet, 1978). For more ambitious efforts, some of the ethnographic methods used by researchers are appropriate. Aspects of social relations that can be observed include the norms of interaction in home and school, the contexts in which bilingual children choose to use different languages, and the duration of teacher contacts with individual children and groups (Erickson, 1981; Heath, 1983). For most teachers, monitoring the quantity and quality of their interactions with students is a good place to start; this can be done by counting interactional behaviors and through note taking.

Frequency of Interaction

A very general overview of classroom interaction can be obtained by the simple technique of determining frequencies of student-teacher interactions. Sadker and Sadker (1982) used such frequencies as numerical indicators of teacher attention directed at boys and girls. In this approach, the number of times a teacher elicits a response (e.g., asks a question, issues a directive) from male and female students is counted on several different occasions. The individual counts are adjusted to the same time period and then averaged. In this type of frequency monitoring, no record is kept of the comments themselves nor of the students involved (except for their gender).

Frequency monitoring can also be used to examine teacher interactions with students who differ along other dimensions such as ethnicity and socioeconomic status. It is suitable for monitoring specific teacher communication behaviors (e.g., questioning strategies, overt and covert corrections, praise, criticism, and feedback) and student interaction with peers. It can also be used to examine whether interaction is distributed evenly in different areas of the classroom (e.g., table groupings, front and back, center and sides). One foreign language teacher used this approach to analyze the proportion of Spanish and English spoken in classroom interactions and the functions for each language (e.g., routines, instructions, humor).

Quality of Interaction

Verbatim notes of specific facets of interaction can be used to describe the nature of discourse between teachers and students in greater detail. One primary grade teacher used this approach to examine the feedback given to pupils in small reading groups and to assess its influence on their participation. By keeping track of specific comments provided as feedback, he was able to determine which seemed to encourage and discourage pupil contributions and which were neutral. In bilingual classrooms, teachers have kept notes on use of each language for specific cognitive, affective, and management purposes (e.g., explaining, questioning, expressing feelings, disciplining). Such notes can provide a rough indication of the balance achieved in the use of both languages by function.

The interaction between teachers and students is at the heart of the educational process in most classrooms.

SOCIAL DIMENSION

Language Attitudes

Language attitudes—the feelings, the beliefs, and values associated with one's own language and/or dialect and those spoken by others—influence perceptions regarding the social identity, status, and ability of the speakers of a given language (Ramírez, 1985). All speakers of English reveal a particular dialect or variety of the language. Chaika (1982) observes that regional dialects traditionally have symbolized allegiance to a region; conveyed positive, shared connotations associated with valued traits; and signaled social bonding within class and ethnic groups. Accents and dialectal variations, however, also can have negative connotations and in many societies are impediments to access to social, educational, and economic opportunity.

Attitudes and values attached to some features of language (e.g., regional accent) are evident and widely acknowledged. These are often captured in humor and parodies. However, people rarely are aware of the depth of reactions to divergent language styles and the speakers who use them. "The ideal of linguistic democracy, in which the speech of every citizen is regarded with equal respect by all others, is perhaps the most unrealistic of all social ideals. Speech is one of the most effective instruments in existence for maintaining a given social order" (Christian, cited in Peñalosa, 1980, p. 183). *My Fair Lady* illustrates some of the language attitudes and the resulting social consequences to which Christian is alluding.

Sociolinguistic research has provided considerable insights about the nature, incidence, and implications of these attitudes. For example, many adults and children display well-defined evaluational reactions to spoken language (Lambert, Hodgson, Gardner, & Fillenbaum, 1972). In Canadian research, speakers of English and French were asked to evaluate the personality characteristics of individuals speaking both languages. The raters did not know that they were listening to the same individuals speak both languages. Ratings were more favorable when the individual spoke English than French; this was true whether the raters were French or English Canadians. Dialect surveys also have revealed hidden attitudes toward ethnicity, region, and gender—attributes that often are reflected in speech patterns (Chaika, 1982). Those who have grown up in families speaking certain varieties of English or other languages are likely to recall situations in which their ability and competence were equated, perhaps negatively, with features of their speech. In the United States, attitudes toward ethnic languages also appear to be influenced by the number of speakers residing in a given community. According to Kjolseth (1982), "The more locally irrelevant an ethnic language and culture is, the higher its social status, and the more viable it is locally, the lower its social status" (p. 7).

In general, those who achieve the highest degree of success in U.S. society tend to have the least accented speech (González, cited in Peñalosa, 1980). The significance of this reality has not gone unnoticed among speakers of different varieties of English. Few television newscasters, for example, speak with a distinctive accent, and some have consciously eliminated certain regional characteristics from their speech. Although existing attitudes may change, achievement-oriented Chicanos have "traditionally made an effort to erase all traces of Spanish influence from their English" (Tovar, cited in Peñalosa, 1980, p. 191).

Language attitudes—both positive and negative—also operate within the classroom and can affect the teaching and learning process. Language plays a major role in establishing the social identity and relationships of teachers and students in the classroom. As Ramírez (1985) observed, the initial impressions teachers form about students are often based upon features of their speech. Once established, these views appear to remain relatively fixed and may influence initial assessments of student ability as well as teacher expectations. Moreover, negative teacher attitudes may reinforce similar student attitudes toward their own or others' nonstandard language use. Thus, students may be subjected to teacher and peer prejudice because of the dialect they speak (Hall & Guthrie, 1981).

Because of the prestige associated with standard English, many teachers accept the premise that equality of opportunity is impossible unless all English speakers can use standard English at the level required for high status jobs or professions. Those who accept this premise are faced with a dilemma, however.

As Chaika (1982) observes, the speech of children and adolescents resembles that of the people with whom they identify. Black English (also referred to as African American English and African American language), for example, is strongly valued by many African Americans as a symbol of intimacy and solidarity—it represents "intergroup distinctiveness from the white community" (Beebe, 1988, p. 65). Differences between Black English and standard English are constantly reinforced and, according to Beebe, apparently increasing among many African Americans. Students who do not identify with speakers of standard English are not likely to emulate their speech patterns. In addition, students who choose to use standard English must often confront peer pressure and accept corrections they may interpret as insulting to their own speech patterns and self-identity.

Research on Black English reported by LeMoine (1993), and Lee and Slaughter-Defoe (1995) suggests the following:

◇ There are standard and vernacular forms of Black English, the former closer to standard English than the latter. Both forms share common features in areas such as phonology, intonation, discourse, and semantics.

◇ Although research on the implications of Black English for teaching and learning is limited, it is clear that teachers can draw upon the strengths of Black English (e.g., expository structure, topic-associative narrative) to enhance literacy and academic competence.

◇ There is no substantive support for assertions that the use of Black English interferes with children's learning to read.

◇ Insights drawn from the research on different language varieties and their effect on teaching and learning have had little influence on instruction at the classroom level.

◇ For children whose primary language is Black English, the kind of natural language learning environment most typically associated with instruction for language minority students is best.

One approach reported to be effective with inner-city high school students is sociodrama. This technique can help students develop proficiency in standard English appropriate to various situations without relying on excessive use of grammar and pronunciation exercises (Chaika, 1982). In a typical sociodrama exercise, students are asked to assume roles and act out situations in which they would be using standard forms of the language (e.g., interviewing for a job, complaining to someone in authority). A similar technique can be applied to writing (e.g., newspaper articles) and used in combination with group work and peer editing.

Student Status

Within the social environment of the classroom, the status of students is determined by and manifested in various ways (Cohen, 1986). At the elementary level, for example, academic status is determined largely by competence in

reading and mathematics. Furthermore, students ranked high on reading ability in the minds of teachers and fellow students are generally also expected to
do well in unrelated school tasks; conversely, those who are regarded as poor
readers are not expected to do well. Peer status at all grade levels also is associated with other characteristics: individual traits (e.g., athletic ability, attractiveness, popularity) and societal distinctions related to class, race, ethnicity,
exceptionality, and sex.

Cohen (1982) reported that in interracial schools, interactions are dominated by Whites when valued intellectual tasks are involved and that the participation and task engagement of minority students in school activities generally is less than that of Whites. Both patterns reflect and reinforce teacher
and student expectations that minority students will be less competent and
successful. These patterns have been observed for students clearly identifiable as members of minority groups. In the classroom, teachers must deal
with multiple status characteristics. In combination, these factors interact and
have a powerful effect on the nature and extent of participation in the classroom and on expectations for competence held by teachers and students. In
general, the higher the status of students, the higher the expectations and vice
versa.

Teachers can modify expectations in interracial educational settings in several
ways (Cohen, 1982). For example, teachers can influence expectations through positive evaluations of student competence. Because of their high status as evaluators,
teachers—especially those from the same ethnic group as students—can affect how
students see themselves in relation to others. The presence of individuals with different ethnic and cultural characteristics in positions of high status and authority
(teachers, administrators) also can alter student perceptions. Finally, use of special
norms (e.g., listening to peers, allowing all students to contribute) in cooperative
group activities appears to promote equality of interaction.

MANAGEMENT DIMENSION

In today's classrooms, teachers are faced with an ever expanding spectrum of
student needs and abilities. To respond effectively to this heterogeneity requires
adaptations in how the total curriculum is implemented and the complementary use of teaching and behavior management techniques.

Hoover and Collier (1986) describe one approach used with minority and
minority students with disabilities that integrates classroom management and
curricular adaptation. In this approach, adaptations are based on analysis of
four basic elements individually and in relation to one another: (a) *content*
(subject-specific knowledge, attitudes, and skills); (b) *instructional strategies*
(teacher repertoires of instructional and management methods and techniques);
(c) *instructional settings* (teaching contexts or groupings); and (d) *student behaviors* (individual abilities to manage and control learning and comportment
in diverse situations, activities, and groups).

According to Hoover and Collier (1986), the interaction of these curricular elements has important consequences for classroom management, as outlined in Figure 5.3. For example, content may directly influence the selection of instructional strategies and settings; it is also influenced by student behaviors. Likewise, the choice of strategy affects setting and student behaviors, which in turn also influence each other. Suppose, for example, that individual students display disruptive behaviors in small-group situations; with this type of student behavior, strategies maximizing active involvement for all group members are likely to be more effective than those requiring turn-taking. Because of the

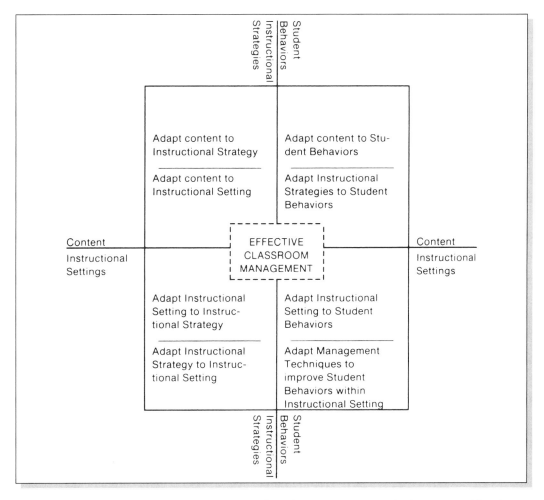

FIGURE 5.3 Model of classroom management based on interactions and adaptations of four basic elements: content, instructional strategies, instructional settings, and student behaviors.
Source: J. J. Hoover and C. Collier, *Classroom Management Through Curricular Adaptations.* Copyright © 1986 by Hamilton Publications. Reprinted by permission.

reciprocal interactions between curricular elements, learning or behavior problems usually are related to more than one element.

Although Hoover and Collier (1986) focus primarily on minority and minority students with disabilities, their approach is applicable to other learners. The important point to remember is that adaptations in one element—content, setting, strategies, or student behaviors—are likely to have a reciprocal effect on other elements. Thus, changes in content may require concurrent accommodations in strategies or setting; changes in group size and composition may affect choice of strategy and student behavior.

Hoover and Collier (1986) describe specific teaching and behavior management techniques that are helpful in adapting curriculum to meet student needs. For adapting instructional techniques, they suggest the following:

1. Provide alternate modes of response (oral rather than written; visual or graphic rather than verbal).
2. Shorten assignments by abbreviating the task given or dividing more complex tasks into segments.
3. Ensure that students experience success and develop self-confidence by initially assigning relatively easy tasks or assignments and then gradually increasing the level of difficulty as they progress.
4. Incorporate student input in curricular planning in ways that promote students' sense of ownership in the process and decision-making skills.
5. Let students choose among alternative activities and assignments.
6. Negotiate verbal or written contracts with students to improve motivation and to clarify responsibilities (expectations, assignments, rewards).
7. Modify the presentation of abstract concepts by using concrete learning activities, teaching the vocabulary required for cognitive academic tasks, and incorporating visual aids, objects and materials (manipulatives), and student experiences.
8. Select written texts with an appropriate reading level in terms of complexity of vocabulary and concepts and/or provide first-language materials for English language learners.
9. Use clues or prompts to assist students working on assignments.
10. Use academic and behavioral expectations and communicate these clearly and concisely to students.

Hoover and Collier (1986) suggest complementing instructional adaptations with specific behavior management techniques. Of primary importance is positive reinforcement that provides feedback or rewards for appropriate responses and behavior in ways that are culturally and personally relevant. They also suggest using nonverbal signals and cues that do not draw attention to individual students (e.g., flicking lights on and off; ringing a bell) when classroom behavior becomes inappropriate. They caution that proximity (strategic positioning) and touch control, while widely used and often effective, are culturally sensitive forms of nonverbal communication. Teachers must remember that personal space is defined differently across cultures. Standing behind students to monitor behavior or within a certain distance can convey very different messages from those intended. Likewise, a gentle tap on the shoulder or head could violate accepted norms of interpersonal contact for some students. Teachers can decide to ignore certain behaviors to reduce the likelihood of confrontations over minor instances of misbehavior. Finally, student accountability and recognition of their responsibility for performance and actions should be promoted. Hoover and Collier offer teachers using this approach the following advice: Make only those modifications that are indicated and be flexible, consistent, and persistent in trying different techniques.

ORGANIZATIONAL DIMENSION

Classroom organization refers to how teachers organize students for instruction—the social structure they create, the social relationships and academic outcomes they produce. Ames and Ames (1984) have described the structure of classrooms as competitive, cooperative, and individualistic. Each structure is based on a different value orientation with its own way of evaluating the performance of individual students both in relation to instructional goals and in relation to other students. Within a competitive structure, achieving a goal or reward is related—implicitly or explicitly—to how other students perform, whereas in a cooperative structure students work with each other toward a common goal. By contrast, when the structure is individualistic, students work toward independent goals. Within these varied structures, students learn to interpret how they perform on academic tasks differently and attach different meanings to success and failure on academic tasks. Not surprisingly, how teachers structure the learning environment affects academic achievement, motivation, and instructional behavior.

In this section, competitive, cooperative, and individualistic structures provide the framework for a discussion of classroom organization and its interaction with social and cultural factors (especially socioeconomic status and ethnicity). Then attention is focused on two strategies used in adapting organization in heterogeneous classrooms. These are cooperative learning and tutoring.

Within-Classroom Groups

Competitive Structure

Competition is a basic element in American culture: it has been described as the primary method used by Americans to motivate members of groups (Stewart, 1979). Most classrooms in the United States have a learning environment with a competitive structure, and given the value placed on individualism and achievement, many students respond well to competition as a motivating force.

There is evidence that within a competitive structure, student perceptions of their own ability and their feelings of personal satisfaction are related to how well they perform as compared to other children (Ames, 1984; Ames & Ames, 1984). When they succeed, children's assessment of their ability is high; when they fail, it is low. On the positive side, competition can enhance the social status and self-esteem of high-achieving learners. On the negative side, most studies suggest that the impact of competitive structures on motivation tends to be negative—particularly for low-achieving children (Ball, 1984). Children learn to attribute success and failure primarily to ability, rather than effort, the nature of the task, or other factors: "We cannot help but speculate that declines in children's self-perceptions of their ability over the elementary school years, may, in part, be a consequence of the competitive nature of many classrooms and the increased emphasis placed on social comparison as children progress through school" (Ames & Ames, 1984, p. 45). In essence, children's affective reactions to success and failure in the competitively structured classroom are closely related to perceptions of their own ability, their performance relative to other children, and their feelings of personal satisfaction.

Students whose value orientations differ are not as likely to respond to a competitive structure with the same enthusiasm as members of the dominant culture. Some researchers have even argued that the value orientations of some groups may interact with competitive classroom structures to produce "negative academic and social schooling outcomes" (Kagan, 1986, p. 268). Socioeconomic status and ethnicity are among the social and cultural factors which appear to influence social orientation. In some non-Western cultures, an intense attachment to family and community can preclude the incentive to excel over others (Stewart, 1979). Moreover, although the motivation to achieve varies across settings in different cultures, its relationship to socioeconomic status is strong; in the United States the effect of socioeconomic status on achievement motivation is larger than that attributed to ethnic differences (Ball, 1984; Cooper & Tom, 1984).

Cooperative Structure

Ames and Ames (1984) suggest that in a learning environment with a cooperative structure, children focus attention not only on personal achievement, but also on group performance and individual effort toward the common goal. How high- and low-achieving students evaluate their own performance is considerably influenced—in a positive or negative direction—by the group's overall performance: "Social context is a potent factor in children's affective reactions to success and failure" (p. 45). Kagan (1986) has found that cooperatively oriented students perform better in cooperatively structured classrooms, although competitively oriented students seem to prefer competitively oriented classes. Group interaction provides a way of challenging and changing expectations for competence based upon status char-

Cooperation can have a positive influence on academic achievement, intergroup relations, self-esteem, and prosocial development.

acteristics (i.e., "agreed-upon social rankings") related to academic, peer, and societal characteristics such as race, social class, and sex (Cohen, 1986). These social rankings, which operate to the disadvantage of students assigned low status within the classroom are less likely to be reinforced within cooperative structures than in other organizational settings. Hence, at an interpersonal level, students appear to minimize perceptions of differences in ability and performance.

On the plus side, cooperation can have positive effects on academic achievement, intergroup relations, self-esteem, and social skills. Ethnic minority students generally show significantly greater academic gains in cooperative settings than in traditional classrooms; other students show equal or somewhat greater gains. Although average and low achievers benefit most in learning environments with a cooperative structure, it is not at the expense of high achievers, whose performance is comparable to that in traditional classrooms (Kagan, 1986). The positive effects of cooperation on student achievement have been reported at elementary and secondary levels, in urban, suburban, and rural schools, among diverse populations, and across subject areas such as mathematics, language arts, social studies, and reading (Slavin, 1981). On the minus side, teachers are advised against using cooperative strategies in situations when group failure can "undermine the potentially positive effects of this noncompetitive structure" (Ames & Ames, 1984, p. 45).

Individualistic Structure

As described by Ames and Ames (1984), a noncompetitive individualistic structure is characterized by continuity of performance over time, self-improvement, and task-orientation. Within this type of structure, children's success and failure on academic tasks is independent of others. Each student has an equal opportunity to achieve success when goals are based on their own performance, and progress on tasks is at their own rate. Mastery learning, for example, assumes that all students are capable of attaining acceptable levels of achievement. Proponents of mastery learning argue that this is especially critical for students who are not achieving academically (Bennett, 1986). However, as Ames (1984) points out, elements of an individual perspective (e.g., self-improvement, performance over time) can also be effectively incorporated within nonmastery approaches.

Ideally, an individualized structure creates an orientation in which effort is valued and students are attentive to the learning strategies they use to achieve success. Ames and Ames (1984) have found that students in individualistic structures tend to relate success or failure on tasks to their own performance over time. When this happens, students are less likely to view current performance as isolated from the effort they put forth to accomplish a task and their performance on related activities. Teacher perceptions are also affected by a task-oriented, individualistic structure, as teachers place greater emphasis on student performance in relation to specific goals and individual effort.

In summary, interpreting the effects of social structures is a complex aspect of classroom process. Research reveals that how classrooms are organized affects student learning, as individuals respond differently to the various structures teachers create. In essence, the structure of the learning environment—competitive, cooperative, or individualistic—provides students with opportunities "to realize certain goals and not others by influencing student motivational processes and achievement patterns" (Ames, 1984, p. 204).

Adapting Organization

Although individual teachers may emphasize different structures, most are likely to use all three structures—competitive, cooperative, and individualistic—in their classrooms at one time or another (Ball, 1984). Hence, from a practical standpoint, teachers need alternative strategies to adapt organization in heterogeneous classrooms. Cooperative learning and tutoring exemplify two of the many strategies teachers can use.

Cooperative Learning

As described by Kagan (1986) and Slavin (1981), cooperative learning methods generally have three features in common:

1. The class is divided into small teams whose members are "positively interdependent" (i.e., the achievement of each team member contributes to the rewards of all).

Cooperative learning methods are generally characterized by small teams, whose members are interdependent, and a task and reward structure that makes individuals accountable for their own learning.

2. Task and reward structures also make individuals accountable for their own learning.
3. Improvement over past performance contributes to the entire group's reward.

Kagan (1986) and Slavin (1981) describe numerous specific cooperative learning approaches. All of them promote student interaction, interdependence, and cooperation. In one common approach, the teacher presents material to the entire class and then students assemble in heterogeneous teams of four or five members. Using worksheets, these *student teams-achievement divisions* (STAD) practice and master the information to be learned. Each student takes a quiz on the material individually. Team scores are determined by the extent to which each student improves over past performance. Individuals and teams demonstrating the greatest improvement are recognized. In the *teams-games-tournaments* (TGT) approach, a variation of the STAD approach, students play academic games with members of other teams whose past performance is similar to their own.

In the *jigsaw* approach, students are individually given information that they must master and "teach" to other team members. Teams have three to seven members (preferably five or six). Students are also given training to promote team building, communication, and leadership. Students are individually tested on their mastery of the material. In some cases, teachers give students information to be learned; in other cases, they obtain it from textbooks, narrative materials, short stories, biographies, or other sources.

The *group investigation* approach requires students to accept considerable responsibility for deciding what they will learn and how they will organize themselves to master the material and communicate what they have learned to other class members. In this approach, students identify the topic to be investigated, organize into research groups, plan the learning task, prepare and present a final report, and evaluate their efforts.

Team-assisted individualization combines features of cooperative and individualized learning. In this approach, group support is provided to assist students in completing individual learning modules. Another cooperative approach called *Finding Out/Descubrimiento* is designed specifically for use in bilingual classrooms. This method is organized around 170 mathematics and science activities in multiple-learning centers. Linguistically heterogeneous groups work cooperatively and interact to complete the activities. For more information on these and other approaches to cooperative learning, see JoAnne W. Putnam, *Cooperative Learning in Diverse Classrooms* (1997).

Tutoring

The notion of one-to-one teaching makes tutoring arguably the oldest form of instruction (Shanahan, 1998). Salomon and Perkins (1998) characterize one person helping another to learn as one of the "most fundamentally social forms of learning" (pp. 3–4). At its core, tutoring involves both cognitive processes and social relations, engaging tutor and tutee in the "active social mediation of individual learning" (p. 3). Tutoring is one of those strategies that is as contemporary as it is traditional.

Shanahan suggests that tutoring has acquired a narrower meaning in U.S. schools in recent years. Thus, although the spectrum of possible applications is very broad, most teachers will associate tutoring with remedial instruction delivered by a professional teacher, paraprofessional, parent, volunteer, or student.

Research on tutoring reveals findings that have implications for educational policy and practice (Shanahan, 1998). In the period from 1970 to 1985, most studies investigated the efficacy of peer or cross-age tutoring: children helping children. In the ensuing years, there has been considerable interest in tutoring as a part of specialized intervention programs for low-achieving children. Shanahan's review of research on the effectiveness and limitations of tutoring in reading indicates that although tutoring works, it should not be considered a panacea. Findings of particular interest to teachers are summarized in Figure 5.4.

1. *Tutoring is an effective strategy for improving academic achievement.* "Research clearly supports the use of many forms of tutoring with a wide range of students" at a variety of grade levels (pp. 220, 226).

2. *Peer tutoring can lead to significant gains in reading, math, and other areas* (p. 219).

3. *Tutoring does not always work.* "Tutoring programs usually lead to at least small residual gains in achievement beyond that accomplished through regular classroom instruction, but tutoring in no way guarantees improved learning. In establishing tutoring programs, care must be taken to ensure adequate time on tasks for students, high quality of instruction, and appropriateness of curriculum. Otherwise, tutoring can actually lead to lower rather than higher achievement " (p. 223).

4. *Tutoring works better for some students than others; at the individual level, outcomes will vary.* For certain low-achieving readers (even children in Reading Recovery programs), tutoring is not a particularly effective strategy (p. 223). However, for low achievers individual instruction seems more effective than group instruction as a whole (p. 229).

5. *Tutoring is not necessarily superior to other forms of intervention.* "Tutoring makes greater sense in the context of improvements designed to raise average achievement than solely as a method for helping just the lowest readers to attain average, but possibly mediocre, outcomes" (p. 225).

6. *Although widely used to help improve reading achievement, tutoring has generally been found to be more beneficial and consistent in areas of the curriculum other than reading (e.g., mathematics)* (p. 226). The influence of tutoring programs on reading achievement is often modest, and sometimes nil (p. 231). It has not been established whether tutoring is more effective with higher or lower level skills.

7. *Although interventions employing tutoring by peers, parents, and volunteers have been successful, the more significant gains were reported in those models using professional teachers as tutors* (p. 227). While training and experience enhances tutoring effectiveness, young children have been effective tutors in some programs (p. 230). In some situations, tutor training appears to be less critical if close and careful supervision and instructional guidance is provided by professional teachers (p. 228).

8. *Gains in learning may not remain stable over time; tutoring effectiveness appears to be dependent at least in part upon tutor knowledge and the supervision and management structure provided* (pp. 228–229). Some tutoring programs have reported greater gains in the short term, diminishing results over longer periods. Others require continued intervention over a longer period to sustain benefits. "With well-trained tutors working with a well-structured curriculum, it is possible to make longer tutoring programs effective even with nonprofessionals such as college students" (p. 229).

FIGURE 5.4   Research highlights: tutoring.

Source: Drawn from the review of literature by T. Shanahan. On the effectiveness and limitations of tutoring in reading. In P. D. Pearson and A. Iran-Nejad (Eds.), *Review of research in education,* Vol. 23 (pp. 217–234). Washington, DC: American Educational Research Association. 1998.

The positive cognitive and affective effects of peer tutoring can be as significant for tutors as tutees.

Tutoring has gained prominence as a strategy that helps students—including those at risk of school failure—attain individual, academic goals. As noted in the previous chapter, tutoring is an integral element in many of the alternative models used by schools that are moving away from more traditional approaches to ability grouping, tracking, and retention. From a teacher perspective, it is especially important that the cognitive and affective effects of tutoring can be as significant and positive for the tutors as for the tutees. When older students serve as tutors, the process often produces "achievement gains for the tutors as well as for the tutees" (Slavin, 1987, p. 113).

The positive role of tutoring in multicultural education has been well established with students across the spectrum of socioeconomic levels and ethnic backgrounds as well as those with learning disabilities (Bennett, 1986; Saunders, 1982). In a discussion about multicultural teaching in England, Saunders observed that cross-age tutoring enhances the identity and learning of children from minority groups. Advantages accrue to both tutor and tutee as basic skills are practiced and repeated, social interaction skills are fostered, and, in the case of bilingual students, language options are provided. Working in tandem, students can also share teaching responsibilities on a common learning task.

According to Jenkins and Jenkins (1987), research and experience suggest that the successful peer tutoring programs at the elementary and secondary levels are characterized by certain features. These include the features highlighted in Figure 5.5.

1. Use of highly structured and carefully prescribed lesson format.

2. Definition of objectives in terms of teachers' own classroom curricula and evaluations of student performance based upon those classroom materials.

3. Careful selection of tutoring content by teachers and monitoring to ensure that students achieve mastery.

4. Careful consideration of the frequency and duration of tutoring lessons.

5. Provision of systematic training for tutors.

6. Creation of a positive class climate and provision for active supervision.

7. Measurement of student progress on a daily basis.

FIGURE 5.5   Characteristics of successful peer-tutoring programs.
Source: Drawn from J. R. Jenkins and L. M. Jenkins. Making peer tutoring work. *Educational Leadership*, 1987, 44(6), 64–68.

SUMMARY

◇ Classrooms are socially and culturally organized learning environments in which the behaviors of and interplay between teachers and learners are paramount. The "hidden curriculum" enacted through classroom processes is evidenced in dimensions such as interaction, social context, management, and organization.

◇ Classroom interaction encompasses many interrelated patterns of teacher and student behavior. Teacher expectations are revealed to students verbally and nonverbally, directly and indirectly. The differential communication patterns that convey these expectations affect high and low achieving students—and those in between—in ways that influence academic performance and learners' self-perceptions. Cultural differences in norms of communication and differential patterns of treatment related to gender and ethnicity are two other factors that make each student's learning experience in the same classroom uniquely their own. Given the implications, teachers need to be cognizant of and monitor the interactional patterns in their classrooms.

◇ Language attitudes and student status are important dimensions of the social context within classrooms. Possibly the most powerful of social markers, language influences social identities, relationships between teachers and students, and academic achievement. In the eyes of teachers and peers, the status of students is determined by a combination of factors including academic achievement, individual traits, and sociocultural factors. Status attributions are related to expectations as to which learners are competent and successful and which are not. Status characteristics can be modified, to some extent, through positive evaluations, the presence of role models, and cooperative group activities.

◇ The challenge of addressing the wide range of student abilities and needs in heterogeneous classrooms demands that teachers approach management with an eye to curricular adaptation. This requires consideration of content, instructional strategies and settings, and student behaviors. Individually and in combination these elements are central to the process of accommodating diverse student requirements.

◇ Traditional classroom organization emphasizes individualistic, competitive values. However, alternative approaches to classroom organization, based on a cooperative orientation, can produce positive academic and social outcomes for nearly all students. Models for cooperative learning feature positively interdependent teams of students, individual accountability, and self-improvement.

◇ Cooperative learning and tutoring are two strategies that teachers can use to adapt organization in heterogeneous classrooms. Particularly effective with average and low achievers, cooperative learning is appropriate for diverse student populations and applicable across grade levels and subject areas. Peer tutoring also has been shown to provide significant cognitive and affective benefits for both tutors and tutees. It is an integral element in many of the alternative models used by schools that are moving away from more traditional approaches to ability grouping, tracking, and retention.

APPLICATION, EXTENSION, AND REFLECTION

1. *Classroom Interaction.* Using the Good and Brophy (1997) behaviors in Figure 5.1 as a guide, observe the classroom interaction between one or more teachers and their students. You may want to begin in your own classroom. Identify the most prominent behaviors and analyze the information collected. Reflect on the findings. Are teacher expectations reflected in the observed behaviors? If so, in what ways? Do your observations suggest that expectations are appropriately high for all students? Why or why not?

2. *Tutoring at Your School.* Use the characteristics of successful tutoring programs as a guideline for examining how tutoring is used in your school. What are the strongest features of your program? What specific areas need to be improved? What kinds of changes would you recommend? Consider the process by which such changes might be implemented?

3. *Competitive, Individualistic, and Cooperative Structures.* Ask several teachers for their perspectives on the relative advantages and disadvantages of competitive, individualistic, and cooperative structures. Which structures have been most effective for their students? Why? Which structures do students seem to prefer? In what ways does the choice of structure affect student performance?

REFERENCES

Ames, C. (1984). Competitive, cooperative and individualistic goal structures: A cognitive-motivational analysis. In R. Ames & C. Ames (Eds.), *Research on motivation in education,* Vol. 1 (pp. 177–207). Orlando, FL: Academic Press.

Ames, C., & Ames, R. (1984). Goal structures and motivation. *The Elementary School Journal, 85*(1), 39–52.

Au, K. Hu-Pei, & Jordan, C. (1981). Teaching reading to Hawaiian children: Finding a culturally appropriate solution. In H. T. Trueba, G. P. Guthrie, & K. Hu-Pei Au (Eds.), *Culture and the bilingual classroom* (pp. 139–152). Rowley, MA: Newbury House.

Ball, S. (1984). Student motivation: Some reflections and projections. In R. Ames & C. Ames (Eds.), *Research on motivation in education,* Vol. 1 (pp. 313–327). Orlando, FL: Academic Press.

Beebe, L. M. (Ed.). (1988). *Issues in second language acquisition.* New York: Newbury House.

Bennett, C. I. (1986). *Comprehensive multicultural education.* Boston: Allyn and Bacon.

Brophy, J. E. (1985). Interactions of male and female students with male and female teachers. In L. C. Wilkinson & C. B. Marrett (Eds.), *Gender influences in classroom interaction* (pp. 115–142). Orlando, FL: Academic Press.

Cazden, C. B. (1986). Classroom discourse. In M. C. Wittrock (Ed.), *Handbook of research on teaching* (3rd ed., pp. 432–463). New York: Macmillan.

Chaika, E. (1982). *Language: The social mirror.* Rowley, MA: Newbury House.

Cohen, E. G. (1982). Expectation states and interracial interaction in school settings. *Annual Review of Sociology, 8,* 209–235.

Cohen, E. G. (1986). *Designing groupwork.* New York: Teachers College Press.

Cooper, H., & Tom, D. Y. H. (1984). Socioeconomic status and ethnic group differences in achievement motivation. In R. Ames & C. Ames (Eds.), *Research in motivation in education,* Vol. 1 (pp. 209–242). Orlando, FL: Academic Press.

Eggleston, J. (1977). *The sociology of the school curriculum.* London: Routledge & Kegan Paul.

Erickson, F. (1981). Some approaches to inquiry in school-community ethnography. In H. T. Trueba, G. P. Guthrie, & K. Hu-Pei Au (Eds.), *Culture and the bilingual classroom* (pp. 17–35). Rowley, MA: Newbury House.

Erickson, F. (1986). Qualitative methods in research on teaching. In M. C. Wittrock (Ed.), *Handbook of research on teaching* (3rd ed., pp. 119–161). New York: Macmillan.

Gay, G. (1996). A multicultural school curriculum. In C. A. Grant & M. L. Gomez (Eds.), *Making schooling multicultural: Campus and classroom* (pp. 37–54). Englewood Cliffs, NJ: Merrill/Prentice Hall.

Gollnick, D. M., & Chinn, P. C. (1994). *Multicultural education in a pluralistic society* (4th ed.). New York: Merrill.

Good, T. L. (1981). Teacher expectations and student perceptions: A decade of research. *Educational Leadership, 38*(5), 415–422.

Good, T. L., & Brophy, J. E. (1997). *Looking in classrooms.* 7th ed. New York: Longman.

Hall, W. S., & Guthrie, L. F. (1981). Cultural and situational variation in language function and use—Methods and procedures for research. In J. L. Green & C. Wallat (Eds.), *Ethnography and language in educational settings* (pp. 209–228). Norwood, NJ: Ablex Publishing Co.

Heath, S. B. (1983). *Way with words.* New York: Cambridge University Press.

Hoover, J. J., & Collier, C. (1986). *Classroom management through curricular adaptations.* Lindale, TX: Hamilton Publications.

Hymes, D. (1981). Ethnographic monitoring. In H. T. Trueba, G. P. Guthrie, & K. Hu-Pei Au (Eds.), *Culture and the bilingual classroom* (pp. 56–68). Rowley, MA: Newbury House.

Jenkins, J. R., & Jenkins, L. M. (1987). Making peer tutoring work. *Educational Leadership, 44*(6), 64–68.

Kagan, S. (1986). Cooperative learning and sociocultural factors in schooling. In *Beyond language: Social and cultural factors in schooling language minority students* (pp. 231–298). Los Angeles: Evaluation, Dissemination and Assessment Center, California State University—Los Angeles.

Kjolseth, R. (1982). Bilingual education programs in the United States. In P. R. Turner (Ed.), *Bilingualism in the Southwest* (2nd ed., pp. 3–28). Tucson: University of Arizona Press.

Ladson-Billings, G. (1994). *The dreamkeepers: Successful teachers of African American children.* San Francisco, CA: Jossey-Bass.

Lambert, W. E., Hodgson, R. C., Gardner, R. C., and Fillenbaum, S. (1972). Attitudinal and cognitive aspects of intensive study of a second language. In R. C. Gardner & W. E. Lambert, *Attitudes and motivation in second-language learning* (pp. 293–305). Rowley, MA: Newbury House.

Legarreta-Marcaida, D. (1981). Effective use of the primary language in the classroom. *Schooling and language minority students: A theoretical framework* (pp. 83–116). Developed by California State Department of Education Office of Bilingual Bicultural Education Sacramento, CA. Published by Evaluation, Dissemination and Assessment Center, California State University—Los Angeles, CA.

LeMoine, N. (1993, August 8). *Mainstream English as a second language: Focus on linguistically different African American students.* Paper presented at the Tenth Annual Summer Seminar for Foreign Language Teachers, University of California, Santa Barbara.

Lee, C. D., and Slaughter-DeFoe, D. T. (1995). *Historical and sociocultural influences on African American education.* In J. A. Banks (Ed.) and C. A. McGee Banks (Assoc. Ed.), *Handbook of research on Multicultural education* (pp. 348–371). New York: Macmillan.

Lewis, A. C. (1999). Washington Commentary, Time for schools to perform. *Phi Delta Kappan, 81*(2), 99–100.

Lindow, J., Marrett, C. B., & Wilkinson, L. C. (1985). Overview. In L. C. Wilkinson & C. B. Marrett (Eds.), *Gender influences in classroom interactions.* Orlando, FL: Academic Press.

Longstreet, W. S. (1978). *Aspects of ethnicity.* New York: Teachers College Press.

Mehan, H. (1988, April). Teacher education issues session. Linguistic Minority Project Conference, Sacramento, CA.

Mohatt, G., & Erickson, F. (1981). Cultural differences in teaching styles in an Odawa school: A sociolinguistic approach. In H. T. Trueba, G. P. Guthrie, & K. Hu-Pei Au (Eds.), *Culture and the bilingual classroom* (pp. 105–119). Rowley, MA: Newbury House.

Morine-Dershimer, G. (1985). *Talking, listening, and learning in elementary classrooms.* New York: Longman.

National Institute of Education (1974). *Teaching as a linguistic process in a cultural setting: Conference on Studies in Teaching, Panel 5.* Washington, DC: National Institute of Education.

Peñalosa, F. (1980). *Chicano sociolinguistics.* Rowley, MA: Newbury House.

Philips, S. U. (1983). *The invisible culture.* Research on Teaching Monograph Series. New York: Longman.

Putnam, JoAnne, (1997). *Cooperative learning in diverse classrooms.* Upper Saddle River, NJ: Merrill/Prentice-Hall.

Ramírez, A. G. (1985). *Bilingualism through schooling: Cross-cultural education for minority and majority students.* Albany: State University of New York Press.

Rosenthal, R., & Babad, E. (1985). Pygmalion in the gymnasium. *Educational Leadership, 43*(1), 36–39.

Sadker, M. P., & Sadker, D. M. (1982). *Sex equity handbook for schools.* New York: Longman.

Sadker, M. P., & Sadker, D. M. (1986). Sexism in the classroom: From grade school to graduate school. *Phi Delta Kappan, 67* (7), 512–515.

Sadker, M. P., Sadker, D. M., & Klein, S. (1991). The issue of gender in elementary and secondary education. In G. Grant (Ed.), *Review of research in education,* Vol. 17 (pp. 269–334). Washington, DC: American Educational Research Association.

Sadker, M. P., Sadker, D. M., & Long, L. (1997). Gender and educational equality. In J. A. Banks & C. A. McGee Banks (Eds.), *Multicultural education: Issues and perspectives* (3rd ed., pp. 131–149). Boston, MA: Allyn and Bacon.

Salomon, G., & Perkins, D. N. (1998). Individual and social aspects of learning. In P. D. Pearson and A. Iran-Nejad (Eds.), *Review of research in education,* Vol. 23 (pp. 1–24). Washington, DC: American Educational Research Association.

Saunders, M. (1982). *Multicultural teaching.* London: McGraw-Hill.

Schwanke, D. (1980). Interracial classroom interaction: A review of selected literature. *Journal of Classroom Interaction, 15*(2), 11–14.

Shanahan, T. (1998). On the effectiveness and limitations of tutoring in reading. In P. D. Pearson and A. Iran-Nejad (Eds.), *Review of research in education,* Vol. 23 (pp. 217–234). Washington, DC: American Educational Research Association.

Shulman, L. (1986). Paradigms and research programs in the study of teaching: A contemporary perspective. In M. C. Wittrock (Ed.), *Handbook of research on teaching* (3rd ed., pp. 3–36). New York: Macmillan.

Slavin, R. E. (1981). Synthesis of research on cooperative learning. *Educational Leadership, 38* (8), 655–660.

Slavin, R. E. (1987). Making Chapter 1 make a difference. *Phi Delta Kappan, 69*(2), 110–119.

Stewart, E. C. (1979). American assumptions and values: Orientation to action. In E. C. Smith & L. F. Luce (Eds.), *Toward internationalism* (pp. 1–22). Rowley, MA: Newbury House. (Reprinted from *American Cultural Patterns: A Cross-Cultural Perspective,* 1972; copyright by Edward C. Stewart.)

Stubbs, M. 1976. *Language, schools and classrooms.* London: Methuen.

U.S. Commission on Civil Rights. (1973). *Teachers and students. Report V: Mexican American education study.* Washington, DC: U.S. Government Printing Office.

Wilkinson, L. C. (1981). Analysis of teacher-student interaction: Expectations communicated by conversational structure. In J. L. Green and C. Wallat (Eds.), *Ethnography and language in educational settings* (pp. 253–268). Norwood, NJ: Ablex Publishing Co.

PART
IV
CONTENT

Textbooks and Other Instructional Materials

*Curriculum materials profoundly affect learners and their
learning—in the way they view themselves and their social
groups; . . . in the way they are motivated to work and play
and learn and live.*

M. Rosenberg (p. 44)

Implementation of a multicultural curriculum requires instructional materials that reflect the diverse character of American society. The "density of
diversity"—to borrow from Cortés (1981a)—is a reality in the twenty-first
century, one that cannot be ignored. At the national level, the U.S. population is
becoming increasingly diverse along many dimensions, including ethnicity. On
a global scale, interdependence is a major characteristic of relationships among
nations and peoples of the world. Students' knowledge of and attitudes toward
people in other parts of the world have greater implications than ever. Moreover, as students from all ethnic groups find themselves in classrooms with

students whose backgrounds are considerably different from their own, "global understanding and related intercultural sensitivity attain a growing significance here at home, as well as in our relations with the rest of the world" (Cortés & Fleming, 1986a, p. 384).

Although teachers cannot control what students know and learn about diversity, they will have to deal with it. It's inescapable. The purpose of this chapter is to assist teachers in looking at textbooks and other instructional materials with an eye to dealing with diversity. Because of the centrality of textbooks and other materials in the teaching of content, teachers must be aware of the inherent attitudes, values, and perspectives these materials convey to students. Skills are needed to examine and analyze materials for manifestations of bias—overt and covert—toward various ethnic, gender, class, age, religious, and other groups. Teachers should attempt to provide students with accurate, fair, and objective representations of diverse groups in content, illustrations, and language. They should also help students develop the skills needed to be critical users of instructional materials.

TEXTBOOKS: DIVERSITY AND CONTROVERSY

Instructional materials in general and textbooks in particular are central to the educational process. In the nineteenth century, reliance upon textbooks set U.S. schools apart from the educational establishment in other countries. An estimated 80–90% of the school curriculum is based upon textbooks (Honig, 1985). Textbook-oriented activities account for about 75% of all classwork and 90% of all homework. By the time students complete high school, they will have read about 32,000 textbook pages (Black, cited in U.S. Commission on Civil Rights, 1980). Altbach (1991) accounts for the preeminence of textbooks, explaining that "they are the least expensive, most reliable means of transmitting knowledge and providing coherence to the curriculum" (p. 237). Textbooks significantly influence the very nature of education by defining what constitutes legitimate knowledge, and by influencing what is taught in the schools and how (p. 243). This has political and social ramifications well beyond the obvious educational implications.

Public Concern Over Textbook Content

Historically, textbooks have been a focal point of public attention. This is understandable when one considers the political, social, cultural, and economic content, values, and beliefs that textbooks convey. Following World War I, for example, the mayor of Chicago and the Hearst newspapers led a major public protest over charges of pro-British bias in history texts. To please critics, one author is said to have offered to change part of his account of the battle of Bunker Hill, transforming "Three times the British returned courageously to the attack" into "Three times the cowardly British returned to the attack"

It is estimated that 80–90% of the school curriculum is based upon textbooks.

(FitzGerald, 1979, p. 35). According to FitzGerald, over the years the range of issues exciting public interest has varied from emphasizing military history and temperance to promoting the interests of utilities, advertising, and industry; in science, protests over evolutionary theory—past and present—have been well publicized and documented.

How different groups are portrayed in textbooks has also been a concern for many years. In 1939, the National Association for the Advancement of Colored People (NAACP) issued a statement highly critical of the treatment of Blacks in textbooks. A decade later the American Council on Education undertook the first major study of how minorities were being portrayed. Depictions were found to be "distressingly inadequate, inappropriate, and even damaging to intergroup relations" (cited in Kane, 1970, p. 1). In the same period, an examination of reading textbooks indicated that females were also underrepresented and stereotyped (Child, Potter, & Levine, cited in U.S. Commission on Civil Rights, 1980).

With the civil rights and women's movements of the 1960s, awareness turned to action. This period was marked by the first successful, large-scale protests by minority groups. In 1962, the Detroit Board of Education withdrew a textbook because it was racially biased against Blacks; a short time later, the Newark Textbook Council took a similar action. Native Americans, Mexican Americans, Puerto Ricans, Asian Americans, Armenian Americans, and others soon protested biased textbook portrayals in school districts across the nation (FitzGerald, 1979; U.S. Commission on Civil Rights, 1980). In the ensuing years, individuals, groups, and organizations undertook literally hundreds of studies analyzing textbooks. Attention also focused on how textbooks portrayed older persons, religious minorities, and people with disabilities.

Today, the proposition that the United States is a multicultural, multilingual, and multiracial society and should be represented as such in textbooks has gained greater acceptance. State laws to ensure fair textbooks, although not always enforced, have been enacted. A multitude of guidelines have been drafted and implemented by those selecting, evaluating, and developing textbooks and other instructional materials. Although recent studies show that textbooks published in recent decades are more accurate, fair, and objective than those from previous decades, they also reveal areas in which bias persists (e.g., Wieder, 1997). Hence, it is imperative that teachers regard instructional materials from a multicultural perspective, with a critical eye to the multiple messages they convey.

Effect of Textbooks on Student Attitudes and Achievement

How minorities, women, and members of other groups are treated in textbooks is of considerable importance to teachers. If textbooks taught only "factual information," their impact on students' attitudes and beliefs would be limited, their content less controversial. In reality, however, textbooks also influence ideas and transmit "officially-sanctioned" cultural values. "The words and pictures children see in school influence the development of the attitudes they carry into adult life. These words and pictures not only express ideas—they are part of the educational experience which shapes ideas" (Association of American Publishers, 1984, n.p.).

The United States Commission on Civil Rights (1980) examined the treatment of minorities, women, religious groups, and the elderly in textbooks. In its review of research on the effects of textbooks, the Commission found studies indicating that textbooks affect student attitudes; personality development and behavior; academic achievement; and career aspirations and attainment.

The influence of textbooks on student attitudes is significant. It appears, not surprisingly, that children's attitudes are affected by what they read. Perceptions of specific minorities are influenced by whether the treatment in reading material is positive or negative. Favorable stories engender more positive attitudes, unfavorable stories more negative perceptions. This also applies to attitudes toward cultural pluralism in general. In one study, for example, the attitudes of 6- and 7-year-old children exposed to different types of reading material were compared. Materials emphasizing cultural pluralism promoted acceptance of diversity as normal. Those reflecting what was described as a "culturally parochial" viewpoint reinforced existing prejudicial attitudes (Trager & Yarrow, cited in Saunders, 1982). It appears that children recognize a story for what it is but absorb without question "the values and attitudes of the author" (Klein, 1985, p. 14).

How children react to characterizations in textbooks is influenced by a number of factors, according to studies cited in U.S. Commission on Civil Rights

Textbooks can influence student attitudes, personality development, and behavior; academic achievement; and career aspirations and attainment.

(1980). First, the extent to which attitudes and stereotypes are internalized and retained seems to be determined, at least in part, by the amount of time spent interacting with materials. As one would suspect, the longer the contact, the greater the effect. Second, children vary in their emotional involvement and identification with individuals and situations portrayed. In reading, mathematics, and social studies, for example, student performance is enhanced when content is perceived to be relevant and interesting. On the positive side, culturally relevant materials can facilitate the process of learning to read, making it both easier and faster. On the negative side, the absence of characters and situations with which children are able to identify may contribute to and reinforce feelings of insecurity, inferiority, or superiority depending upon an individual's group identity. These nonacademic aspects of textbook content affect variables associated with academic achievement (e.g., motivation, retention, and skills development).

Finally, the career aspirations and attainment of students are sensitive to representations in textbooks ranging from messages about occupational interests (especially for girls, minorities, and children from low-income backgrounds) to perceptions related to future employment and expectations for success. What students see and don't see in teaching materials affects the way in which they define the possibilities and opportunities available to them. Rosenberg (1974) summed up these effects on students as follows:

> [Instructional] materials are relevant to the students' life experiences, or they are not. These materials give the students the clear feeling that this education is intended for them, or it is not. These materials make the students aware that they are part of the mainstream of American education and American life, or that they are not. (p. 44)

Bias in Instructional Materials

In that textbooks and other instructional materials inevitably reflect a point of view—a particular perspective that determines what is to be included and how material is to be presented to a specific student population—all are biased. The bias may be positive or negative, intentional or unintentional, subtle or pronounced. Such bias often reflects particular social and cultural values and beliefs associated with ethnicity, gender, religion, class, age, region, and exceptionality.

In recent decades, many forms of bias in educational materials have been reduced significantly. A teacher need only compare contemporary textbooks with those of a generation ago to see that important changes have taken place. Even though current texts are generally more accurate and representative of cultural diversity, however, problems remain: some groups continue to be underrepresented; imbalances, omissions, and problems with perspective still exist. As a result, ongoing evaluation of educational materials is as relevant and necessary today as in the past. Teachers using newer textbooks and other materials need to be aware of the persistence of more subtle forms of bias; those using older instructional materials must also be sensitive to the presence of more overt forms of bias.

Under ideal circumstances, replacement cycles would provide current textbooks in every classroom. Unfortunately, timely replacements are not a reality in all schools; outdated and obsolete texts often remain in use years beyond "retirement" age (Luty, 1982). Thus, teachers are likely to encounter examples of social and cultural bias that have disappeared from more contemporary texts. In addition, teachers using classical works of children's and adolescent literature or original historical documents need to consider how these and similar materials reflect the attitudes and values of the period in which they were written.

Types of Bias

Bias in textbooks and other instructional materials is conveyed in several different ways. The intent of this section is to help teachers recognize four of the most common forms of bias: inaccuracy, stereotyping, omissions and distortions, and biased language usage.

Inaccuracy

Sometimes the information contained in textbooks is simply inaccurate, undocumented, or untrustworthy (also known as "lies and cherished myths"). This remains an important issue, most specifically with respect to history textbooks (Loewen, 1996; Shenkman, 1988, 1991). As Loewen observes, "only in history is accuracy so political" (p. 292).

To illustrate his point, Loewen writes a collective account on Christopher Columbus based upon content traditionally found in American history textbooks. He italicizes only those pieces of historical information he believes to be true and verifiable:

Born in Genoa, of humble parents, *Christopher Columbus grew up to become an experienced seafarer, venturing as far as Iceland and West Africa.* His adventures convinced him that the world must be round and that the fabled riches of the East—spices and gold—could be had by sailing west, superseding the overland routes, which the Turks had closed off to commerce. *To get funding for his enterprise, he beseeched monarch after monarch in Western Europe.* After at first being dismissed by Ferdinand and Isabella of Spain, Columbus finally got his chance when *Isabella decided to underwrite a* modest *expedition. Columbus outfitted three* pitifully small *ships, the Niña, the Pinta, and the Santa María, and set forth from Spain. After an* arduous *journey* of more than two months, during which his mutinous crew almost threw him overboard, Columbus discovered the *West Indies on October 12, 1492.* Unfortunately, although *he made three more voyages to America,* he never knew he had discovered a New World. *Columbus died* in obscurity, unappreciated and penniless. Yet without his daring *American history would have been very different,* for in a sense he made it all possible. (p. 54)

Although you wouldn't know it from the "authoritative" accounts presented in most textbooks, many of the controversies surrounding the life of Christopher Columbus have never been resolved by historians, and much of the information in traditional accounts is either wrong or unverifiable. On this topic, Loewen (1996) characterizes what passes for history in most textbooks as a concoction of lies, half-truths, facts, and omissions (p. 39). The traditional account is more than inaccurate, however. By comparison, the myth makes the real story seem trivial and simplistic. It obfuscates the real significance of events leading up to 1492, and the profound cultural changes set in motion on that date. A more accurate historical account is compelling, complex, emotional, contradictory, but never boring. It depicts human beings at their best and at their worst.

Stereotyping

Before proceeding, take a moment to complete the following sentences with the first words that come to mind:

Girls are _____.
Boys are _____.
Older persons are _____.
Members of group X are _____.

How did you respond? If children were asked to complete these sentences with information gleaned only from their textbooks, which, if any, specific attributes and characteristics do you think would prevail?

The presence of stereotyping in textbooks has been well documented. *Stereotyping* occurs when all individuals in a particular group are depicted as having the same attributes; the result is that diversity *within* groups is obscured, whereas differences between them are exaggerated (Klein, 1985). In textbooks, stereotyping has been common in the portrayal of ethnic minorities, women, elderly persons, and members of other groups. For example, Native Americans have been stereotyped as warlike; Puerto Ricans, as violent and poor. Stereo-typing by role has been particularly widespread in reading materials (e.g., Blacks depicted only in service work, sports, and entertainment). Depictions provide for limited development of characters, and a narrow range of activities, occupations, and experiences (U.S. Commission on Civil Rights, 1980). Al-though there is less stereotyping now than in the past, it has not yet disappeared (Sadker, Sadker, & Klein, 1991).

Omissions and Distortions

In this context, *omission* refers to information left out of an account presented in a textbook. *Distortions* often result from the lack of balance occasioned by sys-tematic omissions. Because of omission, members of certain groups have re-mained virtually "invisible" in textbooks. Even today, efforts at inclusion and integration have been more balanced and thorough for some groups than oth-ers. Hispanic Americans, Asian Americans, Native Americans, and women con-tinue to be among those commonly underrepresented in educational materials. As an example, one student's analysis of a widely used U.S. history text at the college level revealed a generic entry in the index for "women," but no coun-terpart for "men."

When the impression conveyed through the omission of information is in-accurate or unbalanced, distortions occur. For example, history and reading ma-terials that ignore the presence and realities of certain groups in contemporary society, confine treatment to negative experiences, or provide only a single point of view on events and issues may be technically correct but nevertheless mis-leading. What is left unsaid can be as important as the information actually pre-sented. For example, the use of general referents (e.g., Native American, His-panic American, Asian American) when the specific names of ethnic groups or Native nations (e.g., Navajo, Hopi, Mexican American, Cuban American, Puerto Rican, Japanese American, Chinese American) are called for gives a false im-pression of uniformity in heritage, culture, values, and beliefs.

Biased Language Usage

Specific aspects of language usage can convey bias in subtle, often unintended ways. Of particular importance in relation to textbook bias are the nuances of meaning associated with particular words, selection of proper nouns to refer to groups, and the gender attitudes reflected in language.

Words or phrases with the same denotative meaning often convey quite dif-ferent connotations reflecting positive or negative evaluations or an implicit viewpoint. For example, the impression created about a particular group differs substantially depending on whether members are referred to as "terrorists" or "freedom fighters." In many situations, several different words or phrases can be used to identify or denote the same referent, and the writer's specific choice of words carries meaning above and beyond simple identification.

Descriptions of conflicts are particularly sensitive to word choice: the "Yom Kippur War" and the "Ramadan War" refer to the same conflict; and religious differences dictate whether Richard the Lionhearted battled in a "Christian Crusade" or Saladin in an "Islamic Holy War" (Griswold, 1986). Did the European powers "colonize" or "invade" the Americas? (Cruz-Janzen, 1998). In terms of U.S. history, consider the different perspectives embodied in the terms "Civil War," "the Rebellion," and "War Between the States." What about Bull Run and Manassas (First and Second)? Antietam and Sharpsburg? How many students realize that the same battles were given different names by the armies involved—one side using adjacent towns, the other the streams that marked the landscape?

Other good examples of the influence of word choice can be found in accounts of the outcomes of struggles for basic rights and independence. The difference between women being "given" the right to vote as opposed to their "winning" it is perhaps subtle, but definitely significant (Gollnick, Sadker, & Sadker, 1982). Such differences in connotation also occur in descriptions of national independence movements, in which colonial powers "give" or "grant" independence as opposed to people having struggled to achieve or regain their freedom (Crofts, 1986).

In some instances, proper names have not been used appropriately in identifying certain peoples. In essence, the name people use to refer to themselves is replaced by one ascribed to them by others. With respect to groups of people in Africa, for example, the San have often been referred to as Bushmen. The latter term, however, comes from the Afrikaans "boesman," and is a name Europeans gave to the people they encountered in the bush (Klein, 1985). Similarly, the Mbuti and Khoi peoples have often been referred to as Pygmies and Hottentots (Bennett, 1986).

Language has been described as a "social mirror" (Chaika, 1982). It is not the cause of societal attitudes but rather a reflection of the prevailing and changing attitudes and realities of society. Teachers can demonstrate one effect of linguistic bias relating to gender by asking students to draw an "early caveman" (Gollnick et al., 1982). The completed drawings are then examined to see whether males or females are portrayed and the types of activities represented. The results of such an exercise generally suggest that terms traditionally considered generic are apparently less all-encompassing than once assumed, at least in the minds of children. For example, especially at the elementary school level, children given this task draw only pictures of cavemen. In contrast, when instructed to draw "cave people," the children generate drawings of men, women, and children. In classrooms, teachers can point out to students words that appear to exclude women as full participants in society or to limit their occupational options. This includes sensitivity to occupational terms (e.g., mail carrier and police officer as alternatives to mailman and policeman) and use of the generic *he* pronoun (Gollnick et al., 1982).

Although considerable attention has been focused on avoiding language that stereotypes and deprecates women (e.g., pronouns, job titles/descriptions, expressions), it should be noted that concern has also been expressed regarding language-bias that denigrates males (August, 1992; The University of Wisconsin, 1992). August takes issue with anti-male usage, language that he regards as gender-exclusive (e.g., *mammal, alma mater, mother tongue*), gender-restrictive (e.g., *coward, nerd*), and promoting negative male stereotypes (e.g., the masculinization of crime and evil).

Portrayal of Various Groups

In addition to the forms of bias just described, teachers also need to be cognizant of group-specific concerns regarding treatment in textbooks and other instructional materials. As members of multiple groups defined according to ethnicity, gender, class, and other dimensions, students may be sensitive about how the groups to which they belong are depicted in history, literature, and other areas of the curriculum. Teachers, however, need a broader awareness, one that provides the basis for incorporating content reflecting this diversity.

In 1980, the U.S. Commission on Civil Rights reviewed hundreds of studies on the treatment of minorities, religious groups, older persons, and females in textbooks. The findings of the Commission are summarized in Figure 6.1.

More recently, Sleeter and Grant examined social studies, reading/language arts, science, and mathematics textbooks used in grades 1–8. Copyright dates for the textbooks they analyzed were from 1980 to 1988. They determined that the "treatment of diversity in textbooks has not improved much over the past fifteen years or so, generally, although a few textbooks have improved in specific limited ways" (cited in Grant & Tate, 1995, p. 149). Grant and Tate's review of various studies of textbook bias related to sexism indicates that while the presence of females has increased, males still dominate. The portrayal of some women in nontraditional roles is still offset by roles that are frequently stereotyped. They argue that "females continue to serve as the index to frame what is considered a male role. That is, males are active, and do science, business, and athletics, whereas females are active and passive, and do art and science, language and math, and cheerleading" (p. 149).

History Textbooks

Studies of textbooks in the 1980s suggest both change and persistence in some of the patterns outlined in Figure 6.1. A study of U.S. history textbooks by Davis, Ponder, Burlbaw, Garza-Lubeck, & Moss (1986) rated most 1986 texts as very good and some as excellent. These researchers found that although the United States was consistently presented in a positive light, the country's history was described in human terms with credibility and generally without obscuring the blemishes. On the other hand, the treatment of minorities (specifically, Hispanics, Asians, and Native Americans) and women continued to perpetuate "their invisible roles in building this nation" (Davis et al., p. 51). These researchers call for greater recognition of women in history textbooks and more emphasis on the roles of ordinary women in America's development:

Blacks

◇ Persistence of stereotypes in occupational roles, primarily in service work, sports, and entertainment
◇ Continued tendency to present romanticized versions of Black life
◇ Avoidance or denial of the actual conditions in which many Blacks have lived
◇ "Token" representation

Native Americans

◇ Inclusion limited primarily to historical contexts
◇ Rarely depicted in contemporary settings
◇ Failure to present the rich intragroup diversity of cultures and traditions
◇ Failure to include the group's own perspective of its history and cultures in accounts of events and experiences

Hispanics (Puerto Ricans and Mexican Americans)

◇ Generally depicted as living in poverty in segregated neighborhoods
◇ Frequent associations of both groups with violence

Asian and Pacific Island Americans

◇ Depictions in reading and social studies textbooks often stereotypic and limited
◇ Representations of contemporary Asian Americans promoting the image of a "model minority"
◇ Occupational roles most commonly portrayed are service work (e.g., laundry, culinary skills) and railroads

Religious Groups

◇ Rarely depicted

Older Persons

◇ Portrayed in children's literature mostly by images of individuals described as little, old, and poor; individuals neither as healthy nor as self-reliant as younger adults
◇ Failure to feature a full range of behaviors and roles; employment limited to a number of occupations, mostly service-related
◇ Impression that old age is not an enjoyable time of life

Females

◇ Central characters in stories with themes of dependency and domesticity; portrayed in a limited range of occupational roles
◇ Some stereotyping in mathematics texts (particularly in word problems and illustrations) but less than in past
◇ In science, indications of stereotyping in types of activities and occupations (e.g., girls cast more often in the role of observers rather than scientists, as recipients rather than initiators of actions)

FIGURE 6.1 Portrayal of groups in U.S. textbooks before 1980.
Source: U.S. Commission on Civil Rights, 1980.

Textbooks must portray how women have engaged in the roles they have, how they have influenced and participated in the great sweep of historical events, and how they have felt and feel about their lives. The ever-changing roles that average as well as exceptional women have played in our society are no less important to our nation's development than those of ordinary as well as exceptional men. (Davis et al., 1986, p. 52)

Others also are challenging traditional historical perspectives and conceptualizations. In an analysis of high school history textbooks, Tetreault (1984, 1986) found that women were indeed incorporated in the textbooks examined. However, these accounts inevitably emphasized contributions, movements, and events limited to the public arena. What is needed, Tetreault argues, is an approach that would integrate the experiences of men and women into a more holistic view of the human experience. Knowledge of events in the public sphere would be balanced with greater knowledge of the private sphere. Such an approach would avoid the impression that the relationship of men and women throughout American history has been an adversarial one.

The content of history textbooks continues to be the subject of considerable controversy. In California, for example, seven of the nine history textbooks submitted by publishers for state adoption failed to meet criteria addressing diversity (Reinhold, cited in Grant & Tate, 1995, p. 149). In her criticism of content, King (cited in Grant & Tate, 1995, p. 149) found that the textbooks were limited in their representations of diverse ethnic groups. They had inaccurate information, racial stereotypes, and negative representations of African American people; and were biased with regard to omissions and distortions.

Moreover, more recent national efforts to institutionalize the study of history from multiple perspectives have met with strong resistance. McGee Banks' (1999) account of what happened to the National History Standards (NHS) is illustrative. Despite strong support from the American Historical Association and the Organization of American Historians, the version of history standards published in 1996 was subjected to such attack by critics objecting to the attention accorded "women and people of color" and the emphasis on "what was negative in America's past" and on " 'politically correct' culture and causes" that the standards were eventually "officially repudiated" by Congress:

The attacks on the history standards helped to maintain the established history curriculum and to halt efforts to legitimize the histories, voices, and experiences of groups who traditionally have been excluded from school history. (p. 89)

With respect to religious groups, studies representing both liberal and conservative views have agreed that textbooks "largely ignore the importance of religion and religious freedom in U.S. history and life" (American School Board Journal, 1987, p. 46). Overall, references to contemporary religious events, church state issues, and the concept of religious liberty (except during the colonial period) are rare or nonexistent. One study characterized the general treatment of religion in history textbooks as brief and simplistic at best, exclusionary at worst: "Honest treatment of religion in American history seems to be equated with advocacy of particular religious ideas and practices" (Davis et al., 1986, p. 50).

Textbooks and literary works inevitably reflect the attitudes and values of the period in which they were written.

Reading Materials

Some researchers have focused upon the treatment of minority groups and women in reading materials. García and Florez-Tighe (1986) analyzed the portrayal of three minority groups—Blacks, Hispanics and Native Americans—in basal readers. They concluded that the percentage levels of minority content were acceptable but that the portrayals were less than fully accurate and balanced. There seemed to be a tendency, for example, to overrepresent members of minority groups in certain contexts (e.g., Hispanics in rural settings; Native Americans as a pre-Columbian phenomenon).

A review by Bordelon (1985) of studies on sexism in reading materials suggests that basal material in the 1970s and 1980s reflected more equal male-female representation than in the past but no substantial changes in the nature of female activities. Independence, initiative, strength, and ambition remained exclusively male traits. Others also have found changes in the numbers of minorities and females depicted as major characters but not in the types of choices presented as career role models (Britton & Lumpkin, 1984). Although the proportion of female to male central characters in basal readers had more than doubled since the 1960s, the ratio in the 1980s was still not representative of the population as a whole.

It should be noted that teachers must also take cultural considerations into account in dealing with some of the values and attitudes inherent in the changes reflected in today's instructional materials. For some students, for example, the nonsexist orientation emphasized in current children's literature may reflect a set of values incompatible with those in their traditional home community

(Cantoni-Harvey, 1987). In such communities, Cantoni-Harvey observes, boys may be reticent to participate in activities involving cooking and dishwashing, and girls may find it difficult to identify with female characters aspiring to non-traditional roles. She suggests that teachers faced with such situations may want to explain that although equality of the sexes is valued in American society, family members can establish and enact the roles they feel are most appropriate for themselves from the many options available.

Ethnocentric Perspectives: Effects and Limitations

Ethnocentrism is the belief that one's culture is superior to the cultures of others and that the perspective it provides is the optimal platform from which to view and evaluate other people. Because members of all groups tend to perceive their own culture as primary and superior, ethnocentrism is not unique to any particular cultural groups. The essence of an ethnocentric's attitude is captured in the following description: "The ethnocentric says: our religion is the only true one, our language is more refined, our material objects are more sophisticated, our artifacts are more beautiful, we have better clothes, food, literature and theatre" (Preiswerk, cited in Klein, 1985, p. 59).

Educators face a troublesome paradox in dealing with ethnocentrism in the classroom. At one end of the spectrum, as García (1984) notes, ethnocentrism can reflect a "mild ethnic pride," which may be "benevolent" and a positive, cohesive societal force. However, taken to extremes, ethnocentrism has negative social implications, which often are manifested as stereotyping, bias, and discrimination. In response to this paradox, García (1984) suggests that teachers "learn to understand the many forms of ethnocentrism; through understanding perhaps we can better control ethnocentrism among ourselves and our students" (pp. 105–106).

Ethnocentrism can be perpetuated in textbooks and other instructional materials in ways that may be difficult for teachers to recognize. After all, a perspective consonant with one's own attitudes and values is likely to be accepted at face value and not be questioned. It may not even occur to teachers that another perspective even exists. Geography provides some interesting examples. The common terminology used to refer to regions of the world still reflects Eurocentric views: "When the British Empire stood at the heart of matters geographical, the Holy Land was 'Near,' the Persians were 'Middle,' and India and China were 'Far' east of the Greenwich Meridian" (Griswold, 1986, p. 357). To this day, these regions are referred to as the Near East, the Middle East, and the Far East. Along similar lines, the Orient (and hence Orientals) were "east" of the Mediterranean from a European perspective (Anglesey, 1998, p. 13). (This explains why Asia and Asian are preferred terms.) That New Zealand is "down under" is a matter of perspective, ours not theirs. Americans and Europeans are accustomed to maps of the world that split "Asia in half in order to put Europe and the Americas front and center" (Levstik, 1985, p. 42). In fact, different map projections of the world (Figure 6.2) may seem strange and unsettling to some.

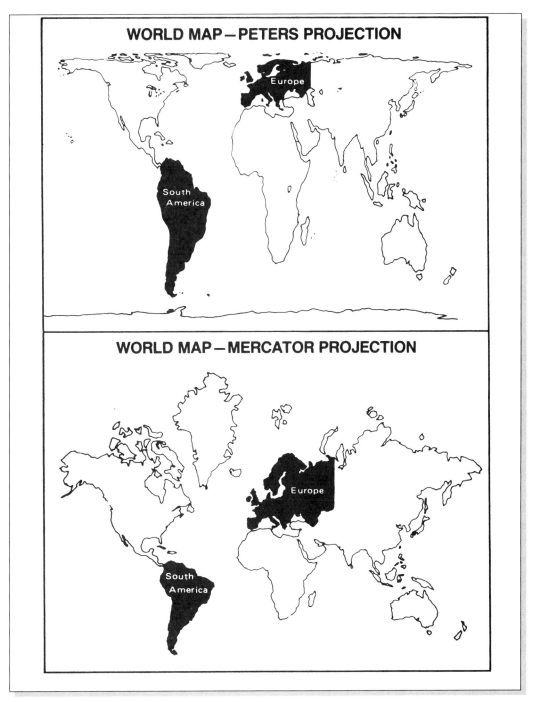

FIGURE 6.2 Different map projections convey different impressions of the relative size, shape, and importance of various regions.
Source: From A. Peters, *The New Cartography.* Copyright © 1983 by Friendship Press. Reprinted by permission.

The powerful impact of such ethnocentric perceptions can be demonstrated to students through an exercise described by Mukhopadhyay (1985). When asked to draw maps of the world from memory, most students depict the United States as considerably larger than it should be in relation to the rest of the world, and they ignore or recall inaccurately areas of the world with which they are less familiar. Students need to recognize how the common perceptions of American society can influence their conceptions of the relative importance of different countries and their notions of what is near and far, familiar and strange (Levstik, 1985). The 7-year-old Korean child's drawing of the world shown in Figure 6.3 dramatically illustrates how ethnocentric societal perceptions can influence views of the world.

That ethnocentrism affects how students perceive other nations has been documented in several countries. In the 1960s, an international study reported on the nationality preferences of U.S. children (Lambert & Klineberg, cited in Cortés & Fleming, 1986b). Children in elementary grades responded that if they were not Americans, they would most prefer to be British, Canadian, or Italian; they would least like to be Chinese, Russian, German, Indian, or Japanese. Older students (age 14) indicated that they would least like to be Russian or African. In a more recent British study, children age 9 to 10, were asked to think about countries they would like to visit; Europe, America, and the "White" Commonwealth were by far the most popular choices. Given an opportunity to write about a place in which they did not want to land by mistake, "they produced a narrow range of stereotype descriptions of jungles, 'primitive' natives brandishing spears and dirty thin people" (Worral, cited in Klein, 1985, p. 8).

Geocultural and Global Perspectives

Perspective is a critical element in how content is treated in any subject area. Dealing with cultural diversity sometimes requires that teachers use a frame of reference different from the one traditionally used. Ideally, the way teachers organize concepts should facilitate incorporation of the myriad cultural experiences that make up the history and heritage of the United States. Ethnocentric perspectives, like blinders, can limit rather than expand this vision. The geocultural and global perspectives described in this section are educationally and conceptually valid alternatives to ethnocentric points of view, which distort views of American society and the rest of the world. Both are appropriate for elementary and secondary levels and useful in subject areas such as history, literature, economics, music, and art.

The history and heritage of the United States have traditionally been characterized as largely the product of a movement of people and European culture from east to west—the Atlantic coast westward to the Pacific coast and beyond (Cortés, 1976, 1981a). For years, this unidirectional approach has permeated the curriculum in U.S. schools. This approach, by limiting discussion of historical developments primarily to those falling within existing national political boundaries, has imposed constraints on thinking and teaching.

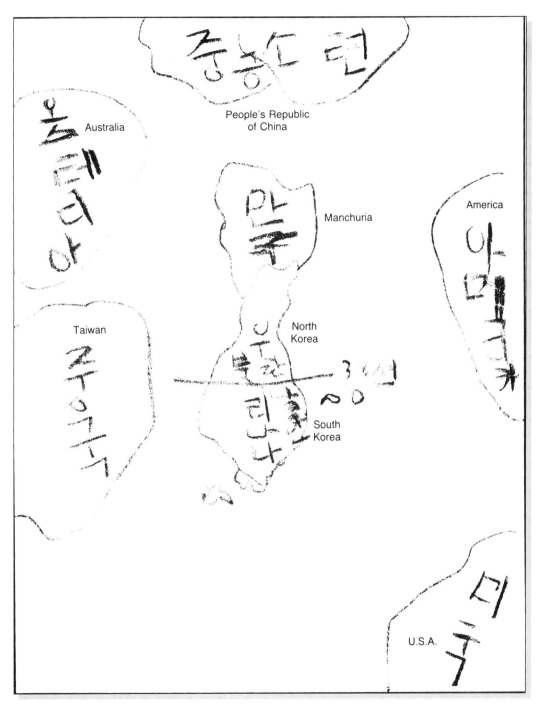

FIGURE 6.3 Map of the world as drawn by a 7-year-old Korean child.
Source: T. W. Johnson, personal collection. Reprinted by permission.

Describing this common conceptual framework as a "straightjacket," Cortés contends that its effect has been twofold. *First, some aspects of the history and heritage of the United States have been largely ignored in the curriculum.* For example, the treatment of Native American, African, Asian, Hawaiian, Hispanic, and Mexican cultures and civilizations prior to their incorporation into the fabric of the nation has generally been limited and without depth. In a review of history texts, FitzGerald (1979) found that the real distortion was less in what textbooks said than in what they did not say. For example, students reading a typical history textbook would have no way of knowing that while English settlers struggled to survive on Roanoke Island, 300 poets were in competition for a prize in Mexico City, or that when Jefferson was President, Mexico City was regarded by a leading European scientist as having "the most solid scientific institutions" of any city in the Western Hemisphere (FitzGerald, 1979, p. 96).

Second, inherent in the theme of an advancing frontier is the tendency to describe established territorial groups (e.g., Native Americans and Mexicans) first as obstacles to westward progress and later as problems in society. From this perspective, resistance to encroachment and territorial conflicts cast those obstructing the westward advance in a negative light.

There is an alternative to this European-oriented, westward-bound perspective—one based upon a multidirectional frame of reference. As defined by Cortés, this *geocultural perspective* encompasses the entire area now part of the United States, subsuming all of the cultures and experiences therein. Such an approach traces "the northwesterly flow of civilization from Africa to America, the northerly flow of Hispanic and Mexican civilization into what is today the U.S. Southwest, and the easterly flow of civilization and cultures from Asia" (Cortés, 1981a, p. 15). The geocultural approach also allows for greater continuity in dealing with multiple group perspectives (e.g., racial, ethnic, cultural, gender, age, religious) as an integral part of the nation's development, not merely as addendums.

Working from a geocultural perspective, Cortés (1981a) suggests, teachers can deal effectively with the following topics, which often are overlooked or treated in a culturally biased way:

1. the varieties of Native American civilizations in what was to become the United States;
2. the northward movement of men and women to explore and establish communities in northern New Spain and Mexico (later the U.S. Southwest) westward movement of English, French, and Dutch, in parallel with the other European and African peoples onto the Atlantic coast;
3. the relations of Native American civilizations with expanding U.S. society from the east and Mexican society from the south;
4. the westward expansion of the United States, including the relations of Anglo-Americans and Mexicans as the United States took over half of northern Mexico by conquest and annexation;

5. the continuous immigration of peoples from Asia, Africa, Latin America, Europe, and Australia, including the adaptations and perspectives of immigrant women and men of diverse national, religious, and linguistic heritages;
6. the response to immigration and to increasing ethnic diversity by U.S. institutions and people (including former immigrants and their descendants).

Just as a geocultural perspective can enhance teaching of the American experience, so too a *multiple-faceted global perspective* can facilitate students' understanding of the world's many complexities. Unfortunately, ethnocentrism continues to pervade the treatment of other peoples and nations, particularly those involving the Third World, in U.S. curricula. When textbooks overemphasize modernization in their treatment of other nations, for example, students learn to define cultures solely or primarily in terms of technological and material achievements and to devalue other important aspects of culture, such as the positive aspects of tradition (Cortés & Fleming, 1986a; Crofts, 1986). Societies that are highly technical and productive are assumed, from this perspective, to be "superior" and "better"; those that are "less advanced" technologically are also considered to be "less civilized."

Often more subtle than in the past, ethnocentrism remains a powerful influence on how areas outside the United States are presented in instructional materials. Partly as the result of such curricula, "many students come to view the world with knowledge drawn almost entirely from Western and middle-class perspectives. But the majority of Earth's people are not white; although they may be influenced by the West, their cultures are neither Western nor dominated by a middle class" (National Council for the Social Studies, cited in Cortés & Fleming, 1986b, p. 340).

Some of the specific effects and limitations of ethnocentric textbooks and curricula were described in the previous section. One antidote to such ethnocentrism is the inclusion of a better balance between the outsider perspective of Americans toward other countries and the insider perspectives of the inhabitants of those countries. Although the use of one's own cultural frame of reference to present realities, events, and experiences of other cultural groups and nations appears "logical" and "normal," it is not always conducive to understanding what is observed (Cortés & Fleming, 1986a). Customs, attitudes, and actions that from the vantage points of American society may seem shortsighted, senseless, or simply exotic may appear perfectly rational and appropriate when viewed from within another society. Inclusion of such insider perspectives offers American students an opportunity to understand how people in other countries see themselves; how groups within other countries see each other; and how they see the outside world, including their neighbors and the United States (Cortés & Fleming, 1987).

All societies hold somewhat inaccurate views of people living far away: "Accounts report that some early Japanese authors described Americans as people who 'had bushy tails somewhere hidden in [their] garments' " (Bullard, 1986, p. 367). If this outsider view seems preposterous to us as Americans, consider our outsider view of the Middle East. What physical resource do you believe is most important to inhabitants of the region? Did you say "oil"? Griswold (1986) points out that the resources that appear most important to the West (e.g., oil, minerals, agricultural products) are not necessarily the most valued by inhabitants of other regions. In many countries of the Middle East, "water exceeds oil in importance because its scarcity limits the growth of . . . economies, both agricultural and industrial" (Griswold, 1986, p. 358). Obviously, the misrepresentations that may result from an outsider's view can extend to all aspects of another country's culture and society. The growing recognition of the importance of insider views to a true understanding of other countries has led to guidelines for curricular reform that stress teaching about cultural and national groups from within their own perspective.

Both geocultural and global perspectives provide numerous and different interpretations of reality. The dilemma that faces teachers is perhaps best expressed in the words of Ortega y Gasset: "Reality happens to be, like a landscape possessed of an infinite number of perspectives, all equally veracious and authentic. The sole false perspective is that which claims to be the only one there is" (cited in Smith & Otero, 1982, p. 10).

Guidelines for Bias-Free Instructional Materials

Implementation of a multicultural program requires instructional materials that provide for fair treatment of all people. As the previous discussion in this chapter indicates, many of today's textbooks are strong in a number of areas but uneven in others: "In the 1990s studies have continued to call attention to the need for greater and more accurate inclusion of people of color, women, people with disabilities, and people living at or below poverty" (Grant & Tate, 1995, p. 149). General guidelines can help teachers to evaluate and select textbooks that are relatively free from bias and to develop their own materials. The guidelines in Figure 6.4, adapted from the Association of American Publishers (1984), address the content, illustrations, and language of instructional materials.

CRITICAL USE OF INSTRUCTIONAL MATERIALS

From a teacher's perspective, providing students with all available information in any subject area is neither feasible nor even desirable. Gone are the days in which defining what was to be taught and how learning outcomes were best assessed seemed an easy and clear-cut task. Not surprisingly, some critics of the current state of education long for what they perceive as the rigor and simplicity of bygone eras. In my local newspaper, for example, one such critic extolled the merits of an 1895 graduation test from Saline County, Kansas (Schreck, 1998). The graduation examination questions encompassed grammar, arithmetic, U.S.

Content

1. Represent diverse groups of people in a variety of activities, occupations, and careers, including positions of leadership.

2. Represent fairly and accurately the historic and contemporary achievements of people in society within a wide range of areas.

3. Integrate materials by and about minorities, women, and members of other cultural groups that provide a range of perspectives and reflect intragroup diversity.

4. Include materials that honestly convey the positive and negative political, social, and economic realities that have been part of the American experience for members of various cultural groups and segments of society.

5. Depict all men and women as displaying a full range of human emotions and behaviors.

6. Represent all groups in a variety of settings—urban, suburban, and rural—and socioeconomic levels.

Illustrations

1. Provide a fair, reasonable, and balanced representation with respect to race, religion, ethnicity, age, socioeconomic level, sex, and national origin.

2. Include positive role models for male and female students of different ethnic backgrounds.

3. Avoid stereotyping groups and individuals.

4. Show men and women from different cultural groups in positions of prominence and leadership.

Language

1. Encompass members of both sexes by (1) avoiding use of terms that exclude women and (2) designating occupations by work performed.

2. Reflect cultural diversity through inclusion of varied ethnic names as well as more common Anglo-Saxon ones.

3. Avoid words that are loaded or convey biased connotations and assumptions.

FIGURE 6.4 Publishers' guidelines.

Source: From Association of American Publishers, *Statement on Bias-Free Materials*. Copyright © 1984 by Association of American Publishers. Used by permission.

history, orthography, geography, and health; reading and penmanship were also evaluated. In the U.S. history segment, students were allowed 45 minutes to respond to the following:

1. Give the epochs into which U.S. History is divided.
2. Give an accounting of the discovery of America by Columbus.
3. Relate the causes and results of the Revolutionary War.
4. Show the territorial growth of the United States.
5. Tell what you can of the history of Kansas.
6. Describe three of the most prominent battles of the Rebellion.
7. Who were the following: Morse, Whitney, Fulton, Bell, Lincoln, Penn, Howe?
8. Name the events connected with the following dates: 1607, 1620, 1800, 1849, and 1865? (p. 5B)

The reality is that we live in a different world, one in which we understand that history is more than names, dates, battles, and epochs, and more than the perspective of one group and one gender. Lest there be any doubt, compare the 1895 graduation test to the types of questions and tasks that challenge today's graduates.

Strategies for Using History Textbooks

In the absence of a single, universally accepted body of knowledge that all students must learn, textbooks play a critical role in defining the ideas, concepts, and skills that constitute a major part of the curriculum. Based on studies in several areas including social studies, researchers have concluded that textbooks are the dominant instructional tool for most teachers. Moreover, "teachers tend not only to rely on, but to believe in, the textbook as the source of knowledge" (Shaver et al., cited in FitzGerald, 1979, p. 19).

This reliance on textbooks is arguably more worrisome in teaching history than in any other subject area. Teachers' tacit acceptance of inaccurate, biased, and distorted content, and the authority they bestow on the information they impart has serious implications. Loewen (1996) contends that the performance differential is greater in history than other subject areas, greater gaps between rich and poor, between Native Americans, African Americans, and Hispanic Americans and other groups. Even along gender lines, girls appear to regard social studies and history with greater aversion than boys (p. 302).

What happens when students realize that their teachers have lied to them? Loewen describes how one of his students reacted when she learned that a much cherished myth—George Washington chopping down the cherry tree—was unfounded. She wrote about "feeling bitter and betrayed by my earlier teachers who had to lie to build up George Washington's image, causing me to question all that I had previously learned" (p. 295). I still recall the disillusionment one of my students expressed when he talked about how the Abraham Lincoln he had idolized in school was not the figure he encountered in his college history class. Loewen suggests that the alienation of minority students is even greater (e.g., when African Americans learn that Washington and Jefferson owned slaves;

when Native Americans learn about Washington and the Iroquois): "the way American history is taught particularly alienates students of color and children from impoverished families. Feel-good history for affluent white males amounts to feel-bad history for everyone else" (p. 301). Loewen tells of an exchange between a student teacher and an Abenaki fifth grader in his class in Swanton, Vermont, a community with a substantial Native American population. Asked by the teacher why he was inattentive when the subject of Thanksgiving came up, the student answered, "My father told me the real truth about that day and not to listen to any white man scum like you!" (p. 301). While most students do not react openly or with anger, the effect on them may be subtle and cumulative.

Loewen questions why teachers continue to use history textbooks that are "overstuffed, overlong, often wrong, mindless, boring and all alike"? He then proceeds to cite studies indicating that many teachers

◇ have a limited knowledge of history;
◇ are not current in their reading in this area;
◇ are frightened of and avoid discussing controversial issues (topics like the Vietnam War, race relations, politics, and religion) in class; and
◇ find it difficult to teach "open-endedly," that is, unwilling to grapple with uncertainty and risk losing authority by admitting that there are gaps in their knowledge—that they just don't know. (pp. 286–287)

Additional factors include time constraints, workload, resources, and fear of the controversy that may be generated by teaching against the textbook. If nothing else, both teachers and students find that depending on textbooks makes it easier to minimize the amount of effort put forth in teaching and learning (Loewen, 1996). Not surprisingly, "the same teachers who are 'vital, broadminded, and immensely knowledgeable in private conversations' nonetheless come across as 'narrow, dull, and rigid in the classroom' " (Shanker, cited in Loewen, 1996, p. 288).

Teachers are not alone in accepting and maintaining the status quo. In the 1970s, public opinion as expressed by lay reviewers of the social studies assessment instruments from the National Assessment for Educational Progress favored elimination of "references to specific minority groups . . . whenever possible" and judged that "exercises which show national heroes in an uncomplimentary fashion though factually accurate are offensive" (cited in Loewen, 1996, p. 292). History is inextricably tied to our allegiance, basic ideals, and socialization processes.

Nonetheless, given the ever-expanding nature of information in today's society, students must learn to use history textbooks analytically and to develop skill in evaluating materials for accuracy and perspective, to examine arguments and evidence, and make rational decisions (Cortés & Fleming, 1986a; Klein, 1985; Loewen, 1996). This is essential if schools are to teach students how to ask questions about society and how to get the answers for themselves; the real power of history is in students' ability to use an understanding of the past to inspire and legitimize their actions in the present (Loewen, 1996, p. 318).

There is agreement that teaching such critical skills is a most significant component of multicultural education, not only in history but in other content areas as well. If critical literacy skills are not taught, the product is a generation of "adults who believe everything they read—or read only what they wish to believe" (Klein, 1985, p. 115).

However, if teachers are to instill critical thinking skills in their students, they, too, must learn to deal with instructional materials analytically. For many teachers, a critical approach is already at the heart of their teaching. FitzGerald (1979) describes a teacher in rural Maine who intentionally uses a "conservative," 10-year-old history text because its viewpoint is diametrically opposed to his own.

For other teachers, however, using textbooks critically, as they would other readings, represents a major departure from their usual practices. Loewen offers some practical suggestions for making the most of the textbook and other available resources. These are presented in Figure 6.5.

---

1. "Introduce fewer topics" and examine these in greater depth.

2. "Delve into historical controversies."

3. Maximize use of resources at school (books, maps, and people) and in the community (family members, older citizens, leaders).

4. Teach history backwards, that is, beginning with the present and relating it to the past.

5. Teach students how to learn history. Even teachers unprepared or unwilling to challenge textbook doctrine, need to help their students learn to ask the right questions:

    a. Ask about the social context of the text: "Why was it written (or painted, etc.)?" Where does the audience fit in the social structure? What was the speaker trying to accomplish?

    b. Whose viewpoint is presented? "Where is the speaker or writer located in social structure?" "What interests—material or ideological—does the statement serve?" "Whose viewpoints are omitted?"

    c. "Is the account believable? Does each acting group behave reasonably—as we might, given the same situation and socialization?" "Does it cohere? Do some of its assertions contradict others?"

    d. "Is the account backed up by other sources? Or do other authors contradict it?"

    e. "After reading the words or seeing the image, how is one supposed to feel about the America that has been presented? "

FIGURE 6.5   Making the most of textbooks.
Source: Adapted from suggestions in J. W. Loewen. *Lies My Teacher Told Me: Everything your American history textbook got wrong.* New York: Touchstone, 1996, pp. 315–317.

Strategies for Teaching Insider Perspective

Teachers need to reconsider how they portray different peoples and cultures, and look for ways that are more consistent with perspectives within the cultures themselves. This is no less important in dealing with perspectives involving people living in the United States. Using the American Indian perspective as an example, Haukoos and Beauvais (1998) describe the kind of rethinking and the changes that this entails. More specifically, they suggest that teachers, particularly at the elementary level, restructure the knowledge base to teach that

1. *Most American Indian and Alaska Native people prefer to be identified by the name of their nation and use American Indian in reference to Native peoples collectively.*

2. *Although tribes is acceptable to some Native people, most prefer to be recognized as belonging to a distinctive nation of people rather than a tribe,* since the latter term encompasses both social and political institutions.

3. *American Indian culture differs across and within nations, over time, and in relation to place.* Teaching must be specific to the culture: "All Native peoples cannot and should not be lumped together." (p. 163)

4. *The traditional Pilgrim-Indian image, more myth than reality, perpetuates stereotypes of Native peoples.* (See number 1 in Application, Extension, and Reflection, at the end of this chapter.)

5. *Certain symbols and names are derogatory to American Indian people; use of such symbols is not acceptable.* Among these are degrading referents (e.g., squaw), representations denigrating sacred rituals and social ceremonies (e.g., war dancing), and mythical images of Native people frozen in time (e.g., stereotypic depictions with bows and arrows, tipis, tomahawks, etc.). (Cruz-Janzen, 1998, p. 222)

6. *The Native peoples' provided early models for democracy.* The nation's democratic institutions are indebted to the uniquely democratic systems established by many Native peoples. Native peoples provided successful models of government characterized as "decentralized, self-ruling, and loosely confederated" (e.g., Iroquoian Confederacy of Nations).

7. *The Native peoples' legacy to world commerce is significant.* The contributions of Native peoples to the global economy, as great as they are, have been little recognized. A most important part of this legacy is the plants used for food (e.g., corn, potatoes, squash, beans, pumpkins, melon, and peanuts) and drugs (e.g., in excess of 200 listed in the American pharmacopoeia) and as building supplies.

8. *The American Indian peoples' have a rich cultural heritage.* To respect all living things and live in harmony with nature is a philosophy or world view common to the cultures of indigenous peoples around the world—from the Inuit of the Arctic and the Ainu of northern Japan to the Lapps in Scandinavia, the Bedouins of the Middle East, and the mountain people of Switzerland and Taiwan (Wideman, cited in Haukoos & Beauvais, 1998). This and other facets of Native cultures provide models for dealing with social, spiritual, physical, environmental, and other issues.

1. *Select one nation as the focus of study.* Guiding questions draw students' attention from the past to the present (e.g., where the people live, how they make a living, how their government is structured, where their children go to school and to college, what family or national traditions are observed).

2. *Study in greater depth what Native people in a specific region have in common.* Guiding questions draw students' attention to factors influencing the culture (e.g., why the Native nations of the Great Plains were so mobile in the past and how that mobility influences them in the present, what factors have influenced the cultures, nations, and peoples of particular regions).

3. *Use children's literature rather than social studies textbooks to study Native people.* Consistent with Native peoples' use of stories to teach, teachers can use a variety of stories from many Native nations to explore social messages they convey (e.g., stories about Spider, Coyote, Deer or Badger, the tricksters in most Native cultures) and a better understanding of cultural development.

4. *Study one critical event having a major impact on Native people.* Suggested topics include the Trail of Tears, the Black Hawk Wars, President Andrew Jackson's administration, and the reduction of American Indian populations from 1769 to 1890.

5. *Visit a Native nation or community to develop an understanding of modern Native people.* Activities might include visits to a cultural center, and school or community events.

FIGURE 6.6   Teaching strategies: Native people.
Source: Adapted from suggestions in G. D. Haukoos and A. B. Beauvais (1998). "Creating positive images: Thoughts for teaching about American Indians." In F. Schultz (Ed.), *Multicultural Education* 1998/1999, Annual Editions Series, pp. 162-167. Guilford, CT: Dushkin/McGraw-Hill.

Haukoos and Beauvais (1998) are specific as to how teachers can help students construct knowledge in ways that dispel myths and avoid creating stereotypes. This requires replacing the general study of American Indians and Alaska Natives with specific topics that allow for more in-depth study. The basic set of strategies they provide is applicable to teaching about other cultures as well. They emphasize use of the five strategies highlighted in Figure 6.6.

Strategies for Teaching About Religion

Teaching about religion is defined as encompassing consideration of "the beliefs and practices of religions; the role of religion in history and contemporary society; and religious themes in music, art, and literature" (*Religion in the Public School Curriculum: Questions and Answers,* n.p.) In order to help you assess what you already know in this area, try to answer the following questions:

When finished, compare your answers with those in Figure 6.7. Which of your answers agreed with those provided by the sponsors? Which of your answers were not in agreement? Why?

---

1. Is it constitutional to teach about religion in public schools?

2. Why should study about religion be included in the public school curriculum?

3. Where does study about religion belong in the curriculum?

4. Do current textbooks teach about religion?

5. How does teaching about religion relate to the teaching of values?

6. Do religious holidays belong in the curriculum?

7. How should religious holidays be treated in the classroom?

8. When should teaching about religious holidays take place?

9. May students be absent for religious holidays?

Source: *Religion in the Public School Curriculum: Questions and Answers,* n.d.; *Religious Holidays in the Public Schools: Questions and Answers,* n.d.

The following questions and answers address some of the most basic concerns that school boards, administrators, and teachers have in regards to teaching *about* religion. They are intended to help define what is "constitutionally permissible, educationally sound, and sensitive to the beliefs of students and parents."

1. *Is it constitutional to teach about religion in public schools?*

Yes. In the 1960s school prayer cases (which ruled against state-sponsored school prayer and Bible reading), the U.S. Supreme Court indicated that public school education may include teaching about religion. In *Abington v. Schempp,* Associate Justice Tom Clark wrote for the Court:

[I]t might well be said that one's education is not complete without a study of comparative religion or the history of religion and its relationship to the advancement of civilization. It certainly may be said that the Bible is worthy of study for its literary and historic qualities. Nothing we have said here indicates that such study of the Bible or of religion, when presented objectively as part of a secular program of education, may not be effected consistently with the First Amendment.

(continued)

FIGURE 6.7   Teaching about religion.

FIGURE 6.7 *(continued)*

2. *Why should study about religion be included in the public school curriculum?*

Because religion plays a significant role in history and society, study about religion is essential to understanding both the nation and the world. Omission of facts about religion can give students the false impression that the religious life of humankind is insignificant or unimportant. Failure to understand even the basic symbols, practices, and concepts of the various religions makes much of history, literature, art, and contemporary life unintelligible.

Study about religion is also important if students are to value religious liberty, the first freedom guaranteed in the Bill of Rights. Moreover, knowledge of the roles of religion in the past and present promotes cross-cultural understanding essential to democracy and world peace.

3. *Where does study about religion belong in the curriculum?*

Wherever it naturally arises. On the secondary level, the social studies, literature, and the arts offer many opportunities for the inclusion of information about religions—their ideas and themes. On the elementary level, natural opportunities arise in discussions of family and community life and in instruction about festivals and different cultures. Many educators believe that integrating study about religion into existing courses is an educationally sound way to acquaint students with the role of religion in history and society.

Religion also may be taught about in special courses or units. Some secondary schools, for example, offer such courses as world religions, the Bible as literature, and the religious literature of the West and of the East.

4. *Do current textbooks teach about religion?*

Rarely. Recent textbook studies conclude that most widely used textbooks largely ignore the role of religion in history and society. For example, readers of high school U.S. history texts learn little or nothing about the great colonial revivals, the struggles of minority faiths, the religious motivations of immigrants, the contributions of religious groups to many social movements, major episodes of religious intolerance, and many other significant events of history. Education without appropriate attention to major religious influences and themes is incomplete education.

5. *How does teaching about religion relate to the teaching of values?*

Teaching about religion is not the same as teaching values. The former is objective, academic study; the latter involves the teaching of particular ethical viewpoints or standards of behavior.

There are basic moral values that are recognized by the population at large (e.g., honesty, integrity, justice, compassion). These values can be taught through discussion, by example, and by carrying out school policies. However, teachers may not invoke religious authority.

Public schools may teach about the various religious and non-religious perspectives concerning the many complex moral issues confronting society, but such perspectives must be presented without adopting, sponsoring, or denigrating one view against another.

6. *Do religious holidays belong in the curriculum?*

The study of religious holidays may be included in elementary and secondary curricula as opportunities for teaching *about* religions. Such study serves the academic goals of

FIGURE 6.7 *(continued)*

educating students about history and cultures, as well as the traditions of particular religions within a pluralistic society.

7. *How should religious holidays be treated in the classroom?*

Teachers must be alert to the distinction between teaching *about* religious holidays, which is permissible, and *celebrating* religious holidays, which is not. Recognition of and information about holidays may focus on how and when they are celebrated, their origins, histories, and generally agreed-upon meanings. If the approach is objective and sensitive, neither promoting nor inhibiting religion, this study can foster understanding and mutual respect for differences in belief.

Teachers will want to avoid asking students to explain their beliefs and customs. An offer to do so should be treated with courtesy and accepted or rejected depending upon the educational relevancy.

Teachers may not use the study of religious holidays as an opportunity to proselytize or to inject personal religious beliefs into the discussions. Teachers can avoid this by teaching through attribution, i.e., by reporting that "some Buddhists believe . . ."

8. *When should teaching about religious holidays take place?*

On the elementary level, natural opportunities arise for discussion of religious holidays while studying different cultures and communities. In the secondary curriculum, students of world history or literature have opportunities to consider the holy days of religious traditions. Teachers find it helpful when they are provided with an inclusive calendar noting major religious and secular holidays with brief descriptions of their significance.

9. *May students be absent for religious holidays?*

Sensitive school policy on absences will take account of the religious needs and requirements of students. Students should be allowed a reasonable number of excused absences, without penalties, to observe religious holidays within their traditions. Students may be asked to complete makeup assignments or examinations in conjunction with such absences.

Sources: *Religion in the Public School Curriculum: Questions and Answers,* n.d., sponsored jointly by the American Academy of Religion, American Association of School Administrators, American Federation of Teachers, American Jewish Congress, American United Research Foundation, Association for Supervision and Curriculum Development, Baptist Joint Committee on Public Affairs, Christian Legal Society, First Liberty Institute at George Mason University, The Islamic Society of North America, National Association of Evangelicals, National Conference of Christians and Jews, National Council of Churches of Christ in the U.S.A., National Council on Religion and Public Education, National Council for the Social Studies, National Education Association, National School Boards Association, and The Church of Jesus Christ of Latter-day Saints. Used with permission.
Religious Holidays in the Public Schools: Questions and Answers, n.d., sponsored jointly by American Academy of Religion, American Association of School Administrators, American Federation of Teachers, American Jewish Committee, American Jewish Congress, American United Research Foundation, Association for Supervision and Curriculum Development, Baptist Joint Committee on Public Affairs, Christian Legal Society, The Islamic Society of North America, National Association of Evangelicals, National Conference of Christians and Jews, National Council of Churches of Christ in the U.S.A., National Council on Religion and Public Education, National Council for the Social Studies, National Education Association, and National School Boards Association. Used with permission.

The First Amendment to the U.S. Constitution states the following: "Congress shall make no law respecting an establishment of religion, nor prohibiting the free exercise thereof . . .". Three principles consistent with these Religious Liberty clauses provide a useful civic framework for teachers to use in teaching about religion. These principles center on rights, responsibilities, and respect:

◇ *Rights:* Religious liberty, or freedom of conscience, is a precious, fundamental and inalienable right.
◇ *Responsibilities:* Religious liberty places on all people a universal responsibility to protect that right for others.
◇ *Respect:* Living with our deepest differences requires a principled respect for persons and truth, and for the guidelines by which we can conduct arguments robustly but civilly whenever those differences are in question. (Haynes, Cassity, & Stone, 1993, pp. 1–4)

These principles are in the Williamsburg Charter, a national compact reaffirming the contemporary significance of First Amendment principles safeguarding religious liberty and respect for our deepest differences. The Williamsburg Charter Foundation has defined what it means to teach about religion in the public schools as follows:

The school

◇ takes an *academic,* not *devotional,* approach to religion;
◇ strives for student *awareness of religions,* but does not promote student *acceptance of any one religion;*
◇ sponsors *study about religion,* not the practice of religion;
◇ exposes students to a *diversity of* religious *views,* but *does not impose any particular view;*
◇ educates *about all religions;* it does not *promote or denigrate any religion;*
◇ *informs* students about various *beliefs;* it *does not seek to conform* students to *any particular belief.* (Haynes, 1991, pp. 2–3).

Leading educational and religious organizations agree that teaching about religion in the public schools is constitutional and necessary if students are to understand and appreciate history and cultures (First Amendment Center, 1999). There is also consensus that this must be done objectively and with religious neutrality: "The purpose of the public schools is to educate students about a variety of religious traditions, not to indoctrinate them into any tradition" (p. 2).

Working within the civic framework just described, teachers can make teaching about religion an integral and important part of the curriculum (Haynes, 1998). The guidelines described in Figure 6.8 can help teachers and students to find common ground in addressing our most profound differences.

Natural Inclusion (p. 7.5)

◇ Content related to religion should be presented within a historical and cultural context.

◇ Only content essential to understanding the history and culture of people and events should be taught. Academic requirements should be used to determine which religions are included and what is discussed.

◇ Teachers should explain why specific religious influences and themes have been selected for inclusion in their study of history and culture.

◇ Teachers also need to make students aware of the diversity of opinion that exists within as well as across religions.

Fairness and Balance (p. 7.5)

◇ Discussions of religious traditions must be conducted in an atmosphere free of advocacy.

◇ While presenting divergent perspectives, teachers should neither advocate a particular point of view nor inject their own personal religious beliefs.

◇ Critical thinking is an essential part of the fair and balanced study of historical events involving religious traditions. Comparing and contrasting the different perspectives of religious groups on historical and current events is just one of many appropriate strategies. However, attacks on religion or teaching that condemns the theology or practice of any faith are inappropriate in the public school curriculum.

Respect for Differences (p. 7.5)

◇ In teaching about the major faiths in world history, teachers must not present religious truth claims as relative, represent all faiths as "basically the same," or explain religion as simply a social or psychological phenomena. Such views are neither neutral nor compatible with the way members of faith communities regard their religious practices and beliefs.

◇ It is appropriate to introduce students to the various theories of religion and to explain the social, economic, and cultural contexts in which religions developed and changed. This includes how people interpret the practices and belief of their faith, and how these have affected their lives, past and present.

◇ The key to helping students understand the beliefs of the world's religious traditions and appreciate how each faith understands itself is teaching respect for differences. In the public schools, the teacher's task is to teach about divergent approaches to religious truth without advocating one position over another.

Use of Religious Scriptures (p. 7.7)

◇ Exposing students to the classical religious texts of the world's major faith communities is appropriate in the study of history, literature, art, and law. When used, selections from sacred accounts must be treated with respect, and presented only in historical and cultural contexts. Students should also be made aware of the differing interpretations of scripture that exist within each religious tradition.

(continued)

FIGURE 6.8 Basic guidelines.

FIGURE 6.8   *(continued)*

Role-Playing (p. 7.7)

◇ There is no place in the public school classroom for role-playing that recreates religious practices or ceremonies. Such role-playing activities are problematic for a
number of reasons. They may unintentionally mock or oversimplify the meaning
of rituals that are sacred to those who practice them. They may also violate the con-
sciences of students (and teachers) required to participate in practices contrary to
their own beliefs.

◇ Teachers are encouraged to use audio-visual resources and primary documents to
present the ceremonies and rituals of the world's religious traditions.

Guest Speakers (p. 7.7)

◇ Used selectively and appropriately, guest speakers can contribute to students' understanding of religious traditions. Those invited must be able to discuss religious
traditions within the historical and cultural context under study in a way that is
academic, scholarly, and objective. Moreover, invited speakers also need to understand that the nature of their role and task is educational, and that they are operating within a civic framework defined by First Amendment guidelines on
teaching about religion in the public schools.

Student Beliefs (p. 7.8)

◇ Teachers should not elicit information about students' religious affiliations or beliefs, nor should students be asked to explain their own religious beliefs and practices for the class. It is appropriate, however, for students to express their religious
views voluntarily when these are relevant to the topic, and appropriate for the discussion or assignment.

◇ For class discussions about religion, teachers may want to establish ground rules
emphasizing the civic framework embedded within the First Amendment principles of rights, responsibilities, and respect. These can be useful in creating a classroom environment in which our deepest differences are explored in ways that are
nonjudgmental and nonthreatening.

Adapted from Charles C. Haynes and Oliver Thomas (Eds.), 1998. "Rationale and Guidelines for Teaching
about Religion." *Finding Common Ground: A First Amendment Guide to Religion and Public Education*, (3rd. ed.).
Nashville, TN: First Amendment Center, pp. 7.5–7.9. Used with permission.

Nord and Haynes (1998) assert that "we don't take religion seriously in the
public school curriculum" (p. 201). Teachers ready to take teaching about religion more seriously may want to consider what is currently left out of the curriculum and what ought to be included. Those who teach social studies and
literature, especially at the secondary level, are most likely to find that "without proper attention to the role of religion, the story of America is incomplete
and distorted" (Haynes, 1990, p. 3). For these teachers in particular, the 29 significant religious influences in American history identified by an ASCD panel
of teachers and professors are most relevant (Haynes, 1990). Appropriate
study of the areas highlighted in Figure 6.9 can enrich the curriculum in ways

1. Religious motivations in Spanish, English, and French exploration and colonization. (p. 3)

2. The existence of Native American religions and civilization prior to and during European settlement. (p. 4)

3. The role of Spanish missions are social institutions in the first Spanish settlements and in expanding the Hispanic frontier northward, 1550–1848, in which is now the southwestern and western United States. (p. 4)

4. The role of Puritan religion in the foundation of the Bible Commonwealths of New England and in the shaping of the later nation's sense of mission. (p. 4)

5. The development of religious pluralism in the colonies of Rhode Island, New York, New Jersey, Pennsylvania, Maryland, and to a large degree, in the Southern colonies. (p. 5)

6. The work of Indian missions in shaping the relationships of the colonists with Native Americans, from John Eliot in New England through the Quakers, peace churches, and Methodists to Roman Catholic missions on the northern plains and in Alaska after the Civil War. (p. 5)

7. The influence of the great colonial revivals, often called "The Great Awakening," 1728–1790, in the making of an independent republic and in the realignment of the denominations. (p. 5)

8. The contribution of the Enlightenment's ideals of religious liberty and "civic virtue" to the thinking of the Founding Fathers, especially Thomas Jefferson, James Madison, and George Mason. (p. 6)

9. The growth of the anti-Catholic and antiforeign nativist movement in the first half of the 19th century, culminating in the 1840s and 1850s in the Know-Nothing party. (p. 6)

10. The place of religiously inspired moralism, Protestant millennialism, Methodist perfectionism, and the Christian Utopianism (exhibited by such groups as the Shakers) in 19th century movements for social reform. (p. 6)

11. The role of Protestantism in the founding of American colleges and in the shaping of the common school movement. (p. 6)

12. The part played by religion, as practiced by both whites and blacks, in the movement to abolish slavery, 1825–1866. (p. 7)

13. The function of religion, Catholic and Jewish as well as Protestant, in the formation of new communities on the frontier—as seen especially in the settlements of western New York, the Shenandoah and Mississippi valleys, Utah, and the Great Northwest Territory—and religion's place in the emergence of a mixed English and Hispanic culture in the Southwest. (p. 7)

14. The significance of the great revivals of religion led by Charles G. Finney, Dwight L. Moody, and the Catholic Redemptorist fathers, 1810–1890. (p. 7)

(continued)

FIGURE 6.9   Religious influences in American history.

FIGURE 6.9 *(continued)*

15. The rise of indigenous religious movements in 19th century America, such as the Latter-day Saints (Mormons), Disciples and churches of Christ, Seventh-Day Adventists, Christian Scientists, and Jehovah's Witnesses. (p. 8)

16. The centrality of religion in African American culture after the Civil War and the implications of this religious tradition for the history of African American schooling. (p. 8)

17. The place of the Bible in American literature and the law. (p. 8)

18. The place of overseas missions, Catholic as well as Protestant, in American foreign relations, from the first expressions of national interest in the Near East in the 1830s to such events as the Boxer Rebellion in China, the Spanish-American War, and the modern involvement of black and white Americans in shaping our nation's policies toward Africa and Latin America. (p. 9)

19. Moral and religious consensus in the Progressive Era. (p. 9)

20. The centrality of religion in the new immigrant subcultures formed in America between 1880 and 1910, including Czech Roman Catholic, Ukrainian Greek Catholic, Romanian Orthodox, Hungarian and Finnish Protestant, and Asian Buddhist (especially in Hawaii). Many Jewish subcommunities existed, among them one comprised primarily of German immigrants ("Reform") and another of Jews from central and eastern Europe ("Orthodox"). (p. 9)

21. The role of religion in providing health care to the urban poor in the 19th century, including the Lutheran, Methodist, and Baptist deaconess movements; Roman Catholic sisterhoods; Seventh-Day Adventist sanatoriums; and Jewish hospitals. (p. 10)

22. The significance of Fundamentalists to the restructuring of evangelical movements in the 20th century. (p. 10)

23. The place of religion in the civil rights crusade surrounding Martin Luther King, Jr., and especially the roles of American Protestant, Jewish, and Catholic clergy in it. (p. 10)

24. The work of Reinhold Niebuhr and the "political realists," before and during World War II, in opposing the pacifism and isolation that had penetrated American religious communities. (p. 11)

25. The recent revival of the religiously based peace movement, based on a convergence of religious forces from all faiths. (p. 11)

26. The revitalization of Judaism continues. (p. 12)

27. Developments within the Roman Catholic faith, especially since the Second Vatican Council, such as the spread of a biblical approach to piety, liturgical renewal, ecumenical involvement, and the charismatic movement. (p. 12)

FIGURE 6.9   *(continued)*

---

28. The involvement of American religious communities in international controversies, such as apartheid in South Africa and the many conflicts in Central America and the Middle East. (p. 13)

29. Expanding religious pluralism in the United States, as revealed in the expansion of the numbers of American Muslims and Buddhists, and in the rise of new religious movements. (p. 13)

Source: Adapted from D. Berreth, E. Gaustad, H. Greenhut, C. C. Haynes, M. J. Karlinger and T. Smith. "Religious influences in American history." (1990). *Religion in American History: What to Teach and How.* Alexandria, VA: Association for Supervision and Curriculum Development, pp. 3–14. Used with permission.

that enhance students' understanding of history and society. (For a more detailed discussion of each topic and recommended readings, see Berreth, Gaustad, Greenhut, Haynes, Karlinger, & Smith, 1990, *Religion in American history: What to teach and how.*)

Meeting the challenge of incorporating the study of religion in the public school curriculum can be an engaging and rewarding opportunity, a major contribution to preparing students to live and work together in a pluralistic society. For most teachers, this will require additional study focused on teaching about religion in ways that are "constitutionally permissible, educationally sound, and culturally sensitive" (Haynes, 1998, pp. 7.10). To this end, Haynes encourages teachers to participate in professional development opportunities offered by national and state institutes, local school districts, and through universities and colleges. They are also advised to become familiar with state and local guidelines in this area. He also advises teachers to be very clear as to their educational goals and objectives, and prepared to explain why, how, and when they will teach about religion to students, parents, and administrators.

Strategies for Demystifying Print

Teachers have found several strategies effective in the process of "demystifying print" (Klein's term is apropos). One is to help students learn to challenge what they read through guided questioning: Do you believe that is true? Why did the author say that . . . ? More probing questions can be used to direct analysis of specific topics in different content areas (Klein, 1985).

Another strategy is to make published writing accessible to students, their families, and communities. In many elementary and secondary schools, student efforts are compiled into class and school "publications." My bilingual high school students translated children's stories for use by pupils in elementary schools. In some English schools, parents and community members write and

Demystifying print includes making published writing accessible to students.

illustrate stories for children which are bound, laminated, and displayed in classrooms and school libraries (Klein, 1986). Such texts, Klein observes can provide a wide range of languages, dialects, orthographies, and viewpoints.

Analyzing, comparing, and contrasting texts and readings is a third strategy teachers can use. This technique requires "the application of critical thinking to the reading process" (Saunders, 1982, p. 114). Through critical reading, students become actively involved with a written text by examining its attitudinal, functional, and evaluative elements. According to Saunders, critical reading encompasses a range of skills from distinguishing between factual information, opinions, and propaganda to analyzing the language used to convey ideas. On occasion, for example, accounts in different textbooks, particularly in history, appear to be contradictory. Such discrepancies can be revealed by analyses of different textbooks published during the same period, different editions of the same text, and texts selected from different periods. To illustrate this point, consider the following excerpts about the beginning of the Crusades from two different sources:

Text One

The first Crusade . . . was the result of an appeal for Western help from the hard-pressed Emperor Alexius of Byzantium. His territories in Asia Minor had been captured by the Moslems in 1071, and the Saljuk's spreading power had put [an end] to the relatively peaceful relations he had enjoyed with the Arab occupiers of Palestine . . . He was attracted by the idea of getting foreigners to recapture his territories for him. (*The Invaders,* cited in Klein, 1985, p. 118)

Text Two

About 900 years ago, the Christian pilgrims met trouble in the Holy Land. They were cruelly treated by the Saracens who had conquered Jerusalem. This made Christian people everywhere very angry. Alexius sent to the Head of the Christian Church, Pope Urban II, for help against the Saracens. (*The Crusades*, cited in Klein, 1985, p. 118)

One variation on this strategy involves its use with textbooks and materials from other countries. In accordance with local guidelines and practices, students could compare accounts of periods, events, and individuals in U.S. textbooks with appropriate materials from other nations. They may be intrigued by the English version of the American Revolution (or was it a rebellion?) or the War of 1812. How are past and present leaders and events portrayed? Students might also find it useful to compare the treatment of countries like Canada, Australia, and New Zealand in foreign and domestic texts. Bilingual students can assist in doing the same with comparable texts in other languages.

Finally, students can analyze how various evaluative terms are used in depictions of different groups in textbooks and readings. In general, approximately 300 common nouns and adjectives are believed to account for about 88% of the evaluative terms (favorable and unfavorable) commonly found in textbooks (Saunders, 1982). One list developed in the early 1970s included brave, civilized, hardworking, intelligent, honorable, proud, honest, bold, clean, noble, and victorious as examples of positive terms; negative terms included hostile, ignorant, primitive, savage, backward, barbarian, blood-thirsty, corrupt, dirty, lazy, warlike, and treacherous. By using scales of such evaluate terms, students can rate how different groups are depicted along various dimensions. As an example, the following scale could be used to assess how the elderly are portrayed (Sorgman & Sorenson, 1984, p. 122):

Kind .Mean
Healthy . . . . .Sick
Happy . . . . .Sad
Quiet . . . . .Aggressive
Poor .Rich
Wise .Senile

Strategies for Media Analysis

Students receive a multicultural education both in and out of schools. Outside of schools, they learn through that all-encompassing, dynamic, informal curriculum of family, peers, neighbors, institutions, organizations, mass media, and other socializing forces Cortés calls the "societal curriculum" (1995, p. 169). From this societal curriculum, students learn about themselves and others, about diversity in its many manifestations, including race, ethnicity, culture, gender, religion, exceptionality, region, and nationality. Through interactions with the societal curriculum, students learn fact and fiction, consciously and unconsciously.

Most relevant to this discussion is the mass media. On a daily level, ideas are communicated in a variety of forms that include television, motion pictures, radio, magazines, newspapers, and more recently, via information networks such as the Internet. These constitute an educationally powerful force within society. Media use accounts for a significant proportion of students' time away from school; by the time they graduate, for example, average high school seniors will have spent more time watching television than in the classroom—about 20% more (Cortés, 1983). The media is a most powerful "multicultural educator," contributing to and also reflecting existing societal views regarding different groups within American society and in foreign countries.

> By participating in the social construction of knowledge about race and ethnicity, media multicultural education both interacts with and affects personal identity, both challenges and reinforces intergroup prejudice, contributes to both intergroup understanding and intergroup misunderstanding, and influences public norms, expectations, hopes, and fears about diversity. (Cortés, 1995, p. 169)

In one second-grade classroom, a teacher discovered that her pupils believed "all Indians were dead" because no one they knew resembled the "image" of Native Americans evoked by television westerns.

The pervasiveness of the media in American society and its ability to shape users' attitudes and beliefs pose an important challenge for teachers. Research on the impact of media on intergroup and intragroup perceptions and self-identity reveals that

◇ media influences intergroup and intragroup perceptions; viewers learn about ethnicity and race from news and entertainment media;
◇ individual responses to media vary; the influence—conscious and unconscious—differs as to degree, content, and persistence; and
◇ the influence of media can be positive or negative. (Cortés, 1995, p. 176)

Although the media influence the social construction of multicultural knowledge, learners are generally unaware of how media teaching/learning works (p. 179). Teachers cannot expect to influence students' construction of racial, cultural, and ethnic knowledge, perceptions, beliefs, and attitudes while ignoring media's contribution.

> The communications revolution has given us a new student and new means for communicating with that student . . . We must acknowledge the existence and influence of this new media culture and enable the child to master its codes and to control its impact. We should want them to be active, intelligent, appreciative, and selective consumers of the total media culture. (Culkin, cited in Los Angeles County Superintendent of Schools, 1981a, p. 1)

As a primary source of ideas and information, both the fictional and nonfictional media should be examined analytically. The need to improve critical thinking in this area is well established (Cortés, 1995). Consider that learners may not be cognizant of media-fostered prejudices toward a particular group until these beliefs and attitudes are aroused through interaction with individuals from that group. Also consider that television viewers find it difficult to distinguish between news and entertainment as evidenced by a survey in which there was disagreement as to whether *America's Most Wanted* is a news or entertainment program—50% said it was news, 28% thought it was entertainment (Rosentiel, cited in Cortés, 1995).

From a teacher's perspective, the purposes of including media analysis in the curriculum is to develop the following (Cortés, 1980):

◇ An awareness of the multicultural content conveyed by the media and its impact on how individuals view themselves and others as members of specific groups.
◇ "Media literacy" (i.e., critical skills in evaluating the various media as sources of information and ideas).
◇ An understanding of how previous knowledge, attitudes, and experiences influence an individual's ability to interpret and respond to what they encounter as readers, listeners, and viewers.

Cortés (1980) has outlined four approaches teachers can use in teaching media analysis in the context of multicultural education; these approaches focus on content, communication structure, causation, and self as viewer. Each approach deals with a different aspect of the media and requires its own set of strategies for classroom analysis.

Media Content

Analysis of media content from a multicultural perspective has two major components: (a) to examine how various groups and foreign nations are portrayed in different media and (b) to identify the underlying viewpoint of various presentations. As with other sources of information, presentations in the media—even "factual" accounts of events—are subjective. Overtly or covertly, they mirror a particular point of view; intentionally and unintentionally, they are subject to varying degrees of distortion. Content analysis research indicates that the information transmitted may or may not be correct, balanced, or contextualized (Cortés, 1995, p. 173).

Having students do a content analysis of a television program is a good initial eye-opener in developing their media literacy. Subjecting a program to analysis is a much different experience than watching it solely for its entertainment value. In examining how different groups are portrayed, many elements such as the following are relevant (McGee Banks, 1977; Cortés, 1983; Smith & Otero, 1982):

1. Generalizations and stereotypes
2. Representations of social status (e.g., class, occupation, professional, rural/urban)
3. Attributions (e.g., intelligence, abilities, language, values, attitudes, behaviors, interpersonal relations, sense of humor)
4. Problems and issues (e.g., types, scope, solutions)
5. Degree of group identification
6. Topic, theme, point of view, perspective (e.g., group members and nonmembers)

Numerous sources are suitable for content analysis, from children's literature and animated films at the elementary level to newspaper stories, television series, and movies at the secondary level (Cortés, 1980). In my class, I introduce the process of media analysis using the "Teacher's Beau" episode of the classic *Little Rascals* comedies. It is a short episode set in a 1935 school context that provides numerous examples of many of the elements identified. In areas where television newscasts are available from other countries (e.g., Canada or Mexico) or in other languages, a comparative study of how the same events are covered for different audiences can be quite revealing. The selection of stories originating in Mexico City or Montreal, for example, use of film footage, and accompanying narration makes for a most interesting contrast with coverage on newscasts in the United States. Such a project also can capitalize on ethnic language skills not often tapped in the regular curriculum. Using stories featured on the major network news, students can compare and contrast the treatment given the same individual, issue, or event as well as the time allocated for coverage (Cortés, 1983). Subsequent comparisons can then be made with coverage in print media (e.g., local newspapers and national news magazines).

Media Communication Structure

The various media differ in the communication modalities used to present messages. Some are visual, some auditory; others are multidimensional. When words, sounds, and images are juxtaposed, as in films and television, students must be able to recognize what each component contributes to the whole and how it does so. They also need to know how the various components can be examined separately.

DeVaney (1996) teaches the analysis of structure in television beginning with the smallest unit—a frame. She develops image-reading skills by asking students to look at what is and is not included in the images, by projecting what lies beyond the frame, etc. She also has students focus on angle (e.g., looking up to or down on people); lighting (e.g., from low to convey a quiet, sad, or fearful mood to bright for a cheerful or joyous mood); and distance (e.g., close to define detail, medium to compare and contrast, long to establish setting or provide overview). Analysis of motion and shots (a sequence of frames) complete her examination of structure. In considering television as visual text, DeVaney asserts that "the camera always lies"; for even when recording an actual event, the technology of television recasts that event in presenting the story (p. 357).

Teachers can use several strategies to facilitate an analysis of visual and auditory messages. Cortés (1980) suggests drawing attention separately to each element. One technique is to show a news story or documentary in which ethnic groups or foreign nations are represented. The account is presented to one group of students with the sound track and to another group without the sound track. After viewing the story or documentary, students are asked to compare how their group interpretations differ and to assess the influence of the narration on how the visual material is interpreted.

Other strategies also can enhance students' ability to critically view films (Los Angeles County Schools, 1981a, 1981b). For example, teachers can show a 2- or 3-minute excerpt from a film, directing students' attention to the visual material. In discussion, students are asked to summarize information and highlight main points. When the same segment is shown a second time, students are instructed to focus on the narrative, concentrating on what is said and how (e.g., wording and attitudes). An alternative approach is to contrast the spoken text and film sequence by taking an excerpt and recording the two messages side by side in separate columns for comparison. Some questions to consider when using films that portray cultures and populations are presented in Figure 6.10. Having students analyze and compare several films, using these questions as a guide, will sharpen their critical viewing skills.

Overall Presentation

Does the film:

1. Offer a positive image of cultures or populations portrayed?

2. Show basic similarities among all groups of people without making value judgments?

3. Present factual information objectively?

4. Portray one segment of the population and their activities as representative of the entire culture or population?

5. Provide a comprehensive view of cultures and populations which allows students to identify and appreciate characteristic modes of behavior and adaptation?

6. Present information in a manner that is balanced and unambiguous, (i.e., present positive and negative elements as appropriate, avoiding distortions and stereotypes)?

7. Provide an accurate and balanced representation of the historical development of the cultures and populations depicted?

8. Examine historical and/or contemporary forces and conditions contributing to advantages and disadvantages faced by the cultures and populations portrayed?

9. Explore intergroup conflict and tension in a balanced and objective manner?

Photography

1. How do the camera angles, types of shots, distance, and movement affect the way information is communicated by the camera? What is the message communicated through the photography?

(continued)

FIGURE 6.10   Questions for critical viewing of films.

FIGURE 6.10   *(continued)*

---

2. How and when are long shots used? Are they supported by appropriate close-ups?

3. How and when are close-ups used?

Sound Track

1. Are "buzz" words used to describe people, living conditions, heritage?

2. To what extent does the narration convey a sense of respect for the culture?

3. To what extent does the presentation of content in the film depend on narration as opposed to visual material?

4. What words does the narrator emphasize? How is this done?

5. How is point of view reflected in the choice of words used in the narration?

6. How are music and sound effects used to enhance the message, set the scene, and affect the pace?

7. To what extent does the film appear to be authentic and accurate?

Source: Adapted from J. N. Hawkins and J. Maksik, 1976. *Teacher's Resource Handbook for African Studies* (Occasional Paper No. 16). African Studies Center, University of California—Los Angeles. Cited in Los Angeles County Superintendent of Schools (1981b).

Causation

To be multicultural media literate, students must be aware of the reasons for variations in the treatment of different groups and foreign nations. This awareness comes from knowledge of the historical forces and societal conditions that influence media and account for changes in treatment over time (Cortés, 1980). How groups and nations are depicted is sensitive toward international diplomacy, ethnic politics, economic conditions, and changing social attitudes. For example, the September 1941 issue of *Time* magazine carried an article offering "guidelines" for distinguishing between individuals who are Chinese and Japanese (Smith & Otero, 1982). Polls consistently reveal shifts in public attitudes toward different groups nationally and internationally.

At this level of analysis, relevant activities include the following (Cortés, 1980):

1. Identification of the period in which something was written or produced.
2. Investigation of the social conditions of the period using other sources (e.g., historical accounts, literature).
3. Examination of changes in the treatment of groups within a single genre (e.g., westerns in television and movies).
4. Comparison of the treatment of specific groups or nations in different media during the same historical period or within a particular type of media over time.

Self as Viewer

Individuals' own knowledge, attitudes, and experiences influence how they perceive and interpret messages conveyed through the media. As Cortés (1980) has observed, the media are only part of the experience; "viewers and readers are the other critical aspect of the complex process of communication" (p. 45). How individuals respond to media messages is in many ways a reflection of themselves.

In the classroom, teachers can use different types of media to promote student awareness of their own reactions to media as viewers and readers. Cortés (1980) has found media presentations involving foreign areas, multiple ethnic groups, and intergroup relations especially useful for this purpose because they tend to generate a diversity of responses. As different group perspectives emerge, students can compare and contrast these reactions and explore why reactions differ.

SUMMARY

◇ Textbooks and other instructional materials are fundamental components in the implementation of a multicultural curriculum. Historically, textbooks have occupied a major role in classrooms across the United States. Student involvement with textbooks accounts for major portions of students' time in class and almost all of the time engaged in homework. The fact that textbooks and other instructional materials overtly and covertly convey political, social, and cultural values and beliefs generates considerable debate from a wide range of groups.

◇ Within multicultural education, particular interest has been directed at how different cultural groups are portrayed in textbooks. The civil rights movement brought attention to bear on the treatment of ethnic groups, especially African Americans, Hispanics, Native Americans, and Asian Americans. The women's movement emphasized bias in the depiction of females. Consideration of social content now covers a broad range of categories, including age, exceptionality, religion, and socioeconomic level. Concern over the effects of how issues and groups are depicted goes beyond mere academic debate. The implications are serious because student attitudes, personality development and behavior, academic achievement, and career aspirations are affected by the instructional materials they use.

◇ Bias in textbooks has traditionally taken a variety of different forms. From a teacher's perspective, perhaps the most important practices that contribute to bias are inaccuracies, stereotyping, omissions and distortions, and biased language usage. Although bias in textbooks, especially in its most blatant forms, has been considerably reduced in recent years, some remains. Its manifestations are often subtle and differ to some extent depending on the group involved. The effects and limitations of ethnocentrism can be mitigated to some extent by adopting geocultural and global perspectives, which recognize the existence of diverse viewpoints.

◇ As teachers use textbooks and other instructional materials they need to examine and use them critically and analytically. This requires the evaluation of content, illustrations, and language. Some of the limitations in current texts and instructional materials can be addressed using a variety of strategies related to insider perspective, demystifying print, and media analysis. Strategies specific to teaching about religion and teaching history also contribute to the incorporation of multicultural perspectives. This process also entails empowering students as critical users of texts, reading materials, and media—learners willing to challenge what they see and what they read by questioning, contrasting, comparing, analyzing, and evaluating information from different sources.

APPLICATION, EXTENSION, AND REFLECTION

1. *Rethinking What We Teach.* I first began to explore Thanksgiving from a multicultural point of view a few years ago, after I was given a children's book on a thanksgiving celebration that took place on the Rio Grande years before the Pilgrims arrived in Massachusetts. Since then, I have been collecting information and exploring how Thanksgiving might be treated from many different perspectives. I have also discovered that this is a topic that engenders strong reactions in some teachers, as they are asked to grapple with historical information that challenges deeply ingrained myths and misconceptions.

   Larsen (1986) suggests that the "first" Thanksgiving probably dates back some 30,000 years, while the tradition of giving thanks for the harvests of the land dates back at least 10,000 years: "Every last Thursday in November we now partake in one of the *oldest* and most *universal* of human celebrations, and *there are many thanksgiving stories to tell*" (p. 4). Clearly, this is a topic with real possibilities, an event so widely yet so poorly taught that it can provide the impetus teachers need to rethink events of the past and their meaning for the present.

   Shenkman is right in observing that "Thanksgiving is the source of bountiful misconceptions" (1988, 139). It's now time for you to consider how many of these you recognize. How well can you separate cherished myths from historical record? When you teach about Thanksgiving, are you teaching history or are you teaching myths and misconceptions? (See figure 6.11.)

   Having distinguished between historical fact and myth, what will you teach about Thanksgiving and how will you teach it? Be advised that Figure 6.11 was not designed to address substantive issues such as religious intolerance and the plagues that the textbooks largely ignore. To learn more, consult other resources. As an example, Loewen's (1996) chapter, "The Truth About the First Thanksgiving," is a useful source of historical information and an eye opener for many teachers. If you are looking for a starting point, one of my students found information and a lesson

Indicate whether or not each of the following statements is TRUE or FALSE by placing a "T" or "F" in the blank.

The Event

_____**1.** No one knows exactly when the first Thanksgiving in Plymouth took place. In Massachusetts, it was made a legal holiday on December 21 in 1895, and three years later, the federal government established the legal holiday on the last Thursday in November.

_____**2.** Thanksgiving was an annual event for the Pilgrims.

_____**3.** The Pilgrims regarded Thanksgiving as a family celebration.

_____**4.** For the Pilgrims, Thanksgiving was a secular festival, not a religious holiday.

_____**5.** With respect to the food eaten by the Pilgrims and Wampanoag, scholars know only that they ate "fowl" and "deer".

_____**6.** No one knows for sure whether turkeys were consumed.

_____**7.** Thanksgiving became a religious and family event during the Victorian era.

_____**8.** There is historical evidence of an earlier "thanksgiving" event during the colonial period—a celebration and feast on the Rio Grande near El Paso shared by 400 colonists (including 135 families) from New Spain (now Mexico) and Native Americans—23 years before the Mayflower landed.

The Pilgrims

_____**9.** The Pilgrims enjoyed complete freedom of worship in Holland.

_____**10.** In addition to wanting a place of their own in which to practice their faith, the Pilgrims left Holland because they feared that their children would adopt the Dutch language, manners, and ideas.

_____**11.** Only about one third of the Mayflower's passengers and crew came to America for religious reasons; the others came to better their fortunes.

_____**12.** It is not clear exactly when the Pilgrims arrived in Plymouth.

_____**13.** The Pilgrims did not land on Plymouth Rock.

_____**14.** The Pilgrims were neither partial to black nor did they wear tall hats with shiny buckles.

_____**15.** The Pilgrims lived in clapboard houses with thatched roofs.

_____**16.** The Pilgrims were not revered nationally until the nineteenth century.

The Wampanoag

_____**17.** The Wampanoag were Algonkian-speaking people, members of an extensive confederacy known as the League of the Delaware.

(continued)

FIGURE 6.11   Self-test: Thanksgiving.

FIGURE 6.11   *(continued)*

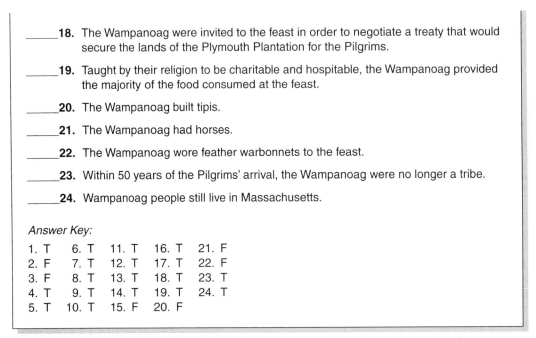

_____**18.** The Wampanoag were invited to the feast in order to negotiate a treaty that would secure the lands of the Plymouth Plantation for the Pilgrims.

_____**19.** Taught by their religion to be charitable and hospitable, the Wampanoag provided the majority of the food consumed at the feast.

_____**20.** The Wampanoag built tipis.

_____**21.** The Wampanoag had horses.

_____**22.** The Wampanoag wore feather warbonnets to the feast.

_____**23.** Within 50 years of the Pilgrims' arrival, the Wampanoag were no longer a tribe.

_____**24.** Wampanoag people still live in Massachusetts.

Answer Key:

1. T	6. T	11. T	16. T	21. F
2. F	7. T	12. T	17. T	22. F
3. F	8. T	13. T	18. T	23. T
4. T	9. T	14. T	19. T	24. T
5. T	10. T	15. F	20. F	

Sources: Bragg, Bea. (1989). *The Very First Thanksgiving: Pioneers on the Rio Grande.* Tucson, AZ: Harbinger House, p. 55.

Crawford, James. (1991), *Bilingual Education: History, Politics, Theory, and Practice.* Los Angeles, CA: Bilingual educational services.

Larsen, Chuck. (September 1986). An introduction for teachers. Teaching about Thanksgiving, Center For World Indigenous Studies, Olympia, WA, pp. 3–4. http://www.night.net/thanksgiving/lesson-plan/html

Ross, Cathy; Robertson, Mary; Larsen, Chuck; and Fernandez, Roger. (1986). Teaching about Thanksgiving, Center for World Indigenous Studies, Olympia, WA, pp. 6, 9–11. http://www.night.net/thanksgiving/lesson-plan/html

Shenkman, Richard. (1988). *Legends, Lies, and Cherished Myths of American History.* New York, NY: Harper & Row, pp. 139–140.

Shenkman, Richard. (1991). *"I Love Paul Revere Whether He Rode or Not"—Warren Harding.* New York, NY: Harper Perennial, pp. 16, 17–18, 20–21.

plan available on the Internet through The Center for World Indigenous Studies at http://www.night.net/thanksgiving/lesson-plan.html.

To take this process one step further, identify an event or prominent national figure of your choice, and do some research on your own. Begin your own professional process of sorting out the myths from what historians can substantiate as having transpired. Explore different perspectives on the particular individual or event you selected. Reflect on what should be taught and how it might be done.

"Literacy" tests are an effective technique for drawing attention to what students know and do not know about different groups in American society.

2. *"Literacy" Tests.* Time for a test! "Literacy" tests are an effective way to draw attention to what students know and do not know about different groups in American society. By addressing those groups whose textbook treatment has traditionally been limited and uneven, such exercises provide opportunities for discussion of common misconceptions about the nation's development as a pluralistic society. Such literacy tests are readily available, applicable in most content areas at the secondary level, and versatile.

   The two variations reprinted here will also enable teachers to "test" their own knowledge of history from what is perhaps a different perspective than usual. After completing the exercises, compare your performance on the two tests and, if possible, discuss the results with others. Which test was easier? Why? How well did you know the material? How would you rate your knowledge in these areas?

   The Ethnic Literacy Test developed by Banks (1987) assesses knowledge about specific historical events related to ethnic groups in the United States and some aspects of their culture and role in American society. This test is presented in Figure 6.12.

   The "Susan B. Who?" test, developed by Gollnick et al. (1982), assesses knowledge about the contributions of specific women to the development of the United States. This test is presented in Figure 6.13.

Directions: Indicate whether each of the statements is TRUE or FALSE by placing a "T" or "F" in the preceding space.

_____ **1.** The percentage of Whites in the United States, relative to non-Whites, decreased between 1970 and 1980.

_____ **2.** The first Chinese immigrants who came to the United States worked on the railroads.

_____ **3.** In 1980, there were more than 26 million African Americans in the United States.

_____ **4.** Puerto Ricans on the island of Puerto Rico became U.S. citizens in 1920.

_____ **5.** Between 1970 and 1979, the Mexican American population increased by slightly more than 60%.

_____ **6.** Between 1820 and 1930, 15 million immigrants came to the United States.

_____ **7.** White Anglo-Saxon Protestants are the most powerful group in the United States.

_____ **8.** Rosh Hashanah, which in Hebrew means "end of the year," is a Jewish holiday that comes early in the fall.

_____ **9.** Between 1820 and 1971, Germans were the largest European group immigrating to the United States.

_____**10.** The first law to limit immigration to the United States was passed in 1882 to restrict the number of African immigrants.

_____**11.** Puerto Ricans in New York City tend to identify strongly with African Americans in that city.

_____**12.** Between 1820 and 1971, more individuals from Canada and Newfoundland immigrated to the United States than from Mexico.

_____**13.** Most African Americans came from the eastern parts of Africa.

_____**14.** The internment of the Japanese Americans during World War II was opposed by President Franklin D. Roosevelt.

_____**15.** In 1980, there were more than 14 million Hispanic Americans in the United States.

_____**16.** More than 270,000 immigrants came to the United States from the Philippines between 1971 and 1980.

_____**17.** Congress passed a Removal Act that authorized the removal of American Indians from east to west of the Mississippi in 1830.

_____**18.** A Japanese settlement was established in California as early as 1869.

_____**19.** The United States acquired a large part of Mexico's territory under the terms of the Treaty of Guadalupe Hidalgo in 1848.

_____**20.** Agriculture dominates the economy of the island of Puerto Rico.

(continued)

FIGURE 6.12   Ethnic literacy test.

FIGURE 6.12 *(continued)*

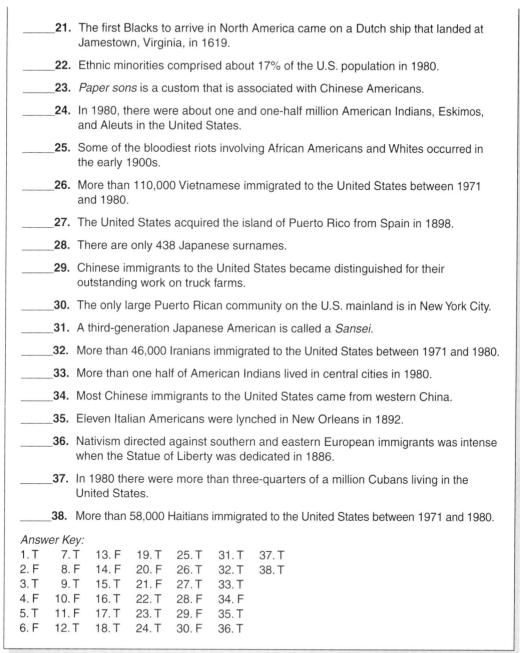

_____**21.** The first Blacks to arrive in North America came on a Dutch ship that landed at Jamestown, Virginia, in 1619.

_____**22.** Ethnic minorities comprised about 17% of the U.S. population in 1980.

_____**23.** *Paper sons* is a custom that is associated with Chinese Americans.

_____**24.** In 1980, there were about one and one-half million American Indians, Eskimos, and Aleuts in the United States.

_____**25.** Some of the bloodiest riots involving African Americans and Whites occurred in the early 1900s.

_____**26.** More than 110,000 Vietnamese immigrated to the United States between 1971 and 1980.

_____**27.** The United States acquired the island of Puerto Rico from Spain in 1898.

_____**28.** There are only 438 Japanese surnames.

_____**29.** Chinese immigrants to the United States became distinguished for their outstanding work on truck farms.

_____**30.** The only large Puerto Rican community on the U.S. mainland is in New York City.

_____**31.** A third-generation Japanese American is called a *Sansei.*

_____**32.** More than 46,000 Iranians immigrated to the United States between 1971 and 1980.

_____**33.** More than one half of American Indians lived in central cities in 1980.

_____**34.** Most Chinese immigrants to the United States came from western China.

_____**35.** Eleven Italian Americans were lynched in New Orleans in 1892.

_____**36.** Nativism directed against southern and eastern European immigrants was intense when the Statue of Liberty was dedicated in 1886.

_____**37.** In 1980 there were more than three-quarters of a million Cubans living in the United States.

_____**38.** More than 58,000 Haitians immigrated to the United States between 1971 and 1980.

Answer Key:

1. T	7. T	13. F	19. T	25. T	31. T	37. T
2. F	8. F	14. F	20. F	26. T	32. T	38. T
3. T	9. T	15. T	21. F	27. T	33. T	
4. F	10. F	16. T	22. T	28. F	34. F	
5. T	11. F	17. T	23. T	29. F	35. T	
6. F	12. T	18. T	24. T	30. F	36. T	

Source: From J. A. Banks, *Teaching Strategies for Ethnic Studies* (4th ed.). Copyright © 1987 by Allyn and Bacon. Reprinted with permission.

Directions: Match each individual with her contributions and achievements by placing the appropriate letter before her name.

_____ **1.** Prudence Crandall

_____ **2.** Mary Berry

_____ **3.** Sor Juana Inés de la Cruz

_____ **4.** Patricia Harris

_____ **5.** Dixie Lee Ray

_____ **6.** Harriet Tubman

_____ **7.** Alice Paul

_____ **8.** Lupe Anguiano

_____ **9.** Susan B. Anthony

_____**10.** Betty Friedan

_____**11.** Maria Tallchief

_____**12.** Maria Goeppert-Mayer

_____**13.** Wilma Rudolph

_____**14.** Chien-Shiung Wu

_____**15.** Margaret Mead

a. An organizer of the Underground Railroad during the Civil War

b. First woman president of a major state university

c. Nuclear physicist

d. Winner of Nobel Prize for Physics in 1963

e. Established a school for Black girls in Connecticut prior to the Civil War

f. Responsible for the creation of several Hispanic women's coalitions

g. Classic ballet dancer in the 1940s and 1950s

h. Author of a rationale for educating women in the fifteenth century

i. Governor of Washington, former head of Atomic Energy Commission

j. Anthropologist, psychologist, writer, lecturer, and teacher

k. Leader in the struggle for women's rights during the nineteenth century

l. U.S. runner who won three Olympic gold medals in 1960 for field and track

m. Militant suffragist who organized parades and demonstrations in the nation's capital

n. First Black woman to be appointed an ambassador and later a member of the U.S. Cabinet

o. Author of *The Feminine Mystique* and one of the founders of the National Organization for Women

Answer Key:

1. e	4. n	7. m	10. o	13. l
2. b	5. i	8. f	11. g	14. c
3. h	6. a	9. k	12. d	15. j

FIGURE 6.13 "Susan B. Who?"
Source: From D. M. Gollnick, M. P. Sadker, and D. Sadker, "Beyond the Dick and Jane Syndrome: Confronting Sex Bias in Instructional Materials." Cited in M. P. Sadker and D. M. Sadker (1982).

3. *Then and Now.* Figure 6.1 highlights research findings on the portrayal of various groups in U.S. textbooks before 1980. Select one or more current textbooks and compare the treatment of various groups in pre-1980s texts with those in use today. Apply the guidelines provided in this chapter. In what important ways are the textbooks different? In what ways are they similar? In what ways might the textbook treatment of different groups be improved?

4. *Observing the Societal Curriculum.* Education is a lifelong process, a complex combination of formal and informal learning and experiences. That portion of an individual's education acquired outside the classroom is transmitted via the "societal curriculum"(Cortés, 2000). As described by Cortés, it comprises the massive, informal curriculum of home, community, and society—the sum total of socializing forces that "educate" individuals throughout their lives. For each individual, the societal curriculum embodies the lessons learned from family, peer groups, neighborhood, institutions, organizations, mass media, and personal experiences. Because it involves elements that are of primary importance to individuals, the societal curriculum exerts considerable influence (both positive and negative) on intercultural and interethnic attitudes, values, and beliefs. Its effects are felt before one reaches school age and continue beyond the period of formal education throughout one's entire life.

    Because of its pervasiveness and influence, the societal curriculum must be given serious consideration in the design and implementation of multicultural education. Awareness of its existence and content is the first step. To this end, Cortés (1981b) suggests that teachers observe and keep a record (perhaps even a journal) of the number and variety of topics they encounter in the course of daily contact with different sources: family members, friends, community organizations, media, and so forth. From my own experience, teachers have found this activity to be quite revealing. Building on this initial level of awareness, teachers can use strategies (such as the multicultural analysis of media highlighted in this chapter) to integrate elements of the societal curriculum into the school program.

5. *Media Analysis.* Select one or more of the strategies presented in this chapter and use these to analyze selected films, radio or television programs. What did your analysis reveal? What are the implications for you as a teacher? How might you apply the critical analysis of media as part of your own curriculum? (For more information, see Cortés, *The Children Are Watching*.)

REFERENCES

Altbach, P. G. (1991). The unchanging variable: Textbooks in comparative perspective. In P. G. Altback, G. P. Kelly, H. G. Petrie, & L. Weis (Eds.), *Textbooks in American society: Politics, policy, and pedagogy* (pp. 237–254). Albany, NY: State University of New York Press.

American School Board Journal. (1987). Textbooks ignore religion in American
    history. *Education Digest, LII*(7), 46–47.

Anglesey, Z. (1998). "Moving from an Obsolete Lingo to a Vocabulary of Respect."
    In F. Schultz (Ed.), *Multicultural Education 1998/99,* Annual Editions Series, 5th
    ed. (pp. 8–13). Guilford, CT: Dushkin/McGraw-Hill.

Association of American Publishers. (1984). *Statement on bias-free materials* (rev. ed.).
    Brochure available from School Division, AAP, 220 E. 23rd St., New York, NY
    10010.

August, E. R. (1992). Real men don't: Anti-male bias in English. In G. Goshgarian
    (Ed.), *Exploring language* (6th ed., 238–249). New York: HarperCollins.

Banks, C. A. McGee. (1977). A content analysis of the treatment of Black Americans
    on television. *Social Education, 41*(4), 336–339, 344.

Banks, C. A. McGee. (1999). The challenges of national standards in a multicultural
    society. In F. Schultz (Ed.), *Multicultural education 99/00,* Annual Editions
    Series, (pp. 88–92). Guilford, CT: Dushkin/ McGraw-Hill.

Banks, J. A. (1987). *Teaching strategies for ethnic studies* (4th ed.). Boston: Allyn
    and Bacon.

Bennett, C. I. (1986). *Comprehensive multicultural education.* Boston: Allyn and Bacon.

Berreth, D., Gaustad, E., Greenhut, H., Haynes, C. C., Karlinger, Sister M. J., and
    Smith, T. (1990). Religious influences in American history. (pp. 3–14). In C. C.
    Haynes. *Religion in American history: What to teach and how.* Alexandria, VA:
    Association for Supervision and Curriculum Development.

Bordelon, K. W. (1985). Sexism in reading materials. *The Reading Teacher, 38*(8),
    792–797.

Bragg, B. (1989). *The very first Thanksgiving: Pioneers on the Rio Grande.* Tucson, AZ:
    Harbinger House.

Britton, G., & Lumpkin, M. (1984). Females and minorities in basal readers.
    Education Digest, L(2), 48–50.

Bullard, B. M. (1986). Asia. *Social Education, 50*(5), 367–375.

Cantoni-Harvey, G. (1987). *Content-area language instruction.* Reading, MA:
    Addison-Wesley.

Chaika, E. (1982). *Language: The social mirror.* Rowley, MA: Newbury House.

Cortés, C. E. (1976). Need for a geo-cultural perspective in the bicentennial.
    Educational Leadership, 33(4), 290–292.

Cortés, C. E. (1980). The role of media in multicultural education. *Viewpoints in
    Teaching and Learning, 56*(1), 28–49.

Cortés, C. E. (1981a). Dealing with the density of diversity: Groupness and
    individuality in the California history/social science framework. *Social Studies
    Review, 21*(1), 12–18.

Cortés, C. E. (1981b). The societal curriculum: Implications for multiethnic
    education. In J. A. Banks (Ed.), *Education in the 80's: Multiethnic education*
    (pp. 24–32). Washington, DC: National Education Association.

Cortés, C. E. (1983). The mass media: Civic education's public curriculum. *Journal
    of Teacher Education, XXXIV*(6), 25–29.

Cortés, C. E. (1995). Knowledge construction and popular culture: The media as
    multicultural educator. In J. A. Banks (Ed.) & C. A. McGee Banks (Assoc. Ed.),
    Handbook of research on multicultural education (pp. 169–183). New York: Macmillan.

Cortés, C. E. (2000). *The Children Are Watching: How the Media Teach about Diversity.* New York: Teachers College Press.

Cortés, C. E., & Fleming, D. B. (1986a). Changing global perspectives in textbooks. *Social Education, 50*(6), 376–384.

Cortés, C. E., & Fleming, D. B. (1986b). Global education and textbooks. *Social Education, 50*(5), 340–344.

Cortés, C. E., & Fleming, D. B. (1987). Social studies texts need a global perspective. *Education Digest, LII*(7), 42–45.

Crofts, M. (1986). Africa. *Social Education, 50*(5), 345–350.

Cruz-Janzen, M. I. (1998). Invisibility: The language bias of political control and power. In F. Schultz (Ed.), *Multicultural education 1998/99,* Annual Editions Series (pp. 219–222). Guilford, CT: Dushkin/McGraw-Hill.

Davis, O. L., Jr., Ponder, G., Burlbaw, L. M., Garza-Lubeck, M., & Moss, A. (1986). A review of U.S. history textbooks. *Education Digest, LII*(3), 50–53.

DeVaney, A. (1996). Television and film in the classroom: The presence and absence of people of color. In C. A. Grant & M. L. Gomez (Eds.), *Making schooling multicultural: Campus and classroom* (pp. 349–367). Englewood Cliffs, NJ: Merrill/Prentice Hall.

First Amendment Center. (1999) *A Teacher's Guide to Religion in the Schools.* Nashville, TN: First Amendment Center.

FitzGerald, F. (1979). *America revisited.* Boston: Atlantic Monthly Press/Little, Brown.

García, R. (1984). Countering classroom discrimination. *Theory Into Practice, XXII*(2), 104–109.

García, J., & Florez-Tighe, V. (1986). The portrayal of Blacks, Hispanics, and Native Americans in recent basal reading series. *Equity and Excellence, 22*(4–6), 72–76.

Gollnick, D. M., Sadker, M. P., & Sadker, D. (1982). Beyond the Dick and Jane syndrome: Confronting sex bias in instructional materials. In M. P. Sadker & D. M. Sadker (Eds.), *Sex equity handbook for schools* (pp. 60–95). New York: Longman.

Grant, C. A., & Tate, W. F. (1995). Multicultural education through the lens of the multicultural education research literature. In J. A. Banks (Ed.) & C. A. McGee Banks (Assoc. Ed.), *Handbook of research on multicultural education* (pp. 145–166). New York: Macmillan.

Griswold, W. J. (1986). Middle East. *Social Education, 50*(5), 357–366.

Haukoos, G. D., & Beauvais, A. B. (1998). Creating positive cultural images: Thoughts for teaching about American Indians. In F. Schultz (Ed.), *Multicultural education 1998/1999,* Annual Editions Series (pp. 162–167). Guilford, CT: Dushkin/McGraw-Hill.

Haynes C. C. (1991). *A Teacher's Guide to Study about Religion in Public Schools.* Boston, MA: Houghton Mifflin Co.

Haynes, C. C., Cassity, M. D., and Stone, M. S. (1993). The State of California *Three Rs Project Manual.* Fairfax, VA: First Liberty Institute at George Mason University.

Haynes, C. C. (1998). Rationale and guidelines for teaching about religion (pp. 7.1–7.18). In Haynes, C. C. , and Thomas O. (Eds.). (1998). *Finding common ground: A First Amendment guide to religion and public education* (3rd.). Nashville, TN: The First Amendment Center.

Haynes, C. C. (1990). *Religion in American History: What to Teach and How.* Alexandria, VA: Association for Supervision and Curriculum Development.

Honig, W. (1985, November 18). "Last chance" to teach culture. Interview. *U.S. News and World Report, 99*(21), 82.

Kane, M. B. (1970). *Minorities in textbooks.* Chicago: Quadrangle Books.

Klein, G. (1985). *Reading into racism.* London: Routledge and Kegan Paul.

Levstik, L. S. (1985). Literary geography and mapping. *Social Education, 49*(1), 38–43.

The Little Rascals. (1935). "Teacher's Beau" in *The Little Rascals* series, Vol. 2. Cabin Fever Entertainment.

Loewen, J. W. (1996). *Lies my teacher told me: Everything your American history textbook got wrong.* New York: Touchstone.

Los Angeles County Superintendent of Schools. (1981a). *There's more to television and films than meets the eye.* Unpublished annotated list of films. Coordinated by P. Seeley. Los Angeles: Office of the Los Angeles County Superintendent of Schools, Educational Services Group.

Los Angeles County Superintendent of Schools. (1981b). *Films on Africa . . . Another Look.* Project of the Administrative Committee for Program Development. Coordinated by J. B. Perez & P. Seeley. Downey, CA: Author.

Luty, C. (1982). Tight budgets keep outdated texts in use past normal "retirement" age. *NEA Today,* December, p. 5.

Mukhopadhyay, C. C. (1985). Teaching cultural awareness through simulations: Bafa Bafa. In H. Hernández & C. C. Mukhopadhyay, *Integrating multicultural perspectives into teacher education* (pp. 100–104). Chico: California State University—Chico.

Nord, W. A. and Haynes, C. C., (1998). *Taking religion seriously across the curriculum.* Arlington, VA: Association for Supervision and Curriculum Development.

Peters, A. (1983). *The new cartography.* New York: Friendship Press.

Religion in the Public School Curriculum: Questions and Answers. (nd). Arlington, VA: The Freedom Forum. [Sponsors of the brochure are identified in Figure 6.7]

Religious Holidays in the Public Schools: Questions and Answers. (nd). Arlington VA: The Freedom Forum. [Sponsors of the brochure are identified in Figure 6.7]

Rosenberg, M. (1974). Evaluate your textbooks for racism, sexism. In M. Dunfee (Ed.), *Eliminating ethnic bias* (pp. 43–47). Washington, DC: Association of Supervision and Curriculum Development.

Sadker, M., Sadker, D., & Klein, S. (1991). The issue of gender in elementary and secondary education. In G. Grant (Ed.), *Review of research in education,* Vol. 17 (pp. 269–333). Washington, D. C.: American Educational Research Association.

Saunders, M. (1982). *Multicultural teaching.* London: McGraw-Hill.

Schreck, R. E. (1998, June 7). A graduation test from 1895. Public Forum section, *Enterprise-Record,* Chico, CA, p. 5B.

Shenkman, R. (1988). *Legends, lies, and cherished myths of American history.* New York: Harper & Row.

Shenkman, R. (1991). *"I love Paul Revere whether he rode or not"—Warren Harding.* New York: HarperPerennial.

Smith, G. R., & Otero, G. (1982). *Teaching about cultural awareness.* Denver: University of Denver, Center for Teaching International Relations.

Sorgman, M. I., & Sorenson, M. (1984). Ageism. *Theory Into Practice, XXIII*(2), 17–123.

Tetreault, M. K. (1984). Notable American women: The case of United States history textbooks. *Social Education, 48*(7), 546–550.

Tetreault, M. K. (1986). Integrating women's history: The case of United States history high school textbooks. *The History Teacher, 19*(2), 211–262.

University of Wisconsin-Extension. (1992). Guide to nonsexist language. In G. Goshgarian (Ed.), *Exploring language* (6th ed., 250–256). New York: HarperCollins.

U.S. Commission on Civil Rights. (1980). *Characters in textbooks.* Clearinghouse Publication 62. Washington, DC: U.S. Government Printing Office.

Wieder, A. (1997). South Carolina unrevised: Portrayals of race in current South Carolina history textbooks. In F. Schultz (Ed.), *Annual editions: Multicultural education, 1997/98* (pp. 68–73). Guilford, CT: Dushkin/McGraw-Hill.

CHAPTER 7 Development of a Multicultural Curriculum

No one should make the claim of being educated until he or she has learned to live in harmony with people who are different.

A. H. Wilson
(cited in Cole, 1984, p. 151)

The purpose of this chapter is to facilitate development of an integrated, interdisciplinary multicultural program appropriate to classroom settings in elementary and secondary schools. To accomplish this task, teachers must adopt a sound and systematic approach. As Gay (1977) observes, "It will be virtually impossible for [multicultural] programs to command academic respect if their formulation ignores the acceptable principles of curriculum design" (p. 94). Thus, teachers involved in the development of multicultural programs must consider the accepted components of curriculum design: needs assessment; goals and learning outcomes; implementation; teaching strategies; and evaluation (Gay, 1977). In developing a multicultural curriculum, teachers will also want to examine the level of content integration and uses of technology.

NEEDS ASSESSMENT

Teachers integrating multicultural perspectives into an existing curriculum need to examine various facets of the existing program. This examination usually includes an initial assessment of student knowledge, attitudes, and skills and an evaluation of the curriculum as a whole. To proceed without such assessment can result in programs that are less sensitive than they otherwise could be to variations in student population, school environment, and community setting.

Assessing Student Attitudes and Perceptions

In general, two key questions underlie the assessment of student knowledge, attitudes, and skills in relation to multicultural education. They can be stated as follows (California State Department of Education, 1979):

◇ What knowledge, attitudes, and skills do students already demonstrate in areas identified within multicultural education?
◇ What knowledge, attitudes, and skills do they need to develop?

Although assessment of knowledge and skills is an accepted part of teaching, assessment of attitudes and perceptions is much less common. Many of the goals and objectives in multicultural education involve efforts to examine and even change how students see themselves, how they are viewed by others and, in turn, how they view others. Needs assessment, especially as it relates to student attitudes and perceptions, is a critical, yet often ignored aspect of program development (Kehoe, 1984a).

Information regarding student attitudes about ethnicity, cultural diversity, and self-concept is particularly relevant to curriculum development. Kehoe (1984a) has found that the more negative the attitudes of students are toward a specific minority group, the less receptive they will be to inclusion of that group's history and culture in the curriculum. In one study involving Canadian high school students, for example, student attitudes differed toward the inclusion of history and culture related to Japanese, Chinese, and East Indian immigrant groups in the curriculum. Minority-group students overwhelmingly supported incorporation of ethnic content about all groups; majority-group students were favorably disposed to including content related to the Japanese and Chinese but not to East Indians. In view of these attitudes, Canadian educators designed an elementary curriculum that emphasized cultural differences in the Japanese-Canadian content and cultural similarities in the East Indian-Canadian content (Kehoe, Echols, & Stone, cited in Kehoe, 1984b).

Teachers also need to be sensitive to student self-concept. In some schools, students belonging to identifiable groups—whether defined by ethnicity, ability, class, or other dimensions—may view themselves quite differently. This was the case in a Canadian study of junior high school students (Perry, Clifton, & Hryniuk, cited in Kehoe, 1984a). In this study, British-Canadian students rated themselves very positively, whereas Native Indian students rated themselves less positively on several measures and were rated by others in some relatively negative terms. When educators developing a multicultural program are faced with this type of situation, Kehoe suggests that they include in the program (a) culturally appropriate ways to promote self-esteem among those who rate themselves less positively and (b) strategies to change the attitudes of other students. In such cases, improving the self-evaluations of students whose self-concept is high and who are favorably perceived by others would not appear to be a major priority.

Student attitudes—positive and negative—are likely to influence how specific ethnic material in a multicultural program is received. For this reason, curriculum development must involve not only selection of appropriate content but also identification of student attitudes toward culturally relevant concepts. Formal and informal indicators of prevailing attitudes in the classroom, school, and community are needed in order to select the combination of strategies and materials most likely to be effective. Although there are limitations and problems inherent in the assessment of attitudes, a number of measures can provide teachers with useful information. Among these, Kehoe recommends opinion questionnaires, semantic differentials, social distance scales, and surveys. Two of these techniques are featured here.

In an *opinion questionnaire*, students are asked to indicate the extent to which they agree or disagree (e.g., strongly, moderately, slightly) with a series of 15 to 20 statements. In the context of multicultural education, statements such as the following would be relevant (Kehoe, 1984a, pp. 131–132):

1. Foreign languages often sound pleasing to the ear.
2. I enjoy being around people who are different from me.
3. You can learn a lot from people whose backgrounds are different from yours.
4. People with different backgrounds don't usually have a great deal in common.
5. A country where everyone has the same background is a lot better off than a very mixed one.
6. Because differences among people mainly divide them, people should try to be more alike.

Positive responses to items 1–3 indicate a generally favorable attitude toward cultural diversity; students with this type of attitude are likely to be receptive to program content related to different ethnic and cultural groups. In contrast, positive responses to items 4–6 indicate a negative attitude toward diversity; students with this attitude are likely to be disinterested in, perhaps even hostile toward, minority-oriented content.

An *information survey* can be used to assess student willingness to have the ethnic history and culture of specific groups incorporated into the curriculum. Such surveys can be used to provide information about the extent to which students in a particular school or school district are willing to have the history and culture of a specific group included and the specific topics that students consider most interesting and relevant. The two following questions are examples of the type of questions an information survey contains (Kehoe, 1984a, pp. 141–142):

1. It would be better if the history (or present-day culture) of East Indians in Canada (a) was omitted, (b) was given brief mention, or (c) was given a lot of attention in the curriculum.
2. If East Indian history and culture are included in the curriculum, then the following topics should receive mention:
   (a) The performance of East Indian soldiers on the side of Canadians during World War II.
   (b) A discussion of the East Indian concept of beauty in men and women.
   (c) Possible conflict between East Indians and majority Canadians because of differences in social customs (e.g., East Indians sometimes go to the front of lined-up people).
   (d) A discussion of physical attacks against East Indians in Toronto.

As these sample questions indicate, an information survey can be designed to provide specific information relevant to a particular school and community and to students of different age levels.

In addition to formal measures of prevailing attitudes, informal observation, discussion, and interviews can uncover helpful supplementary information. The objective of both formal and informal assessment is to gather information useful in developing programs that are culturally and locally relevant in terms of goals and objectives, content, strategies, and evaluation procedures.

Assessing Program Needs

Evaluation of the strengths and weaknesses of the existing curriculum as it relates to multicultural education can help educators identify the types of changes that are needed. Initially, general questions such as the following can be asked (California State Department of Education, 1979): How is the current program helping students develop knowledge, attitudes, and skills relevant to individual and group differences? How effective is the current program? In what ways is it effective? In what ways is it not effective?

From these general questions, assessment can move to more specific areas of the curriculum. The multicultural needs assessment survey presented in Figure 7.1 was designed to identify special program needs at the elementary level. It provides elementary teachers with a practical tool for examining their school's multicultural program and serves as a model for those wishing to develop their own.

Surveys in the early 1980s found fairly consistent patterns in the nature of multicultural programs in secondary schools (Freedman, 1983). The findings indicate that, although proponents of multicultural and multiethnic education emphasize the importance of systematic integration across the disciplines, the

Multicultural Instruction

Content related to human dignity and self-worth:

1. To what degree do pupils exhibit pride and acceptance of self and abilities?

2. To what degree do pupils recognize the basic similarities among members of the human race and the uniqueness of individuals?

3. To what degree do pupils accept each other on the basis of individual worth regardless of gender, race, religion, or socioeconomic background?

4. To what extent do pupils have opportunities to experience success in learning?

Content related to ethnic studies:

1. To what extent do pupils know about their own heritage, history, and contributions to America?

2. To what degree do pupils feel pride in their ethnic heritage?

3. To what degree do pupils recognize and accept the fact that America has been enriched by the contributions of all its ethnic groups?

Content related to intercultural studies:

1. To what extent do pupils have knowledge of universal characteristics of cultures?

2. To what extent do pupils have knowledge of the various groups (religious, ethnic, cultural, etc.) in the United States?

3. To what extent do pupils have positive attitudes toward ethnic groups that are not based on stereotypes?

4. To what extent do pupils recognize and know the significance of events, customs, and traditions that are special for different groups?

5. To what degree do pupils accept and appreciate the diversities of the American culture?

Content related to understanding and acceptance of differences and similarities:

1. To what extent do pupils participate in activities in which they learn to value both individual and group differences?

2. To what extent do pupils have knowledge of similarities and differences in ways individuals express themselves (e.g., in art, music, literature)?

3. To what degree do pupils recognize and accept differences as positive?

Content related to human and intergroup relations:

1. To what extent do pupils engage in positive social interaction among all students of the school?

2. To what extent do pupils have knowledge and understanding of cultural pluralism?

(continued)

FIGURE 7.1 Multicultural needs assessment (elementary).

FIGURE 7.1   *(continued)*

3. To what extent do pupils recognize prejudice as a block to communication and interaction?

4. To what extent do pupils acknowledge that people of different backgrounds have common concerns and can work together to solve common problems?

Instructional Approaches and Strategies

1. To what extent is multicultural instruction in your classroom cross-disciplinary, drawing from and contributing to other curriculum areas?

2. To what extent is multicultural instruction in your classroom cross-cultural in nature instead of structured around separate ethnic groups?

3. To what extent does the multicultural instruction in your classroom involve acquisition of knowledge and attitudes?

4. To what extent is multicultural instruction in your classroom appropriate to the maturity level of the pupils?

School Climate

1. To what extent are the multicultural classroom experiences interrelated with school-wide experiences?

2. To what extent are the approaches and strategies for multicultural classroom instruction evident in the total school multicultural program?

3. To what extent are self-concept and attitudes toward learning equally positive in all pupils at the school?

4. To what extent do students of all ethnic groups have the opportunity to be integrated into the social system of the school so that they share comparable status and roles within the school?

5. To what extent does the physical environment of the school (bulletin boards, displays, etc.) reflect the racial/ethnic composition of the student population?

Parent/Community Involvement

1. To what extent have multicultural resources among parents and in community been identified?

2. To what extent have such resources been utilized at the school?

3. To what extent do the multicultural objectives of the school reflect the concerns of the parents and community surrounding the school?

Source: Adapted from *Multicultural Needs Assessment—Teacher Survey.* Long Beach (CA) Unified School District, Education Department, Special Projects Branch. Used with permission.

majority of programs were confined to one area, namely, social studies (primarily, American history and ethnic studies classes). Only one fourth of the schools responding to surveys indicated that a multicultural approach was included in the area of English literature. As Freedman (1983) puts it, most programs are "serially mono-ethnic": that is, specific groups are treated sequentially and in isolation from one another.

Freedman found, however, that programs differed greatly with respect to the priority given specific educational objectives. Although the highest-ranking general objective was the development of attitudes associated with tolerance and mutual respect, specific objectives varied considerably depending on the composition of the student population. Schools with significant numbers of racial minorities tended to emphasize enhancing the self-esteem of minority-group students; those with large nonminority enrollments gave priority to changing student perceptions and images of minority groups and to understanding the causes of prejudice. In most programs, understanding ethnicity and culture, stereotyping, and intergroup perceptions were the least important objectives.

Freedman (1983) concluded that the primary focus of the programs evaluated was narrowly defined, being directed primarily at racial prejudice and injustice. Consistent with this focus, content emphasis was on minority groups. Unless a specific group was numerically significant within the local community,

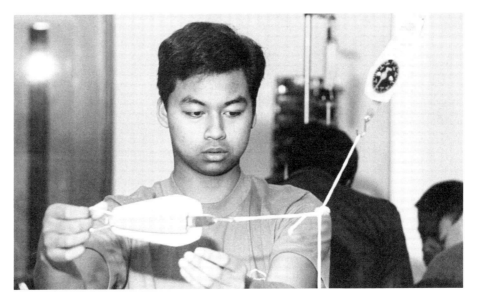

Multicultural perspectives can be integrated across content areas such as mathematics, science, foreign languages, home economics, and physical education, as well as social studies, literature, art, and music.

White ethnic groups were considered only in the treatment of immigration. Issues related to cultural groups along dimensions defined by gender or socioeconomic status, for example, were not usually included.

Given this background, teachers at all levels may find the checklist in Figure 7.2 useful for evaluating existing programs from a multicultural perspective (the applicability of specific items may vary according to grade level or subject area).

Rating Scale

1 = *Ineffective:* This guideline is either entirely lacking, or it is producing no results.
2 = *Somewhat effective:* The program does address this guideline, but it is not accomplishing fully the desired results.
3 = *Effective:* The program is doing a quite satisfactory job here, but there are ways for doing even better.
4 = *Very effective:* The program is doing an outstanding job in addressing the guideline so rated.

This checklist contains guidelines that serve as criteria for evaluating the effectiveness of the multicultural education components established by the National Council for the Social Studies.

Rating

1	2	3	4			
☐	☐	☐	☐	1.0		Does ethnic and cultural diversity permeate the total school environment?
☐	☐	☐	☐		1.1	Are ethnic content and perspectives incorporated into all aspects of the curriculum, preschool through 12th grade and beyond?
☐	☐	☐	☐		1.2	Do instructional materials treat racial and ethnic differences and groups honestly, realistically, and sensitively?
☐	☐	☐	☐		1.3	Do school libraries and resource centers offer a variety of materials on the histories, experiences, and cultures of many racial, ethnic, and cultural groups?
☐	☐	☐	☐		1.4	Do school assemblies, decorations, speakers, holidays, and heroes reflect racial, ethnic, and cultural group differences?
☐	☐	☐	☐		1.5	Are extracurricular activities multiethnic and multicultural?

1	2	3	4			
☐	☐	☐	☐	2.0		Do school policies and procedures foster positive interactions among the various racial, ethnic, and cultural group members of the school?
☐	☐	☐	☐		2.1	Do school policies accommodate the behavioral patterns, learning styles, and orientations of those ethnic and cultural group members actually in the school?
☐	☐	☐	☐		2.2	Does the school provide a variety of instruments and techniques for teaching and counseling students of various ethnic and cultural groups?
☐	☐	☐	☐		2.3	Do school policies recognize the holidays and festivities of various ethnic groups?
☐	☐	☐	☐		2.4	Do school policies avoid instructional and guidance practices based on stereotyped and ethnocentric perceptions?

(continued)

FIGURE 7.2   Checklist for assessing a school's multicultural education program.

FIGURE 7.2 *(continued)*

☐ ☐ ☐ ☐ 2.5 Do school policies respect the dignity and worth of students as individuals *and* members of racial, ethnic, and cultural groups?

1 2 3 4 3.0 Is the school staff (administrators, instructors, counselors, and
☐ ☐ ☐ ☐ support staff) multiethnic and multiracial?
☐ ☐ ☐ ☐   3.1 Has the school established and enforced policies for recruiting and maintaining a staff made up of individuals from various racial and ethnic groups?

1 2 3 4 4.0 Does the school have systematic, comprehensive, mandatory,
☐ ☐ ☐ ☐ and continuing multicultural staff development programs?
☐ ☐ ☐ ☐   4.1 Are teachers, librarians, counselors, administrators, and support staff included in the staff development programs?
☐ ☐ ☐ ☐   4.2 Do the staff development programs include a variety of experiences (such as lectures, field experiences, and curriculum projects)?
☐ ☐ ☐ ☐   4.3 Do the staff development programs provide opportunities to gain knowledge and understanding about various racial, ethnic, and cultural groups?
☐ ☐ ☐ ☐   4.4 Do the staff development programs provide opportunities for participants to explore their attitudes and feelings about their own ethnicity and others?
☐ ☐ ☐ ☐   4.5 Do the staff development programs examine the verbal and nonverbal patterns of interethnic group interactions?
☐ ☐ ☐ ☐   4.6 Do the staff development programs provide opportunities for learning how to create and select multiethnic instructional materials and how to incorporate multicultural content into curriculum materials?

1 2 3 4 5.0 Does the curriculum reflect the ethnic learning styles of students
☐ ☐ ☐ ☐ within the school?
☐ ☐ ☐ ☐   5.1 Is the curriculum designed to help students learn how to function effectively in various cultural environments and learn more than one cognitive style?
☐ ☐ ☐ ☐   5.2 Do the objectives, instructional strategies, and learning materials reflect the cultures and cognitive styles of the various ethnic and cultural groups within the school?

1 2 3 4 6.0 Does the curriculum provide continuous opportunities for
☐ ☐ ☐ ☐ students to develop a better sense of self?
☐ ☐ ☐ ☐   6.1 Does the curriculum help students strengthen their self-identities?
☐ ☐ ☐ ☐   6.2 Is the curriculum designed to help students develop greater self-understanding?
☐ ☐ ☐ ☐   6.3 Does the curriculum help students improve their self-concept?
☐ ☐ ☐ ☐   6.4 Does the curriculum help students to better understand themselves in light of their ethnic and cultural heritages?

FIGURE 7.2   *(continued)*

1	2	3	4		
☐	☐	☐	☐	7.0	Does the curriculum help students understand the wholeness of the experiences of ethnic and cultural groups?
☐	☐	☐	☐	7.1	Does the curriculum include the study of societal problems some ethnic and cultural group members experience, such as racism, prejudice, discrimination, and exploitation?
☐	☐	☐	☐	7.2	Does the curriculum include the study of historical experiences, cultural patterns, and social problems of various ethnic and cultural groups?
☐	☐	☐	☐	7.3	Does the curriculum include both positive and negative aspects of ethnic and cultural group experiences?
☐	☐	☐	☐	7.4	Does the curriculum present people of color both as active participants in society and as subjects of oppression and exploitation?
☐	☐	☐	☐	7.5	Does the curriculum examine the diversity within each group's experience?
☐	☐	☐	☐	7.6	Does the curriculum present group experiences as dynamic and continuously changing?
☐	☐	☐	☐	7.7	Does the curriculum examine the total experiences of groups instead of focusing exclusively on the "heroes"?
1	2	3	4		
☐	☐	☐	☐	8.0	Does the curriculum help students identify and understand the ever-present conflict between ideals and realities in human societies?
☐	☐	☐	☐	8.1	Does the curriculum help students identify and understand the value conflicts inherent in a multicultural society?
☐	☐	☐	☐	8.2	Does the curriculum examine differing views of ideals and realities among ethnic and cultural groups?
1	2	3	4		
☐	☐	☐	☐	9.0	Does the curriculum explore and clarify ethnic alternatives and options within U.S. society?
☐	☐	☐	☐	9.1	Does the teacher create a classroom atmosphere reflecting an acceptance of and respect for ethnic and cultural differences?
☐	☐	☐	☐	9.2	Does the teacher create a classroom atmosphere allowing realistic consideration of alternatives and options for members of ethnic and cultural groups?
1	2	3	4		
☐	☐	☐	☐	10.0	Does the curriculum promote values, attitudes, and behaviors that support ethnic and cultural diversity?
☐	☐	☐	☐	10.1	Does the curriculum help students examine differences within and among ethnic and cultural groups?
☐	☐	☐	☐	10.2	Does the curriculum foster attitudes supportive of cultural democracy and other unifying democratic ideals and values?
☐	☐	☐	☐	10.3	Does the curriculum reflect ethnic and cultural diversity?
☐	☐	☐	☐	10.4	Does the curriculum present diversity as a vital societal force that encompasses both potential strength and potential conflict?

FIGURE 7.2 *(continued)*

1	2	3	4	
☐	☐	☐	☐	**11.0** Does the curriculum help students develop decision-making abilities, social participation skills, and a sense of political efficacy necessary for effective citizenship?
☐	☐	☐	☐	11.1 Does the curriculum help students develop the ability to distinguish facts from interpretation and opinions?
☐	☐	☐	☐	11.2 Does the curriculum help students develop skills in finding and processing information?
☐	☐	☐	☐	11.3 Does the curriculum help students develop sound knowledge, concepts, generalizations, and theories about issues related to ethnicity and cultural identity?
☐	☐	☐	☐	11.4 Does the curriculum help students develop sound methods of thinking about issues related to ethnic and cultural groups?
☐	☐	☐	☐	11.5 Does the curriculum help students develop skills in clarifying and reconsidering their values and relating them to their understanding of ethnicity and cultural identity?
☐	☐	☐	☐	11.6 Does the curriculum include opportunities to use knowledge, valuing, and thinking in decision making on issues related to race, ethnicity, and culture?
☐	☐	☐	☐	11.7 Does the curriculum provide opportunities for students to take action on social problems affecting racial, ethnic, and cultural groups?
☐	☐	☐	☐	11.8 Does the curriculum help students develop a sense of efficacy?

1	2	3	4	
☐	☐	☐	☐	**12.0** Does the curriculum help students develop skills necessary for effective interpersonal and intercultural group interactions?
☐	☐	☐	☐	12.1 Does the curriculum help students understand ethnic and cultural reference points that influence communications?
☐	☐	☐	☐	12.2 Does the curriculum help students participate in cross-ethnic and cross-cultural experiences and reflect upon them?

1	2	3	4	
☐	☐	☐	☐	**13.0** Is the multicultural curriculum comprehensive in scope and sequence, presenting holistic views of ethnic and cultural groups, and an integral part of the total school curriculum?
☐	☐	☐	☐	13.1 Does the curriculum introduce students to the experiences of persons of widely varying backgrounds in the study of each ethnic and cultural group?
☐	☐	☐	☐	13.2 Does the curriculum discuss the successes and contributions of group members within the context of that group's values?
☐	☐	☐	☐	13.3 Does the curriculum include the role of ethnicity and culture in the local community as well as in the nation?

FIGURE 7.2   *(continued)*

1	2	3	4	
☐	☐	☐	☐	**14.0** Does the curriculum include the continuous study of the cultures, historical experiences, social realities, and existential conditions of ethnic groups with a variety of racial compositions?
☐	☐	☐	☐	14.1 Does the curriculum include study of several ethnic and cultural groups?
☐	☐	☐	☐	14.2 Does the curriculum include studies of both white ethnic groups and ethnic groups of color?
☐	☐	☐	☐	14.3 Does the curriculum provide for continuity in the examination of aspects of experience affected by race?

1	2	3	4	
☐	☐	☐	☐	**15.0** Are interdisciplinary and multidisciplinary approaches used in designing and implementing the curriculum?
☐	☐	☐	☐	15.1 Are interdisciplinary and multidisciplinary perspectives used in the study of ethnic and cultural groups and related issues?
☐	☐	☐	☐	15.2 Are approaches used authentic and comprehensive explanations of ethnic and cultural issues, events, and problems?

1	2	3	4	
☐	☐	☐	☐	**16.0** Does the curriculum use comparative approaches in the study of racial, ethnic, and cultural groups?
☐	☐	☐	☐	16.1 Does the curriculum focus on the similarities and differences among and between ethnic and cultural groups?
☐	☐	☐	☐	16.2 Are matters examined from comparative perspectives with fairness to all?

1	2	3	4	
☐	☐	☐	☐	**17.0** Does the curriculum help students view and interpret events, situations, and conflict from diverse ethnic and cultural perspectives and points of view?
☐	☐	☐	☐	17.1 Are the perspectives of various ethnic and cultural groups represented in the instructional program?
☐	☐	☐	☐	17.2 Are students taught why different ethnic and cultural groups often perceive the same historical event or contemporary situation differently?
☐	☐	☐	☐	17.3 Are the perspectives of each ethnic and cultural group presented as valid ways to perceive the past and the present?

1	2	3	4	
☐	☐	☐	☐	**18.0** Does the curriculum conceptualize and describe the development of the United States as a multicultural society?
☐	☐	☐	☐	18.1 Does the curriculum view the territorial and cultural growth of the United States as flowing from several directions?
☐	☐	☐	☐	18.2 Does the curriculum include a parallel study of the various societies that developed in the geo-cultural United States?

FIGURE 7.2 *(continued)*

1	2	3	4	
☐	☐	☐	☐	19.0 Does the school provide opportunities for students to participate in the aesthetic experiences of various ethnic and cultural groups?
☐	☐	☐	☐	19.1 Are multiethnic literature and art used to promote empathy and understanding of people from various ethnic and cultural groups?
☐	☐	☐	☐	19.2 Are multiethnic literature and art used to promote self-examination and self-understanding?
☐	☐	☐	☐	19.3 Do students read and hear the poetry, short stories, novels, folklore, plays, essays, and autobiographies of a variety of ethnic and cultural groups?
☐	☐	☐	☐	19.4 Do students examine the music, art, architecture, and dance of a variety of ethnic and cultural groups?
☐	☐	☐	☐	19.5 Do students have available the artistic, musical, and literary expression of the local ethnic and cultural communities?
☐	☐	☐	☐	19.6 Are opportunities provided for students to develop full literacy, and musical expression?

1	2	3	4	
☐	☐	☐	☐	20.0 Does the curriculum provide opportunities for students to develop full literacy in at least two languages?
☐	☐	☐	☐	20.1 Are students taught to communicate (speaking, reading, and writing) in a second language?
☐	☐	☐	☐	20.2 Are the students taught about the culture of people who use the second language?
☐	☐	☐	☐	20.3 Are second language speakers provided opportunities to develop full literacy in their native language?
☐	☐	☐	☐	20.4 Are students for whom English is a second language taught in their native languages as needed?

1	2	3	4	
☐	☐	☐	☐	21.0 Does the curriculum make maximum use of local community resources?
☐	☐	☐	☐	21.1 Are students involved in the continuous study of the local community?
☐	☐	☐	☐	21.2 Are members of the local ethnic and cultural communities continually used as classroom resources?
☐	☐	☐	☐	21.3 Are field trips to the various local ethnic and cultural communities provided for students?

1	2	3	4	
☐	☐	☐	☐	22.0 Do the assessment procedures used with students reflect their ethnic and community cultures?
☐	☐	☐	☐	22.1 Do teachers use a variety of assessment procedures that reflect the ethnic and cultural diversity of students?
☐	☐	☐	☐	22.2 Do teachers' day-to-day assessment techniques take into account the ethnic and cultural diversity of their students?

FIGURE 7.2 *(continued)*

1	2	3	4	
☐	☐	☐	☐	23.0 Does the school conduct ongoing, systematic evaluations of the goals, methods, and instructional materials used in teaching about ethnicity and culture?
☐	☐	☐	☐	23.1 Do assessment procedures draw on many sources of evidence from many sorts of people?
☐	☐	☐	☐	23.2 Does the evaluation program examine school policies and procedures?
☐	☐	☐	☐	23.3 Does the evaluation program examine the everyday climate of the school?
☐	☐	☐	☐	23.4 Does the evaluation program examine the effectiveness of curricular programs, both academic and nonacademic?
☐	☐	☐	☐	23.5 Are the results of evaluation used to improve the school program?

Follow-up After marking the checklist as objectively as possible, a summary of the results can prove helpful in identifying areas to be developed and in planning modifications to further enhance existing components. The following format can facilitate this process:

1. The checklist indicates that our program is very effective in the following areas:

   a.

   b.

   c.

2. The checklist indicates that we need to work to become more effective in the following areas:

   a.

   b.

   c.

3. The checklist indicates that we lack the following aspects of a completely effective multicultural education program:

   a.

   b.

   c.

4. We have the following specific plans for improving the effectiveness of our program:

   a.

   b.

   c.

Sources: From J. A. Banks. (September 1992). Curriculum Guidelines for Multicultural Education. *Social Education,* pp. 274–294. National Council for the Social Studies. Rating scale adapted from Checklist for Assessing a School's Foreign Language Program, *Handbook for Planning an Effective Foreign Language Program,* 1985.

EDUCATIONAL GOALS AND LEARNING OUTCOMES

Any instructional program that is multicultural should be consistent with the following general guidelines (Banks, 1981; California State Department of Education, 1977, 1979):

1. *Emphasize multiple groups (e.g., ethnic, religious, regional, socioeconomic, language) rather than treating individual groups separately or in isolation.* Such multiple-group emphasis diminishes the likelihood of stereotyping and facilitates integration of multicultural content into the overall curriculum.
2. *Provide an interdisciplinary focus for the integration of multicultural perspectives, as appropriate, in all content areas.* Although most frequently associated with the social sciences, language, literature, art, and music, multicultural perspectives are valid and applicable in areas such as mathematics, science, home economics, and physical education.
3. *Use a variety of instructional approaches and materials appropriate to the maturity level of students.* In particular, teaching strategies should aim to accommodate differences in learning styles and to maximize academic achievement.
4. *Focus on the development of both cognitive and affective skills.* Learning outcomes should be assessed in terms of knowledge, attitudes, and skills.
5. *Emphasize school and area populations, locally oriented activities, and community resources.*

Articulating goals and desired learning outcomes is an essential part of developing instructional programs. Gay (1977) recommends that the curriculum teachers develop include both general goals and specific objectives (as determined by programmatic emphases and the needs of the student population to be served). The statement of goals and objectives in Figure 7.3 illustrates the types of learning outcomes frequently specified in multicultural education programs.

As teachers embark on the process of what Gay (1996) refers to as "multiculturalizing" the curriculum, she suggests that teachers use four key questions to guide and direct their reform efforts, be they modest or major revisions. By design, the process of answering these questions within the framework of subject areas and skills taught in K–12 schools requires that teachers address specific goals and objectives, rationale, content, activities, and evaluation (p. 46). Keeping in mind that the focus is the inclusion of "ethnically, culturally, and socially pluralistic content, experiences, and perspectives," the key questions are:

1. What do you want students to learn?
2. Why are these learnings especially beneficial for students and an integral component of the particular subjects and skills taught?
3. How will these learnings be facilitated and accomplished within culturally (socially, ethnically) relevant contexts?
4. How will appropriate strategies and techniques be used to determine if and when the specified learning outcomes have been achieved?
(Adapted from Gay, 1996, p. 46)

General Goals

Goal 1.0   To be aware of ethnic ancestry and cultural heritage in relation to self-definition

Objectives:

1.1   To demonstrate appreciation of the characteristics of one's own ethnic, cultural, and linguistic heritage
1.2   To analyze the influence of one's ethnic/cultural heritage and experiences on one's values and lifestyle
1.3   To define personal strengths, capabilities, and limitations (self-esteem)
1.4   To demonstrate the ability to present to others aspects of one's own cultural heritage

Goal 2.0   To be aware of the similarities and differences among individuals from diverse ethnic, cultural, linguistic, and religious groups within the community, the United States, and the world

Objectives:

2.1   To recognize similarities and differences among diverse socioeconomic, ethnic, cultural, linguistic, and religious groups
2.2   To recognize similarities and differences in sex roles within diverse groups in society
2.3   To tolerate alternative beliefs, manners, customs, linguistic traditions, and lifestyles of individuals and groups different from self
2.4   To develop an awareness of and appreciation for cultural diversity in our society and globally
2.5   To understand how people within the United States and from various places in the world differ in their views on issues (e.g., resource use, environmental pollution)

Goal 3.0   To be aware of the elements of different cultures

Objectives:

3.1   To describe the elements that make up different cultures and recognize those that are common to all humanity
3.2   To compare the elements of diverse cultures
3.3   To recognize that cultures change over time and as the result of contact with other cultural groups

Goal 4.0   To demonstrate skills in maintaining positive relationships with other individuals or groups and in responding constructively to conflict in relationships

Objectives:

4.1   To develop sensitivity to problems of others through learning and practicing interpersonal skills
4.2   To analyze factors that contribute to conflicts
4.3   To demonstrate the ability to cooperate with others (e.g., males and females; mainstreamed students; members of diverse racial, ethnic, cultural, linguistic, and religious groups) in performing a variety of tasks

(continued)

FIGURE 7.3   Multicultural goals and objectives.

FIGURE 7.3　*(continued)*

Goal 5.0　To identify various forms of stereotyping, prejudice, and discrimination

　Objectives:

　　5.1　To identify causes and consequences of stereotyping, prejudice, and discrimination
　　5.2　To confront behavior in self and others that is based on stereotyping, prejudice, and discrimination
　　5.3　To identify biases in textbooks and other instructional materials and in the media

Goal 6.0　To achieve academically in all basic subject areas

Specific Content-Area Goals

Literature and Fine Arts

Goal 6.0　To develop knowledge of and appreciation for the multicultural nature of the literary and fine arts (literature, art, theater, and music) in our society, historically and currently

　Objectives:

　　6.1　To develop an awareness of the major movements, traditions, and cultural contexts of various forms of expression, past and present
　　6.2　To explore how the writer, artist, dramatist, and musician (male and female) have communicated the timelessness and universality of the human condition
　　6.3　To develop the ability to use awareness of multicultural history and tradition in literary and artistic expression
　　6.4　To recognize the value and role of the literary and fine arts in the lives of individuals in different cultural groups

Foreign/Second Language

Goal 7.0　To appreciate the similarities and diversities among languages, cultures, and value systems within the United States and throughout the world

　Objectives:

　　7.1　To recognize language patterns that are different from the native language
　　7.2　To recognize behavioral patterns (attitudes, values, customs, traditions, and taboos) of cultures that are different from the native culture
　　7.3　To function in the sociocultural contexts in which the language is used

Mathematics

Goal 8.0　To develop an appreciation for and understanding of the contributions that various cultures have made to mathematical concepts and applications

　Objectives:

　　8.1　To relate the contributions of other cultures to the development of the modern Western number system and other areas of mathematics
　　8.2　To recognize similarities and differences between the counting system used in the United States and systems used in other countries

FIGURE 7.3   *(continued)*

    8.3 To identify variations in computational algorithms as performed in different cultures
    8.4 To use computational instruments from other cultures
    8.5 To play mathematical games from other cultures

Science

Goal 9.0   To develop appreciation for and understanding of the contributions that various cultures have made to scientific concepts and applications

   Objectives:

    9.1 To give attention to and value science as an endeavor of human beings from all ethnic and cultural backgrounds
    9.2 To demonstrate knowledge of contributions to science and technology made by men and women of various nationalities

Social Sciences

Goal 10.0   To enable and encourage students to understand and respect individual and cultural differences and similarities

   Objectives:

    10.1 To understand and appreciate the United States in particular and the world in general as multicultural phenomena
    10.2 To understand and appreciate universal as well as alternative ideas about beauty, ideological beliefs, sex roles, moral standards, and value systems
    10.3 To be aware of the wide diversity of occupational choices available and the ways in which individuals make these choices
    10.4 To analyze behavior and attitudes for biases against the characteristics of specific groups (e.g., sexual, ethnic, economic)
    10.5 To understand different units of human organizations such as world organizations, nation states, ethnic groups, business and labor groups, kin groups, and families

---

Source: Adapted from J. Browne and J. P. Perez, *Multicultural Education Course of Study for Grades Kindergarten Through Twelve 1979–1981.* Used with permission of the Los Angeles County Superintendent of Schools.

IMPLEMENTATION

Many options are available to teachers interested in integrating multicultural content into the elementary and secondary curriculum. This section focuses on several principles that are critical to the effective integration of multicultural perspectives into the curriculum.

Balance and Complementarity

Teaching that is multicultural is eclectic by nature. It involves a balanced use of approaches in which the relative strengths of one complements the relative weaknesses of another. According to Nixon (1985), the critical task centers on integration: how to combine and coordinate approaches, faculty, and resources to fashion an effective cross-curricular response. Because multicultural education must be responsive to the uniqueness of each school and each classroom, the development and application of a single, all-encompassing model is precluded. Teachers must use elements of different approaches in tandem to achieve a balance of essential concepts, perspectives, and experiences, which are incomplete when presented in isolation.

For example, teachers can promote more positive attitudes toward cultural diversity by focusing less attention on differences that appear exotic and bizarre (and conducive to stereotyping) and greater attention on similarities among people and cultures in terms of family life and everyday living. It is also advantageous to balance treatment of historical and contemporary hardships and injustices with consideration of positive achievements and developments associated with various groups (Kehoe, 1984b). An effective multicultural curriculum is likely to include the following balanced elements:

◇ content about racism awareness and cultural diversity;
◇ experiential learning and the acquisition of facts and skills;
◇ contemporary perspectives and historical perspectives; and
◇ content about local issues and global issues (Nixon, 1985).

The planning matrix presented in Figure 7.4 can help educators to achieve balance and complementarity in terms of the basic types of learning, specific topics addressed, and subject areas that are incorporated into a multicultural curriculum.

Structure and Organization

It bears repeating that teachers need to systematically incorporate multicultural content into the curriculum. The question is how this can best be accomplished. Over the years, some of the curricular design approaches used in multicultural education have been criticized because they lead to poorly integrated, narrowly focused programs (Gay, 1977). Among the least acceptable are approaches that include content about specific ethnic groups by use of separate components and those that deal with social, economic, and political realities from a "problems" perspective.

Gay (1975, 1977, 1979) has described several basic organizational strategies appropriate for incorporating multicultural content at the elementary and secondary levels. The curriculum emphasis and basic instructional approach for each of these design strategies are summarized in Table 7.1. Gay regards the thematic and conceptual strategies as most promising. The first provides a framework based on recurrent universal themes; the second, a framework based on concepts drawn from different disciplines. Both have the advantage of allowing for multiple perspectives and comparative, interdisciplinary analyses.

Kind of learning	TOPIC	Academic activities									
		Reading	Oral, written language	Mathematics	Social studies	Science	Health	Foreign language	Art, music, drama, dance	Physical education	Practical arts, vocations
I. Understand concepts	A. Self B. Lifestyle C. Culture D. Changes in individuals and groups E. Cultural contact as agent in change F. Personal heritage G. Similarities/differences among individuals and groups H. Competence I. Occupational diversity J. Stereotypes/prejudice/discrimination										
II. Acquire values	A. Self-esteem B. Appreciation of self and others C. Respect for values/dignity/worth of self and others D. Respect for similarities/differences E. Acceptance of cultural pluralism F. Acceptance of diversity of lifestyles G. Desire to bring about equity/reduce stereotypes H. Positive attitude toward school and life										
III. Develop skills	A. Analyzing influence of heritage B. Analyzing similarities/differences C. Distinguishing between myths/stereotypes and facts D. Recognizing prejudiced behavior E. Identifying biases in media F. Interpreting personal heritage G. Clarifying personal values H. Using skills of conflict resolution										
IV. Demonstrate behaviors, personal and social	A. Working to reduce inequities B. Confronting prejudiced behavior C. Cooperating with diverse others D. Using community persons as resources E. Using persons in school as resources F. Working to resolve conflicts G. Participating/involving others in life of school H. Using interpersonal skills										

FIGURE 7.4 Planning matrix for multicultural curriculum development.

Source: California State Department of Education, 1979, *Planning for Multicultural Education as a Part of School Improvement*. Reprinted by permission.

TABLE 7.1 *Strategies for Incorporating Multicultural Content into Curriculum*

Approach	Emphasis	Basic Features
Integrative Multicultural Basic Skills (elementary)	Social skills Intellectual skills Literacy skills Functional survival skills	Use cultural perspectives content, material, and experiences to teach basic educational skills
Modified Basic Skills	Fundamental skills Social action skills Decision-making skills Ethnic literacy	Use ethnic materials to teach basic skills, enhance student ethnic identity, and expand awareness of multiethnic perspectives; address ethnic/gender stereotypes and racial attitudes
Conceptual Approach	Concepts from multiple disciplines (e.g., social sciences, such as power, identity, ethnicity, culture, survival, communication, change, racism, socialization, acculturation)	Analyze concepts within an interdisciplinary framework using comparative and multiethnic perspectives
Thematic Approach	Themes characterizing the human condition, social realities, and cultural experiences of ethnic groups in the United States (e.g., ethnic identity; the role of ethnic groups in society; struggles against injustice; the quest for freedom)	Focus on themes rather than ethnic groups and treat themes from interdisciplinary perspectives; examine inter- and intragroup diversity
Cultural Components	Culture and traditions of ethnic groups including perceptions, behavior and communication patterns, socialization processes, value systems, interpersonal interaction styles	Emphasize identification of cultural features for specific groups; rely on ethnic source materials (e.g., literature, histories, folklore, customs, traditions, religious heritage)
Branching Designs	Idea, issue, concept, or problem extended from one discipline to another (e.g., analysis of protest as manifested in civic, literary, and artistic areas)	Organize the curriculum to allow for more integrated, in-depth, and cohesive treatment of content

Source: G. Gay, "Organizing and Planning Culturally Pluralistic Curriculum," 1975, *Educational Leadership*, *33*(3), 176–183; and G. Gay, "On Behalf of Children: A Curriculum Design for Multicultural Education in the Elementary School," 1979, *Journal of Negro Education, XLCIII*(3), 324–340.

TEACHING STRATEGIES

Given the nature of its curricular goals and objectives and the commitment to meeting the needs of a diverse student population, multicultural education requires a broad repertoire of instructional methods and techniques. Because teaching methods are culturally influenced, certain methods work better with some students than others. Teachers who assume that the same methods work effectively with all students ignore the influence of culture as well as other factors on the instructional process.

To identify methods that work for students in a particular classroom, teachers must use strategies with an analytical eye. Although research may suggest what works, it often does not indicate what works for whom, when, and under what specific conditions. When selecting and applying a particular instructional method, teachers should consider whether it works effectively with all students or only with certain groups of students (as defined by culture, gender, ability, age, learning style, or other relevant dimensions). For example, the inquiry method, though widely used, is based upon assumptions about questioning and problem solving that are not universally shared (Payne, 1977). Consequently, as presently implemented, the inquiry method may be quite effective in certain cultural contexts but relatively ineffective in others. In general, attainment of instructional objectives depends in large part on the use of teaching strategies that are suitable and effective for a specific purpose, time, and student population. The effective

Effective teachers are skilled in choosing instructional strategies that are appropriate for a specific purpose, time, and student.

teacher "is the one who can make the right judgment as to what teaching device is the most valuable at any given moment" (Politzer, 1970, pp. 42–43).

Joyce and Weil (1986) observe that *"when we teach well, we help students learn well"* (p. iii). They suggest that effective teaching strategies

(a) help students learn academic skills, ideas, and information; develop values and social skills; and understand themselves and their environment; and

(b) provide students with repertoires of powerful tools for acquiring education.

Among the wide variety of effective teaching strategies used in multicultural education are the four discussed here: concept attainment, advance organizers, role playing, and simulations.

Concept Attainment

The teaching strategy known as concept attainment is designed to facilitate the learning of concepts through concept formation and hypothesizing (Joyce & Weil, 1986; Tenenberg, 1978). A teacher using this strategy presents examples, some of which have attributes of a well-defined target concept. Students are asked to compare and contrast the examples, attempting to distinguish those containing essential characteristics of the target concept from those that do not. Through this process students eventually learn the attributes that define the concept. Figure 7.5 presents an illustration of concept attainment in which visual examples are used to convey attributes of the target concept.

In some cases, verbal examples are used. For example, if the concept to be taught is "doublespeak" (i.e., deceptive language that is evasive and euphemistic), the following exemplars and nonexemplars might be used (Lutz, cited in Shearer, 1988).

Exemplars	Nonexemplars
incomplete occurrence	failure
safety-related occurrence	accident
experienced automobile	used car
unauthorized withdrawal	bank robbery
downsizing personnel	firing employees
ultimate high-intensity warfare	nuclear war
advanced downward adjustments	budget cuts
digital fever computer	thermometer
social-expression products	greeting cards

In this case, the teacher presents a few examples in random order and encourages students to compare them and begin hypothesizing about which essential attributes differentiate one group from the other. As the activity continues, additional examples are provided and hypotheses tested until the concept is identified. Students then are given a chance to practice and think of examples of their own. In the final phase of the exercise, students can discuss their individual strategies for developing and testing hypotheses. Additional information on

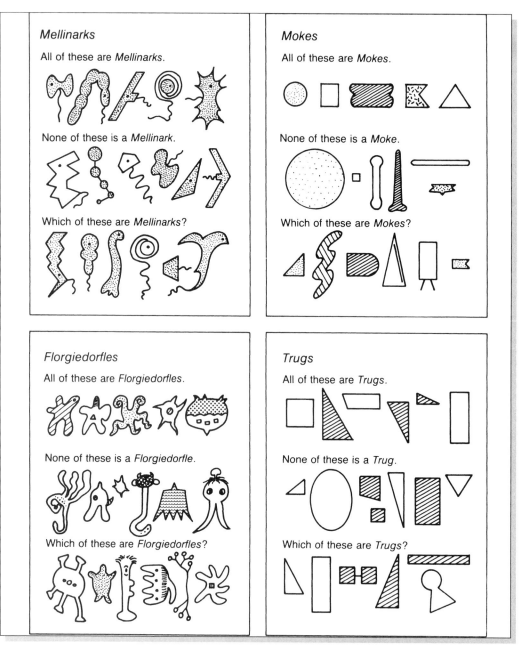

FIGURE 7.5 Sample visual exemplars and nonexemplars used with concept attainment approach. The criterial attributes of Mellinarks are spots, a black dot, and a tail. Mokes share only one defining attribute—height. All the Florgiedorfles have the same height and number of arms. Trugs may be either shaded triangles or unshaded quadrilaterals.

Source: *Teachers Guide for Attribute Games and Problems.* Copyright © 1968 by McGraw-Hill. Used with permission.

concept attainment and related generic teaching strategies is presented by Tenenberg (1978) and Joyce and Weil (1986).

Advance Organizers

Advance organizers are structured overviews describing the hierarchy of related concepts within a discipline or subject area (Joyce & Weil, 1986). These "intellectual maps" can facilitate student acquisition and retention of new, abstract information by providing a visual, conceptual framework for learning activities. By enhancing the clarity and organization of knowledge, they enable students to better relate, integrate, and remember new information.

Earle and Barron (cited in Smith & Kepner, 1981) have outlined a procedure for developing structured overviews. The first four steps focus on the preparation of instruction; the last two promote active student involvement in the lessons presented.

Developing and Using an Advance Organizer

1. Analyze the learning task and required vocabulary. List key words representing the major concepts to be learned.
2. Arrange the key words in a diagram that displays the relationship among concepts.
3. Add familiar vocabulary concepts to illustrate the relationship between what students know and what they are to learn.
4. Examine the advance organizer. Are major relationships depicted clearly and concisely? Does it focus only on the most essential relationships between concepts?
5. In introducing the content, display the diagram and briefly explain the arrangement of the key words. Ask students to contribute as much information as they can.
6. During the presentation and related activities, make the connection between new information and the structured overview.

Advance organizers have been used in a variety of subject areas. They are also effective in adapting instruction at more advanced levels to meet the needs of English language learners (Cantoni-Harvey, 1987). Figure 7.6 is an example of an advance organizer dealing with mathematical concepts. In Figure 7.7, Tompkins and Hoskisson (1995, p. 366) illustrate the use of graphic organizers in relation to five expository text structures.

Role Playing

Role playing is an experiential learning activity in which students act out behavior in real-life situations. In theory, "dramatizing" problems enables students to scrutinize feelings, attitudes, and values; develop problem-solving strategies; and experience greater empathy toward others (Joyce & Weil, 1986). Classroom re-creations elicit responses that can be directed purposefully in subsequent

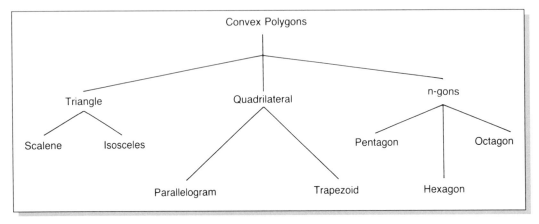

FIGURE 7.6   Advance organizers for presentation on convex polygons.
Source: C. F. Smith, Jr., and H. S. Kepner, Jr., *Reading in the Mathematics Classroom.* Copyright (1981 by National Education Association. Reprinted by permission.

group discussions of human relations and intercultural communication. Role playing provides a way of integrating social and personal as well as emotional and intellectual elements. In fact, students appear to experience greater changes in attitude when they voluntarily assume roles opposed to their own beliefs (Kehoe, 1984a).

Role plays are appropriate for presenting a number of topics at both elementary and secondary levels. For example, Hoopes and Pusch (1979) use role play to demonstrate that social status is culturally based and manifested in behavior on a daily basis. To make their point, they suggest that teachers themselves role play the following encounters (pp. 148–149):

◇ Going before a judge in traffic court for running a red light.
◇ Requesting an extension on a term paper from a professor.
◇ Ordering a sandwich at a small restaurant.
◇ Ordering dinner with wine at an elegant restaurant.
◇ Scheduling an appointment with a busy doctor, dentist, or lawyer.
◇ Meeting the Governor at an official occasion.
◇ Discussing a disciplinary problem in your classroom with the principal.

Simulations

Simulations are a second type of experiential learning activity widely used in multicultural education, most often in the social sciences. These activities are designed to be used as a basis for viewing human behavior and examining situations in the real world. Psychologically, effective simulations provide sensory learning, insight about the consequences of one's behavior, and an opportunity for self-correction (Joyce & Weil, 1986). They range from short, simple exercises to complex activities requiring extended periods of time and can be applied to diverse areas such as competition and cooperation, critical thinking and decision making, and development of concepts and skills.

Pattern	Description	Cue Words	Graphic Organizer	Sample Passage
Description	The author describes a topic by listing characteristics, features, and examples.	*for example* *characteristics are*		The Olympic symbol consists of five interlocking rings. The rings represent the five continents—Africa, Asia, Europe, North America, and South America—from which athletes come to compete in the games. The rings are colored black, blue, green, red, and yellow. At least one of these colors is found in the flag of every country sending athletes to compete in the Olympic games.
Sequence	The author lists items or events in numerical or chronological order.	*first, second, third* *next* *then* *finally*	1. _____ 2. _____ 3. _____ 4. _____ 5. _____	The Olympic games began as athletic festivals to honor the Greek gods. The most important festival was held in the valley of Olympia to honor Zeus, the king of the gods. It was this festival that became the Olympic games in 776 B.C. These games were ended in A.D. 394 by the Roman Emperor who ruled Greece. No Olympic games were held for more than 1,500 years. Then the modern Olympics began in 1896. Almost 300 male athletes competed in the first modern Olympics. In the games held in 1900, female athletes were allowed to compete. The games have continued every four years since1896 except during World War II, and they will most likely continue for many years to come.
Comparison	The author explains how two or more things are alike and/or how they are different.	*different* *in contrast* *alike* *same as* *on the other hand*	Alike / Different	The Modern Olympics is very unlike the ancient Olympic games. Individual events are different. While there were no swimming races in the ancient games, for example, there were chariot races. There were no female contestants and all athletes competed in the nude. Of course, the ancient and modern Olympics are also alike in many ways. Some events, such as the javelin and discus throws, are the same. Some people say that cheating, professionalism, and nationalism in the modern games are a disgrace to the Olympic tradition. But according to the ancient Greek writers, there were many cases of cheating, nationalism, and professionalism in their Olympics, too.
Cause and Effect	The author lists one or more causes and the resulting effect or effects.	*reasons why* *if . . . then* *as a result* *therefore* *because*	Cause → Effect #1, Effect #2, Effect #3	There are several reasons why so many people attend the Olympic games or watch them on television. One reason is tradition. The name *Olympics* and the torch and flame remind people of the ancient games. People can escape the ordinariness of daily life by attending or watching the Olympics. They like to identify with someone else's individual sacrifice and accomplishment. National pride is another reason, and an athlete's or a team's hard earned victory becomes a nation's victory. There are national medal counts and people keep track of how many medals their country's athletes have won.
Problem and Solution	The author states a problem and lists one or more solutions for the problem. A variation of this pattern is the question-and-answer format in which the author poses a question and then answers it.	*problem is* *dilemma is* *puzzle is* *solved* *question . . . answer*	Problem → Solution	One problem with the modern Olympics is that it has become very big and expensive to operate. The city or country that hosts the games often loses a lot of money. A stadium, pools, and playing fields must be built for the athletic events and housing is needed for the athletes who come from around the world. And all of these facilities are used for only 2 weeks! In 1984, Los Angeles solved these problems by charging a fee for companies who wanted to be official sponsors of the games. Companies like McDonald's paid a lot of money to be part of the Olympics. Many buildings that were already built in the Los Angeles area were also used. The Coliseum where the 1932 games were held was used again and many colleges and universities in the area became playing and living sites.

FIGURE 7.7 Five expository text structures with corresponding graphic organizers.
Source: G. E. Tompkins and K. Hoskisson, *Language Arts: Content and Teaching Strategies.* Copyright © 1995 by Merrill/Prentice Hall., pp. 367-368.

Among the simulations most frequently associated with multicultural education are Bafa Bafa, Star Power, Win As Much as You Can, and Albatross. Other commercially prepared and teacher-developed simulation games also are available (for a guide to references on simulation games, see Mukhopadhyay & Cushman, 1985). Descriptions of existing simulation games, instructions for teachers interested in developing their own, and critiques of some of the most widely used models are presented in Batchelder and Warner (1977), Hoopes and Ventura (1979), Mukhopadhyay (1985), Mukhopadhyay and Cushman (1985), Pusch (1979), and Sawyer and Green (1984).

ASSESSMENT AND EVALUATION

After a multicultural education program is developed and implemented, its effectiveness can be assessed in several ways. A relatively simple evaluation method is teacher observation of student behaviors. For purposes of informal evaluation, a sampling of students is sufficient. The following examples illustrate how attainment of specific program objectives is indicated by various student behaviors (California State Department of Education, 1979):

Objective 1:	The student will demonstrate recognition of the dignity and worth of individuals and groups different from himself/herself.
Behaviors:	Interacting with students within same group and from different groups. Interacting cooperatively in small groups. Sharing of materials, time, and space.
Objective 2:	The student will develop feelings of self-worth and self-acceptance.
Behaviors:	Requesting assistance when needed. Participating voluntarily in a range of activities. Providing assistance to other students (e.g., tutoring).
Objective 3:	The student will desire and be willing to reduce or eliminate inequalities and conflicts caused by stereotyping, prejudice, discrimination, and inequality of opportunity.
Behaviors:	Choosing partners freely regardless of their ethnicity, gender, socioeconomic status, etc. Participating in activities across lines defined by socioeconomic level or other factors. Avoiding behaviors demeaning to other students (e.g., jokes, name calling).

Other recommended measures of program effectiveness include oral and written tests (teacher-made and standardized), sociograms, questionnaires, surveys, student projects, interviews, anecdotal information, and discussion groups.

Indicators such as attendance records, class participation, and incidence of disruptive behavior also provide clues about student acceptance of and interest in the program. Many of these procedures are conducive to staff, parent, and student involvement. Whatever combination of evaluation tools is used, the information collected should be well documented, relevant, and useful. The validity of evaluation depends upon the questions asked, behaviors observed, and effort made to sample randomly apply common standards (California State Department of Education, 1979).

THE INTEGRATION OF MULTICULTURAL CONTENT

As teachers embark upon development of a multicultural curriculum, they will want to consider how they approach the integration of multicultural content. Banks (1997) identifies basic approaches at four increasingly sophisticated levels of integration—approaches that are frequently used in combination and found in actual classrooms across the nation. Banks cautions that the transition from one level to another is likely to be incremental and cumulative. "It is unrealistic to expect a teacher to move directly from a highly mainstream-centric curriculum to one that focuses on decision making and social action" (p. 242). With this in mind, the various approaches and levels provide a useful "yardstick" by which to measure existing curriculum and projected curriculum development efforts.

Level 1: *The Contributions Approach (pp. 232–235)*

Description   The *contributions approach* is characterized by an emphasis on ethnic heroes and heroines, contributions, holidays, events, and celebrations, and discrete cultural elements and artifacts such as foods, dance, music, etc. This approach is widely used—particularly by teachers with a limited knowledge of multiethnic/multicultural content. Because it is the easiest approach to use, it is often the starting point of efforts to integrate content into the mainstream curriculum.

The contributions approach does not change the basic curriculum in any substantial way. The individuals selected for inclusion are those whose ideas and contributions are generally "acceptable" to the larger society; individuals representing what are regarded as more divergent or extreme views are largely ignored. The selection of cultural events and elements follows similar lines.

Limitations   Among the limitations, Banks includes the tendency to avoid or minimize addressing issues such as racism, poverty, power, and discrimination. By treating people and contributions as marginal to the greater scope of the core curriculum, this approach tends to trivialize the study of ethnic cultures, and reinforce stereotypes and misconceptions. The fact that heroes and heroines are successful takes precedence over the process or struggle required to reach their goals, and this limits the students' depth of understanding.

Level 2: *The Additive Approach (pp. 235–237)*

Description   The *additive approach* is similar to the contributions approach in that it also represents an attempt to integrate multicultural content into the mainstream curriculum without changing the basic structure, and design. In this model, content takes the form of concepts, themes and perspectives, often presented via a unit, book, film, or additional course. One reason teachers opt for this approach is because it demands less time and effort than approaches that involve restructuring the curriculum.

Limitations   As with the contributions approach, the perspective that the additive approach offers students is still limited—the mainstream perspective is central and paramount. Content selected for inclusion must accommodate the existing schema. In teaching history, for example, most of the geocultural perspectives discussed in Chapter 6 remain largely outside the well-established unidirectional ("westward") view of history. When other perspectives are relegated to adjunct status, students are less likely to develop a genuine understanding of different cultural and ethnic perspectives, and an appreciation for their interconnections with other people and events. In fact, such efforts to integrate content at levels that deal with more difficult and complex issues (e.g., the book *The Color Purple*, the movie *Miss Jane Pittman*) can have unanticipated consequences: "Adding ethnic content to the curriculum in a sporadic and segmented way can result in pedagogical problems, trouble for the teacher, student confusion, and community controversy" (p. 237).

Level 3: *The Transformation Approach (pp. 237–239)*

Description   The *transformation approach* is significantly different from the preceding approaches in that it represents a basic change in goals, structure, and perspective. Multiple perspectives that allow for the examination of issues, events, and problems from the point of view of the groups most affected or involved supersede the traditional structure of the mainstream core curriculum. According to Banks, this serves to ensure that content, perspectives, and frames of reference are expanded so as to better represent the dynamic character, growth, and complexity of our nation, and thus, to enable students to develop a greater understanding of diverse groups. ". . . the emphasis should not be on the ways that various ethnic and cultural groups have contributed to mainstream U.S. society and culture. *The emphasis, rather should be on how the common U.S. culture and society emerged from a complex synthesis and interaction of the diverse cultural elements that originated within the various cultural, racial, ethnic, and religious groups that make up U.S. society*" (p. 239).

   A failure to integrate diverse perspectives is regarded as tantamount to providing an incomplete and limited view of history, literature, language, art, music, mathematics, and science. As an example, Gay and Banks (cited in Banks, 1997) suggest that teaching the American Revolution would require treatment of political, military, social, economic, philosophical, and geographical aspects that involve groups such as Anglo revolutionaries and loyalists, the British, other Europeans, American Indians, African Americans, and others.

Limitations   This approach is limited only in the sense that students may or may not develop the skills and capabilities to use the knowledge they acquire in ways that empower them socially, politically, and culturally. This capacity characterizes only the highest level of multicultural content integration.

Level 4: *The Social Action Approach (pp. 239–242)*

Description   The *social action approach* encompasses the transformation approach and further extends its goals in the direction of applying what students learn to effect social change. The emphasis is on decision-making skills, reflective thinking, and political and social efficacy. Students engage in activities directed toward improving their schools, neighborhoods, and communities, and society as a whole through social action. The role of the teacher in this approach is fundamentally different than in the previous approaches, as "teachers are agents of social change who promote democratic values and the empowerment of students" (p. 240).

Limitations   Banks does not identify any specific limitations for this approach.

Moving toward a multicultural curriculum that provides students with the highest level of knowledge and skills is increasingly a necessity rather than an option. As Cummins and Sayers (1997) observe, "the changing cultural, economic/scientific, and existential realities that we are currently experiencing highlight the importance of promoting students' capacity for collaborative

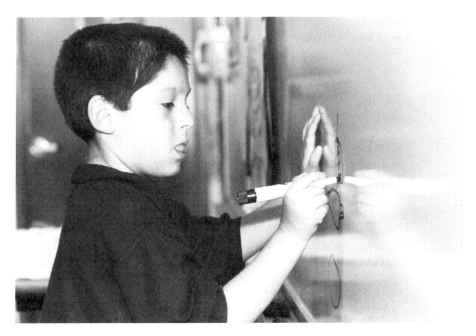

Effective teaching helps students develop repertoires of powerful strategies for academic success and lifelong learning.

critical inquiry of immediate relevance to their lives" (p. 220). This generation of learners will inherit a world of increasing cultural diversity in the United States and increasing international interdependence with other countries, deal with an explosion of information and disinformation, and grapple with complex social and environmental issues in domestic and global arenas. Put most succinctly by Hughes, "In the world that is coming, if you can't navigate difference, you've had it" (cited in Cummins & Sayers, p. 220).

Technology is an inescapable facet of this new world. As we shall see in the section that follows, it can and should be an integral part of a dynamic multicultural curriculum that contributes to addressing these challenges and those yet to come.

TECHNOLOGY IN MULTICULTURAL EDUCATION

Cole and Griffin (1987) address the impact of computer technology on education, specifically in relation to redefining connections between the contexts in which learning takes place—most especially, the classroom, school, and community. They assert that computers hold the promise of creating powerful learning environments characterized by stronger linkages between the educational contexts highlighted previously in Figure 4.1. Facilitating such linkages, however, requires that educators view the computer as a "medium" rather than as an "agent." That is, the computer is not a replacement for people such as the teacher, but rather a means for reorganizing human interactions, creating new milieus for learning, and expanding access to the world outside the classroom: "it involves teachers in a new system of possibilities and social demands in the education of their students" (p. 45).

As with other educational innovations, teachers are central to the efficacy of instructional computer use. For example, teachers determine the participant structures (e.g., same- or cross-age dyads; same- or cross-ability dyads; same- or cross-sex dyads) utilized in their own classrooms, and these in turn influence the effectiveness of computer use in instruction: "there is reason to worry that a laissez-faire attitude toward social organization during computer introduction may contribute to the recapitulation of the status quo, including less effective education for women and minorities" (Cole & Griffin, 1987, p. 53). According to Cole and Griffin, findings from the limited number of research studies available appear to suggest that students benefit from working on computers in pairs rather than independently or in small groups. In dyads, students seem to complement each other's strengths, make fewer simple mistakes, and provide each other support in doing higher level tasks.

Taking advantage of the promise of technology is not without its challenges, however, particularly for women and minorities. Cole and Griffin cite research done in the 1980s which suggests that the manner in which computers are being used in the schools puts women and minorities at a disadvantage in relation to nonminorities and males. They attribute this to:

Teachers are central to the efficacy of instructional computer use.

(a) the greater access to computers afforded to children from upper- and middle-class backgrounds than to those from low income homes;

(b) the differential patterns of computer use associated with socioeconomic status (drill and practice for poor children; "cognitive enrichment" for children from the middle- and upper-classes); and

(c) the greater involvement of male students with computers than females, regardless of ethnicity or class. (Cole & Griffin, 1987, pp. 43–44).

Simply stated, "wealthier schools get more computers and they do more interesting things with them. Within each school, access and patterns of usage favor males over females and higher achieving children over lower achievers" (p. 54). Of special concern is the tendency to limit the applications of technology to lower-level basic skills (drill-and-practice programs) for children perceived to be "behind," thus delaying or even denying them opportunities for engagement in the use of computers for higher order problem solving. Used in this manner, computers "make the academically rich richer without increasing significantly the academic capital of the poor" (p. 59).

Cole and Griffin describe what it will take to exploit the full potential of computers in reorganizing the context of education to enhance learning, particularly for women and minorities:

These include changing the social organization of the classroom; changing the goal of educational activity; changing the relationship between the classroom, the school, and the community; and changing the lesson activity itself to give each student a supportive environment for learning. The introduction and use of computers in classrooms must be seen as part of such systems, not as independent innovations, if they are not to introduce new problems. (p. 56)

For students caught in the drill and practice trap, this means tasks that enable learners to acquire basic knowledge in the process of accomplishing higher order goals: tasks that embed rote learning within activities at higher levels of the curriculum (pp. 58–59).

Internet resources for achieving these goals are highlighted in Figure 7.8. Sayers (1999) focuses on "challenging cultural illiteracy" by providing teachers with Internet tools for involving students in global learning networks. According to Sayers, the ever-changing and growing community of information and human resources available via the Internet is "an ideal technological tool for multicultural education practitioners" in their search for access to current and accurate information on a myriad of topics.

Searching Launchsite Webpages

Sample webpages
- "Internet Navigation" at Rice University (http://riceinfo.rice.edu/Internet/)
- *ClNet's Search.Com* (http.//www.search.com/

Search Engines: Subject-Oriented

Less labor-intensive

Yahoo! (http://www.yahoo.com)

The following are illustrative of the links found using "multicultural education" as a descriptor:

Descriptor ⇨ *Education: K-12: Organizations*
Example: *A World Aware: Reality Education (A.W.A.R.E.)*

Descriptor ⇨ *Education: Teaching: Organizations*
Example: *American Association of Colleges for Teacher Education(AACTE)*

Descriptor ⇨ *Regional: U.S. States: Virginia; Cities; Charlottesville; Education; Colleges
        and Universities; University of Virginia; Departments and Programs*
Example: *Multicultural Pavilion*
        (http://curry.edschool.virginia.edu/go/multicultural)

Descriptor ⇨ *Society and Culture: Diversity*
Example: *Multicultural Alliance*

Descriptor ⇨ *Society and Culture: Diversity: Organizations*
Examples: *Multicultural Centre, The National MultiCultural Institute*

More labor-intensive

Excite's NetReviews (http.//www.excite.com)

The Argus Clearinghouse University of Maryland (http.//www.clearinghouse.net)

(continued)

FIGURE 7.8   Internet resources for multicultural education.

FIGURE 7.8 *(continued)*

Search Engines: Full-Text

Alta Vista (http://altavista.digital.com)
Infoseek (http://www.infoseek.com)
Excite (http://www.excite.com)

Other

Metacrawler (http://www.metacrawler.com) Searches major search engine databases such as:

• *Open Text*	• *Inktomi*	• *Excite*	• *Galaxy*
• *Lycos*	• *InfoSeek*	• *Yahoo!*	• *Alta Vista*

Search Engines: People Resources

Electronic mail-based discussion groups

• Listserv	• Listproc	• Majordomo

• *Liszt.Com* (http://www.liszt.com/)

USENET newsgroup-based discussion groups
  Accessed through Internet Service Provider's subscription (e.g., AT&T, America Online, Compuserve, Prodigy)

DejaNews (http://search.dejanews.com)
  Also available through many search engines including
  • *Alta Vista* (http://altavista.digital.com)
  • *Infoseek* (http://www.infoseek.com)
  • *Excite* (http://www.excite.com)

Individuals
• *WhoWhere?* (http://www.whowhere.com/)
• *Yahoo!'s People Search* (http://www.yahoo.com/search/people/)

Source: Drawn from D. Sayers. (1999). Mining and Refining the Information Lode: Internet Search Tools for Multicultural Education. In *Annual Editions: Multicultural Education, 1999/2000*, pp. 160–165.

SUMMARY

◇ Teachers committed to the development of a multicultural curriculum that adheres to accepted principles of curriculum design must take the following five components into account: needs assessment, goals and learning outcomes, implementation, teaching strategies, and evaluation.

◇ Needs assessment is a twofold process. In addition to identifying the knowledge, attitudes, and skills that students already demonstrate, assessment reveals those that have yet to be developed. Student attitudes and perceptions are especially important because they directly and indirectly influence the teaching of content and skills. By the same token, analysis of the existing curriculum is part of a recursive process in which teachers identify the strengths and weaknesses of what is already in place, and prioritize curriculum areas that require modest or major revisions.

◇ As teachers focus on educational goals and learning outcomes, they ask themselves what students are to learn, why these outcomes are salient, and how they are to be achieved (specifying relevant contexts and appropriate strategies) and then evaluated. Program goals and objectives should incorporate a multiple-group approach in an integrative, interdisciplinary framework emphasizing cognitive and affective skills. Special attention should be given to school populations, locally-oriented activities, and community resources.

◇ During implementation, teachers draw on several principles critical to the effective integration of multicultural perspectives into the curriculum. Among these are balance and complementarity and structure and organization. Concepts, themes, and basic skills need to be brought together in a cohesive, well-integrated program of instruction. Among the organizational strategies suitable for incorporating multicultural content, frameworks that are thematic and conceptual promise to be the most effective in addressing multiple perspectives and allowing for comparative, interdisciplinary analyses.

◇ Given the nature of its curricular goals and objectives, and the commitment to meeting the needs of a diverse student population, multicultural education requires a broad repertoire of instructional methods and techniques. Effective strategies foster development of academic and social skills; foster an understanding of self and environment; and provide powerful tools for the continued acquisition of knowledge. With this in mind, teachers must select and use strategies with a critical eye toward using those that are most suitable and effective for a specific purpose, time, and student population. Concept attainment, advance organizers, role playing, and simulations exemplify the variety of strategies used in multicultural education.

◇ Once a program is developed and implemented, its effectiveness can be assessed in a number of ways. Formal measures and informal indicators include but are not limited to teacher observation of student behaviors, anecdotal information, attendance records, class participation, interviews, tests, projects, surveys, and discussion groups. Whatever combination of evaluation tools is used, the information collected should be well documented, relevant, and useful.

◇ Existing curriculum and projected curriculum development efforts can also be evaluated according to their level of sophistication in approaching the integration of multicultural content, from contributions and additions to transformation and social action.

◇ In a world that is increasingly dependent upon technology, teachers must be prepared to take advantage of the promise that it holds while, at the same time, avoiding potential pitfalls. Central to this challenge is the use of technology to create powerful learning environments that serve all students well, including women and minorities.

APPLICATION, EXTENSION, AND REFLECTION

1. *Program Self-Assessment.* The purpose of this activity is to help you identify the relative strengths and weaknesses of the multicultural program at your school. Analysis of the results will help you to identify areas for program development and prioritize program needs. If used as a class activity outside the school, you may choose to maintain confidentiality and not identify your consultants or school by name in reporting findings and recommendations.

   a. Do a self-assessment in a school of your choice. Examine the existing program applying criteria from Figure 7.2. Remember that although the guidelines are intended to assist you in the self-assessment process, specific items may not be applicable to all settings.

   b. After checking all of the questions that do apply, use the follow-up analysis format to organize your findings.

   ◇ *The self-assessment indicates that our program is very effective in the following areas:*
   Explain why the program is particularly effective in these areas and provide specific examples.

   ◇ *The self-assessment indicates that we need to work to become more effective in the following areas:*
   Explain why these are areas that need to be improved and provide specific examples.

   ◇ *The self-assessment indicates that we are not currently providing the following components of an effective program:*
   Explain why these elements are essential.

   ◇ *Based upon your self-assessment, what changes would you recommend to make the program more responsive to diverse populations?*
   Provide a rationale or other justification for your recommendations.

   c. Reflect on the insights that emerge from this assessment and their implications.

2. *Integrating Multicultural Content.* Compare the curriculum in your classroom or school to the approaches described by Banks (1997).

   a. Which of the four approaches best characterizes the integration of multicultural content in the existing curriculum?

    b. Identify the kinds of changes that might be made to bring the curriculum into closer alignment with the higher levels.

    c. Describe the steps that need to be taken in order to implement these changes.

3. *Interdisciplinary Thematic Unit: Making It Multicultural Too!* An important part of teaching from a multicultural perspective is seeing what is as well as what is not included in the content presented to students. Figure 7.9 is a sample interdisciplinary thematic unit as it appears in *Effective Teaching Methods* (Borich, 1996). Examine and analyze this unit outline carefully from a multicultural perspective. After you consider what is included in the unit and what is not, develop a set of specific recommendations as to changes that could be made in objectives, content, activities, assessment, or other components to enhance the incorporation and treatment of multicultural issues and perspectives. In making your recommendations, provide a rationale (justification, basis) for each change.

4. *Multicultural Education: Using the Internet.*

    a. In the dictionary, prejudice is defined as a negative opinion based upon inadequate knowledge; one type of prejudice is "hatred or dislike directed against a racial, religious, or national group" (Flexner, 1983, 714). Use the statements in Figure 7.10 to focus on selected research about prejudice. Were you able to identify all of the statements that were true?

       With this as a starting point, search the Internet for information, ideas, and teaching strategies appropriate for addressing prejudice in the context of your own classroom. Compare notes with peers and colleagues.

    b. Read the information on cross-cultural awareness in Figure 7.11 and Table 7.2. Search the Internet for activities that would foster cross-cultural awareness for learners at one or more of Hanvey's (1979) levels of cultural awareness. Compare notes with peers and colleagues.

Did you find "gold" when you mined the "information lode"?

Grade: 5
Unit Topic: Gold Rush
Course Subject:

Approximate Time Required: One Month

1. **Main Purpose of the Unit**

   The main purpose of this unit is to acquaint the students with the excitement, the hardships and the challenges of the nineteenth century gold rush.

2. **Behavioral Objectives**

   The student will be able to:

   A. *History/Social Science*—Give reasons why people came to California in the 1840s.

   B. *History/Social Science*—Describe the three routes the pioneers took to California.

   C. *History/Social Science*—Compare life in the United States in the 1840s to life in the United States now.

   D. *History/Social Science*—List supplies brought by the pioneers on the trip West.

   E. *Language Arts*—Write a journal entry to describe some of the hardships associated with the trip West.

   F. *Science*—Research and write a report on how gold is mined.

   G. *Math*—Weigh gold nuggets (painted rocks) and calculate their monetary value.

   H. *Art*—Design a prairie quilt pattern using fabric scraps.

3. **Content Outline**

   A. Reasons why people came to California in the 1840s
      1. Gold
      2. Job opportunities
      3. Weather
   B. Supplies for trip
      1. Tools
      2. Personal supplies
      3. Food
      4. Household items

   C. Life on the trip West
      1. Weather conditions
      2. Roles of men, women, children
      3. Hazards of the trail
   D. Life in California after arrival
      1. Inflated prices
      2. Staking a claim
      3. Striking it rich
      4. A typical day in the life of a miner

4. **Procedures and Activities**
   A. Read aloud
   B. Small-group reading
   C. Independent reading
   D. Discussion
   E. Journal entries
   F. Measurement
   G. Cooking
   H. Singing

5. **Instructional Aids and Resources**
   A. Literature selections
      1. *Patty Reed's Doll*
      2. *By the Great Horn Spoon*
      3. *If You Traveled West in a Covered Wagon*
      4. *Children of the Wild West*
      5. *Joshua's Westward Journal*
      6. *The Way West, Journal of a Pioneer Woman*
      7. *The Little House Cookbook*
   B. **Items indicative of the period (if obtainable)**
      1. Cast iron skillet
      2. Bonnet or leather hat
      3. Old tools

6. **Assessment/Evaluation**

   Develop a rubric to grade these.

   A. Essay—Choose one route that the pioneers took to get to California and describe the journey.

   B. Gold Rush Game Board—Design a board game detailing the trip to California. The winner arrives in California and strikes it rich!

FIGURE 7.9   Interdisciplinary thematic unit: making it multicultural too.

Source: Figure 5.9, example interdisciplinary thematic unit, written by Cynthia Kiel, teacher, Glendora, CA. In G. D. Borich, 1996, *Effective Teaching Methods*, 3rd ed., Prentice Hall, p. 201. Reprinted by permission.

A number of research findings in regards to prejudice are contained in the following statements. See if you can determine which of the statements are consistent with the research and which are not. Circle T if you believe that the statement is TRUE, and F if you think it is FALSE.

T   F   **1.** Stereotypes are generally learned within family and school settings.
T   F   **2.** Prejudice is frequently learned without conscious intent.
T   F   **3.** Individuals generally do not realize how prejudiced they actually are.
T   F   **4.** Individuals prejudiced against members of one ethnic group are likely to be prejudiced against members of other groups as well.
T   F   **5.** Prejudice is an excellent predictor of discriminatory behavior.
T   F   **6.** There is considerable agreement within a society regarding specific stereotypes assigned to particular groups.
T   F   **7.** Individuals expressing antagonistic attitudes toward an ethnic group believe that the group has many objectionable qualities.
T   F   **8.** Stereotypes are almost always the result of direct contact.
T   F   **9.** Individuals not in direct competition with minority group members tend to be less prejudiced toward them.
T   F   **10.** Stereotypes resist change.
T   F   **11.** Changes in established social and economic conditions—especially those that modify relations among groups—can alter stereotypes over extended periods of time.
T   F   **12.** The beliefs of individuals about their own ethnic group tend to be more positive than the beliefs of those outside the group.

Key:
1. T   2. T   3. T   4. T   5. F   6. T   7. T   8. F   9. T   10. T   11. T   12. T

FIGURE 7.10   Prejudice: What Do You Think?
Source: The questions are based on a summary of research findings that appear in J. Kehoe. (1984). *Achieving Cultural Diversity in Canadian Schools,* Cornwall, Ontario, Vesta Publications.

Piaget and Weil are credited with being among the first to study children's development of concepts related to foreign people and countries (Saunders, 1982). Working with children 5 to 10 years of age, they concluded that such concepts are developed early in life and become increasingly sophisticated as children pass through various stages of development. In Stage 1 (egocentric stage), the focus is on oneself as the center of the world. In Stage 2 (sociocentric stage), the focus is on one's own group as the center of attention. Stage 3 is marked by reciprocity and the realization that "one's people are foreigners in other countries, foreigners are not foreign at home and that they too have feelings about belonging to their homeland" (p. 114).

Cross-cultural awareness is a primary objective of education that is multicultural, but it is a difficult goal to attain. As Hanvey (1979) observes, it is relatively simple to gain some knowledge of other cultures; it is considerably more difficult to comprehend and appreciate the human capacity for creating cultures and the profound differences in perspective and experience that result. When such differences are identified at a superficial level only, neither understanding nor true acceptance is likely.

Cross-cultural awareness has been described as operating at several levels, which are broadly defined according to competency in recognizing and interpreting cultural elements that contrast with one's own behaviors, values, and beliefs. The four levels defined by Hanvey (1979) are summarized in Table 7.2.

Observations at Levels I and II are likely to be characterized by varying degrees of ethnocentrism and stereotyping. Ethnocentrism is the belief that one's cultural ways are not only valid and superior to those of others but also universally applicable in evaluating and judging human behavior. All human beings have a natural tendency to be ethnocentric. For example, in many languages, speakers of the language are referred to as "the people"; all others are denoted as strangers, foreigners or outsiders (Alameda County School Department, 1969; Hanvey, 1979). Persons with strong ethnocentric attitudes and beliefs, especially when these are unconscious, may have considerable difficulty in appreciating and accepting the range of cultural differences that exists in human societies (Arvizu et al., 1980).

Stereotypes are predispositions and general attitudes toward particular groups. They influence perceptions of and behaviors toward different groups and often reflect the information to which individuals have been exposed (Smith & Otero, 1982). Stereotypes, positive as well as negative, affect how members regard their own group(s) as well as other groups.

When individuals' cross-cultural awareness reaches Level III and higher, they begin to develop a sense of cultural relativity. Striving to understand another people in terms of their own outlook and situation is at the heart of cultural relativism. It is an attitude that can best be described in the words of the Native American proverb, "Never judge another man until you have walked a mile in his moccasins" (Gollnick & Chinn, 1994, p. 9).

The process of acculturation is central to what happens at Level IV. In general terms, acculturation occurs when intercultural contact between different cultural groups influences the cultural patterns of one or both groups. At the individual level, the critical element is a person's acceptance and adoption of behaviors and values from the new culture. As Johnson (1977) explains, "To 'learn' a culture means to internalize often unstated assumptions and rules for appropriate behavior [and] . . . to interpret and predict the behavior of others as well as to appropriately respond" (p. 13).

(continued)

FIGURE 7.11 Cross-Cultural Awareness

FIGURE 7.11   *(continued)*

Within the classroom environment, teachers may exhibit these various levels of cultural awareness. For example, teachers may observe that students from different cultural, ethnic, or social groups exhibit cultural traits that differ significantly from their own. If teachers' understanding of other cultural, ethnic, and social groups is limited, however, such behaviors and contexts will seem unrelated, and students' actions will be evaluated only from the teachers' cultural perspective (Levels I and II). On the other hand, teachers at Levels III and IV of cultural awareness know that culture affects how individuals act in virtually all aspects of their life, and that its influence is reflected in language, nonverbal communication, behavior, and values. Such teachers recognize, for example, that nonverbal behaviors are not identical across cultures; that children from many Mexican American, Native American, Punjabi, and African American homes are taught different rules governing eye contact. They realize that such behaviors are cultural traits, and understand how to interpret the meaning of what they observe.

Level III teachers cognitively accept that many behaviors learned in one's own culture are arbitrary and not universally shared. Level IV individuals have moved one step further and begun to acculturate to other cultures; for them, strangeness gives way to greater insight and familiarity. Teachers should strive to develop their cultural awareness to Levels III and IV. For most, Level III is a practical and attainable goal, conducive to implementing an educational program that is multicultural. Ideally, most teachers will also achieve some aspects of Level IV awareness.

TABLE 7.2   *Cross-Cultural Awareness*

Level	Information	Mode	Interpretation
I	Awareness of superficial or very visible cultural traits; stereotypes	Tourism, textbooks, *National Geographic*	Unbelievable (i.e., exotic, bizarre)
II	Awareness of significant and subtle cultural traits that contrast markedly with one's own	Culture conflict situations	Unbelievable (i.e., frustrating, irrational)
III	Awareness of significant and subtle cultural traits that contrast markedly with one's own	Intellectual analysis	Believable cognitively
IV	Awareness of how another culture feels from the standpoint of the insider	Cultural immersion; living the culture	Believable because of subjective familiarity

REFERENCES

Alameda County School Department. (1969). *Cultural understanding.* Hayward, CA: Author.

Arvizu, S. F., Snyder, W. A., & Espinosa, P. T. (1980, June). *Demystifying the concept of culture: Theoretical and conceptual tools.* Bilingual Education Paper Series, 3(11). Los Angeles: Evaluation, Dissemination and Assessment Center, California State University—Los Angeles.

Banks, J. A. (1981). *Multiethnic education.* Boston: Allyn and Bacon.

Banks, J. A. (September 1992). Curriculum guidelines for multicultural education. *Social Education.* National Council for the Social Studies.

Banks, J. A. (1997). Approaches to multicultural curriculum reform. In J. A. Banks & C. A. McGee Banks (Eds.), *Multicultural education: Issues and perspectives* (3rd ed., pp. 229–250). Needham Heights, MA: Allyn and Bacon.

Batchelder, D., & Warner, E. G. (Eds.). (1977). *Beyond experience.* Brattleboro, VT: The Experiment Press.

Borich, G. D. (1996). *Effective teaching methods.* (3rd ed.). Englewood Cliffs, NJ: Merrill-Prentice Hall.

California State Department of Education. (1977). *Guide for multicultural education.* Sacramento: CA State Department of Education.

California State Department of Education. (1979). *Planning for multicultural education as a part of school improvement.* Sacramento, CA.

Cantoni-Harvey, G. (1987). *Content-area language instructions.* Reading, MA: Addison-Wesley.

Cole, D. J. (1984). Multicultural education and global education: A possible merger. *Theory Into Practice, XXIII* (2), 151–154.

Cole, M., & Griffin, P. (Eds.). (1987). Laboratory of Human Cognition. *Contextual factors in education.* Prepared for Committee on Research in Mathematics, Science, and Technology Education, Commission on Behavior and Social Sciences and Education, National Research Council. Madison, WI: Wisconsin Center for Education Research, School of Education, University of Wisconsin—Madison.

Cummins, J., & Sayers, D. (1997). Multicultural education and technology: Promise and pitfalls. In F. Schultz (Ed.), *Multicultural education 1997/98* (pp. 218–224). Guilford, CT: Dushkin/McGraw-Hill. (Reprinted from *Multicultural education,* Spring 1996, 4–11; National Association for Multicultural Education).

Flexner, S. B. (Ed.). (1983). *The Random House dictionary.* New York: Oxford University Press.

Freedman, P. I. (1983). A national sample of multiethnic/multicultural education in secondary schools. *Contemporary Education, 54*(2), 130–133.

Gay, G. (1975). Organizing and planning culturally pluralistic curriculum. *Educational Leadership, 33* (3), 176–183.

Gay, G. (1977). Curriculum design for multicultural education. In C. Grant (Ed.), *Multicultural education: Commitments, issues and applications* (pp. 94–104). Washington, DC: Association for Supervision and Curriculum Development.

Gay G. (1979). On behalf of children: A curriculum design for multicultural education in the elementary school. *Journal of Negro Education, XLCIII* (3), 324–340.

Gay, G. (1996). A multicultural school curriculum. In C. A. Grant & M. L. Gómez (Eds.), *Making schooling multicultural: Campus and classroom* (pp. 37–54). Englewood Cliffs, NJ: Merrill/Prentice Hall.

Gollnick, D. M., & Chinn, P. C. (1994). *Multicultural education in a pluralistic society* (4th ed.). New York: Merrill.

Hanvey, R. G. (1979). Cross-cultural awareness. In E. C. Smith & L. F. Luce (Eds.), *Toward internationalism* (pp. 46–56). Rowley, MA: Newbury House. (Reprinted from *An attainable global perspective*, 1976; New York: Center for Global Perspectives).

Hoopes, D. S., & Pusch, M. D. (1979). Teaching strategies: The methods and techniques of cross-cultural training. In M. D. Pusch (Ed.), *Multicultural education: A cross-cultural training approach* (pp. 104–204). LaGrange Park, IL: Intercultural Network.

Hoopes, D. S., & Ventura, P. (Eds.). (1979). *Intercultural sourcebook: Cross-cultural training methodologies*. LaGrange Park, IL: Intercultural Network.

Johnson, N. B. (1977). On the relationship of anthropology to multicultural teaching and learning. *Journal of Teacher Education, XXVIII*(3), 10–15.

Joyce, B., & Weil, M. (1986). *Models of teaching* (3rd ed.). Englewood Cliffs, NJ: Prentice-Hall.

Kehoe, J. (1984a). *Achieving cultural diversity in Canadian schools*. Cornwall, Ontario: Vesta Publications.

Kehoe, J. (1984b). Achieving the goals of multicultural education in the classroom. In R. J. Samuda, J. W. Berry, & M. Laferriere (Eds.), *Multiculturalism in Canada* (pp. 139–153). Toronto: Allyn and Bacon.

Long Beach Unified School District. (n.d.). *Multicultural needs assessment—teacher survey*. Long Beach, CA: Special Projects Branch, Education Department.

Los Angeles County Superintendent of Schools. (1979). *Multicultural education course of study for grades kindergarten through twelve 1979–1981*. J. Browne and J. B. Perez (developers). Los Angeles: Office of the Los Angeles County Superintendent of Schools, Educational Services Group.

Mukhopadhyay, C. C. (1985). Teaching cultural awareness through simulation: Bafa Bafa. In H. Hernández & C. C. Mukhopadhyay, *Integrating multicultural perspectives into teacher education: A curriculum resource guide* (pp. 100–104). Chico: California State University—Chico.

Mukhopadhyay, C. C., & Cushman, R. (1985). A guide to references on simulation games. In H. Hernández & C. C. Mukhopadhyay, *Integrating multicultural perspectives into teacher education: A curriculum resource guide* (pp. 291–293). Chico: California State University—Chico.

Nixon, J. (1985). *A teacher's guide to multicultural education*. Oxford: Basil Blackwell.

Payne, C. (1977). A rationale for including multicultural education and its implementation in the daily lesson plan. *Journal of Research and Development in Education, 11*(1), 33–45.

Politzer, R. L. (1970). Some reflections on "good" and "bad" language teaching behaviors. *Language Learning, XX* (1), 31–43.

Pusch, M. (Ed.). (1979). *Multicultural education: A cross-cultural training approach*. LaGrange Park, IL: Intercultural Network.

Saunders, M. (1982). *Multicultural teaching*. London: McGraw-Hill.

Sawyer, D., & Green, H. (1984). *The NESA activities for Native and multicultural classrooms*. Vancouver, British Columbia: The Tillacum Library.

Sayers, D. (1999). Mining and refining the information lode: Internet search tools for multicultural education. In F. Schultz (Ed.), *Annual editions: Multicultural education, 1999/2000* (pp. 160–165). Guilford, CT: Dushkin/McGraw-Hill. (Reprinted from *Multicultural Education,* Summer 1997, 36–39; National Association for Multicultural Education).

Shearer, L. (1988, January 10). Intelligence report. *Parade Magazine,* p. 16.

Smith, C. F., Jr., & Kepner, H. S. (1981). *Reading in the mathematics classroom.* Washington, DC: National Education Association.

Smith, G. R., & Otero, G. (1982). *Teaching about cultural awareness.* Denver: University of Denver, Center for Teaching International Relations.

Tenenberg, M. (1978). *Generic teaching strategies series: Module and videotapes.* Hayward: California State University, Department of Education.

Tompkins, G. E., & Hoskisson, K. (1995). *Language arts: Content and teaching strategies.* Englewood Cliffs, NJ: Merrill/Prentice Hall.

Teaching From a
Multicultural Perspective

*The success of education depends on adapting teaching to
individual differences among learners.*

L. Corno and R. E. Snow (1986, p. 605)

On a daily basis, teachers in regular classrooms are challenged to provide
an educational environment and experience that meets the individual
needs of students from diverse cultural, social, and linguistic backgrounds, including students with disabilities; students achieving at levels not
commensurate with their abilities; and students with unique talents and capabilities. This central challenge to the educational enterprise has been recognized
for many centuries and in diverse cultures:

> The success of education depends on adapting teaching to individual differ-
> ences among learners. This thought, and the admonition to teachers it carries,
> can be found expressed in some detail in the fourth century B.C. Chinese

treatise by Yue-Zheng entitled *Xue Ji,* in the ancient Hebrew Haggadah of Passover, and in the *De Institutione Oratoria* of Quintilian in first century Rome. (Corno & Snow, 1986, p. 605)

In this final chapter, the emphasis is on teaching and learning. Focusing on teachers, we explore the teaching strategies that comprise a basic repertoire for effective instruction with diverse populations. Focusing on learners, we examine their uniqueness in terms of learning strategies, learning styles, and multiple intelligences.

EFFECTIVE INSTRUCTION FOR ALL LEARNERS

In recent years, educators have made considerable progress in identifying the essential attributes of effective instruction for students from a multitude of cultural, ethnic, linguistic, and socioeconomic backgrounds. The reality is that educators now know how to teach students successfully: "there can no longer be any excuses for continued failure to do so" (Johnson, ASCD, 1995, p. 177). In 1995, the Association for Supervision and Curriculum Development (ASCD) synthesized research and practice on improving student achievement into a comprehensive set of teaching strategies for "educating everybody's children." Predicated on the belief that "as our students become more and more diverse . . . so must our ways of teaching them," the strategies are intended to help teachers provide students traditionally on the academic margins with the kind of instruction generally reserved for the most privileged.

As one educator noted in her response to the recommended strategies, internalization is going to require considerable reflection and analysis on the part of teachers. Stevens pointedly reminds us that as teachers, "we know more than we do" (ASCD, 1995, p. 168). It is not enough for teachers to peruse the strategies and summarily dismiss them, having determined that they are already employing all of the effective practices recommended. Many practitioners are not cognizant of how poorly the strategies are actually implemented or how limited the time devoted to their use. Although sincere in their belief that they are teaching diverse learners in an exemplary manner, such teachers' failure to perceive the "cognitive dissonance between their current reality and any vision of a desired state of affairs" renders them ineffective in improving instruction (p. 168). If teachers are to effect change, they need to begin by being honest with themselves about the extent to which they are actually using effective strategies with all of their students.

This line of thinking has been echoed by other educators. Reflecting on potential obstacles to implementation of the strategies, Stewart asserts that teachers are "the biggest barrier to effective instruction":

> Classroom teachers first need to examine themselves carefully and assess their attitudes toward change; then, with their administrators, they need to take a long, hard look at themselves and decide how they are going to influence the performance of those students who do not fit the 'norms'. (ASCD, 1995, p. 176)

The challenge is for teachers to take what they know and use it to create learning environments in which all students can succeed. Teachers need to determine what they are already doing well, identify what they can do better, and chart an effective course for improving instruction.

To facilitate this process, a synopsis of 54 effective instructional strategies identified by ASCD is presented in Figure 8.1. The chart is designed with several objectives in mind. First, the list of strategies serves as a sort of conceptual organizer. It illustrates where many of the strategies highlighted in this text fit within the broader spectrum of effective instruction for diverse populations. Second, the format is intended to invite teachers to actively interact with the effective instructional strategies appropriate to their grade level and subject area. Teachers are asked to reflect upon their own teaching, analyzing which of the strategies are truly characteristic of what they do in the classroom and determining which will be more prominent in the future. In the second column, teachers are invited to note how each strategy is currently being implemented in their classroom. In the third column, there is room to add new ideas, ways of strengthening the implementation of strategies currently in use and introducing new ones, thus reducing the dissonance between vision and reality described earlier by Stevens.

Implementation of the effective instructional strategies described in this section requires that teachers focus on the students in their classroom as learners unique in many ways. For practitioners, learning strategies, learning styles, and multiple intelligences offer powerful tools for meeting the challenge of teaching diverse populations and creating schools of excellence for all.

Effective Instructional Strategies	What I Do Well	What I Can Do More Effectively
1. **Provide opportunities for students to work together** In a variety of flexible social configurations and settings (cooperative learning groups, dyads, independently), students develop proficiencies, skills, and knowledge while accommodating individual differences.		
2. **Use reality-based learning approaches** Learning experiences that have real purposes and audiences, and are based on authentic materials and content enhance meaning, motivation, and satisfaction.		*(continued)*

FIGURE 8.1 Teaching strategies for multicultural classrooms.

FIGURE 8.1 *(continued)*

Effective Instructional Strategies	What I Do Well	What I Can Do More Effectively
3. Encourage interdisciplinary teaching Interdisciplinary teaching enables students to see relationships across subject areas and discover real-life applications of learning.		
4. Involve students actively Since most students tend to be tactile/ kinesthetic learners, teachers use a range of active learning experiences in all areas of the curriculum to provide many opportunities for students to develop their own understandings, produce their own analyses, and find their own solutions to problems.		
5. Actively model behaviors Teachers model the behaviors and processes that students are to assimilate and practice (e.g., sustained silent reading, scaffolding).		
6. Explore the fullest dimensions of thought Teachers provide all students with meaningful opportunities to become critical thinkers and creative problem solvers.		
7. Use alternative assessments Teachers use multiple assessments to evaluate student achievement as well as to examine the effectiveness of instruction (e.g., multiple indicators, individual progress, student self-evaluation).		
8. Use accelerated learning techniques Techniques that accelerate learning are used with students at all ability and performance levels.		
9. Foster strategies in questioning Student-generated questions and student-led discussions promote more active student learning and participation.		
10. Maintain high standards and expectations Teachers convey high achievement expectations for all students, providing challenging instruction and advanced course content.		
11. Use culturally relevant curriculum materials Teachers provide a curriculum and instructional		

FIGURE 8.1   *(continued)*

Effective Instructional Strategies	What I Do Well	What I Can Do More Effectively
materials that recognize, integrate, and accurately mirror student diversity in regards to race and ethnicity, culture and language.		
12. Use sheltered English strategies Teachers use "sheltered English" strategies to make language and content accessible to English language learners.		

Reading Strategies That Promote Achievement	What I Do Well	What I Can Do More Effectively
1. Read aloud By reading aloud to students, teachers provide a good model for the development of accuracy, fluency, and comprehension.		
2. Create a literacy-rich environment The most effective reading materials are generally characterized as motivating, high-quality, developmentally-appropriate (slightly above the student's current reading level), varied in content and difficulty, well organized, suited to diverse reading style preferences, relevant, and reflective of students' cultures, interests, and experiences.		
3. Encourage reading for pleasure Using time and resources, teachers create an environment that promotes reading for pleasure and fosters students' motivation, fluency, and comprehension.		
4. Integrate language activities The integration of listening, speaking, reading, and writing activities enables students to make connections across disciplines while supporting development of oracy[1] and literacy skills.		
5. Accommodate students' interests, backgrounds, abilities, and reading styles Teachers can help students to experience the kind of empowerment that results in more effective learning and enhanced behavior by identifying their interests, backgrounds, abilities, and preferences, and adapting instruction accordingly.		

[1]Oracy is the verbal counterpart of literacy.

FIGURE 8.1 *(continued)*

Reading Strategies That Promote Achievement	What I Do Well	What I Can Do More Effectively
6. Use systematic, varied strategies for recognizing words Teachers foster reading fluency and independence through systematic instruction that uses meaningful and authentic reading situations to help students develop a repertoire of word recognition strategies.		
7. Use a variety of reading methods Teachers accelerate development of reading skills by providing instruction that employs multiple reading methods to accommodate students' interests, backgrounds, and strengths.		
8. Activate students' prior knowledge Teachers promote understanding of and response to reading texts by activating students' prior knowledge and making connections to past experiences.		
9. Provide authentic purposes, materials, and audiences Teachers motivate and engage students using authentic purposes, materials, and audiences in the development of oracy and literacy.		
10. Construct, examine, and extend meaning To promote students' interaction with reading material, teachers provide reading instruction that challenges all readers to construct, interpret, and examine the meaning of texts, and to generate personal and critical responses to texts.		
11. Provide explicit instruction of "what," "when," and "why" Teachers identify the reading strategies that students need to know, demonstrate how, when, and why each strategy is used, and provide opportunities for students to practice applying strategies in context.		

FIGURE 8.1 *(continued)*

Writing Strategies That Promote Achievement	What I Do Well	What I Can Do More Effectively
1. Provide opportunities to write Teachers help students to become competent writers by providing them with a great variety of opportunities to write and share their writing.		
2. Use writing in all subject areas Teachers incorporate writing as a mode of learning in all content areas.		
3. Use authentic writing tasks Teachers engage students in the writing process using authentic tasks with real purposes and audiences.		
4. Use numerous examples of good writing Providing access to a variety of written materials and examples of good writing, teachers make the effective expression of thoughts and ideas primary, and correctness of form (e.g., spelling and grammar) secondary for emergent writers.		
5. Model the writing process Teachers make the writing process visible for students in all content areas.		
6. Use conferencing and peer review Teachers foster the development of writing by providing opportunities for student collaboration and peer review.		
7. Use writing conferences Conferencing individually with students on a regular basis enables teachers to enhance students' self-assessment of their own writing skills and their understanding of the processes involved.		
8. Teach students "how to write" Teachers provide explicit instruction, often in the form of mini-lessons, demonstrating what students are expected to do in their writing.		

FIGURE 8.1 *(continued)*

Writing Strategies That Promote Achievement	What I Do Well	What I Can Do More Effectively
9. Allow time to learn supportive skills Teachers reinforce the supportive writing skills—prewriting, planning, drafting, revising, and editing—on a daily basis, encouraging students to use their own strategies, move naturally between stages, and work at their own pace.		
10. Provide criteria for evaluation Teachers foster independence by providing criteria (e.g., rubrics, exemplars) student writers can use to evaluate and revise their own writing.		
11. Include contextual instruction in grammar To facilitate students' application of skills from one context to another, grammar is taught within the context of writing, emphasizing strategies consistent with observed learner needs.		
12. Use the inquiry method Teachers use structured assignments based upon inquiry to help students produce writing that expands strategy use, accommodates a variety of purposes and audiences, and addresses increasingly complex topics.		
13. Use writing portfolios Teachers use writing portfolios to monitor and evaluate students' writing abilities in different genres, and to provide students with greater responsibility for their progress as writers through the self-assessment of their own work.		
14. Involve students in the evaluation process Teachers hold students accountable for their own growth and employ multiple measures to assess literacy skills.		

Mathematics Strategies That Promote Achievement	What I Do Well	What I Can Do More Effectively
1. Encourage exploration and investigation Teachers use activities that foster mathematical explorations and investigations, promote the construction of mathematical knowledge, and nurture students' curiosity and creativity.		

FIGURE 8.1 *(continued)*

Mathematics Strategies That Promote Achievement	What I Do Well	What I Can Do More Effectively
2. Use manipulatives Teachers enhance conceptual understanding using manipulatives that help students envision the connections between different representations of mathematical ideas (e.g., concrete, linguistic, graphic, symbolic) and internalize the concepts represented.		
3. Use real-world problem-solving activities Teachers provide a variety of authentic problem-solving activities that are interesting and meaningful.		
4. Encourage oral and written expression Teachers facilitate students' construction of mathematical knowledge by making them demonstrate their mathematical understandings orally and in writing.		
5. Use errors to enhance learning Teachers create a learning environment in which students can share, explore, and extend their thinking, in which errors provide opportunities for reflection and are used to enhance student learning in positive ways.		
6. Offer an enriched curriculum and challenging activities Teachers ensure that all students experience mathematics as a discipline characterized by experiences involving inquiry, problem solving, and higher-order thinking.		
7. Use a variety of problem-solving experiences Teachers provide students with challenging tasks that include nonroutine and open-ended problems (e.g., problems with various correct solutions and answers, problems with multiple interpretations).		

FIGURE 8.1 *(continued)*

Communication Strategies That Promote Achievement	What I Do Well	What I Can Do More Effectively
1. Provide ample time for student-generated dialogue and discussion Teachers create a highly interactive environment in oracy skills are encouraged at all grade levels and in all subject areas.		
2. Focus on understanding as a universal goal of communication To achieve competence in oral communication, teachers foster the development of listening and speaking skills that enable students to understand and to be understood.		
3. Reduce students' speaking anxiety Teachers provide a classroom environment and instructional experiences that foster students' confidence in their ability to use language for oral communication.		
4. Encourage the use of both native and standard dialect and language systems Teachers help students to assess the language choices they make in relations to situational appropriateness, enhancing their understanding of the variety of contexts in which native and standard dialects are used in oral communication.		
5. Promote intercultural understanding and communication Teachers help students to develop a multicultural perspective that includes sensitivity to cultural differences in verbal and nonverbal communication, and awareness of the unwritten social and cultural rules that give rise to misunderstandings.		
6. Emphasize higher order thinking For all students at all grade levels, teachers promote the development of analytical and critical thinking through oral communication, utilizing questioning strategies that tap higher cognitive levels and require concomitant student responses.		

FIGURE 8.1   *(continued)*

Communication Strategies That Promote Achievement	What I Do Well	What I Can Do More Effectively
7. Use real-world experiences To help students become effective oral communicators, teachers use instructional strategies that make students more cognizant of the diverse speaking styles used in real-world contexts and help them to develop greater competence in the styles most appropriate to their conversational and academic needs.		
8. Use a wide variety of methods, materials, and technologies Teachers use many different instructional methods, groupings, materials, and technologies to develop students' oral communication skills.		
9. Use both self-assessment and peer evaluations Teachers utilize multiple assessment measures to improve students' effectiveness in oral communication, including various types of feedback from different audiences (e.g., teachers, peers, others), self-assessment, and peer evaluation.		
10. Encourage accurate reporting Teachers address ethical behavior as an integral part of oral communication, emphasizing instructional strategies that address accuracy and related issues (e.g., speaker intent and audience perception); factors that enhance or detract from the impression a speaker makes on an audience and his/her credibility.		

Source: ASCD Improving Student Achievement Research Panel (1995). *Educating Everybody's Children: Diverse Teaching Strategies for Diverse Learners: What Research and Practice Say about Improving Achievement.* Robert W. Cole (Ed.). Alexandria, VA: ASCD (Association for Supervision and Curriculum Development).

Taking advantage of the promise of technology requires access and involvement for all students.

To increase the academic capital of all students, activities must target higher levels of the curriculum and engage learners in challenging tasks.

"As our students become more and more diverse . . . so must our ways of teaching them"

Computers create new milieus for learning and expand access to the world outside the classroom. In doing so, they provide global learning networks that can be used to foster cultural literacy.

Moving toward a multicultural curriculum that provides students with the highest level of knowledge and skills is increasingly a necessity rather than an option.

LEARNING STRATEGIES

Teachers empower students by helping them become more effective learners; teaching students how to use and apply learning strategies can be an important part of this process. The rationale for looking at what students do while learning is simple: "Good teaching includes teaching students how to learn, how to remember, how to think, and how to motivate themselves" (Weinstein & Mayer, 1986, p. 315). Learning strategies have been defined by Weinstein and Mayer (1986) as behaviors and thinking skills utilized during the learning process to influence how information is processed. These involve affective and motivational states as well as the way learners select, acquire, organize, and integrate new information. According to the cognitive model of learning, the learner is viewed as an active participant in the teaching-learning process, one whose use of mental structures and processes in dealing with information plays a critical role. Hence, what students learn depends jointly upon the efficacy and interaction of both teaching and learning strategies.

The learning strategies children use influence how they approach academic learning, as well as general and interpersonal problem-solving situations (Meyers & Lytle, 1986). Moreover, knowledge of these strategies can be developed and taught. In the long run, heightened recognition that learners' knowledge of their own cognitive processes is an important part of the learning process may lead to improved instruction.

Types and Developmental Progression

Eight major categories of learning strategies have been identified: basic and complex rehearsal strategies; basic and complex elaboration strategies; basic and complex organizational strategies; comprehension monitoring strategies; and affective and motivational strategies (Weinstein & Mayer, 1986). Descriptions and examples of these learning strategies are presented in Table 8.1.

Research reveals that there is a developmental progression associated with many of these strategies (Weinstein & Mayer, 1986). Use of rehearsal strategies, for example, generally is acquired and refined as learners progress through the primary and intermediate grades. Other strategies emerge later, as learners grow older. Researchers hypothesize that various learning strategies can be described and taught to students at appropriate levels of maturity. Indeed, students explicitly taught to use various strategies effectively tend to outperform those in control groups. For example, Weinstein and Mayer (1986) report that reading performance can be significantly improved by teaching students comprehension monitoring. Comparisons of good and poor readers reveal that those with poor comprehension skills do not naturally use the active learning strategies required to monitor understanding.

TABLE 8.1 *Learning Strategies*

Category	Example	School Task
Basic Rehearsal Strategies	Repeating names of items in ordered list	Remembering order of planets from sun; order in which characters are introduced in a play
Complex Rehearsal Strategies	Copying, underlining, or shadowing material	Underlining main events in a story; copying portions of a lesson on causes of a war or revolution
Basic Elaboration Strategies	Forming a mental image or sentence relating items in each pair from a list of paired associated words	Forming a phrase or sentence relating the name of a state and its major agricultural product; forming a mental image of a scene described in a poem
Complex Elaboration Strategies	Paraphrasing, summarizing, or describing how new information relates to existing knowledge	Creating an anology between the operation of a post office and a computer; relating the information presented about the structure of complex molecules to that of simple molecules
Basic Organizational Strategies	Grouping or ordering of items to be learned from a list or a section of prose	Organizing foreign vocabulary words into the categories for parts of speech; creating a chronological listing of events leading up to the Declaration of Independence
Complex Organizational Strategies	Outlining a passage or creating a hierarchy	Outlining assigned chapters in a textbook; creating a diagram to show the relationship among the stress forces in a structural design
Comprehension Monitoring Strategies	Checking for comprehension failures	Using self-questioning to check understanding of material presented in class; using textbook questions at beginning of section to guide reading behavior
Affective and Motivational Strategies	Being alert and relaxed to help overcome test anxiety	Reducing external distractions by studying in a quiet place; using thought stopping to prevent thoughts of doing poorly from directing attention away from a test and toward fears of failure

Source: Adapted from C. F. Weinstein and R. F. Mayer, "The Teaching of Learning Strategies." In *Handbook of Research on Teaching* (3rd ed.). Copyright © 1986 by Macmillan. Used by permission.

Classroom Applications

The implications of work on learning strategies are relevant for teachers at all levels. Efforts to implement these learning strategies should extend from elementary through university levels and across content areas. These strategies can benefit students of diverse abilities and talents, and they have been incorporated into programs for gifted and talented learners (Torrance, 1986) and into special education programs (Collier & Hoover, 1987).

One example of the use of learning strategies at the elementary level is Reading Recovery, an early intervention program. Based upon a model developed for use with culturally diverse populations in New Zealand, this program provides short-term, intensive, individualized instruction for first-grade pupils identified at risk of failing (Boehnlein, 1987). Students are given 30 to 40 hours of specific instruction about learning strategies characteristic of good readers, that is, techniques for deriving meaning from structure, self-correcting nonsensical errors, self-monitoring through visual and auditory cues, using book language, and developing memory for text. Rather than asking children to sound out words or giving them the word, teachers ask questions like the following (Boehnlein, 1987):

- ◇ Does it make sense? (for visual and meaning cues)
- ◇ Does that look right? (for visual cues)
- ◇ What would you expect to see or hear? (for letter or sound cues)
- ◇ Can we say it that way? (for structure or grammar cues)

Thus far, research findings on the effectiveness of the Reading Recovery program appear to be positive. Estimates are that after this intervention, 90% of the students involved in the program—those originally in the lowest 20% of their class on the basis of test scores—equal and even surpass the class average in reading (Boehnlein, 1987).

At the secondary level, learning strategies typical of good students have been incorporated into programs such as Learning to Learn (Heiman, 1985). Good students typically generate questions on new material, discuss content, formulate hypotheses, and check for understanding. They also identify specific instructional goals, develop informal ways to assess their progress, and divide complex content principles, ideas, and tasks into smaller, more manageable units. In Learning to Learn, these behaviors provide the basis for training junior and senior high school students in a broad range of content areas (e.g., chemistry, social studies).

One specialized use of learning strategies is in teaching minority students with disabilities. In this context, the purpose of strategy instruction is "to increase student control over and use of strategies which increase the capacity for learning" (Collier & Hoover, 1987, pp. 24–25). The following six strategies have been identified as especially effective with this student population (Collier & Hoover, 1987):

◇ *Active Processing:* Scanning, summarizing, generating questions, clarifying, predicting, and elaborating upon information to be acquired.

◇ *Analogy:* Recall of familiar patterns similar to new ones; identification of analogous elements between concepts, materials, or experiences.

◇ *Coping:* Problem-solving by confronting the problem, planning a strategy, seeking assistance, implementing the solution, developing alternatives, and achieving a solution.

◇ *Evaluation:* Task analysis, strategy identification and implementation, feedback, elaboration, and generalization to other tasks.

◇ *Organization:* Concept development involving data awareness, grouping, labeling, examining groups, and self-testing.

◇ *Rehearsal:* Recall of ideas, reading passages, and related elements; use of self-questioning, visualizing, and summarizing.

For teachers interested in additional information, particularly those working with English language learners, two excellent resources in this area are Oxford's (1990) *Language Learning Strategies: What Every Teacher Should Know* and Chamot and O'Malley's (1994) *The CALLA Handbook.*

LEARNING STYLES

Diversity is manifest not only in the cultural, social, and linguistic backgrounds that students bring to the classroom, but also in their general patterns of response to the instructional environment; these patterns have been termed *learning styles.* From a theoretical standpoint, the concept of learning styles posits that an individual responds to educational experiences using consistent patterns of behavior characterized along cognitive, affective, and physiological dimensions influenced by the interaction of culture, personality, and brain chemistry (Irvine & York, 1995, p. 484). The cognitive dimension encompasses how individuals decode, encode, process, store, and retrieve information. The affective dimension involves emotional and personality characteristics related to motivation, attention, locus of control, interests, willingness to take risks, persistence, responsibility, and sociability. The physiological dimension refers to sensory perceptions (e.g., visual, auditory, kinesthetic) and environmental characteristics (e.g., noise level, light, temperature, room arrangement) (Cornett, 1983). In essence, learning styles are relatively stable indicators of how individuals process information and respond to affective, sensory, and environmental factors in the instructional process.

In addition to converging on the process of learning as a focal point, learning-style theorists also underscore the importance of personality (Silver, Strong, & Perini, 1997). Given that learning styles reflect and are one manifestation of an individual's personality, "learning is the result of a personal, individualized act of thought and feeling" (p. 22). Thus, learning styles are influenced and determined by many of the same elements associated with personality development.

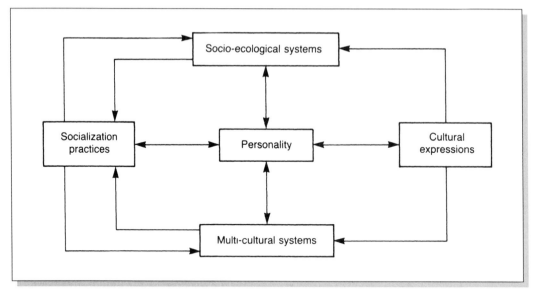

FIGURE 8.2   Interactional model of personality development.
Source: R. T. Garza and J. P. Lipton, "Theoretical Perspectives on Chicano Personality Development," 1982, *Hispanic Journal of Behavioral Sciences,* 4(4), 407–432. Reprinted by permission.

According to the model of Garza and Lipton (1982), personality development in a multicultural society involves the interaction of social, ecological, cultural, personal, and behavioral elements, as illustrated in Figure 8.2. This model relates (a) "personality," which includes affective and cognitive factors, perceptions, aptitudes, and abilities; (b) multicultural systems that bring to bear cultural, social, and environmental influences; and (c) observable behaviors represented through cultural expressions. By focusing on the individual, this model allows for variability within groups: "Even identical cultural, socialization, and situational factors may lead to different personality configurations" (Garza & Lipton, 1982, p. 427). From a teacher's viewpoint, this model is useful because it demonstrates that the personality of each learner is a unique expression of the influence and interaction of various elements. It also emphasizes the interrelationship of elements central to any discussion of personality and learning styles.

A diagrammatic illustration of the elements that affect an individual's learning style, as visualized by Dunn (1984), is presented in Figure 8.3. This graphic representation highlights a number of environmental, emotional, sociological, physical, and psychological elements that can influence the instructional process. (Although the environmental characteristics included in this figure are frequently overlooked, such elements as sound, light, design, and temperature can affect students' performance in the classroom.) A strong advocate of matching teachers' instructional styles to individuals' learning styles, Dunn asserts

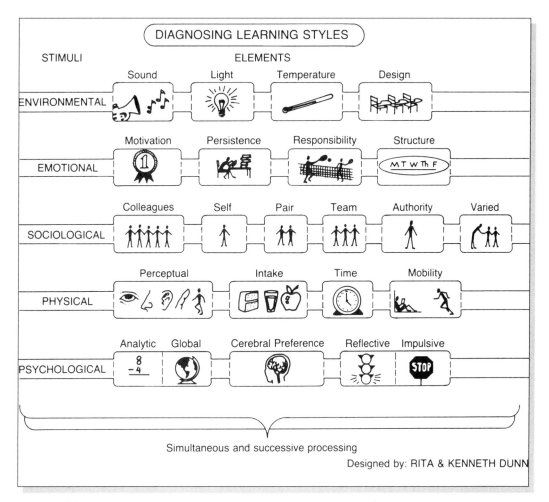

FIGURE 8.3 Component elements characterizing learning-style preferences.
Source: R. Dunn, "Learning Styles: State of the Science," 1984, *Theory Into Practice, XXIII*,(1), 10–19. Published by The Ohio State University, College of Education. Reprinted by permission.

that when strong learning-style preferences are accommodated, academic achievement, attitudes, and behavior will be enhanced. Given the seemingly large number of possible elements to be considered, it is fortunate that the number of elements to which individuals react strongly appears to be relatively small, ranging from 6 to 14 per person (Dunn, 1984).

Effects of Culture on Learning Styles

The relationship between culture and learning styles—although not fully understood—is an important one: "Culture shapes the way we think (Cognition), the way we interact (Behavior), and the way we transmit knowledge to the next generation (Education)" (Collier & Hoover, 1987, p. 7). It defines our beliefs, values, and norms (Owens, cited in Irvine & York, 1995). Cultural and cognitive development are closely intertwined. Social and environmental factors, as well as socialization practices, influence cognitive and affective preferences. These, in turn, are manifested in incentives and motivation, interpersonal relationships, and patterns of intellectual abilities (Ramírez & Castañeda, 1974).

From a multicultural perspective, the promise of learning-styles research is in its potential for explaining "why children of the same culture and ethnicity often employ similar strategies for learning" (Irvine & York, 1995, p. 494). Teachers, for example, have long recognized that all learners do not respond in exactly the same way to instruction, and some have posited the existence of culturally related variability in learning styles. Laosa (1977) is not alone in observing that "different cultural groups exhibit nonsuperficial differences in such educationally important variables as the manner of approaching and coping with cognitive and perceptual tasks and with interpersonal, motivational, and other learning situations" (p. 26).

However, recognizing the existence of individual and group variations is one thing; translating what is known about the relationship and interaction between culture, learning, and personality dynamics into educational practice is something else. Given the complexity of this translation process, it is not surprising that few "learning strategies have been associated validly with ethnic group membership" (Laosa, 1977, p. 27). As Irvine and York observe, although culture and ethnicity provide "frameworks" for the development of our initial learning-style preferences, these early predilections continue to evolve in response to the influence of other important factors (p. 492).

The extent to which members of different cultures and microcultures display certain cognitive and affective tendencies has been the subject of debate among educators for many years. As an example, field sensitivity and field independence are two constructs used to describe certain combinations of cognitive and affective behaviors and preferences. By and large, field-sensitive individuals prefer a more global, holistic, and relational approach, whereas field-independent individuals display a more analytic, verbal, and sequential style (Hatch, 1983). Despite the conceptual and methodological problems inherent in learning-styles research, many researchers continue to characterize most African Americans, Hispanics, Native Americans, and members of other ethnic groups (e.g., Hmong) as field-dependent (field-sensitive) learners (Irvine & York, 1995; Timm, Chiang, & Finn, 1999). Assertions that academic achievement can be enhanced by matching students' learning styles with teaching strategies aligned with cultural or ethnic group preferences are also widespread in the literature. In spite of their intuitive appeal, Irvine and York (1995, p. 484) caution that such efforts are "premature and conjectural":

> One core assumption inherent in the learning-styles research is that children outside of mainstream culture learn better when teaching matches their preferred style. However, research on learning styles using culturally diverse students fails to support the premise that members of a given cultural group exhibit a distinc-

tive style. Hence, the issue is not the identification of a style for a particular ethnic or gender group, but rather how instruction should be arranged to meet the instructional needs of culturally diverse students. (p. 494)

Teachers must remember that "it is risky to generalize from group findings to individuals" (Laosa, 1977, p. 28). Moreover, although some studies have revealed differences in cognitive and affective behaviors or patterns among groups, they have also established that significant differences exist within groups as well. For example, differences in maternal teaching behaviors, in both qualitative and quantitative terms, have been found to be much greater within ethnic groups than between ethnic groups (Laosa, 1977). Preferences within groups are sensitive to variables such as gender and length of residence in the United States, and have been observed to change over time as individuals acculturate (Timm, Chiang, & Finn, 1999).

Learning Styles and Educational Outcomes

"Teachers who understand the preferred style of a student can use that knowledge to design and plan instruction and to encourage students to experiment with a wider repertoire of learning approaches" (Irvine & York, 1995, p. 494). This can best be accomplished if teachers are more cognizant of the strengths and limitations of learning-styles research. Even critics acutely aware of the conceptual, methodological, and pedagogical problems that beset research in the field acknowledge its significant potential "for enhancing the achievement of culturally diverse students" (p. 494). Among the promising aspects of learning-styles research are the following:

◇ emphasis on the cultural context of teaching and learning;
◇ focus on contextualization of the teaching act (that is, examination of teacher actions, goals, methods, and materials in relation to learners, their cultural experiences, and preferred learning environment);
◇ recognition of cultural variables as powerful, explanatory factors in school achievement;
◇ validation of the importance of affective as well as cognitive processes in learning, particularly the emphasis on teaching as social interaction;
◇ recognition that the teacher's responsibility for student learning demands the creation of instructional environments conducive to the variety of learning styles represented in each classroom. (p. 494)

Teachers should keep several caveats in mind when considering the various models proposed to explain and describe learning styles and the relationship of learning styles to academic performance. The first is the danger that constructs may be oversimplified when applied to certain groups (e.g., minority students; males and females) and used to stereotype or label rather than to identify individual behaviors that are educationally relevant. "Negative teacher expectations can be fueled if teachers incorporate generalized and decontextualized observations about children of color without knowledge of the limitations of learning-styles labels" (Irvine & York, 1995, p. 495). This becomes an issue, for example, if

All learners have modality strengths, that is, tendencies to rely on one perceptual channel more than the others.

preferences are used in ways that limit the roles and experiences open to students or generate negative inferences about learners' capabilities.

The second involves limitations in the constructs themselves, some of which involve assumptions regarding the importance and universality of culturally relative values. For example, although independence is highly valued by many persons in American society, for others values such as cooperation, mutuality, and respect may take precedence (Hunt, 1981). Such cultural values may well influence students' learning styles and educators' evaluations of them.

Finally, although learning styles may influence academic behavior and performance, overemphasizing individual preferences is not advisable. First, many of the interactions between learner factors and instructional process are not captured by the concept of learning style. Neither are the variations in learning styles related to different content areas and disciplines. Hence, no single, dominant learner dimension should dictate a specific mode of instruction. Second, most effective teachers intuitively employ multiple teaching approaches, and students demonstrate flexibility and adaptability in dealing with these different modes of instruction (Good & Stipek, cited in Doyle & Rutherford, 1984; Silver, Strong, & Perini, 1997, p. 23).

Instructional Pluralism

Cornett (1983) observes that one's teaching style is influenced to some extent by one's learning style. Under most circumstances, the manner in which individuals

☑ Use all types of questions to promote different levels of thinking.

☑ Provide students with a structured overview of material to be learned using advance organizers (see Chapter 7).

☑ Establish a routine in which students expect to learn at least one new thing every day and are asked to share what they have learned.

☑ Explain the purpose for listening, viewing, and reading activities.

☑ Use brainstorming, pretests, word associations, fantasy journeys, etc., as warm-up activities.

☑ Incorporate intermittent practice (e.g., rehearsal strategies) to promote recall and skills development.

☑ Provide opportunities for students to process and retrieve information using multisensory means (e.g., give written and oral directions).

☑ Bring closure to lessons using different review and reflection techniques such as summarizing, creative writing, reciting, opinion surveys, and drama.

FIGURE 8.4   Accommodating learning styles.
Source: Adapted from C. E. Cornett, *What You Should Know About Teaching and Learning Styles,* 1983.

teach is dictated by the way in which they learn; even the levels and subjects taught can reflect individuals' preferences. For example, field-sensitive individuals tend to gravitate toward elementary teaching; those who are field independent seem to be more attracted to mathematics and science at the secondary level.

Teachers faced with culturally diverse classes and students who differ in their learning preferences must be able to draw upon a variety of teaching strategies appropriate to various learning styles. The suggestions in Figure 8.4 illustrate just a few of the techniques teachers use to create a classroom environment appropriate for different learning styles (Cornett, 1983).

More recently, Shaw (1996) has used the term "instructional pluralism" to capture the essence of what sensitivity to multiple learning styles entails and the variability of instruction it implies (p. 73). Whatever the emphasis, Shaw contends that there are four key elements to style:

◇ Every individual has a learning-style preference;
◇ Although individual learning styles are subject to change, they remain relatively stable over time;
◇ While learning styles may vary in terms of their effectiveness in specific situations, one style is not inherently superior to another;
◇ Style is pervasive, that is, manifest across the myriad of contexts that individuals encounter in their lives. (Shaw, 1996, p. 57)

Providing for the diversity of styles in any classroom draws teachers' attention to consideration of general approaches and broad methods to specific methods and strategies. Illustrative of the instructional practices Shaw recommends as part of a teacher's repertoire for the implementation of instructional

Instructional Practice	Examples
1. Interdisciplinary teaching	Interdisciplinary units focusing on content (e.g., stars—integrating social studies, mathematics, science, language arts); process (e.g., scientific method—incorporating science and language arts); or both (individual American cultures and American Indian culture as a whole—using social studies content and processes from the social studies, language arts, math, science, and art).
2. Cooperative learning	Jigsaw Team World Webbing Three-Step Interview Numbered Heads Together
3. Schema construction	Concept mapping
4. Guided imagery	Guided cognitive imagery (mental journeys to distant places, into the past or future, through the circulatory system) Guided affective imagery (visualization at the beginning of class; mental journeys recalling places and associated feelings)
5. Simulations	*Sound Foundations* *Brown Eyes-Blue Eyes*
6. Perspective and empathy exercises	Debates and interviews Perspective-taking exercises in which students assume different points of view (cultural, individual, physical)
7. Using the concrete as a vehicle to the abstract	Concrete examples → Abstract concept ("your family" → "interdependence") Concrete analogy → Abstract material (football strategy → military strategy)
8. Establishing the relevance of what is learned to students' lives	Introducing *The Secret Garden* by exploring the special places students go when they want to be alone and daydream. In rural areas, using materials that present students with math problems from the farmer's world.

FIGURE 8.5   Instructional pluralism.

Source: Adapted from C. C. Shaw, "Instructional Pluralism: A Means to Realizing the Dream of Multicultural, Social Reconstructionist Education." In *Making Schooling Multicultural: Campus and Classroom,* 1996. C. A. Grant and M. L Gomez (eds.). Merrill/Prentice Hall Englewood Cliffs, N.J. pp. 55–76.

pluralism are those highlighted in Figure 8.5. These have the advantage of engaging all learners while incorporating key elements that are important for students with specific learning-style preferences.

In the section that follows, we will continue the exploration of avenues for furthering our understanding of learners. Multiple intelligences is in many ways separate and distinct from learning styles in regards to theory, research, and application.

> Though both theories claim that dominant ideologies of intelligence inhibit our understanding of human differences, learning styles are concerned with differences in the *process* of learning, whereas multiple intelligences center on the *content* and *products*.(Silver, Strong, & Perini, 1997, p. 22)

In other words, "a person's learning style is *the intelligences put to work*" (Armstrong, 1994, p. 13).

Bearing this in mind, the two fields do share certain commonalities that make them complementary and useful tools for teachers of increasingly diverse populations. Both focus on learning and learner-centered instruction that stresses teaching the whole person. Consistent with this is an emphasis on teachers as reflective practitioners and decision makers enacting a substantive and qualitatively sound curriculum. Their outcomes are active and reflective learners (Guild, 1997). These are neither prescriptive approaches nor panaceas; solid, effective teaching is central to their success. In the final analysis, learning styles and multiple intelligences "offer more students the opportunity to succeed by focusing attention on how they learn" (p. 31).

MULTIPLE INTELLIGENCES

Gardner's theory of multiple intelligences enhances our appreciation of learners in ways that contribute to the creation of school learning environments that enable all students to succeed. Gardner defines intelligence as "the human ability to solve problems or to make something that is valued in one or more cultures" (Checkley, 1997, p. 8). It is a view of human intelligence that challenges traditional views of intelligence, most especially the constructs that dominate "disembodied language-logic instruments" such as IQ tests and the SAT (p. 10). In this view of human intelligence,

◇ All human beings possess the eight intelligences (p. 9);
◇ Abilities are not distributed equally across the intelligence areas, that is, individuals tend to be stronger in some intelligences than others;
◇ The overall configuration of relative strengths is unique for each person, giving each individual a singular profile of intelligences (p. 9); and
◇ Individuals can improve their capabilities in each of the intelligences, although the extent of progress made in each of the different areas may vary. (p. 10)

According to Armstrong, sensitivity to cultural differences is embedded within the criteria used to identify multiple intelligences. By definition, true intelligences must be highly regarded by a culture. Moreover, although the eight intelligences are manifest and practiced in all of the world's cultures, how they are used and the value ascribed to each can vary greatly. To illustrate, the Puluwat culture accords considerable prestige to its chief navigators, given the importance of spatial intelligence to a people living on several hundred islands in the South Seas. Early in life, children learn to recognize the constellations, the profiles of islands on the horizon, and the geographical data conveyed by changes on the water's surface. Among the Anang in Nigeria, musical intelligence is universal, not the purview of a relative few. By age five, children are expected to master hundreds of songs and dances. Along similar lines, children in Hungary receive daily instruction in music; expectations for all include the reading of musical notation. The common thread is that "every culture has and uses all seven [eight] intelligences" (p. 162).

The eight intelligences are highlighted in Table 8.2. For each area, there is brief description, examples of high "end-state" performances and culturally valued expressions of expertise, and a sampling of appropriate teaching strategies.

Campbell (1997) provides a set of instructional menus used to infuse multiple intelligences into lesson planning (Figure 8.6). First, the teacher determines the concept to be taught and selects the intelligences most appropriate in approaching the content. Second, the teacher refers to the menus to generate ideas and provide variety. The menus will grow as the teacher's repertoire of strategies and techniques for each of the intelligences develops and expands.

The conceptualization of human abilities in multiple intelligences does not prescribe what teachers teach nor how they do so. Rather, it offers a model of the mind useful in constructing curriculum and enhancing instruction (Campbell, 1997). The implications for teaching are significant, as teaching in accordance with multiple intelligences impacts instruction, curriculum, assessment, and more. From a multicultural education perspective, multiple intelligences recognizes the challenge that educators face in designing curricula that are both "*content*-sensitive (e.g., exposing students to the beliefs, background, and foundations of individual cultures)" and "*process*-sensitive (e.g., helping students understand the many 'ways of knowing' that different cultures possess)" (Armstrong, 1994, p. 161).

Central to the application of multiple intelligences is an understanding that

1. *Teachers need to change and expand their instructional repertoires.* Important topics in all disciplines can be taught in different ways; new content should be addressed using multiple approaches appropriate for a specific group of learners in a particular setting. (Campbell, Campbell, & Dickinson, 1996, p. 307; Checkley, 1997, p. 10; Latham, 1997, p. 84)
2. *Teachers need to change their perception of students.* Although teachers are aware of and responsive to the diverse intelligences of their students, there is research to suggest that their perceptions of students are influenced most strongly by traditional views of ability that favor verbal and analytic skills. (Campbell et al., 1996, pp. 306–307; Latham, 1997, p. 84)

TABLE 8.2 *The Eight Multiple Intelligences: Overview*

Intelligence	Description	High End-States	Ways That Cultures Value	Teaching Strategies
Linguistic	Sensitivity to the sounds, structure, meanings, and functions of words and language	Writer Orator Journalist Newscaster	Oral histories Storytelling Literature	Storytelling Brainstorming Tape recording Journal writing Publishing
Logical-Mathematical	Sensitivity to, and capacity to discern, logical or numerical patterns; ability to handle long chains of reasoning	Scientist Mathematician Engineer Computer programmer Accountant	Scientific discoveries Mathematical theories Counting and classification systems	Calculations and quantifications Classifications and categorizations Socratic questioning Heuristics
Spatial	Capacity to perceive the visual-spatial world accurately and to perform transformations on one's initial perceptions	Artist Architect Sailor Pilot Painter	Artistic works Navigational systems Architectural designs Inventions	Visualization Color cues Picture metaphors Idea sketching Graphic symbols
Bodily-Kinesthetic	Ability to control one's body movements and to handle objects skillfully	Athlete Dancer Sculptor Surgeons Craftspeople	Crafts Athletic performances Dramatic works Dance forms Sculpture	Body answers Classroom theater Kinesthetic concepts Hands-on thinking Body maps
Musical	Ability to produce and appreciate rhythm, pitch, and timbre; appreciation of the forms of musical expressiveness	Composer Performer Conductor Musician Critic Instrument maker	Musical compositions Performances Recordings	Rhythms, songs, raps, and chants Discographics Supermemory music Musical concepts Mood music

(continued)

TABLE 8.2 (continued)

Intelligence	Description	High End-States	Ways That Cultures Value	Teaching Strategies
Interpersonal	Capacity to discern and respond appropriately to the moods, temperaments, motivations, and desires of other people	Teacher Counselor Politician Actor Social worker	Political documents Social institutions	Peer sharing People sculptures Cooperative groups Board games Simulations
Intrapersonal	Sensitivity to one's feelings and the ability to discriminate among one's emotions; knowledge of one's own strengths and weaknesses	Theologian Philosopher Psychologist	Religious systems Psychological theories Rites of passage	One-minute reflection periods Personal connections Choice time Goal-setting sessions
Naturalist	Capacity to classify nature; ability to recognize and classify plants, minerals, and animals, including rocks and grass and all variety of flora and fauna	Farmer Botanist Chef Naturalist Biologist	Human survival (e.g., hunters, gatherers, farmers) Environmental systems Agricultural systems	Observations Caring for pets and animals Gardening

Sources: Adapted from T. Armstrong, *Multiple Intelligences in the Classroom*, 1994, Association for Supervision and Curriculum Development, Alexandria, VA. Used by permission. Additional information from L. Campbell, "Variations on a Theme—How Teachers Interpret MI Theory," September 1997, *Educational Leadership*, 55(1), 14–19; and K. Checkley, "The First Seven . . . and the Eighth," September 1997, *Educational Leadership*, 55(1), 8–13.

Linguistic Menu

Use storytelling to explain _____

Conduct a debate on _____

Write a poem, myth, legend, short play, or news article about _____

Create a talk show radio program about _____

Conduct an interview about _____ with _____

Logical-Mathematical Menu

Translate a _____ into a mathematical formula.

Design and conduct an experiment on _____

Make up syllogisms to demonstrate _____

Make up analogies to explain _____

Describe the patterns or symmetry in _____

Bodily-Kinesthetic Menu

Create a movement or sequence of movements to explain _____

Make task or puzzle cards for _____

Build or construct a _____

Plan and attend a field trip that will _____

Bring hands-on materials to demonstrate _____

Visual Menu

Chart, map, cluster, or graph _____

Create a slide show, videotape, or photo album of _____

Create a piece of art that demonstrates _____

Invent a board or card game to demonstrate _____

Illustrate, draw, paint, sketch, or sculpt _____

Musical Menu

Give a presentation with appropriate musical accompaniment on _____

Sing a rap or song that explains _____

Indicate the rhythmical patterns in _____

Explain how the music of a song is similar to _____

Make an instrument and use it to demonstrate _____

(continued)

FIGURE 8.6 Multiple intelligences menus.

FIGURE 8.6   *(continued)*

Interpersonal Menu

Conduct a meeting to address _____

Intentionally use _____ social skills to learn about _____

Participate in a service project to _____

Teach someone about _____

Practice giving and receiving feedback on _____

Use technology to _____

Intrapersonal Menu

Describe qualities you possess that will help you successfully complete _____

Set and pursue a goal to _____

Describe one of your personal values about _____

Write a journal entry on _____

Assess your own work in _____

Naturalist Menu

Create observation notebooks of _____

Describe changes in the local or global environment _____

Care for pets, wildlife, gardens, or parks _____

Use binoculars, telescopes, microscopes, or magnifiers to _____

Draw or photograph natural objects _____

Source: L. Campbell, "Variations on a Theme—How Teachers Interpret MI Theory," *Educational Leadership*, September 1997, p. 18. Used by permission.

3. *Classroom assessment practices must undergo considerable transformation.* Assessment practices at the classroom and school level change with the application of multiple intelligences. Performance assessment and the use of multiple measures are fully consistent with the view of human abilities in multiple intelligences. The potential benefits for special populations (e.g., gifted, special education) are significant. (Campbell et al., 1996, pp. 311–312; Checkley, 1997, pp. 12–13)

4. *Curricular adaptations will vary considerably from one school to another.* There is no one model for the application of multiple intelligences; in fact, there are potentially as many models as there are teachers adapting it for use with students in their schools and communities. (Campbell et al., 1996, pp. 308–311; Campbell, 1997, pp. 15, 19)

Teachers embracing multiple intelligences see powerful affirmation of what they know about students and the differences in their capacities for learning in

Teachers embracing multiple intelligences see powerful affirmation of what they know about students and the differences in their capacities for learning in distinct areas.

distinct areas (Campbell, 1997, p. 19; Latham, 1997, p. 84). In the final analysis, Gardner asserts that "you cannot be a good MI teacher if you don't want to know each child and try to gear how you teach and how you evaluate to that particular child" (Checkley, p. 11). The same can be said of good multicultural educators.

As we have seen, there is a synergetic relationship between teaching and learning. In the final analysis, this is why multicultural education is about *students, teachers,* and *educational change.* This is also why making education what it can be, should be, and must be for *all* students is a vision for the present as well as the future.

SUMMARY

◇ Understanding how to meet the needs of students requires insight about the learner's individual abilities, the broader sociocultural context, and the learning environment provided in the classroom. The teacher's task is a challenging one—to create facilitative teaching and learning environments in which all students can achieve academically to their fullest potential.

◇ Knowledge of learning styles can help teachers in designing classroom environments and instructional strategies that are compatible with individual patterns of behavior along cognitive, affective, and physiological dimensions.

◇ Teachers can also use learning strategies to "empower" students, that is, to help them develop effective learning skills so that they can become successful learners.

◇ Learning strategies focus attention on the learner as an active participant and partner in the teaching-learning process. Learning strategies can be used to "empower" students, that is, to help them develop the effective learning skills they need to become more successful learners.

◇ Learning styles recognize how learners are influenced by the complex interplay of individual, cultural, and contextual factors. Knowledge of learning styles can facilitate the design of classroom environments more compatible with the cognitive, affective, and physiological preferences of individual learners. Viewed within the framework of instructional pluralism, sensitivity to learning styles can foster practices that enable teachers to engage all learners by incorporating key features appropriate to distinct preferences.

◇ The theory of multiple intelligences contributes to the understanding of learners by expanding the conceptualization of human abilities. As teachers change their perception of learners, so too, must they expand their instructional repertoire and transform current assessment practices.

◇ In conclusion, it is important to recognize the symbiotic relationship of teaching and learning, for this is central to the vision of multicultural education introduced at the beginning of our journey together. Multicultural education is about *students, teachers,* and *educational change;* it is what education can be, should be, and must be for all students.

APPLICATION, EXTENSION, AND REFLECTION

1. *Teaching Strategies for Multicultural Classrooms.* Select one or more videos that demonstrate effective teaching in multicultural instructional settings. Use appropriate sections of Figure 8.7, to identify specific teaching strategies used by the exemplary teachers in the videos. For example, use "Good Morning, Miss Toliver" (FASE, 1993) to focus on multicultural, communication, and mathematics strategies that promote achievement. Indicate all of the strategies that are evident in Miss Toliver's classroom, and provide specific examples of how each of these is used. Add additional strategies identified in the video as appropriate. Share and compare your observations with others.

Instructions: Select the appropriate categories for the video you are viewing, and check all of the teaching strategies observed. In the adjoining space, identify/describe the specific types of activities used by the teacher to effect each strategy.

Effective Instructional Strategies	Examples from the Video
☐ 1. Provides opportunities for students to work together	
☐ 2. Uses reality-based learning approaches	
☐ 3. Encourages interdisciplinary teaching	
☐ 4. Involves students actively	
☐ 5. Actively models behaviors	
☐ 6. Explores the fullest dimensions of thought	
☐ 7. Uses alternative assessments	
☐ 8. Uses accelerated learning techniques	
☐ 9. Fosters strategies in questioning	
☐ 10. Maintains high standards and expectations	
☐ 11. Uses culturally relevant curriculum materials	
☐ 12. Uses sheltered English strategies	

(continued)

FIGURE 8.7 Teaching strategies: video viewing guide.

FIGURE 8.7 *(continued)*

Reading Strategies That Promote Achievement	Examples from the Video
☐ 1. Reads aloud	
☐ 2. Creates a literacy-rich environment	
☐ 3. Encourages reading for pleasure	
☐ 4. Integrates language activities	
☐ 5. Accommodates students' interests, backgrounds, abilities, and reading styles	
☐ 6. Uses systematic, varied strategies for recognizing words	
☐ 7. Uses a variety of reading methods	
☐ 8. Activates students' prior knowledge	
☐ 9. Provides authentic purposes, materials, and audiences	
☐ 10. Constructs, examines, and extends meaning	
☐ 11. Provides explicit instruction of "what," "when," and "why"	

Writing Strategies That Promote Achievement	Examples from the Video
☐ 1. Provides opportunities to write	
☐ 2. Uses writing in all subject areas	
☐ 3. Uses authentic writing tasks	

FIGURE 8.7 *(continued)*

Writing Strategies That Promote Achievement	Examples from the Video
☐ 4 Uses numerous examples of good writing	
☐ 5. Models the writing process	
☐ 6. Uses conferencing and peer review	
☐ 7. Uses writing conferences	
☐ 8. Teaches students "how to write"	
☐ 9. Allows time to learn supportive skills	
☐ 10. Provides criteria for evaluation	
☐ 11. Includes contextual instruction in grammar	
☐ 12. Uses the inquiry method	
☐ 13. Uses writing portfolios	
☐ 14. Involves students in the evaluation process	
Mathematics Strategies That Promote Achievement	Examples from the Video
☐ 1. Encourages exploration and investigation	
☐ 2. Uses manipulatives	
☐ 3. Uses real-world problem-solving activities	

FIGURE 8.7 *(continued)*

Mathematics Strategies That Promote Achievement	Examples from the Video
☐ 4. Encourages oral and written expression	
☐ 5. Uses errors to enhance learning	
☐ 6. Offers an enriched curriculum and challenging activities	
☐ 7. Uses a variety of problem-solving experiences	

Communication Strategies That Promote Achievement	Examples from the Video
☐ 1. Provides ample time for student-generated dialogue and discussion	
☐ 2. Focuses on understanding as a universal goal of communication	
☐ 3. Reduces students' speaking anxiety	
☐ 4. Encourages the use of both native and standard dialect and language systems	
☐ 5. Promotes intercultural understanding and communication	
☐ 6. Emphasizes higher order thinking	
☐ 7. Uses real-world experiences	
☐ 8. Uses a wide variety of methods, materials, and technologies	

FIGURE 8.7   *(continued)*

Communication Strategies That Promote Achievement	Examples from the Video
☐ 9. Uses both self-assessment and peer evaluations	
☐ 10. Encourages accurate reporting	

Source: ASCD Improving Student Achievement Research Panel, 1995. *Educating Everybody's Children: Diverse Teaching Strategies for Diverse Learners: What Research and Practice Say about Improving Achievement.* Robert W. Cole (Ed.). Alexandria, VA: ASCD (Association for Supervision and Curriculum Development). Used by permission.

2. *Multiple Intelligences: Software.* "Computers themselves . . . are intelligence-neutral mechanisms . . . these software programs can be designed to interface with any or all of the seven [eight] intelligences" (Armstrong, 1994, p. 158). For each of the multiple intelligences and corresponding types of software highlighted in Figure 8.8, identify two or more software programs appropriate for learners at your grade level and/or subject area.

REFERENCES

ASCD Improving Student Achievement Research Panel. (1995). *Educating everybody's children: Diverse teaching strategies for diverse learners: What research and practice say about improving achievement.* Robert W. Cole (Ed.). Alexandria, VA: ASCD (Association for Supervision and Curriculum Development).

Armstrong, T. (1994). *Multiple intelligences in the classroom.* Alexandria, VA: Association for Supervision and Curriculum Development.

Boehnlein, M. (1987). Reading intervention for high-risk first-graders. *Educational Leadership, 44* (6), 32–37.

Campbell, L. (1997, September). Variations on a theme—How teachers interpret MI theory. *Educational Leadership, 55*(1), 14–19.

Campbell, L., Campbell, B., & Dickinson, D. (1996). *Teaching and learning through multiple intelligences.* Needham Heights, MA: Allyn and Bacon.

Chamot, A. U., & O'Malley, J. M. (1994). *The CALLA handbook.* Reading, MA: Addison-Wesley.

Checkley, K. (1997, September). The first seven. . . and the eighth: A conversation with Howard Gardner. *Educational Leadership, 55*(1), 8–13.

Collier, C., & Hoover, J. J. (1987). *Cognitive learning strategies for minority handicapped students.* Lindale, TX: Hamilton Publications.

Linguistic Intelligence
- word processing
- desktop publishing programs
- interactive storybooks

- typing tutors
- electronic libraries
- word games

Logical-Mathematical Intelligence
- math skills tutorials
- science programs
- computer programming tutors

- logic games
- critical thinking programs

Spatial Intelligence
- animation programs
- electronic chess games
- spatial program-solving games
- graphic presentations of knowledge

- draw-and-paint programs
- electronic puzzle kits
- geometry programs
- clip-art programs

Bodily-Kinesthetic Intelligence
- virtual-reality system software
- tools that plug into computers
- hands-on construction kits that interface with computers

- motion-simulation games
- eye-hand coordination games

Musical Intelligence
- musical instrument digital interfaces
- singing software
- tone recognition and melody memory enhancers

- music literature tutors
- composition software

Interpersonal Intelligence
- electronic bulletin boards

- simulation games

Intrapersonal Intelligence
- personal choice software
- any self-paced program

- career counseling software

FIGURE 8.8   Software and multiple intelligences.
Source: Adapted from T. Armstrong, 1994, *Multiple Intelligences in the Classroom,* p. 160. Association for Supervision and Curriculum Development, Alexandria, VA. Used by permission.

Cornett, C. E. (1983). *What you should know about teaching and learning styles.* Bloomington, IN: Phi Delta Kappa Educational Foundation.

Corno, L., & Snow, R. E. (1986). Adapting teaching to individual differences among learners. In M. C. Wittrock (Ed.), *Handbook of research on teaching* (3rd ed., pp. 605–629). New York: Macmillan.

Doyle, W., & Rutherford, B. (1984). Classroom research on matching learning and teaching styles. *Theory Into Practice, XXIII* (1), 20–25.

Dunn, R. (1984). Learning styles: State of the science. *Theory Into Practice, XXIII* (1), 10–19.

Foundation for Advancements in Science and Education (FASE). (1993). *Good morning, Miss Tolliver.* 4801 Wilshire Blvd., Suite 215, Los Angeles, CA 90010.

Garza, R. T., & Lipton, J. P. (1982). Theoretical perspectives on Chicano personality development. *Hispanic Journal of Behavioral Sciences, 4* (4), 407–432.

Guild, P. B. (1997, September). Where do the learning theories overlap? *Educational Leadership, 55*(1), 30–31.

Hatch, E. M. (1983). *Psycholinguistics.* Rowley, MA: Newbury House.

Heiman, M. (1985). Learning to learn. *Educational Leadership, 43* (1), 20–24.

Hunt, D. E. (1981). Learning style and the interdependence of practice and theory. *Phi Delta Kappan, 62* (7), 647.

Irvine, J. J., & York, D. E. (1995). Learning styles and culturally diverse students: A literature review. In J. A. Banks (Ed.) & C. A. McGee Banks (Assoc. Ed.), *Handbook of research on multicultural education* (pp. 484–497). New York: Macmillan.

Laosa, L. M. (1977). Multicultural education—How psychology can contribute. *Journal of Teacher Education, XXVIII* (3), 26–30.

Latham, A. S. (1997, September). Quantifying MI's gains. *Educational Leadership, 55*(1), 84–85.

Meyers, J., & Lytle, S. (1986). Assessment of the learning process. *Exceptional Children, 53* (2), 138–144.

Oxford, R. L. (1990). *Language learning strategies: What every teacher should know.* Boston: Heinle & Heinle.

Ramírez, M., & Castañeda, A. (1974). *Cultural democracy, bicognitive development and education.* New York: Academic Press.

Shaw, C. C. (1996). Instructional pluralism: A means to realizing the dream of multicultural, social reconstructionist education In C. A. Grant & M. L. Gomez (Eds.), *Making schooling multicultural: Campus and classroom* (pp. 55–76). Englewood Cliffs, NJ: Merrill-Prentice Hall.

Silver, H., Strong, R., & Perini, M. (1997, September). Integrating learning styles and multiple intelligences. *Educational Leadership, 55*(1), 22–27.

Timm, J. T., Chiang, B., & Finn, B. D. (1999). Acculturation in the cognitive style of Laotian Hmong students in the United States. In F. Schultz (Ed.), *Annual editions: Multicultural education* 1999/2000 (pp. 188–194). Guilford, CT: Dushkin/McGraw-Hill.

Torrance, E. P., (1986). "Teaching creative and gifted learners." In M. C. Wittrock (Ed.), *Handbook of research on teaching* (3rd ed., pp. 630–147). New York: Macmillan.

Weinstein, C. F., & Mayer, R. F. (1986). The teaching of learning strategies. In M. C. Wittrock (Ed.), *Handbook of research on teaching* (3rd ed., pp. 315–317). New York: Macmillan.

NAME INDEX

SUBJECT INDEX